DIECAST TOY AIRCRAFT

AN INTERNATIONAL GUIDE

Sue Richardson

NEW CAVENDISH BOOKS

LONDON

Dedication

To my husband Mike, whose knowledge of the full-size planes was essential to the understanding of the models, and who proofread the entire book.

First edition published in Great Britain by New Cavendish Books Ltd, 1997

Designed by Jacky Wedgwood

Edited by Narisa Chakra

Typesetting by Adrienne Lee and Dorchester Typesetting

Printed and bound in Spain by Book Print SL

ISBN 1 872727 23 9

Front cover illustration, clockwise from top left: Space Shuttle by Dinky, three Solido Delta-wing fighters, Dinky prototype of the Boeing SST (viewed from below), Corgi Surf Rescue helicopter, Hubley Kiddie Toy P.47 Thunderbolt, Tootsietoy Trimotor.

Back cover illustration:
Crescent Night Raiders board game

Acknowledgements

Since deciding to write this book in 1989, I have been overwhelmed with help from fellow collectors: some have lent models so that I could play with them at my leisure; some have given information ranging from a single interesting nugget to details of virtually a whole range; some have painstakingly double-checked my information against theirs; some have provided me with manufacturers' catalogues; some have rooted around in toy shops in foreign lands to turn up the latest obscure products; some have found models that just had to be bought to increase the collection, or sent a sales list full of interesting toys; some, in the last but essential stage, have lent models for photography. Collectors who live relatively locally (to Windsor) and the members of *The Plane News* have been of extra special help. Before all this, there were authors who had already written books or contributed to the magazine *Modellers' World*, some of whom have sadly died.

Thank you all: Barry Appleyard, David Austin, Derek Barratt, John Beugels, Graham Bridges, David Brooks, Clive Chick, Arthur Close, George Cox, Vic Davey, John de Uphaugh, Alan Dimmock, Michael Driver, Tony Duva, Tom Fisher, John Gay, John Gibson, Lester Harrison, José Heraud, Iain Hines, Philip Jewell, Peter Jongbloed, Norman Joplin, Ian Leonard, Geoff Ligget, Bernard Macaire, Hugo Marsh, Tony Martin, Thomas Wm McGarry, Doug McHard, Maurice Mouraux, Vic Mumby, Nigel Mynheer, Len Nash, Geoff Noble, Colin Penn, Peter Quaile, J M Roulet, Clint Seeley, Brian Smart, David Smith, John Stevens, Jeff Stevenson, Patrick Trench, Graham Turrell, David Vanner, Martin Uden, Matt Vance, Alan and Paul Watkins, Gates Willard.

The auction houses, Christies, South Kensington, and Phillips, Bayswater, have been most helpful.

Contents

Introduction

Flying machines have been part of many toy manufacturers' production since the days of the balloon, the airship and the Wright Flyer. This book aims to cover manufacturers of cast toy aeroplanes throughout the world. It describes the variations and dates of all the models in each range, demonstrating how diecast toys, available from the early years of this century to date, reflect in miniature the history of aviation itself. The attraction of collecting toys made for children, rather than models made as recognition items, or for the collector, is that the toy truly echoes the age in which it was made. Indeed, the development of aeroplanes from 'stick insect' to wide bodied jet, from the Red Baron to the Stealth Fighter, is paralleled by the progress in toy production. From humble beginnings as cheap Penny Toys and Dime Store pieces, toys are today mass-produced and distributed world-wide, backed by high pressure television advertising by multinationals accessing new markets. Of course, toys do not mirror reality in every case. In some instances such as that of Cierva's Autogiro, in reality a developmental dead end, public enthusiasm for the toy led to a production line far above that of the real life plane. In a different case, the shortages of material during World War II meant that there are no diecast toys of that epitome of the heavy bomber, the Lancaster.

Due to the wide scope of the subject, this book concentrates on cast toys that are models of real planes. Tinplate toys have been excluded. Not only are these expensive and less easily available to the collector, but they present neither such good representations of the real thing, nor do they cover such a wide range of real life aircraft manufacture and types.

How to use the book As the contents page shows, the first two chapters deal with Dinky Toys, undoubtedly the most important manufacturer of diecast planes. Generally, a description of the major features of each group is followed by a listing giving details such as the size of wingspan, the production span dates, the colours, the renumbering and other dating aids. In Chapter 1, these listings follow the major sub-sections dividing Dinky production. In Chapter 2, the complete listings are at the end. In Chapter 3, divided alphabetically into countries and sub-divided alphabetically into manufacturers, the listings appear at the end of each manufacturer. For the major ranges, the names in these listings are those used by the manufacturers, but for the smaller ranges the names have, in some cases, been expanded to make the models easier to identify. Relevant picture sections with numbered photographs appear at the end of each chapter. The picture numbers appear in bold in the index for easy reference.

The comprehensive index lists the name of the plane both as used by the toy manufacturer, e.g: Bristol Blenheim Bomber, Dinky 62b, 62d; and as by the lay person, e.g. Blenheim Bomber, Dinky 62b, 62d.

1 Dinky Toys – English

'Not only are Dinky Toys delightful to look at and fascinating to play with, but they have the great virtue of being made with a zinc alloy which is practically unbreakable. They will stand up to all the knocking about and rough usage that may be their lot in the hands of very young children and yet retain their shape and rich colouring.'

1939/40 Meccano Catalogue

Collecting Dinky toy aeroplanes produced in the Binns Road Factory in Liverpool presents a fair challenge, not just to the novice collector but to the expert as well. Their production spans 45 years from the first release in 1934 until 1979, with a break during the Second World War, and their numbers run into approximately 75 basic diecastings: some with casting variations; many with colour variations; some with different versions being issued pre- and post-war. The scale varied at different times from approximately 1/220, which produces pretty models with a wingspan mainly between 75mm and 150mm, at the beginning, to scales around 1/65, with a wingspan up to 200mm, for the very detailed large models produced in the 1970s when the need to standardise box sizes to assist the retailer took precedence over consistency of scale. Enthusiasm within the factory for producing aeroplanes waxed and waned several times over the years and they fall into distinct groups:

a Pre-war production, including Sets and imported French Dinky Toys.
b Post-war (1945–49) re-issue of some of these models.
c Those introduced in the late forties, most of which were renumbered from two-figure plus letter suffix numbers to three-figure numbers. Some of these remained in production until the early sixties.
d The group in production from 1954 to the mid-sixties, all of which were released on three-figure numbers.
e The 'Big Planes' of 1965 to 1980.

Frank Hornby's Meccano Dinky Toys

Frank Hornby, father of the British tinplate and diecast toy industry, dominated the first three quarters of the 20th century despite his death in 1936. It was his invention and development of a constructional toy that formed the basis of the Meccano empire that was to encompass tinplate, clockwork and electric Hornby Trains and diecast Dinky Toys. A flair for knowing what new product would appeal to the market, a willingness to try new production processes, a zeal for the values of education and improvement and an iron will, established classic ranges of toys whose brand names became eponyms for all similar types of toys.

After the establishment of the Binns Road works in Liverpool as the design and manufacturing centre for the Meccano construction system, a factory which thereafter provided a base for most operations until 1979/80, Hornby looked for a method of promoting his products. He came up with the idea of a monthly publication *Meccano Magazine* which would explain the many wonderful gadgets and models that could be made with Meccano and could carry articles of both educational and general interest to boys. The next development was the introduction of a range of clockwork trains modelled on those available from continental manufacturers such as Bing, which were imported by Gamages and other London department stores. Whereas most of the trains were constructed of tinplate pressings, the engines ran on diecast wheels so it was not too much of a jump to produce station accessories in solid metal.

1931 saw the first of the range of cast metal toys that by 1934 had acquired the name 'Dinky Toys'. An adopted daughter of Frank Hornby, Olive, is credited with the first use of the name Dinky, having reputedly looked at the toys and said, 'aren't they Dinky?'. This Scottish word meaning pretty, neat, of engaging appearance, certainly typifies the toys but also had a similar sound pattern to Tootsie, the name already in use in the United States, for a like range of toy vehicles. This similarity is probably more than a coincidence. Made from mazac and with diecasting machines replacing the older, more labour intensive hand-filled dies, Dinky Toys were a success. Following the production of trains, road vehicles and ships, the move to make aeroplanes was a logical commercial decision. By November 1934, there were already 150 varieties of Dinky Toy available.

Meccano Magazine articles often foreshadowed the types of plane that were modelled. Many issues included not only two pages of *Air News*, but one, or even two other two-page articles on aircraft that were new or had gripped the public imagination with their speed and distance record attempts. Often the articles would cover a group of planes, say seaplanes, one of which would subsequently appear in model form. In this way, the magazine kept the boys informed of new developments in aviation and acted as a publicity machine for Dinky Aeroplanes. Some of the articles enthused about planes that were unsuccessful or at a dead end of development and the information printed was sometimes more enthusiastic than accurate. Whatever the reality of the real models, the pre-war toys are a delightful group and constitute perhaps the prettiest range of diecast aeroplanes made to date.

The numbers of Dinky Toys available continued to increase, with an advertisement proclaiming 200 varieties by June 1935, 250 by August 1936 and 300 by April 1938. However, this success story was shortly to be blighted by the outbreak of war and on 15 September 1939 a shortage of materials caused a general price increase.

Very soon, the factory began to be turned over to war work and toy production began to tail off. The imposition of Purchase Tax in October 1940 raised prices by about 20 per cent, making what toys there were very expensive. Around this time, Spitfires, finished in a wide variety of colours and fitted with split rings in their tail so that they could be worn as pendants or pinned onto the lapel, were sold for 2/6d (12.5p). The whole of this amount, with no deductions for cost of materials or Purchase Tax was donated to Lord Beaverbrook's Spitfire Fund to purchase a 'Meccano Spitfire' for the RAF. The advert in the November 1940 *Meccano*

Magazine (and the box lid covered with silvery paper with black lettering, including 'Spitfire' in script) detailed the colours: light grey, red, yellow, magenta, dark blue, light blue, emerald green, medium green and camouflage. The quality of the metal used was very poor, such a simple shape not requiring a very pure mix to ensure a proper cast, and very few indeed have survived. The pendants that have been seen all have roundels and are finished in red with a silver or green propeller, or in chrome with a silver propeller. The latter finish occurs also on one with a brooch pin fitted. The castings are marked underneath 'Meccano Spitfire Fund'.

Toy stocks were eked out as long as possible and the January 1941 catalogue still listed most of the planes, although the supply must have been virtually exhausted. The Government Order of January 1942 that forbade the manufacture of metal toys was more to show that no effort was being wasted in inessential production than a necessary act to increase production itself. Likewise the Order freezing warehouse stocks was more of a propaganda exercise than an effective curb on supplies. Further restrictions from 30 September 1943 forbade even the sale of new and secondhand metal model or toy goods.

By early 1945, it had become obvious that the end of the war was really only a matter of time and as war work was wound down, so the factory dusted off the pre-war drawings and examined the dies to discover which were in a fit state still to be used. By Christmas 1945, 50 different Dinky Toys were on sale, of which 12 were planes. Not only had these dies survived but they had the merit of being easy to run, requiring little metal and very little assembly. The Spitfire was a new casting but the old die had been modified, not replaced. However, there were far too few to supply the home market and, as the government required that priority be given to exports, they were not widely available. It took until August 1946 for the first new plane, the Avro York, 70a, to be released. November of the same year saw the first truly modern plane, the jet-engined Gloster Meteor.

Wars were not at an end and the Korean War of the early 1950s caused a metal shortage and a hiatus in new releases. 1954 is often regarded as an important date in the story of Dinky Toys as it is the year during which most of the Dinky production was renumbered from a two-number plus suffix letter to a three-number catalogue system. This was occasioned by the 'filling up' of the old system and happens to coincide with a change in the type of road vehicle produced and an emphasis on the marketing of 'Supertoys'. However it made little difference to aeroplane releases, a coherent group of which were in production between 1952 and 1965. The cessation of production coincided with a change in the ownership of the firm. Because of the unrecouped expenses of retooling for Dublo Trains in 1959, Meccano Ltd made a trading loss in 1963 and were taken over by Lines Bros Ltd, another important British toy firm of nearly as great longevity. At that time, the machine shop was being turned over to fully-automated Kipps diecasting machines which improved the rate and quality of production. However, these machines could not run the old dies and a new group of planes (in a bigger scale) was introduced.

In 1971, at the beginning of the recession of the 1970s, not long after the renaming of the firm as Meccano-Tri-ang Ltd, the whole of the Lines Bros group went into liquidation. Airfix, a British manufacturer of plastic kits established since the war, bought the Meccano and Dinky Toy part of the empire. However, lack of direction and labour troubles forced the closure of the Binns Road factory in 1979 and the closure of the firm in 1980. Subsequently, a few products appeared mysteriously from Hong Kong, some boxed and some not. The famous name, Dinky Toys, was sold off and in 1989 was being used again by Matchbox Toys Ltd, but to date there are no planes or products in the range.

Pre-war production and post-war re-issues

By the 1930s, aeroplanes and their flyers had all but lost their image of the daredevil 'magnificent men in their flying machines', held together with chewing gum and string. Their enterprises, though no less adventurous and stirring, had the more serious aim of developing air routes around the world for the transportation of people and mail. The development of machines capable of such long journeys at high speed led to air races and exciting attempts at speed and distance records. Press interest in the exploits of the intrepid pilots inspired the public imagination. Indeed, press barons funded prizes for successful first flights and air races to whip up enthusiasm and increase the readership of their newspapers. How fortuitous it was that the new Dinky aeroplane ranges were launched in June 1934 in the midst of such public interest.

SETS AND BOXES The first six models were planned and released together as a set, in line with the marketing tactics of the newly emerging diecast toy division of the great Meccano Empire. The concept of sets was a hang-over from that of the Hornby train set in which a locomotive, rolling stock and rails were sold all in one box, for one was no use without the other though each was also available individually. However, you could play with one aeroplane on its own and the common practice, after this first release, was for the planes to be packed in retailer boxes of six of the same thing, or, for the prestige and larger planes, in individual boxes. These were generally blue with a printed description of the real plane on the lid, usually on the outside but occasionally on the inside, for example, 60h Singapore.

Until 1939, the printing was text only, with a diagram being added later. Yellow boxes of six with the models packed vertically were used for some small planes such as six 62m Airspeed Envoys in a box dated 12.39. Blue, or sometimes yellow or green, display boxes of six were sold as a unit, for instance by mail order from Hamleys, the London toy shop, who for Christmas 1940 offered a yellow box of camouflaged Blenheims 62d (which were laid out 'flying' from bottom right to top left in echelon or a blue box of six Spitfires 62a or six Hurricane 62s (which were laid out in arrowhead formation). The retailer would also sell an individual plane from the box. (See Dealer/Presentation Boxes and contents.) As war approached, shops commonly sold planes loose, e.g. Flying Fortress, even though the item was originally supplied in an individual box. Yellow boxes of six with the models packed vertically were also used for post-war re-issues. The beautifully decorated packaging of the sets with the labelled models corded down in position were by then regarded as prestige gift sets. The popularity of the first set, the 60 Set, and the degree to which they were prized by their child owners, is attested by the number that have survived relatively intact and have turned up at auction, 50 years later, in the second half of the 1980s.

MARKINGS Almost all the toys, (except the Autogiro), were marked with one or more of the following: 'Dinky', 'England', 'Meccano', or 'M.Ltd'. 'Made in England' appeared as well, so there is no doubt about the make and country of origin of this group. The reason for the inclusion of a small number of French Dinky planes in this chapter is that Meccano imported them into the UK and advertised them alongside the domestic product in the catalogue. However, unsurprisingly, the French product seems not to have been so popular as less have survived in England compared with the domestic product. Perhaps children were not sufficiently familiar with French aeroplanes to desire them. Indeed, the vast majority of planes modelled by Dinky in the UK were English and very familiar at the time even though some have now faded into obscurity.

SCALE The scale of the pre-war models is very variable ranging between approximately 1/130 and 1/220.

DATES The introduction and deletion dates of each toy are relatively easy to ascertain because of the wealth of dated catalogues that Meccano published. Most of the castings were simple to produce for they are without the depth or complexity of many of the road vehicles and are fairly light, so most planes remained in the catalogue until 1941, even though the factory was being turned over to war work. The 1941 catalogues are printed as being in effect 'until further notice' but stocks were variable and many items would have run out before sales of metal toys were banned in 1942, freezing what stocks there were in the warehouses. Thus the term 'pre-war', though common parlance, is a slight misnomer. There are casting variations on almost all the models and it can be less easy to place an individual item within these dates but there are some general changes that can be dated and which apply to much of the pre-war production. These are appended here. More information on individual pieces can be found in the numerical listing. Many boxes printed the number of available Dinky varieties – of all types, not just aeroplanes, on their interior. Linking these to the earliest appearance of the particular number in *Meccano Magazine* advertising, and assuming that the box is no earlier than the *Meccano Magazine* date, the number claimed provides a dating guide to the box (and contents if original). Numbers claimed to be available: 150 by November 1934
200 by June 1935
250 by August 1936
300 by April 1938

GENERAL DATING GUIDES

GLIDING GAME In 1937, as part of Meccano's constant attempts to improve the play value of their toys, the Gliding Game was developed. This enabled the planes to be 'flown' down pieces of fine cord which were passed through the eye of a split pin located in a purpose-made hole in the upper wing or fuselage of the larger planes. The split pin is unusual in having a square cross section to locate firmly in the square hole so that the plane flew straight and did not swing on its axis. In 1940 the hole was filled in. The small planes were equipped with a wire hook which located over the wings. The leaflet shows the General Monospar, decorated in the first type bright colours nestling in the hook, but this is an anachronism because by the time the game was introduced, the 60 Set colours had changed and the Monospar was in silver with registration letters. Most of the wires have got lost, or are in the wrong box, so are of little assistance in dating. The leaflet gives detailed instructions on how to rig up the game and, apart from the last paragraph mentioning the planes, is virtually identical to that of the French language version in the French Dinky Gliding Game leaflet. *Meccano Magazine* for March 1938 even printed a suggestion from a Manchester reader that the split pin made a good bomb release mechanism for unleashing airgun pellets from beneath a Whitley Bomber upon a target constructed from wood and Meccano. One suspects that less careful children may have selected other victims!

NAMES

Before 1938, most of the planes were not marked with their names, though some such as the Singapore Flying Boat always were. When the names were added, it was usually the same wording as that in the catalogue, though, for instance, 60w Flying Boat Clipper III is actually marked 'Pan American Airways Clipper III'. Note that it is only the name and not the number that is embossed under the wing. The names were on removable inserts in the dies enabling one die to be used for all the versions. The outline of this insert is often clearly visible particularly on late examples where the die has become worn.

REGISTRATION
LETTERS

Before 1938, the registration letters, if applied, were usually black and slightly smaller and more rounded than subsequently.

PROPELLER PINS

The pins holding on the tinplate propellers were thin with small heads until some time in 1939. Subsequently, thicker and larger ones with hemispherical heads were used. In 1940, flat-headed ones were introduced and these latter two types ran concurrently both during 1940–41 and after the war. Propellers are usually bright metal, referred to as 'silver' but not actually painted silver, while silver planes may have red painted ones.

CAMOUFLAGE
AND ROUNDELS

Although there are earlier examples, camouflage, or 'Shadow Shading' which had been introduced as standard for the RAF in 1937 by the Air Ministry, became more common from 1939. There are two distinct shades of the two hand-applied colours: mid-green with mid-brown and later, dark green with dark brown. The civilian planes, in particular, were renamed when they were camouflaged to something more suitable, e.g. 60a Imperial Airways Liner became 66a Heavy Bomber. At first, and until 1939, the RAF roundels on some models, such as 60h Singapore Flying Boat, which should have been red upon white upon blue were represented by a red roundel and a blue roundel stencilled on the wings with the silver band between them representing the white. Some early issues of, for instance, 60n Fairey Battle or 60p Gloster Gladiator have the dots applied in red paint. Red, white and blue transfers with even width bands were introduced in 1937 and after 1939 became standard. The decal applied to camouflaged planes was normally a red and blue roundel, though red, white and blue ones are found particularly on fuselage sides. Some had a prototypical additional outer ring of a high visibility colour, yellow. (There is a certain irony in camouflaging a plane *and* ensuring the visibility of its roundels.) When the fuselage roundels were changed by the Air Ministry to blue and red in April 1939, it was decreed that the underside of the camouflaged fighters (which Dinky had modelled in white) should be 'dazzle' camouflage of black for the port wing and white for the starboard. The Dinky liveries followed suit. In December 1940, schemes were standardised and 'temperate land' camouflage of dark green and dark earth with black underside was adopted. Again Dinky followed. Generally, models with light camouflage had high visibility roundels and those with dark camouflage had red and blue roundels. The post-war re-issues and issues initially were found with red, white and blue roundels from the camouflaged planes. Then they had roundels with a thin white ring as used by the RAF on uncamouflaged surfaces from 1942 to 1947. Later they were changed to the even width rings used after 1947.

WHEELS   Small, plain, gold-coloured, mazac wheels in one of two diameters, 6mm or 8mm, were fitted as standard though they were subsequently deleted on some military models. According to the factory drawing of the larger wheel, it was made of lead briefly in 1938. Examples have been found but it is important to ascertain whether lead wheels found on models are original or are white metal replacements. Flying Boats were fitted with rollers.

RE-ISSUES   Those castings that were re-issued post-war were often given a new generic name, for example 60g DH Comet became 60g Light Racer – possibly because most of the prototypes had not survived the war in any numbers. Some of the very latest issues of the models that usually had name transfers did not carry them and there are also some unusual registration letters.

METAL FATIGUE   Metal fatigue is unfortunately all too common in the pre-war castings, the Mayo Composite suffering particularly. The break-up of the metal starts as hairline cracks but eventually pieces can fall off and the metal crumbles. There is no cure for this as it is an electro-chemical action within the metal structure caused by impurities in the mazac. It is to be hoped that if the metal is contaminated, this process will take many years to cause destruction, so that these pretty models can be enjoyed for many years to come. It would be a shame for them, with the exception of any tinplate wings, to turn to dust like a collection of ancient flying beetles. Metal fatigue causes the castings to 'grow' and diewear can cause them to become smaller or larger so that the wingspan dimensions given in the tables may be approximate.

GROUPING   The planes are described basically in groups, for example the 60 Set; Civil Aeroplanes; and so on, with all the different issues and liveries grouped together on the earliest name that was issued. The toy's relationship to the real plane and general comments are found next. The French imports are covered in detail in the French Dinky chapter. The detail for more accurate dating is found in the numerical listing at the end of the section. Numerical order is very close to the order of issue of the basic casting. Every attempt has been made to stick rigidly to the titles that Dinky used for the planes in the numerical listing, but for punctuation simplicity, the plethora of quotation marks has been omitted. Thus Fairey 'Battle' Bomber is rendered as Fairey Battle Bomber. Pre-war castings re-issued post-war and included within the pre-war tables are marked re-issue in bold for clarity.

Related items

There are items that appeal to the toy collector even although they are not toys. Some of them aid collecting: copies of manufacturers' catalogues, which Dinky produced virtually every year, and the monthly issues of *Meccano Magazine* which advertise and feature the Dinky product. Some are of interest for the background they provide: the factory drawings of the toys, most of which are lost except for a batch from the 1950s. The drawings were made after wooden prototypes had been accepted by the new products committee. The prototypes were normally the same size as the finished toy and correctly painted. Some of the later ones had brass parts which gives very crisp detail. Once the die drawings had been made, the prototypes were no longer needed and the pattern maker was permitted to take them home. Some have survived and an authenticated batch of pre-war prototypes, with markings in Indian ink, are in various collections: 62s Spitfire, 62b Bristol Blenheim, 62g Boeing Flying Fortress, 62k King's Aeroplane, 63b Seaplane Mercury. The prototype of one plane that was never released, the Boeing SST, was presented by Meccano to its creator, Vic Mumby.

The surviving drawings of toys no longer in production were rescued from the Binns Road factory with management agreement in the late 1970s so that they could be preserved. There are no doubt others that have been taken from the drawing office at various times. Some of the drawings were used to produce the die made of tool steel. It was usually in two pieces, with one fixed to the base of the machine and the other moveable. Mazac, an alloy originally almost pure zinc was forced between the two sections of the die into a toy-shaped cavity. Opening the die enabled the part to be removed. The casting machines were at first hand-operated but later became fully automatic. Other drawings were for non-diecast parts, to show assembly details or paint and decal finishes. All the drawings are dated and are an invaluable aid to research, quite apart from their intrinsic fascination.

Experimental versions were produced as part of research and development: 60az Arc-en-Ciel in white and green, 60e Monospar G-ABVD an unpainted casting, 62h Hawker Hurricane chrome plated, 62m Airspeed Envoy in RAF finish, 62r DH Albatross without wheels and, from the Big Plane Range, a Phantom 725 in Hurricane colours and a Bell Helicopter 732 with added stretchers. Great care must be taken to authenticate such items as these, for it is not too difficult to produce repaints and livery changes.

It is also possible to reproduce, using rubber moulds, models in white metal which can be difficult to distinguish from the original. White metal is much softer than mazac and is easily scratched with a pin. There are souvenir issues made in pewter. A half-size Vulcan Bomber and a post-war Spitfire, usually silver plated, fitted with a ring or pin to represent the Spitfire Fund Souvenir, were produced in 1983 for the exhibition celebrating 50 years of Dinky Toys at the London Toy and Model Museum. Replacement parts are available: propellers and floats in white metal; propellers in tinplate; waterslide transfers. It is possible to reproduce boxes with sophisticated photocopiers. Repaints vary from the ones done by the original owner to match an actual livery or with superdetailing to recent refurbishment of chipped models. Some of these are so good that they appear to be original but often silver repaints can be detected by the thin shiny paint. The originals have thick aluminium-silver paint. Carrier film around the edge of transfers on a pre-war item indicates that they are not original.

Copies of pre-war planes were made in India during and immediately after the war. The quality is frequently good, for example the DC3 and Whitley Bomber, and not all the underneath markings have been removed, nor were they marked made in India. This group was accompanied by others never made by Dinky.

The pre-war models

The 22 pre-war castings with several liveries on each casting at first sight seem a confusing mixture, but they can be broken down quite conveniently into four types: the 60 Set; civil aeroplanes; seaplanes; military aircraft. Some of the planes fit into more than one category and Dinky created some interesting variations with the use of camouflage paint so the edges of the groups tend to merge into one another.

THE 60 SET

The very first group of six models, issued in June 1934, was packaged as a set in a blue presentation box and allocated the number 60, each model being given a letter suffix to distinguish it within the set. The models are a mixture of types ranging from a beautiful airliner, via one based on a prototype that did not go into production and three other monoplanes, to a model of a military prototype, an autogiro, the forerunner of the helicopters. The models were regarded primarily as toys and were painted in bright eye-catching colours designed for instantaneous appeal to the boy in the toyshop who would most likely never have seen an aeroplane and would have gleaned his knowledge from *Modern Boy*, *The Boy's Own Paper*, *Meccano Magazine* or *Arthur Mee's Encyclopaedia*. Each model could be purchased individually. *See also:* 66 Set.

Imperial Airways Liner – 60a, 66a

The 90-foot wingspan of the Armstrong Whitworth AW15 Atalanta means that the Dinky is 1/216 scale, nominally 1/220. The construction consists of a diecast fuselage/tail unit with the high round-tipped tinplate wing tabbed on. Two wheels on a single axle and four diecast engines, with small unpainted tinplate propellers, rivetted to the leading edge of the wing complete this toy which is especially pretty in gold with blue or red sunray pattern, a scheme found commonly on sporting planes, and it is a good model. The later plain colours had the registration G-ABTI, that of Atalanta herself. 66a, the camouflage version, was called a Heavy Bomber.

DH Leopard Moth – 60b, 66b

This fairly good model is 1/145 scale and is constructed from a single diecasting carrying a tinplate wing. The small two-bladed propeller is fitted directly onto the pointed nose and the two wheels share a single axle. Camouflaged as 66b, it was called the Dive Bomber Fighter.

Percival Gull – 60c, 60k, 66c, 60k re-issue

It first appeared in the 60 Set. In 1936, Amy Mollison set a distance record of 6,700 miles to Cape Town in just over three days, so Dinky finished the plane in light blue and silver and gave it Amy's registration letters, in blue, G-ADZO. The very first models were part of a promotion, packed in 60c boxes but with a mention of a special display at Lewis's in Manchester. Later, this, the Percival Gull Monoplane, was numbered 60k and packaged in a little box whose lid bore the legend: 'Scale model of actual Percival Gull Aeroplane flown by Mrs Amy Mollison on her record flight to Cape Town and back'. In 1937, H L Brook took the South African record and Dinky packaged the same plane, but with the registration letters in black, in a yellow box describing it as: 'Scale Model Souvenir of actual Percival Gull Aeroplane flown by Mr H L Brook on his record-breaking South African flight in 1937'. This description bends the truth as this 1/145 scale model is good on the whole, but not too accurate around the windows. The tinplate wing slots through the diecast body just above the undercarriage struts which carry two wheels on a single axle. There is a large two-blade propeller fitted to the nose. 66c Two-Seater Fighter is the camouflaged version. Post-war the toy was re-issued on 60k with 'Light Tourer' instead of 'Percival Gull' impressed in fine letters under the wing and had either a large or small two-bladed propeller.

Low Wing Monoplane – 60d, 66d

Considered to be based on the Vickers Jockey, this was a design that did not go into production. It has the tinplate wing slotted through the diecast body, two wheels on a single axle and a large two-bladed propeller. If it is a model of the Jockey, the scale is 1/130. With its open cockpit it is the most toylike of the Dinky planes, though the later fitting of a pilot's head improved the look slightly. The later version, camouflaged as 66d, had the improbable title of Torpedo Dive Bomber.

General Monospar – 60e, 66e

The Monospar design, by virtue of its lightness and strength, produced fast planes one of which, the ST/25 upon which the Dinky is modelled, won the 1934 King's Cup Air Race. At 1/150 scale, it is a really pretty model of a very pretty plane. The single diecasting of the wings has the engines and undercarriage legs cast in, the latter being fitted with wheels on individual axles, a system which was used as standard on models released subsequent to the 60 Set. The propellers have two small blades. Camouflaged, it was known as 66e Medium Bomber.

Cierva Autogiro – 60f, 60f

Invented by Juan de la Cierva, this revolutionary design had a rotary engine which powered the propeller with the freely rotating, unpowered, rotor above the cockpit providing the lift and enabling near vertical take-off. The one-piece diecasting initially lacked the pilot's head. The undercarriage has a single axle with two wheels. The small two-bladed propeller and the rotor are tinplate. It is a reasonable model, 1/156 scale, with no markings and is difficult to distinguish from the French Dinky except by the colour: the English Dinky, except for 66f, is probably always gold with blue rotor and tail tips. The later slightly longer engine cowling and more oval cockpit hole can be accounted for by routine die maintenance. Dinky painted it silver with RAF roundels on the fuselage and called it Army Cooperation Autogiro, 66f.

CIVIL AEROPLANES

DH Comet Aeroplane – 60g, 60g re-issue

This plane was created to take part in the 1934 MacRobertson Air Race held to commemorate the centenary of the Australian State of Victoria. Several were ordered, amongst others by Jim and Amy Mollison, but the race was won by C W A Scott and T C Black piloting G-ACSS. Despite advertising in *Meccano Magazine* that they were modelling the winning plane, when the registration letters were later applied, Dinky used G ACSR, which had been piloted by Jones and Waller and got no further than Baghdad. G-ACSR was subsequently, however, a very successful plane making record flights to Capetown and back: 14,000 miles piloted by A E Clouston and Mrs Kirby-Green (as publicised in the 1938 Meccano catalogue); and by Clouston again who, accompanied by Ricketts, completed the first round trip of 24,000 miles to New Zealand. This good model, 1/157 scale, is a one-piece casting with small two-bladed propellers and wheels in fairings. At first marked 'Dinky Toys' up inside the fuselage and 'Meccano Made in England' on the tail but without the plane name and with no registration letters, it later acquired both. Judging by the different sizes of ejector pins found and the differing length of the words 'Made in England', there was more than one die in use at the same time. The name was changed to Light Racer after the war and it acquired small three-bladed props and spurious but apt registration letters, G-RACE.

Douglas DC3 Airliner – 60t

The Dinky, PH-ALI, is a model of one used by KLM. BEA used one on its first commercial UK flight. The 1/220 scale, one-piece casting is good but because the fuselage is hollow and open underneath, the sides are moulded rather flatly without the graceful underbelly curve that distinguishes the full-size plane. The first castings had a square gliding game hole set well back along the fuselage and a tiny tail wheel was fitted at the rear. Both of these fittings were later deleted. There were two standard wheels and three-blade propellers. The individual box lid is printed with information about the plane and a line drawing with the parts of the plane labelled. Despite its wartime service, BEA's use of them on its first commercial UK flight and its essential part in the Berlin Airlift which provided a springboard for many an airline, the toy was not re-issued, leading one to suppose that the die was lost during the war.

DH Flamingo Liner – 62f not issued

Publicised in the 1939/40 catalogue as a 'Scale model of the latest British Transport Monoplane. It has a top speed of 245mph and can carry 12 to 20 passengers'. In the Canadian catalogue dated 8 November 1939, it is marked 'suspended'. Though featured on the rear cover of *Meccano Magazine* for a year from late 1943, it was not issued. Any examples of the Flamingo that do exist in metal are from the late 1980s and are models in white metal, made for collectors.

Airspeed Envoy – 62m, 62k, 62m re-issue

One of these adaptable planes was commissioned by the Air Council for the King's Flight. The more luxurious trimmings reduced its passenger capacity to four with three crew: the pilot, Captain of the King's Flight, Wing Commander Fielden, a radio operator and a steward. It was finished in the eye-catching livery of the Brigade of Guards, blue, red and silver. The Dinky is a very pretty 1/180 scale representation of both the standard and the King's Aeroplane, showing the characteristic fluting over the Cheetah IX engine cylinders. A single diecasting, it has two two-blade propellers and two small wheels. 62m is the standard version in a variety of colours, its windows attractively picked out in silver, with a selection of registration numbers. 62k is the authentically finished Airspeed Envoy King's Aeroplane G-AEXX, packed in its own little blue box with printed information on the lid. Incidentally, Dinky had run out of 60 numbers by this time and jumped directly to 62k to designate the King's plane. Re-issued post-war on 62m as Light Transport. Each one is marked under the wing with the relevant name.

Junkers Ju90 Airliner – 62n, 62y, 67a, 62y re-issue

The large one-piece casting of the 1/217 scale model is an imposing representation of the Ju90. It has a distinctive tailfin with the forward part fixed and the larger flap protruding above in an elegant curve. Two wheels and four three-bladed propellers are fitted. The windows are not in the casting but are represented by bluish transfers and the registration number is the prototypical D-AURE. Two-toned officially to please little children, not because the impending hostilities could have made a German machine unpopular, though the finish covered for that as well, the Giant High-Speed Monoplane was numbered 62y. With this name, the casting was re-issued post-war, finished in a similar manner or in silver. Painted black (with white transfers) and blue undersurfaces, the German night raider colours, the Junkers Ju89 Heavy Bomber, 67a, used the same casting and therefore is not a model of the real Ju89. When the second version was released the name was placed on an insert and the 'J.U.90' became 'J.U.9.0.'. Both the pre-war Junkers were packed in individual boxes with details of the actual plane on the lid. Whereas the civilian information on the box lid is good, that for the military plane is imaginative. Not only was the fuselage different from the civilian version, and the engines had different capabilities, but it was not fitted with the armament that Dinky claimed. Perhaps the errors were, for Dinky, a most unusual mistake or perhaps incorrect information was supplied as part of a clever disinformation campaign!

Ensign Class Airliner – 62p, 62x, 68a, 62p re-issue

The Dinky is a good, curvaceous, model of this graceful plane and consists of two castings: the fuselage and tail in one piece with a recess in the top of the casting to take the single-piece wing, engines and undercarriage legs. The two pieces are rivetted together and the ensemble completed with two wheels and four three-blade propellers. The scale is 1/220. G-ADSR, 'Ensign', named as such on a transfer either side of the nose and on a small paper label on the individual box, was released in December 1938, to be quickly followed by several others with authentic names and registration letters, all the names beginning with E. 62x, British 40-Seater Airliner, was called the 'Western' type to indicate the version with the short-haul seating capacity, although indistinguishable from the 27-seater from the outside. It was painted to appeal to children in two bright colours, the second one being applied as a flash along the top of the fuselage and to the ailerons and elevators. 68a is the Ensign Airliner in

Service Camouflage, with the gliding game hole filled in. Post-war, the casting was re-issued as Armstrong Whitworth Airliner, Explorer or sometimes Echo, in silver or in two colours masked in the same way as 62x. Each of the versions carried its own name under the wing.

De Havilland Albatross Mail Liner – 62r, 62w, 68b, 62r re-issue

The Air Ministry decided to promote British research and ordered two DH 91 Albatross experimental mail planes, so named for the resemblance of the long thin wings to those of that long range bird, the Albatross. Imperial Airways received a delivery of five 21-seater short-range versions and designated them the Frobisher Class. G-AFDI made record flights: London to Paris in 53 minutes, London to Brussels in 48. The Dinky is 1/216 scale and a very good neat representation with the two castings, comprising the upper fuselage with tail, and lower fuselage with wings, nesting cleanly together. The circular air intakes for cooling the engines are modelled on the leading edges of the wing though, for lack of clutter, the two innermost ones nearest the fuselage have been omitted. The toy is completed by two wheels and four three-bladed propellers, which for accuracy should have had two blades. The Albatross was painted silver and given the Air Ministry number G-AEVV. Still in silver, but with its authentic individual name and speedbird logo (Frobisher, G-ADFI, being the first real plane to carry this emblem) transferred on either side of the nose, the Imperial Airways Frobisher Class Airliner was numbered 62w. Finished in camouflage, the livery in which it flew when used by the RAF as military transport, 68b was known as Frobisher Class Liner in Service Camouflage. Re-issued post-war under the simplified name Four-engined Liner, 62r, it had all the underwing lettering engraved in a smaller size. It was given a wide variety of finishes. Each is given its name under the wing. The Albatross 62r and the Frobisher 62w came in individual boxes.

FLYING BOATS

Flying Boats now look so antiquated that it is difficult to realise that they were the perfect solution to the exploration of the world before the establishment of international airports in all countries. The concept was that of the ocean-going ship which could travel between seaports over land as well as sea rather than the more modern idea of a rapid transit system linking capital to capital and a country to its holiday resorts. Moreover, flying boats, not needing expensive, clumsy undercarriages, could be far larger and were relatively cheaper to build.

Singapore Flying Boat – 60h, 60m

This biplane with triple tail fins looks about as flight-worthy as a bumble bee, and it buzzed around sedately at a cruising speed of 95mph giving it a range of 1,000 miles. Used by the RAF (hence the roundels) as an anti-piracy patrol flying from Alexandria in Egypt, this gun ship had Lewis gun positions in the nose, amidships and one near the tail. The Dinky Toy is a complex construction of two tinplate wings with diecast fuselage/tail unit, struts, floats and engine pods. The four large propellers are two-bladed. At 1/216 scale, it is quite a fair model, though the fuselage is somewhat long and clumsy and the sweep back on the leading edge of the upper wing is so unpronounced that it tends to look more like a bad pressing than an intentional feature. The strange holes in the upper part of the fuselage are correct representations of the gun emplacements and the pilot sat in the small greenhouse-like protuberance above the main body. The name, after the very first issues, is impressed under the starboard wing. There are several developments in the toy for, when it was first issued, it had the concave undersides of the bows fully modelled; no roller was fitted and there was no gliding hole present in the upper wing. During 1936, a red, green or yellow plastic roller was fitted, which subsequently became green wood in 1940. In 1937, the gliding hole was pierced in the upper wing and in 1940 the hull was simplified by the removal of most of the under-bow keel to make the casting easier to remove from the mould. Other changes also occurred (see table) making this the Dinky plane with the greatest number of variations. The few produced in 1940 and finished in grey had a genuine precursor in the Blackburn Flying Boat that was delivered in 1931 to 209 Sqdn in Battleship Grey. Service Flying Boats often had their hulls painted in bright colours to enable rescue boats to see them and Dinky produced it, without the gliding game hole, in a variety of colourful finishes as 60m, Four-Engined Flying Boat. Early issues have either no roller, or no name impressed under the wing, or neither.

Empire Flying Boat – 60r, 60x, 63a, 60r reissue

228 of these all-metal Short S.23 Flying Boats were ordered by Imperial Airways to comply with the Government's 1935 Empire Airmail Scheme which decreed that mail should be carried by air if possible. A better-known military derivative, the Sunderland, went into service in 1938 and became the mainstay of Coastal Command. The first Dinky Toy, scale 1/220, was named Caledonia after the experimental version. A good model with all the doors and windows correctly marked on the hull, the two castings comprise the hull and tail with a section indented to take the wings and central fuselage section. The diecast floats are rivetted to the wings and it carries four three-bladed propellers. The roller is red, or occasionally yellow, plastic, replaced in 1940 by wood. Initially, the deep keel beneath the bow was cast in but this was removed in 1940, the accuracy of the model suffering considerably. Post-war castings are of the second type. Individually boxed, the names were on transfers applied to the nose. Early ones had larger oblong boxes allowing the plane wing to be parallel to the long edge with their names on card inserts. The lids featured a line drawing and some text. Once six names had been released, the boxes with text only on the lid were decreased in size and the names applied to the box edge with gummed paper strips. The planes fitted diagonally in these square boxes. The box lids detailed the models available, the early oblong ones up to Cambria, the later square ones featured that part of the range that was available. Not all the names were available all the time because three crashed and Dinky renamed them, making 15 in all. Atlantic Flying Boat, 60x, is uncommon and is finished in striking two-tone liveries with individual names and registration letters and the wings a different colour from the fuselage. The same casting was used as part of the Mayo Composite, 63a (see below). Post-war, it was still known as the Empire Flying Boat, 60r, with a reduced number of names and fitted with a brass or red plastic roller.

Mayo Composite – 63 = 63a + 63b

The Air Ministry ordered this piggyback pair from Shorts after its design in 1932 by Major RH Mayo, the Technical General Manager of Imperial Airways. The larger plane was designed to assist the small one into the air and then as soon as the critical speed of 150mph had been reached, the relative lift was such that the small plane continued upwards when the automatic separation device triggered while the lower one dropped down, despite the reduction in overall weight. The system may appear strange until one remembers that a similar system was used to launch the Space Shuttle from the back of a specially-modified jumbo jet for its experimental flights. Shorts modified the Empire Flying Boat by belling out the fuselage to give a more stable base and added 250 square feet, a 16 per cent increase, to the wing area for added lift. Maia, G-ADHK, first flew in August 1937. The Dinky Maia, 63a, is thus not an accurate model, the casting not being modified in any way except for the name cartouche – Mayo Composite – being used and the fitting of the tinplate cradle to take Seaplane Mercury 63b. Maia and Mercury transfers were fitted to the two castings. The pair were regarded as a set and they had a set number, 63, and a box that took the pair, but they were also available separately.

Seaplane Mercury –
63b, 63b re-issue,
700 renumber

This powerful little machine was specially designed to be the upper part of the Mayo Composite. The Dinky, a good, approximately 1/220 scale model, consists of a single hollow fuselage main casting fitted with two diecast floats rivetted on through the wing in the usual manner. The name Mercury is found beneath the wing and transferred on the nose. The correct registration, G-ADHJ, was used. A spring-clip fixed within the length of the fuselage holds the toy on top of Maia. Post-war, without the clip but with the fixing pegs still part of the interior of the casting and with 'Seaplane' beneath the wing and spurious registration letters, it was re-issued still as 63b. Production of planes ceased between 1949 and 1952, but then it was re-released with flat disc propeller pins in black. Re-numbering to 700 took place in 1954 and it was not dropped from the catalogue until 1957, 18 years after its first appearance. Even though most other Dinkies had been boxed individually by this time, a box was not produced for the seaplane.

Pan American Flying Boat Clipper III – 60w, 60w re-issue

Pan Am called all their flying boats 'Clipper', the merchantmen of the air. The Dinky is a good 1/212 scale model of the Sikorsky S-24-B of which only three were made. The fuselage, wing pylon and tail are cast in one piece and the separate wing is rivetted onto the pylon. The two floats are as usual separate castings. Four small three-bladed propellers and a plastic roller are fitted. The registration USA is on the port wing and NC16736 on the starboard. As a waterline model it is very pretty, the distinctive 'vee' on the flightdeck window being well modelled. As a model of the plane in flight it suffers from the technical necessity of not having an undercut on the die so that the sweep of the bow is somewhat truncated. Also because the plane sat down into the water, the fuselage does not look deep enough. They were packed in individual boxes containing a leaflet on the real aircraft. Pre-war it appeared only in this version. It was re-issued post-war as Flying Boat, 60w, with no registration letters and a brass or plastic roller. The name under the wing was changed to suit.

MILITARY AEROPLANES

Fairey Battle Bomber – 60n, 60s

The Dinky is a good model in 1/216 scale, a single casting with a hollow fuselage and the undercarriage legs cast in. The legs were removed in 1940. Initially the toy was not named. A three-bladed propeller was fitted.

Finished in silver with the red dot and blue band of the RAF roundel stencilled on each wingtip. When the camouflaged version with the new Air Ministry Shading was released it was allocated the number 60s and called a Medium Bomber. The high visibility roundel was on one wingtip only. They were available in 'mirror' pairs in which the camouflage was applied in an exactly opposite manner and the roundel to the other wingtip. From 1939, the original title with subtitle, Fairey Battle Bomber, Camouflaged, also 60s, was used for a version with roundels on both tips, which were also available in pairs. In 1940, for the darker camouflage this was changed to a blue circle with a red dot on each wing.

Gloster Gladiator Biplane – 60p

Three examples of this last biplane of the RAF, named Faith, Hope and Charity defended Malta in WWII. The toy is to 1/225 scale and is a good model with a realistic rake to the wings. The smooth metal front section and ribbed fabric-covered rear section of the fuselage are well modelled, but the presence of the pilot's head rather than a cockpit canopy makes it look earlier than it is. The heavy central wing support is the rivet that holds the casting of the upper wing to the lower wing and fuselage casting, with the tinplate oblong strut component sandwiched between them. It is fitted with a two-blade propeller and tiny wheels. The upper wing carried the maker's name and the plane name was added to the lower in 1939. Only available in this finish, it is now difficult to find, as it was so easy to lose such a small item.

Armstrong Whitworth Whitley Bomber – 60v, 62t

The 1/220 scale Dinky is quite a good model which omits the rear gun detail. It is one solid casting with a witness of the slight angling of the wings. Two wheels (the tail wheel being part of the casting) and two three-bladed propellers complete the toy. Finished in silver with RAF roundels on the wings. The drawing, dated 11 August 1937, for the roundels is one of the few pre-war factory drawings extant. As Armstrong Whitworth Whitley Bomber with Shadow Shading, 62t, the first to be so named, it was available first in light, then in dark camouflage, with gliding hole and then without and was individually boxed. The dark camouflage type had the underneath of the wings painted black on the port and white on the starboard wing.

Bristol Blenheim Bomber – 62b, 62d, 62b re-issue

Dinky produced a reasonably accurate, apart from overscale engine cowlings, 1/218 scale one-piece model of the Mark IV without undercarriage and fitted with two three-blade propellers. Finished in silver with RAF roundels, it was named 'Blenheim Bomber' beneath the wing. With no change to the casting, a camouflaged version which ran through the usual painting variations was released as Bristol Blenheim Bomber Camouflaged, 62d. The lid of the wartime box of six remarks on the Wilhelmshaven raid on 3 September 1939. The engine details have been uprated to a more impressive 920hp. The post-war re-issue was renamed Medium Bomber and was given the original number 62b. It can be found with red, white and blue, or red and blue roundels.

Vickers Supermarine Spitfire – 62a, 62e, 62a re-issue

One of the most beautiful and best known fighter planes, the Spitfire became the symbol of the nation's courage. Besides the Meccano Spitfire (see page 4), many others were paid for by public subscription and carried names on the sides of the cockpit such as 'East India Fund Flight', 'North Borneo II' and 'Chorley & District'. The Dinky version is a good model to a scale of 1/202 of the Mk2, a small, solid, one-piece casting without undercarriage fitted with a small three-blade propeller. It was painted silver, though there is a *Meccano Magazine* reference to one in 'service grey', with red, white and blue roundels on the wings or red and blue ones, with high visibility roundels on the fuselage. Vickers Supermarine Spitfire Camouflaged, 62e, came in light or dark camouflage with the appropriate roundels and half black and half white beneath. It is found with red, white and blue or red and blue roundels. The die was modified before it was re-issued as Spitfire, 62a, post-war (see Post-war re-issues).

Hawker Hurricane Single-Seater Fighter – 62s, 62h, 62s re-issue

A reasonably good single-piece casting with an undercarriage, in 1/218 scale, it was fitted with a two-blade propeller. The finish was silver and the red, white and blue roundel drawing is dated 24.11.38. In 1940, the undercarriage was deleted. Hawker Hurricane Single-Seater Fighter Camouflaged, 62h, was available with undercarriage with two wheels on a single axle, but also reportedly in late 1939/early 1940 with wheels on individual axles, in light camouflage and without undercarriage in dark. The post-war re-issue Hurricane, 62s, is finished in silver with a three-bladed propeller and red and blue wing roundels.

Boeing Flying Fortress – 62g, 62g re-issue

Dinky produced a good 1/216 scale model of the B.17D, used by the US Army Air Corps and British units, which is identified by the cooling ribs behind the motor cowlings. The upper fuselage with tail is rivetted to the lower fuselage, wing and undercarriage casting. Three-blade propellers are fitted. Finished in silver with the cockpit and nose canopy blued. The US Army Air Corps insignia, blue roundels carrying a white star with a red dot in the centre, are applied to each wing and the rudder has a blue vertical bar edging red and white stripes. It was usually packed in its own box with details and drawing on the lid. Initially the box had a plain lid and an accompanying leaflet. When it was re-issued post-war it was renamed Long Range Bomber but still utilised the US AAC finish.

The pre-war sets

None of the Dinky aeroplane sets issued between 1934 and 1940 can be regarded as common. It is not known how many of each were produced but they ranged from fairly to very expensive for the time, as the price of each set was the sum of the prices of the individual items. The easiest to find is the second type 60 Set, in which the planes have registration numbers, probably because it was in production for the longest. All the aeroplane sets remained in the catalogue from the time of issue until 1941 but it is not known how readily available they were especially after the start of hostilities. Many of the planes, particularly those in the later sets, suffer from fatigue. It is difficult to tell if a set is original as very few have the planes fixed to the backing card with the original stringing. To authenticate a set, care should be taken to check that the correct plane types of a consistent age are in the box. Luckily each backing card has the name of each aeroplane printed above or below its position in the box. In addition, the overall look and the provenance of the set can go further toward deciding whether the set is as it was originally sold, or whether it has been made up from individual pieces. All the basic castings except that of 62g Boeing Flying Fortress were included in one or other of the sets. The sets range from very pretty to truly magnificent and are scarce and very desirable.

60 Aeroplanes/British Aeroplanes 1934–41

		1st issue	2nd issue
60a	Imperial Airways Liner	gold and blue	gold
60b	DH Leopard Moth	green and yellow	green
60c	Percival Gull	white and blue	white
60d	Low Wing Monoplane	red and cream	red
60e	General Monospar	silver and blue	silver
60f	Cierva Autogiro	gold and blue	gold and blue

First issued (to *circa* 1936) with planes in colourful early livery and subsequently with planes with registration letters, threaded down into a square box with names printed on the backing card. The colours were usually the ones listed above and are thus the commonest found on these castings. The standard blue box carried a colourful, yellow, red and green, label on its lift-off lid. The first printing had 'MECCANO DINKY TOYS' in the top left hand corner but subsequent ones utilised the later logo, 'DINKY TOYS' 'Manufactured by MECCANO Ltd, Liverpool'. The backing card changed as well, the first from *circa* November 1934 being headed 'MECCANO DINKY TOYS no.60' and claiming a production of 150 Varieties (which included Dinky Toys in general, not just planes). The type with the second box lid from *circa* June 1935 which was used for the later plane livery is marked 'DINKY TOYS no.60' with 200 and later, from mid-1938, 300 varieties claimed. (There is also a very early box, probably the first one, with a blue and white label featuring a good line drawing of the Atalanta. The backing card makes no claims to the number of varieties.) Also issued in camouflage as Set 66 Camouflaged Aeroplane Set.

61 RAF Aeroplanes 1937–41
60h Singapore Flying Boat with and, after 1940, without gliding hole
2 x 60n Fairey Battle Bomber
2 x 60p Gloster Gladiator Biplane

Oblong blue box approximately 200mm x 125mm with the contents printed on the lid in black or a plain lid on a '300 varieties' box. (There is a very early, probably the first, box, which is covered in paper with black and gold squiggles and gold and green dashes on a blue ground and contains a card backing claiming 250 models in the range. The label on the edge of the lid is printed with the same information that is on the usual box: A 2185 Dinky Toys RAF Aeroplanes Set 61.) Inside the box, is claimed with some licence that 'Each aeroplane in this set is an exact scale model'. The 1939/40 catalogue proclaims with the full flavour of the times, that 'The outstanding item is a fine model of the Short Singapore III flying boat, a type used by several General Reconnaissance squadrons and by the RAF Iraq Command. The smaller single-engined machines are Fairey Battle two-seater medium bombers, one of the earliest of the modern streamlined monoplanes of this class; and Gloster Gladiator single-seater fighters. The Gladiator is a development of the famous Gauntlet, and is armed with four machine guns. It has a top speed of 250mph.'

63 Mayo Composite Aircraft
63a Maia
63b Seaplane Mercury
See Flying Boats and numerical listing.

64 Presentation Aeroplane Set 1939–41
60g DH Comet
62h Hurricane (camouflaged)/Export: 62a Spitfire
62k King's Aeroplane
62m Airspeed Envoy
62s Hurricane (aluminium)
63b Seaplane Mercury

This is a set made up from the smaller models in the Dinky range and is packed in a small blue box with the contents description on the lid. The inclusion of the red and blue King's Aeroplane makes this unusual set very pretty. A flimsy leaflet dated 4.39 illustrating and describing the planes was enclosed. A Canadian catalogue from 1940 gives a slightly different contents list in which 62h Hurricane Camouflaged is replaced by 62a Spitfire in silver. These names are printed on the backing card. An example of this set has been seen in a box with a New York shop name.

65 Presentation Aeroplane Set 1939–41
60r Empire Flying Boat
60t Douglas DC3
60v Whitley Bomber
60w Clipper III Flying Boat
62n Junkers Ju 90
62p Ensign Class Airliner
62r DH Albatross Mail Liner
62w Frobisher Class Airliner

These are eight of the largest of the Dinky aeroplanes and were all finished in silver. Both this and the previous set were issued the same month, May 1939. The large blue oblong box has a coloured label illustrating six of the models flying through the clouds. The card liner, which was dark blue rather than the usual white, had the names of the planes printed in silver indicating the prestigious nature of the set. A foolscap-sized flimsy leaflet dated 4.39 illustrating and describing the planes was enclosed.

66 Camouflaged Aeroplane Set 1940–41

66a Heavy Bomber	= 60a	Imperial Airways Liner without name
66b Dive-Bomber Fighter	= 60b	Leopard Moth, later version with windows
66c Two-Seater Fighter	= 60d	Low Wing Monoplane, 2nd casting with head, no name
66d Torpedo Dive Bomber	= 60c	Percival Gull
66e Medium Bomber	= 60e	General Monospar with this type name all in dark camouflage with red and blue roundels on the wings
66f Army Co-operation Autogiro	= 60f	Cierva Autogiro with pilot in silver-grey with silver rotor and red, white and blue roundels on the fuselage.

Not released until July 1940 and possibly the scarcest set. The square yellow or green box has the contents printed on the lid in black. The models are laid out in the same formation as in the 60 Set but the names printed on the backing card are the fictitious military ones. Each model was also supplied to the retailer in a yellow box of six.

68 Aircraft in Service Camouflage 1940–41
2 x 60s Fairey Battle Bomber
2 x 62d Bristol Blenheim Bomber
3 x 62e Spitfire
3 x 62h Hurricane
1 x 62t Whitley Bomber
1 x 68a Ensign Class Airliner
1 x 68b Frobisher Class Airliner

Issued in July 1940 as was the previous set. All 13 aircraft were in camouflage, the last two not having been previously available in brown and green. Probably issued briefly in light camouflage but normally in dark. The large square blue box utilises the lid artwork of the 65 Presentation Aeroplane Set, three planes pictured against a cloudy sky either side of a list of the planes in the set. One box has been seen with a label along the edge stating that it is the 'Set of Camouflaged Aeroplanes no.68', while another one reads:

'Made in England
For sale in the United States by
MECCANO COMPANY OF AMERICA INC
200–5th Avenue–New York'

Pre-war dealer/presentation boxes and contents

The planes without individual boxes were packed in presentation boxes which could be sold unbroken or, more usually, used as dealer packs from which items were sold individually. They were not advertised to the public by Meccano, although shops such as Hamleys included them as such in their mail order catalogues. The boxes were usually blue, but green and yellow are also found. The planes, usually six in number, except for the Camouflaged Spitfire 62e of which there could be eight, were usually strung down in flight formation, echelon to the left, arrowhead, reverse arrowhead or line abreast. Some, for example DH Comet, had their wheels nesting in cutouts in the backing card. The box lids varied from (early) completely plain, to (later) having a block of text in the centre, to (later still) very detailed, for example 62h Hurricane Camouflaged with written information including an explanation of high visibility roundels and a labelled drawing. The later box of the 62d Blenheim Camouflaged comments that the planes 'have given splendid service in the present war and took part in the raids on Kiel and Borkum.' (Wilhelmshaven, 3 September 1939). The box printing is usually dated with the month and the year along the edge of the lid.

The following, all scarce, are the versions so far recorded:

60g	DH Comet	63 pairs – facing	blue box, out, in, out
60p	Gloster Gladiator	6 arrowhead	blue box
60n	Fairey Battle Bomber	6 reverse arrowhead	blue box marked 300 varieties
60s	Medium Bomber, mirror image camouflage	2 line abreast	blue box
60s	Fairey Battle Bomber Camouflaged	2 line abreast 6 in echelon	blue box blue box
62a	Spitfire Fighter	6 arrowhead	blue box
62b	Blenheim Bomber	6 echelon	blue or green box
62d	Blenheim Camouflaged	6 echelon	yellow, green or later blue box
62e	Spitfire Camouflaged	6 arrowhead 8 2-3-2 formation	blue box blue box
62h	Hurricane Camouflaged	6 arrowhead	green box
62m	Airspeed Envoy		box dated 12.39
62s	Hurricane	6 arrowhead	blue box

All of 66 The Camouflaged Aeroplane Set a-f were supplied to the retailer in yellow boxes of six with the planes stacked vertically, three and three.

French Dinky toys imported into Britain

The production personnel and facilities of Meccano in France and England were entirely separate. Each factory made its own decisions as to what to manufacture, but it was inevitable that there should be many similarities because of the overall control by Frank Hornby and because the types of toys that appealed to French and British boys in the 1930s were very much the same, though the examples were different being modelled on national prototypes. The planes that the French Dinky factory produced have a distinctly French charm and the early ones are painted in more complex and cheerful colour combinations than the English. This was effective in disguising the fact that several of the castings appear in different guises on different numbers and with different names. The justification for mentioning them in this section is that the ones listed below were imported into England by Meccano and listed in the UK catalogues. Full details can be found in the section on French Dinky.

All the French Dinky models except 60f La Cierva are marked 'Dinky Toys Fab en France' but unfortunately for the collector who is unfamiliar with French planes, none of those in the sets, apart from 61az Dewoitine D338, are named. All were fitted with an undercarriage like the British 60 Set: two legs with one wire axle securing the small wheels against the outside of the legs, except for 60az Arc-en-Ciel which has streamlined fairings enclosing slightly bigger wheels.

The 'z' suffix was added to the French Dinky numbers to distinguish them from the English which used the same digits. Two sets were imported and the two airliners from the sets plus two other models were sold separately. All are difficult to find, the two sets only being imported from 1937 and 1938 respectively and 64a and 64b only in 1939. All except 64b were in 1940 catalogues but there are no records of the stocks that were available. The early 60z box is blue similar to English production. The later is dark green with a yellow inner and a picture on the lid of a boy raising his arm.

60az Arc-en-Ciel
135mm. Gold with red, blue or green wingtips

60z French Aeroplanes
60a Arc-en-Ciel as above
60b Potez 58 75mm. Yellow-orange with grey trim, yellow with white. In different livery as 61d Potez 58 Sanitaire
60c Hanriotpotez H180T 80mm. Green with white or red trim (leading edges of wing and tips of tailplane). Also as 61e Hanriot 180M
60d Breguet Corsaire 78mm. Red with green pattern on wings and tail
60e Dewoitine 500 Chasseur 80mm. White with parts of wing and tailplane red. Also as 61f Dewoitine 500D
60f La Cierva Autogiro rotor 74mm. Casting without pilot's head. Silver fuselage, red tailfins, cream rotor or silver fuselage, green rotor, tailfins and engine cowling. Some rotors black beneath

61az Dewoitine D338
138mm. Second casting with closed windows. Silver with registration in black F-ADBF. The first casting which was that of the Arc-en-Ciel with the addition of three large shiny, turned engine covers was probably not in the imported sets, though *Meccano Magazine* illustrations consistently show the first one (as does its French counterpart).

61z French Aeroplanes
61a Dewoitine D338 above
61b Potez 56 69mm. Blue with silver engines and fuselage top
61c Farman 360 70mm. Silver with yellow or blue flash
61d Potez 58 Sanitaire 75mm. White or silver with red crosses on the wings. *See 60b*
61e Hanriot 180M 80mm. Silver with or without red and blue French Air Force roundels. *See 60c*
61f Dewoitine de Chasse 500D 80mm. Silver with French Air Force roundels. *See 60c*

64az Amiot 370
106mm. Silver with French Air Force roundels

64bz Bloch 220
105mm. Silver with registration in black F-AOHJ

PRE-WAR AND POST-WAR RE-ISSUES

On some of the two-tone planes the colours can look very different in various combinations. There is a 62x British 40-seater Airliner which is a very deep yellow with a maroon trim and almost looks orange. The same yellow is on 60x Atlantic Flying Boat Swiftsure, but in one case it looks pale as the model is fatigued. Describing shades such as mid-blue and dark blue is naturally somewhat subjective.
Each item begins with wingspan measurement.

60 Aeroplanes/British Aeroplanes 1934–41
Set contains: 60a, b, c, d, e, f below
All planes without registration letters.
'150 varieties' on backing card.
c.June 1935: all with registration letter except 60f Autogiro '200 varieties' on backing card.
From mid-1938: '300 varieties' on backing card.
Also as 66 Camouflaged Aeroplanes Set.
See also Sets.

60a Imperial Airways Liner 1934–41
27mm
Gold with blue sunray effect,
silver with blue sunray effect,
white with blue sunray effect,
red with cream sunray effect,
yellow with blue wingtips and tail,
blue with yellow wings with blue tips and yellow fin,
red with cream wingtips and fin, blue with red tips and fin,
white with red tips and fin.
Also seen: white or silver with blue wingtips and fin and three slightly diagonal blue stripes on each wing, blue top of cabin.
Red fuselage and wing tips, cream wing, fin, tailplane and nose.
After 1936: gold, silver, red, white/cream, green, pale blue, mid-blue with registration G-ABTI.
From 1939: Name pressed under wing.
Also in camouflage as 66a Heavy Bomber.

60az Monoplane Arc-en-Ciel 1937/8–40
See Dinky: French Imports and French Dinky

60b DH Leopard Moth 1934–41
76mm
To 1936: green with yellow wingtips and tail,
dark blue with red,
gold with red,
dark blue with orange or silver with green to 1936.
From 1936: green, gold, dark cream, silver, red, beige, mid-blue or pale blue with registration G-ACPT.
1939: name added.
From 1939/40: windows filled in.
Also in camouflage as 66b Dive Bomber Fighter.

60c Percival Gull 1934–41
76mm
To 1936: white with blue wingtips and tail,
cream with blue,
white with green,
buff with red or blue,
mid-blue with white,
golden beige with red,
gold with light green,
or silver with green.
From 1936: white, red, yellow, light blue, gold, or silver with black registration G-ADZO.
From 1939/40: side windows filled in.
Also as 60k Souvenir issues and in camouflage as 66c Two Seater Fighter.
Re-issued post-war as 60k Light Tourer.

60d Low Wing Monoplane 1934–41
76mm
To 1936: red with cream wingtips and tail,
orange with cream,
yellow with green,
gold with blue or silver with red.
From 1936: pilot's head added. Now coloured red, orange, silver or light blue with registration G-AVYP.
Also seen with head and earlier red and cream colour scheme.
Also in camouflage as 66d Torpedo Dive Bomber.

60e General Monospar 1934–41
80mm
To 1936/37: gold with red wingtips and tail
Lilac with blue
Cream with red
Mid-blue with white
or silver with blue.
Thereafter: silver, gold, cream or lilac with registration G-ABVP.
Later: name added.
Also in camouflage as 66e Medium Bomber.

60f Cierva Autogiro 1934–41
(Rotor dia. 72mm) Length 53mm
Gold with blue rotor and tailplane tips, some with light blue edge to engine cowl. Probably most other colours, except 66f below are from French Dinky (see Chapter Two).
c.1936: pilot's head added.
Also in silver-grey with silver rotor and red, white and blue roundels as 66f Army Co-operation Autogiro.

60g DH Comet Aeroplane 1935–41
86mm
To c.1936: red with gold ailerons, elevators and fin,
gold with red,
silver with blue or all red.
From c.1936: red, silver or gold with registration G-ACSR
usually with name under wing. Re-issued post-war as 60g
Light Racer.

60g Light Racer 1945–49
Re-issue of above
Yellow, red or silver with spurious registration G-RACE.
Name under wing.

60h Singapore Flying Boat 1936–41
126mm
Early casting lead hull, with tinplate wings.
Later: mazac hull.
Silver
1940: some grey.
No roller for first few months.
From 1937: gliding game hole in upper wing.
Stencilled roundels until 1939.
Subsequently: red, white and blue transfer roundels.
1940: the hull was simplified, a seat was represented in the
front gun position and the gliding game hole was deleted.
Later: red, green or yellow plastic roller became wood.
Individual boxes.
Also in colours as 60m Four-Engined Flying Boat.

60k Percival Gull Monoplane 1936–41
76mm
60c in commemorative livery of blue with silver wings and
tailplane.
Registration letters G-ADZO in blue for Amy Mollison's
plane or G-ADZO in black for H L Brook's.
Individual yellow boxes.

60k Light Tourer 1945–49
76mm
Re-issue of 60c Percival Gull

60m Four-Engined Flying Boat 1936–41
126mm
Casting of 60h Singapore Flying Boat in civilian colours.
Early: without name impressed under wing.
Later: with name.
Usually with silver propellers and yellow roller, but may have
red or green propellers and green roller.
Letters usually black:
red G-EVCU,
light green G-EVCU,
dark blue, white letters G-EVCU,
dark green G-EYCE,
gold G-EXFE,
gold G-EUTG,
silver G-EUTG,
blue G-EYTV,
red G-EXGF,
cream–fuselage only seen.

60n Fairey Battle Bomber 1937–41
75mm
Silver. Blued cockpit canopy.
1940: some in grey.
1938: name added.
Roundels: early red dots painted. Red and blue stencilled
roundels until 1939. Thereafter: red white and blue transfers.
1940: undercarriage deleted.
Also in camouflage as 60s Medium Bomber.

60p Gloster Gladiator Biplane 1937–41
44mm
Silver
1940: some in grey.
Roundels: early red dots painted. Red and blue roundels
stencilled until 1939.
1939: name added and roundels changed to red, white and
blue transfers.

60r Empire Flying Boat 1937–41
156mm
Silver
Gliding hole in wing until 1940.
Subsequently: the bow casting was simplified, the gliding hole
was deleted.
To 1940: red or yellow, some orange plastic rollers.
From 1940: wood
Pre-war names and registration numbers:
Caledonia G-ADHM.
Followed immediately by:
Canopus G-ADHL,
Corsair G-ADVB,
Challenger G-ADVD,
Centurion G-ADVE,
Cambria G-ADUV,
The above in oblong boxes with name inserts.
From January 1938: whole range in square boxes with name
labels. The following then released:
Calpurnia G-AETW,
Ceres G-AETX,
Clio G-AETY,
Calypso G-AEUA,
Corinna G-AEUC,
Cheviot G-AEUG,
From January 1939:
Capella G-ADUY replacing Calpurnia.
From September 1939:
Cordelia G-AEUD,
Camilla G-AEUB replacing Centurion and Challenger.
Also in bright colours as 60x Atlantic Flying Boat. Also with
tinplate seaplane carrier on top of wing as 63a Flying Boat
Maia.

60r Empire Flying Boat 1945–49
Post-war re-issue of above.
Brass roller.
Caledonia G-ADHM,
Cambria G-ADUV,
unnamed G-ADVB.

60s Medium Bomber 1937–40
75mm
60n in light camouflage with black undersurfaces. Red, white
and blue roundel with yellow outer ring, applied to one wing
only.
Available also in blue box in mirror-image echelon pairs.

Also available as:
Fairey Battle Bomber (Camouflaged) 1939–41
no undercarriage.
As above but with name under wing in light camouflage with
roundels on both wings.
From 1940: darker camouflage.
Blue and red roundels on both wings.
Available also in pairs in a blue box.

60t Douglas DC3 Airliner 1938–41
132mm
Silver with registration PH-ALI.
With small tail-wheel. Later without.
From 1940: no gliding hole. Individual boxes.

60v Armstrong Whitworth 1937–41
Whitley Bomber
116mm
Silver with red, white and blue roundels.
At first with gliding hole, later without.
Individual boxes.
Also in camouflage as 62t.

60w Flying Boat Clipper III 1938–41
164mm
Silver. Registration USA NC 16736.
Gliding game hole.
'Pan American Airways Clipper III' cast under wing.
Red plastic roller.
Individual box.
Re-issued post-war as 60w Flying Boat.

60w Flying Boat 1945–49
Re-issue of above.
No registration or gliding hole.
Brass or plastic roller.
Silver, blue, light or dark green.

60x Atlantic Flying Boat 1937–41
156mm
60r Empire Flying Boat in bright colours.
Name under wing.
Propellers usually silver.
Wings: yellow/dark cream with spurious registration in black.
Dauntless, light blue fuselage G-AZBP.
Endeavour, dark blue or black, red propellers, silver letters G-AZBQ.
Enterprise, royal blue, red propellers, silver letters G-AZBR.
Valorous, red, red propellers G-AZBS.
Whirlwind, green G-AZBT.
Swiftsure, deep yellow or orange, red propellers G-AZBU.

60z French Aeroplanes (Set) 1937/8–40
See Dinky: French Imports and French Dinky.

61 RAF Aeroplanes (Set) 1937–41
See Set text and list

61az Dewoitine D338 1937/8–40
See Dinky: French Imports and French Dinky.

61z French Aeroplanes (Set) 1938–40
See Dinky: French Imports and French Dinky.

62a Vickers-Supermarine
Spitfire Fighter 1940–41
52mm
Silver with red, white and blue roundels.
1st casting: short nose, cockpit flush with rear of fuselage.
Also in camouflage as 62e.
Also with ring on tail for Spitfire Fund.

62a Spitfire 1945–49
Re-issue of above.
Silver.
New casting: long nose, bubble cockpit.

62b Bristol Blenheim Bomber 1940–41
78mm
Silver with red, white and blue roundels.
'Blenheim Bomber' under wing. Also in camouflage as 62d.
Re-issued below

62b Medium Bomber 1945–49
78mm
Re-issue of above.
Silver.
'Medium Bomber' under wing.

62d Bristol Blenheim Bomber 1940–41
Camouflaged
78mm
Casting of 62b. Camouflage with black and white undersurface.
Light camouflage with red, white and blue roundels.
Later, dark camouflage with red and blue.

62e Vickers Supermarine Spitfire Camouflaged
1940–41
52mm
1st casting of 62a in light or dark camouflage with black and white undersurfaces.

62f DH Flamingo
Not issued.

62g Boeing Flying Fortress 1939–41
144mm
Silver with, later without, gliding hole. Also grey with gliding hole.
Name under wing.
USAAC stars on wing, stripes on tail.
Individual box with leaflet, later: without.
Commonly sold without box.
Re-issued below.

62g Long Range Bomber 1945–49
144mm
Re-issue of above in same silver livery.
Some early post-war have blueish canopy and nose.

62h Hawker Hurricane Single Seater Fighter
Camouflaged 1939–41
55mm
Casting of 62s.
With undercarriage in light camouflage, all black undersurface until 1940.
Then: no undercarriage and dark camouflage with half black/half white undersurface.

62k Airspeed Envoy King's 1938–41
Aeroplane
91mm
Casting of 62m.
Silver wings and tailplane, red and blue fuselage and engines.
Registration G-AEXX.
Name under wing.
Individual box.

62m Airspeed Envoy 1938–41
91mm
Name under wing.
Propellers silver but commonly red.
Each colour usually with the same registration:
red, red propellers G-ADBA,
silver G-ACVI,
blue G-ADCA,
green, red propellers G-AENA,
gold, red propellers G-ACMT,
yellow G-ACVJ,
See also 62k King's Aeroplane.,
Re-issued below as Light Transport.

62m Light Transport 1945–49
Re-issue of above.
Red, silver or blue.
Fictitious registration G-ATMH.
Name under wing.

62n Junkers Ju90 Airliner 1938–41
160mm
Silver.
'J.U.90' under wing.
After issue of 62y in 1939, name on insert J.U.9.0.
To 1940 Gliding hole.
Registrations: D-AURE, D-AIVI
(D-AALU shown in literature only).
Window transfers.
Individual box.
Also as 62y Giant High Speed Monoplane and
67a Junkers Ju89 Heavy Bomber.

62p Ensign Airliner 1938–41
173mm
Silver.
Name transfers and registrations:
December 1938: Ensign G-ADSR
From January 1939: individual labels on boxes:
Echo G-ADTB,
Elsinore G-ADST,
Elysian G-ADSZ,
Ettrick G-ADSX,
Explorer G-ADSV,
Gliding game hole until 1940.
Name under wing.
Also as 62x British 40-Seater Airliner,
68a Armstrong Whitworth Airliner in Service Camouflage.
Re-issued below.

62p Armstrong Whitworth Airliner 1945–49
Re-issue of above.
Silver.
Blue with silver trim on top of fuselage, ailerons and
elevators,
green with silver trim,
grey with green trim.
Explorer G-ADSV
or unnamed.
Name under wing.

62r De Havilland Albatross Mail Liner 1939–41
145mm
Silver with G-AEVV.
Gliding hole until 1940.
'DH Albatross' under wing.
Individual box.
Also as 62w Imperial Airways Frobisher Class Airliner,
68b Frobisher Class Airliner in Service Camouflage.
Re-issued below as Four-engined Liner.

62r Four-engined Liner 1945–49
Re-issue of above.
Grey, light blue, silver or green – all with red ailerons and
elevators.
Later, grey, fawn, light blue or silver with spurious registration
G-ATPV.

62s Hawker Hurricane Single Seater Fighter
1939–41
56mm
Silver
Roundels on wings, later also on fuselage.
With undercarriage and wheels until 1940, then without.
Two-blade propeller.
Also in camouflage as 62h.
Re-issued below.

62s Hurricane 1945–49
Re-issue of above without wheels.
Silver.
Three-blade propeller.

62t Armstrong Whitworth 1939–41
Whitley Bomber Camouflaged
116mm
60v Whitley Bomber in camouflage.
Light camouflage with red, white, blue and yellow roundels.
Later dark with red and blue.
Black undersurfaces.
Individual box.

62w Imperial Airways Frobisher 1939–41
Class Liner
145mm
Casting of 62r DH Albatross.
Silver with Frobisher G-AFDI, followed by
Falcon G-AFDJ,
Fortuna G-AFDK.
Gliding hole until 1940.
Name under wing.
Individual labelled boxes.
Also in camouflage as 68b Frobisher.

62x British 40-Seater Airliner 1939–41
173mm
Casting of 62p Ensign Airliner.
Trim consists of flash down centre of fuselage and trailing
edges of wings and tail.
Red with maroon,
light green with dark green,
light green with olive green,
olive green with dark green,
yellow with maroon,
deep orange with maroon,
light blue with dark blue,
medium blue with silver,
dark blue with light blue,
grey with green.
All with spurious registration G-AZCA.
Gliding hole until 1940.
Name under wing.

62y Giant High Speed Monoplane 1939–41
160mm
Casting of 62n Junkers Ju90.
With window transfers.
2nd colour on trailing edges of wings and tail:
blue with brown trim,
light blue with dark blue,
light green with dark green,
grey with green,
blue with cream,
yellow with maroon,
red with maroon.
All with fictitious reg. D-AZBK.
Gliding hole until 1940.
Name under wing.
Individual box. Re-issued below.

62y Giant High Speed Monoplane 1945–49
Re-issue of above without window transfers.
Colour split as above with
2nd colour on trailing edges of wing and tail:
light green with dark green,
mid-green with dark green,
grey with dark green,
all-over silver.
All with fictitious registration G-ATBK.

63 Mayo Composite Aircraft 1939–41
Boxed pair of 63a Flying Boat Maia and 63b Seaplane
Mercury.

63a Flying Boat Maia 1939–41
156mm
Silver with G-ADHK.
Casting of 60r Empire Flying Boat with tinplate frame to hold Seaplane 63b in centre of upper wing.
'Mayo Composite' under wing.
To 1940: full bows and gliding hole, plastic roller.
After 1940: hollowed out bows, no hole and wooden roller.
Individual box.
Also seen: lead fuselage

63b Seaplane Mercury 1939–41
101mm
Silver with registration G-ADHJ.
Mercury transfer.
Name under wing.
Tinplate clip under fuselage.
Gliding hole until 1940.
Re-issued below.

63b Seaplane 1945–49
Re-issue of above but without tinplate clip.
Silver.
Fictional registration G-AVKW.
Name under wing.

1952–57: Re-issue of above.
Renumbered 700 in 1954.

64 Presentation Aeroplane Set 1939–41
See Set list.

64az Amiot 370 1939–39
See Dinky: French Imports and French Dinky.

64bz Bloch 220 1939–40
See Dinky: French Imports and French Dinky.

65 Presentation Aeroplane Set 1939–41
See Set list.

66 Camouflaged Aeroplane Set 1940–41
60 Set in dark camouflage.
Contains 66a,b,c,d,e,f below.
See Set list.

66a Heavy Bomber 1940–41
127mm
Casting of 60a Imperial Airways Liner.
Dark camouflage, dark green underside.

66b Dive Bomber Fighter 1940–41
76mm
Casting of 60b DH Leopard Moth.
Dark camouflage, dark green underside.

66c Two-Seater Fighter 1940–41
76mm
Casting of 60c Percival Gull.
Light or dark camouflage, dark green underside.

66d Torpedo Dive Bomber 1940–41
76mm
Casting of 60d Low Wing Monoplane.
Light or dark camouflage, dark green underside.

66e Medium Bomber 1940–41
80mm
Casting of 60e General Monospar.
'General Monospar' under wing.
Dark camouflage, dark green underside.

66f Army Co-operation Autogiro 1940–41
(Rotor dia. 72mm) Length 53mm
Casting of 60f Cierva Autogiro.
Silver-grey with silver rotor,
red, white and blue roundels.

67a Junkers Ju89 Heavy Bomber 1940–41
160mm
Casting as 62n Junkers Ju90 Airliner with or without gliding hole.
Name under wing.
Black with pale blue underside.
White crosses on wings, black swastikas on white squares on tailfins.
Individual box.

68 Aircraft in Service Camouflage 1940–41
See Set list.

68a Armstrong Whitworth Ensign Liner in Service Camouflage 1940–41
173mm
Casting of 62p with gliding game hole in light camouflage.
Later: without hole in dark camouflage, black underside. Red and blue roundels on wings.

68b Frobisher Class Liner in Service Camouflage 1940–41
145mm
Casting of 62r DH Albatross/62w Imperial Airways Frobisher with gliding game hole in light camouflage.
Later: dark camouflage with or without gliding hole.
Black underside.
Red and blue roundels.

Post-war re-issues 1945–49

After the war, the Meccano factory at Binns Road, Liverpool was returned to toy production with all possible speed, and re-issues of aeroplanes figure prominently in the early production. Indeed, by Christmas, over 10 per cent (12 out of 50) of the Dinky range available was aircraft. This preponderance may be accounted for by the shapes of the planes which made them relatively easy to cast without the use of too much scarce mazac. T he state of the die will also have featured in their selection as it is known that a proportion of the dies were lost or damaged when Liverpool was bombed. Most of the name inserts in the dies were changed to generic names presumably to make the list appear less dated as several of the prototypes were hardly seen after the war. Examples are found still with all the pre-war technical features but in post-war colours, for example 60k marked Percival Gull but painted silver. Many of the registration letters were invented. Varying band widths are found on RAF roundels, those with narrow white bands being the latest.

The Spitfire is a new casting created by modifying the original die by removing metal to lengthen the nose and the rear of the cockpit to simulate a later Mark. Some examples show the outline of the name insert clearly and its length is that of the insert for the Spitfire Fund version. Pre-war, below the port wing the casting has a cigar-shaped oil cooler which in the post-war version has been partially obscured by an oblong protrusion to match the oblong air intake on the starboard wing. The tell-tale front portion of the oil cooler on the post-war die indicated without doubt that the die was not new but modified from the pre-war. High visibility roundels are found on the fuselage.

A thirteenth casting, 62y Giant High Speed Monoplane, was later added to the list. Some of the castings have a considerable amount of flash or file marks indicating just how much wear the dies had suffered. All of these models were withdrawn in 1949 at the same time as the seven 1946/7 new releases. The only one to be re-introduced in 1952 was 63b Seaplane, which was subsequently renumbered 700.

POST-WAR RE-ISSUES 1945–49

Each item begins with wingspan measurement.

60g Light Racer 1945–49
86mm
Re-issue of 60g DH Comet.
'LIGHT RACER' under wing.
Yellow, red or silver.
Some silver have blued cockpit Spurious registration
G-RACE. Three-blade propeller.

60k Light Tourer 1945–49
76mm
Re-issue of 60c Percival Gull/60k Souvenir issues/66c
Two-seater Fighter.
Very early post-war issues have 'PERCIVAL TOURER' impressed
under the wing.
Usually 'LIGHT TOURER' impressed.
Dark green, light green, red or silver.
Large or small two-blade propeller.

60r Empire Flying Boat 1945–49
156mm
Re-issue of later casting of 60r Empire Flying Boat/60x
Atlantic Flying Boat/63a Maia.
'EMPIRE FLYING BOAT' under wing.
Silver with brass roller.
Caledonia G-ADHM,
Cambria G-ADUV,
unnamed G-ADVB.

60w Flying Boat 1945–49
164mm
Re-issue of 60w Clipper III.
'FLYING BOAT' under wing. Brass or plastic roller.
Silver, blue, light or dark green.
No registration.

62a Spitfire 1945–49
51mm
New casting: long nose, bubble cockpit.
Silver with red, white and blue roundels, or red and blue
roundels on wings. High visibility roundels on fuselage.

62b Medium Bomber 1945–49
78mm
Re-issue of 62b Bristol Blenheim Bomber/62b Medium
Bomber.
'MEDIUM BOMBER' under wing.
Silver, with red, white and blue with thick or thin white
bands, or red and blue roundels on wings.

62g Long Range Bomber 1945–49
144mm
Re-issue of 62g Flying Fortress in same silver livery.
'LONG RANGE BOMBER' under wing.
Some early post-war models have blued canopy and nose.

62m Light Transport 1945–49
91mm
Re-issue of 62m Airspeed Envoy/62k King's Aeroplane.
'LIGHT TRANSPORT' under wing.
Silver, some with blued windows,
red or blue with silver windows.
Fictitious registration G-ATMH.

62p Armstrong Whitworth Airliner 1945–49
173mm
Re-issue of 62p Ensign Airliner.
'ARMSTRONG WHITWORTH AIRLINER' under wing.
Silver, blue with silver trim on top of fuselage, ailerons and
elevators, green with silver trim, grey with green trim.
Echo G-ADTB,
Explorer G-ADSV,
or unnamed.

62r Four-engined Liner 1945–49
145mm
Re-issue of 62r De Havilland Albatross Mail Liner/62w
Imperial Airways Frobisher Class Airliner.
'FOUR ENGINED LINER' under wing.
Grey, light blue, silver or green, all with red ailerons and
elevators, without registration.
Some silver have blued cockpit.
Later: grey, fawn, light blue or silver with spurious registration
G-ATPV.

62s Hurricane 1945–49
55mm
Re-issue of 62s Hawker Hurricane Single Seat Fighter.
Without wheels/62h.
Camouflaged.
Silver.
Three-blade propeller.

62y Giant High Speed Monoplane 1945–49
160mm
Re-issue of 62n Junkers JU90/62y Giant High Speed
Monoplane.
'GIANT HIGH SPEED MONOPLANE' under wing.
Colour split as 62y before: 2nd colour on trailing edges of
wing and tail:
light green with dark green,
mid-green with dark green,
grey with dark green,
all-over silver, some with blued cockpit.
Fictitious registration G-ATBK.

63b Seaplane 1945–49
101mm
Re-issue of 63b Seaplane Mercury without tinplate clip.
Two dies: 'MECCANO LTD' 1.17mm, 2.14mm.
'SEAPLANE' under wing.
Flat silver spinners, then flat black.
Silver, early (die 1) with blued cockpit.
Fictional registration G-AVKW.
Two decals: die 1 rounded G, die 2 squared G

1952–57
Re-issue of 2nd version above with no changes.
Renumbered 700 in 1954.

700 Seaplane Renumbering of 63b above.

Issues of the late 40s and early 50s

The principles underlying the design of the mass production war plane contain the seeds of modern production methods. Standardisation and simple construction contributed largely to achieving rapid and relatively cheap production. To this should be added ease of operation, transport, maintenance, and repair. The aeroplane was built up of numbers of components manufactured largely as separate self-contained units which were easy to transport and assemble. While the famed geodetic construction of Barnes Wallace was robust, the structure took up too much of the space within the fuselage. A system was developed in which a skin of aluminium alloy sheets was flush rivetted to ensure a smooth external surface in monocoque fashion and fitted with the internal parts rather than being handcrafted from the framework outwards. The production facility for each type of part was at some distance from the assembly sheds, dispersal minimising vulnerability from enemy bombing. Thus the roots of the intercountry distribution of the European Airbus manufacture and other inter-Europe projects had its roots long ago in the European conflict. The Empire-centred outlook of Britain was replaced by a realisation of the importance of European and world destinations, a change heralded by the 1940 amalgamation of the recently nationalised British Airways and Imperial Airways into British Overseas Airways.

The first new issues of Dinky Toys were road vehicles but these were quickly followed in August 1946 by the release of the initial plane, the Avro York Airliner. 'A striking model of one of the latest British transport aircraft' claimed the advertising in the August 1946 issue of *Meccano Magazine*. The group that followed the Avro consists of planes designed during the war and is an uncomfortable mixture of variously dated designs, from mid-thirties to early jets. All were named under their wings. Articles and snippets of information in the regular 'Air News' column, mostly written by John WR Taylor and published in *Meccano Magazine* during the war, had brought many of the types to the notice of the reader. These were in most cases during 1946/7 supplemented by 'Coming Soon' or 'Now Available' adverts on the inside of the front cover.

In 1949, all this group introduced in 1946/7 was withdrawn as well as all of the re-releases from before the war. No announcement was made and no official explanation was ever offered but with the shortage of materials, Dinky could not keep all the models that they had in the range in production at the same time and presumably the best sellers were the new road vehicles. Supplies of metal remained problematic during the Korean War but by the middle of 1952, Dinky was able to start re-introducing aeroplanes. The first four were 70a York, 70b Tempest II, 70c Viking, 70e Meteor, and one from the Thirties, 63b Seaplane. The number-cum-letter suffix numbering system became overloaded and number blocks for each type of vehicle were introduced gradually during 1953 and 1954. The Shetland Flying Boat being a Supertoy, a name designating the large sized and, therefore, more expensive models, had already been given a three figure number 700 in 1947 indicating that the change of system was long in the planning. The number block 700 was used, the civilian planes having the lower numbers and the military starting at 730. They were mostly painted silver with a finish that changed over the years from 'aluminium' to very shiny. Blued cockpits were the norm on early issues though the blue wears off easily. There is a wide variety of propeller pins which, allied with the other features, can give an indication of dating. Pointed spinners are early. Flat-headed silver pins tend to predate black. The genuine registration letters were invariably black. Withdrawals were spread over several years and overlapped the release of the next group the most old-fashioned looking ones going first. Helpfully, all this group have their names under their wings, but only the York has a number. All were packed in brown or yellow boxes of six except 70a/704 York and 701 Shetland, which had individual ones.

The factory drawings of a few of this group of planes are extant, having been found at Binns Road in 1979. They are the drawings from which the dies were made and any subsequent modifications to the dies were noted on them. They range from drawings of axles through parts such as wings to complete planes and are invaluable in elucidating what Dinky intended. References to drawings are to these. Apart from the Twin-Engined Fighter the scale is approximately 1/200.

A list of drawings for models planned but never issued was found in an old Binns Road record book found by a Meccano staff member of many years standing. None of the actual drawings have survived.

14 June 1939	Reference to	Barrage Balloon
30 March 1940	Drawing prepared for	Heinkel 111
7 March 1940		Blackbird Skua
? Dec 1945		De Havilland Dove
1 Feb 1946		De Havilland Hornet
21 Feb 1946		Bristol Buckmaster
Also listed in 1945		70g Avro Tudor Airliner, the only one to proceed far enough to be allocated a catalogue number

CIVIL AEROPLANES

Avro York Airliner – 70a, 704

The model is to a scale of 1/195. Its construction is remarkably similar to that used pre-war. The fuselage/tail casting which has delicately raised window detail, has a cutout in the top to take the wing, engine and wing-wide fuselage section, the drawing of which, showing the name 'York' cast under the wing, is dated 24.10.45. The two parts locate together well and even in late examples are a firm fit. The hollow square-section fuselage lends itself to the innovation of a tinplate base secured with three rivets. Small wheels are fitted within the undercarriage legs which are integral with the upper casting. The large, red, three-blade propellers are secured with prominent round-headed pins. Finished in silver usually with a blued cockpit window, the model captures the spirit of the York although the wings are not quite right and there is a lack of surface detail. In the manner of the pre-war large planes, it was supplied from the beginning, August 1946, in an individual, brown cardboard box, with a lift-off lid with a yellow label on the end. To improve the reliability of casting for re-introduction in 1952 the centre fin was made thicker than the two at the extremities of the tail. The propeller pins changed to flat-headed black ones and the tinplate pressing of the underbelly had a spare hole amidships. A drawing change dated 9.3.55. puts the new number, 704 under the starboard wing. Some of the later planes have a very shiny finish, 'silver' rather than 'aluminium'. During this second release, the York was still packed in its own box, now all yellow. Some of them feature both numbers, 70a and 704.

Vickers Viking – 70c, 705

The Dinky, an excellent reproduction of the original in 1/195 scale, had its final drawing completed in October 1946, just in time for the December 1946 announcement that the Viking was available. The top casting, comprising the upper half of the fuselage, nose, tailplane and fin, fits snugly over the part comprising the lower half of the fuselage, wings and engines. There is no undercarriage. The windows are not outlined on the castings, though the baggage hatches are. Pointed spinners used on several others in the group hold the red four-bladed propellers in place. Usually painted silver with blued cockpit and square cabin windows stencilled onto the fuselage, some early models were finished in grey with cockpit and windows in silver. The registration, G-AGOL the number of the second prototype, remains the same. The Viking reappeared with no changes except that the pointed spinner was replaced by a smaller domed type or a flat black one. The only colour is aluminium/silver, with the matt finish earlier than the very shiny one. Renumbered to 705 but the casting was not changed. Of this group, it was one of the longest lived as it was not withdrawn until 1962. Despite its size, it was only available in retailer boxes of six, with two stacks of three models packed horizontally.

Avro Tudor Airliner – 70g not issued

Drawing listed in 1945, catalogue number allocated but not produced.

FLYING BOAT

Shetland Flying Boat – 701

At 1/194 scale this is a large model of a large plane, and appropriately it was released as a Supertoy. First advertised in October 1947 it was allocated to the number block 700, which was later used for the renumbering of the ones in the rest of this group. The only extant drawing is that for the propeller which is dated 13.6.47 with an enlargement in the size of the centre hole dated 24.10.47, just after the release of the toy, a change which probably postdates the actual modification. The box boasts that it is a 'Perfect Scale Model' and, indeed, it is good with its distinctive rounded nose, elongated bubble cockpit giving the crew 360-degree vision and with the outlines of windows, doors and hatches providing plenty of detail on the tall flat sides. This 240gm (over 0.5 lbs) toy is made up of three main castings. The massive, hollow fuselage and tail section has a recess in the top to take the wing and the planing surface has the shape of a keel fitting up under the hull. The rivets holding the ensemble together can be seen on the top of the wing section. A pair of floats are rivetted through the wings and the toy is finished with four very large four-blade propellers held on with standard-sized pointed spinners. The whole is finished in silver with the black registration letters of the second prototype G-AGVD. The propellers are usually black but they are found in red and the cockpit is blued. As befits its size and importance as a Supertoy, the Shetland has an individual box, plain brown with a lift-off lid and a red, white and black paper label on the top featuring a drawing of the plane. Taking into consideration the size and weight of the toy and the disappearance from the skies of the type of plane, it is not surprising that the Shetland was withdrawn in 1949 and not re-released.

MILITARY AEROPLANES

**Tempest II
– 70b, 730**

The toy, drawn in December 1945 at 1/197 scale, is quite a good model clearly showing the radial engine. The realistic effect is heightened by the large pointed spinner securing the red four-blade propeller. This simple single casting without undercarriage, painted silver with blued canopy was advertised in the December 1946 *Meccano Magazine* as already available and as a model of one of the fastest piston-engined machines in the world. The wings and fuselage have RAF roundels, red, white and blue on the wings and on the fuselage, red, white and blue, surrounded with a yellow band. There are two sizes of roundel, the later being smaller with a thicker blue outer band. Dropped from the catalogue in 1949, the model was reinstated with the main batch by June 1952, the only differences being that the propeller was now held on by a black flat-headed spinner and the cockpit blueing was deleted. When the number was changed to 730, the first of a combat plane block, still no alteration was made to the die. Old-fashioned in appearance, it was dropped after 1955. It was supplied to the retailer in boxes of six, with the planes dropped in vertically as were the other small planes.

**Twin-engined
Fighter – 70d, 731**

The drawing of the Messerschmitt Bf.110, commonly called the Me.110, was complete on 25 April 1940. The decision to release the model without fanfare and anonymously as Twin-Engined Fighter was made in October 1945 and the drawing name was changed. It is not a particularly good model for the wings are somewhat too long and too rounded at the tips but presumably the very existence of the drawing and perhaps the partly finished die was a factor in enabling the plane range to be put back into production quickly, a bonus being the small size. At 1/213 scale, the thin fuselage and wings mean that even complete with three-bladed propellers and one of the variety of propeller pins, round-headed silver or flat headed silver or later black, it weighs little more than 10gms. A late reintroduction after the 1949-52 break, by August 1952 it was figuring in *Meccano Magazine* advertising. The drawing has a queried note on it that the sales number, 731, was added in November 1954. The underwing engraving was modified with the result that the spacing on the name 'Twin Engined Fighter' was altered and the letter N in the word Meccano became reversed! These little silver models were undecorated apart from the blueing of the long cockpit canopy of the earlier models and were supplied to the retailer in boxes of six.

**Gloster Meteor
– 70e, 732**

The Dinky drawing for Gloster Meteor, the first operational British jet plane and the most talked about plane of its day, was completed in November 1945 and there are no changes on it. Introduced in November 1946, it was a one-piece casting with no undercarriage but good undersurface detail. An attractive model in 1/197 scale, it is a good representation of the original capturing the shape of the wings with the jet outlets of its turbo-jet engines protruding beyond their trailing edges, and its high tail clear of the jet thrust. It is finished in aluminium, with black air intakes and blueing of the cockpit on early models. There are large RAF roundels on the wings and small yellow-bordered ones on the fuselage. As time passed, including the same withdrawal period as the others, the wing roundels were replaced with smaller ones. After renumbering to 732 the finish became distinctly more shiny, particularly towards its deletion time in 1962 and some had roundels (from the Hawker Hunter, 736) even larger than the original ones. Boxed in half-dozens.

Shooting Star Jet Fighter – 70f, 733

The Dinky drawing, begun at the end of 1945 was finalised in May 1947 and the model was released some nine months after the first batch, with advertising stating that one had 'recently attained a speed of 623.8mph which, subject to official confirmation, is a world record'. A reasonably good one-piece casting for the fuselage and wings, which are a little too tapered, is fitted with separate drop tanks at the wing ends. There is little detail on this small, 1/201 scale model. The undersurface is almost entirely taken up with two lines of wording, all in block capitals, which, under the port wing reads 'MADE IN ENGLAND BY MECCANO LTD.'. The whole is painted silver with a blued canopy. Picked out in black are the twin air inlets for the engine on either side of the fuselage. Three black dashes below the nose on either side indicate the position of the six M-3 machine guns. The US Air Force star marking in light blue and white, is found transferred on the port wing and either side of the rear fuselage. During its withdrawal, from 1949 to late 1952, the tooling, but not the drawing, was slightly changed. This meant that the legend below the port wing loses the word 'BY' and reads 'MADE IN ENGLAND MECCANO LTD', the letters of the three words on the top line being eased apart to use up the space. The cockpit blueing was dropped. Later issues have decals in a darker blue. Packed in retailer boxes of six.

ISSUES OF THE LATE 40s AND EARLY 50s 1945–49 and 1952–62

All are named under the wing

70a Avro York Airliner 1946–49
160mm
Silver with blued cockpit, registration G-AGJC
Individual plain box numbered 70a

1952–59
As above but thicker centre fin on tail. Box numbered 70a.
1953/4: renumbered 704, 704 added under wing.
Individual plain box numbered 70a and 704.

70b Tempest II Fighter 1946–49
63mm
Silver with blued canopy.
RAF roundels.
Yellow band on fuselage roundels. Large pointed spinner.

1952–55
As above but no blueing, flat spinner.
1953/4: renumbered 730.

70c Viking Airliner 1947–49
140mm
Silver with blued windows, grey with silver windows stencilled on fuselage. Registration G-AGOL.
Large pointed spinner.

1952–62
Silver with blued windows.
Registration as above. Flat spinner.
1953/4: renumbered 705.

70d Twin-Engined Fighter 1946–49
76mm
Silver with blued cockpit canopy.

1952–55
As above, but no blueing.
1953/4: renumbered 731.
Some late issues have the 'N' in Meccano back to front.

70e Gloster Meteor Twin-JetFighter 1946–49
67mm
Silver usually with blued cockpit canopy. Black engine intakes.
Large RAF roundels on wings.
Yellow band on fuselage roundels.

1952–62
As above but no blueing and with smaller roundels on wings.
1953/4: renumbered 732.
Later: shiny silver some with largest wing roundels from 736 Hawker Hunter.

70f Shooting Star Jet Fighter 1947–49
61mm
Marked: MADE IN ENGLAND 'BY' MECCANO LTD.
Silver early with blued cockpit.
Cannon positions, engine intake, blackened.
USAF markings: star on port wing only
Small stars on sides of fuselage.

1952–62
As above but no blueing.
'BY' omitted and letters respaced.
Darker blue USAF markings.
1953/4: renumbered 733.

70g Avro Tudor
Not issued.

700 Seaplane 1952–55
Renumbering of 63b.
See Post-war re-issues.

701 Shetland Flying Boat 1947–49
236mm
Silver with blued cockpit, registration G-AGVD.
Individual brown box with 'Supertoy' and drawing on lid.

704 Avro York Airliner
Renumbering of 70a with 704 cast under wing.

705 Viking Airliner
Renumbering of 70c.

730 Tempest II Fighter
Renumbering of 70b.

731 Twin-Engined Fighter
Renumbering of 70d.

732 Gloster Meteor Twin-JetFighter
Renumbering of 70e.

733 Shooting Star Jet Fighter
Renumbering of 70f.

Issues of the late 50s and early 60s

The expansion of civil aviation into a means of moving armies of travellers rather than as a diversion for the wealthy, the inception of the commercial helicopter and the development of post-war military planes went ahead quietly during the late 1940s. Although each type became more specific in its uses, the development of each affected the others to a greater or lesser degree. The Dinky planes that represented these three groups, four airliners, two helicopters and six military jets were introduced from 1954 to 1962.

Toys were beginning to sell well as the post-war shortages reduced and rationing came off. With the ending of the Korean War, materials became plentiful again. The upturn enabled Dinky to invest in new premises at Speke. They announced in 1953, 'We have built a new works where we have installed the most up-to-date plant, resulting in improved methods of production which have enabled us to reduce prices' and an across the board reduction of 9 per cent rounded to the nearest penny was implemented. This, allied with growing demand, had some unforeseen results and on the inside front cover of the December 1954 *Meccano Magazine*, there was an important announcement: 'The growing popularity of Dinky Toys often results in dealers being short of supplies. Output has been increasing continuously in an attempt to keep up with the demand.' Economic circumstances were improving so much that there was scope for creative marketing, and in January 1955 it was announced that the name 'Dinky Supertoys' was being re-introduced for some models. Among the first to be reclassified and renumbered to the 900 block was the Comet Airliner. By now all the reallocation from number plus suffix letter to three-figure designations had been completed. Subsequently, the smaller planes had 700 numbers, the larger, 900. All have individual boxes. In an attractive advert, the January 1955 *Meccano Magazine* trumpets the praises of the DH Comet Jet Airliner, and claims that this and subsequent planes '... will be made and finished more beautifully than ever, and will be remarkable for the wonderfully brilliant finish that will be given to them ... by the use of a new range of enamels'. Most have individual boxes and the smaller, cheaper, military planes packed in yellow boxes were supplied to the retailer in a flimsy greyish card outer carton containing six planes of the same type. Sometime after 1960, transfer roundels changed to Permagrip self-adhesive paper. The factory drawing of the small 4mm diameter ones is dated 12.2.60. The date of implementation is unknown. All the fixed-wing planes have their names under the starboard wing. In 1963/4, all silver models changed to metallic silver-grey, a more accurate colour with a higher gloss. *Circa* 1965, cast metal wheels were replaced by black plastic. In 1968, some Dinky dies were sold to Atamco Ltd in India and became part of the Nicky Toy range.

CIVIL AEROPLANES

DH Comet Jet Airliner – 702, 999

Dinky launched the DH Comet Jet Airliner, originally the world's first jet airliner, with a full page advert in the October 1954 *Meccano Magazine*. The 1/190 scale model which captures the look of the Comet to perfection consists of two castings, one for the nose, upper fuselage and tail and the other for the wings and underfuselage which extends far enough forward to carry the front undercarriage leg as well as the two underwing pairs. This tricycle format was standard by this time as it enabled the floor of the plane to be level and avoided the uphill climb necessitated by the fitting of a tail wheel. Cast double wheels are fitted to all the legs. This was the first Dinky airliner to be sprayed in a full airline livery and the painting is fairly good. The join line between the silver lower and white upper fuselage is camouflaged by a sprayed on royal blue line. The cockpit and passenger windows are painted silver on top of the blue. The thin letters BOAC are blue also. The starboard wing carried, in black, G-ALYV the registration of one of the early ones which had crashed after metal had fatigued at the square corners of the windows. Presumably the transfers were already printed. The white painted tail carried the registration between two bands topped by the Speedbird logo, all in blue. The wheels were gold and the casting carried its number, 702, under the port wingtip. The individual box with its lift-off lid has the Comet surrounded by the blue stripes that usually designate a Supertoy though the name was not actually in use at the time. But a mere three months after its introduction, the name 'Dinky Supertoys' was reintroduced with the new number 999 allocated to the Comet. There seem to exist more 702s than you would expect from the brief time the model was in use. Unfortunately, the production records are no longer extant. The under-wing casting was altered to read 999 instead of 702 and Supertoys added to Dinky. The box number was changed to 999 retaining the now appropriate Supertoy stripes. Later a new box still labelled Dinky Supertoys featured an aerial view of a river flowing through countryside, on the left side with a panel of yellow on the right.

In 1959/60 the registration number was changed to G-ALYX which had belonged to one of the planes that had been destruction tested to establish the cause of the accidents in 1955. The wheels were now silver and the box art was modified to G-ALYX. On the introduction of the Comet 4 in 1958, BOAC changed their tail decoration: the fin now all blue with the registration, horizontal banding and Speedbird in white. Dinky belatedly followed suit with a blue and white transfer, a slight mismatch to the fuselage stripe but the original drawing continued to be used in the catalogue. The lettering BOAC is slightly thicker and on later models, very thick. In 1963/4, the silver was changed to a more realistic metallic grey. In 1968, after the model had been dropped from the range, the dies were sent to India: *see* Nicky Toys.

Handley Page Herald – 703 – not issued

The reference to the name and number only was found in Meccano records and it is surprising that it should have got far enough to have acquired a Dinky number and yet not be produced, especially since Meccano would have been concerned at throwing away such costs as would normally have been incurred in, say, creating the drawing, before number allocation.

Vickers Viscount Airliner – 706 Air France, 708 BEA

The Dinky Toy was modelled on the Viscount 701, the fuselage having 10 windows. The construction is exactly the same as that of the Comet: two castings, the main fuselage nose and tail piece being rivetted to the underfuselage, wing and engine piece which has a hole midwing to fix it onto the painting spigot during manufacture. The technical details on the back of the box are not 100 percent accurate but the scale is 1/190. Twin wheels are fitted to simple undercarriage legs and red four-bladed propellers are held on with dome-headed propeller pins. Perhaps to emphasise its widespread use in Europe, Air France livery was chosen. Finished in silver with a white upper fuselage, the window line is a blue transfer with the windows picked out in silver. The line incorporates the registration and the circular logo of winged horse is backed with white. 'Air France' and the Tricolour surmount it and are all on the same transfer. The tail is covered by a blue shark's tail on an aluminium ground. The port wing carries, in black, part of the registration, F-B, and the starboard the rest, GNL. A triangle on top of the nose is painted blue. This version was withdrawn after a year when the beautiful French Dinky 60E Viscount Air France was released. There is no doubt that this casting is different and that it originates from the French factory, being so marked. Its replacement, the Vickers Viscount 800 Airliner – BEA, 708, uses exactly the same casting but it has had the number 706 removed from beneath its wing and not replaced. What makes it a model of the 800 series (in fact, an 802 fitted with Dart 510 series turbo-props giving it an increased cruising speed) as claimed on the box, is that the transfers show it with 12 side windows and a rectangular door. The only other metal detail that has changed is the fitting of flatter headed propeller pins. The propellers are still red which goes with the rest of the scheme quite nicely. BEA's colours at the time were silver lower half of fuselage and wings with a white upper half and tail. The transfer has the windows in black on the silver and the three red lines and British European Airways on the white of the fuselage. Below the line and behind the rear door is BEA in a red-outlined square and a tiny representation in yellow and red of a crown with a post horn suspended from it to indicate that it was a carrier of the Royal Mails. The tail fin carries the Union Jack above the red registration. BEA in red on the port wing is balanced by the red registration G-AOJA on the starboard. The upper-nose triangle is painted red. After 1963, the silver was changed to metallic grey, producing an even prettier model. The initials on the port wing changed format also and became upright instead of sloping – B E A. In 1965, the wheels went to black plastic. All of these types were packed in yellow flap-ended boxes. After the models were withdrawn from the UK market, the die was sent to India: *see* Nicky Toys.

Caravelle SE210 Airliner – 997

There had been a 1/190th Caravelle in the French Dinky range for several years when Dinky introduced the Caravelle SE210 Airliner, 997 in January 1962. It looks as if the factory at Bobigny sent the die over to England as virtually all of the external details are exactly the same. The nose, upper fuselage and tail are one piece and the wings and lower fuselage another. When these are rivetted together the separate engine-pod unit, which on early issues has a cone within the air intake, is held in place. The front undercarriage leg is part of the lower casting but, in a new manner, the twin rear legs are separate pieces of pressed steel rivetted on. A 'first' is the set of stairs that can be hinged down from beneath the fuselage and can be held open with a spring. The later English version had a hole mid-wing on the lower fuselage for it to be balanced on the finishing jig, 'Made in France' has been changed to 'Made in England' by the use of an insert for the last word (port wing), and 997 has been added to the starboard. In all other respects the lettering is still the same, right down to the French number 60F under the port wing. The English wheels are smaller, whether metal, or as fitted in 1965, black plastic. The plane is finished in silver with a white upper fuselage. A new set of transfers were made, very similar to the French but with slightly different colours: the side stripes are a dark blue that is almost green, with light green banding at the edges and light green triangular windows, Air France, the Tricolour and registration below the tail are all on the same decal which merges into a blue-painted band across the nose. The tail flash is straight edged. The registration F-BGNY is stamped on the starboard wing. Initially the box had Supertoy stripes; later it was yellow with a view over an airport and a close-up illustration of the fold down steps.

Bristol Britannia Airliner – 998

The Dinky drawings of wing with tail plane and the fuselage with tail fin for the Bristol Britannia Airliner, 998 (the 'Whispering Giant') were completed in September and October 1956 respectively and had no significant changes. But, it was not until April 1959 that the toy was released. The construction of this Supertoy was much the same as before but the tail plane was incorporated into the lower casting which is a neat fit to the upper. The castings are very smooth and the thin wing sections are quite an achievement, though later examples betray heavy file marks and some flash on mould split lines. There is a standard tricycle undercarriage with double wheels at the front of the fuselage and two pairs of double wheels at the rear of the inner engine pods. The large red propellers held on with small domed pins are those that were used on the Sunderland Flying Boat. The model, which is finished in Canadian Pacific livery of silver below the window line and white above with a blue (sprayed) nose and a black overpainted radome, was fittingly included in an advert on the inside front cover of the January 1960 *Meccano Magazine* headed 'Supertoys – are more than realistic – they're real'. The registration CF-CZA applied to the starboard wing is stamped on in blue. The whole of the side lining in colour and silver with Canadian Pacific in blue script is one transfer and the tail stripes another. The transfer drawing is dated 4.1.59 and the first material change was made on 23.5.59, one month after the release of the toy, from the incorrect blue lining on fuselage and tail to the correct red, and it was some time before the red was substituted. The January 1960 *Meccano Magazine* still shows the lines as blue, but the 1960 catalogue has them in red. The next, and only other change, was a technical one, dated 14.12.61 when the transfers were changed from spirit fixing to waterslide, the backing film of which tends to yellow with age. In 1964, the silver paint on the lower half was replaced with the more realistic silver-grey. The sturdy cardboard box with lift-off lid initially carried the blue Supertoy stripes but later it became yellow with an aeriel picture of the Canadian Rockies with the plane depicted with red stripes.

HELICOPTERS

Bristol 173 Helicopter – 715

The assembly drawing is dated March 1955 and with an average time lapse, the 1/190 scale representation was introduced in November 1956. The simple one-piece hollow casting was not altered during its seven-year life in the catalogue. Below the stub wings are basic undercarriage legs which take two two-wheel undercarriage assemblies, each consisting of a short axle with two little wheels, reminiscent of the original 60 Set. The rotors are the tinplate three-blade rotor from the Autogiro. Dinky publicity describes the colour as 'light blue' but shades vary and some are quite turquoise, probably late examples. The bright red rotor blades match the red fuselage stripe. The whole of the side decoration of stripe, aluminium windows and spurious black registration, G-AUXR, are on one decal. The cockpit windows and clear nose bubble are silvered. The first yellow, flap-ended boxes have, on the back, details of its range, size, etc, and the information that the 191 'is on order for the Fleet Air Arm for service on anti-submarine duties, and for the RAF for general duties.' Later, as by 1957 the first part was incorrect, all the description was deleted.

Westland-Sikorsky S51 Helicopter – 716

The Dinky drawing was completed in January 1955, with the 1/190 scale model being released in February. 1957. A single solid casting, so small that it was only possible to mark 'England' beneath the fuselage, 'Dinky

Toys Sikorsky S51' having to fit across the undercarriage legs, it was fitted with a nose wheel and twin rear wheels on a wire axle. The incorrect three-blade rotor (it should have had four) is from the Cierva and the tail rotor is a small three-blade propeller. The finish is bright red with the rotor pylon and spurious registration, G-ATWX, in cream with the plexiglass area painted silver.

MILITARY AEROPLANES

The release of most of the military aeroplane models before the development of the planes was completed suggests that the manufacturers supplied information to Meccano. There is no undersurface detail on the castings – just the name of the plane and the manufacturer of the toy. All the planes in this group have three stubby undercarriage legs and small metal wheels. 1955 was a good year for the release of Dinky fighters for as many as three appeared, such profligacy in production no doubt being allowed by the small size and simplicity of the castings. Never the most exciting of Dinky Toys, they may have been helped by the colour advertising that first appeared that year on the *Meccano Magazine* rear cover.

Vickers-Supermarine Swift Fighter – 734

The Dinky drawing dated June 1953 is of the first version. Although the wings of the full size had been changed to a crescent shape, the drawing was not modified. The nose is a little too long but otherwise the 1/194 scale model is good. Some of the wording on the drawing is also in French so there must have been an unfulfilled intention to send it to the French factory. The upper surface of this reasonably attractive little item is detailed and the exhaust orifice is quite deeply hollowed. Finished in grey with green camouflage oversprayed through a mask on the upper surfaces, it was featured in colour on the rear cover of *Meccano Magazine*. RAF roundels decorate the wings and the tail fin carries a red, white and blue flash. The cockpit is silvered.

Gloster Javelin Delta Wing Fighter – 735

When Dinky released the model in May 1955, development of the prototypes had not yet been completed and details had not yet been released. The 1/192 scale model is a good one and replicates the slight crescenting of the leading edge of the wings. Two castings fit neatly together, the upper consisting of nose, upper fuselage and tail with the lower made up of the underfuselage and wings. This construction enables the whole of the jet engines to be hollow so that inlet and outlet orifices cast well. Fitted with metal wheels until 1965, thereafter with small black treaded plastic ones, the finish is medium grey oversprayed on the upper surface with camouflage green. The RAF roundels sit inside a cast circle on the wing and the tail carries an RAF flash. The die was sent to India in 1968 when it became part of the Nicky Toy range. The Javelin featured in an article in the March 1958 *Meccano Magazine* entitled 'Dinky Toy Flies Faster than Sound' which explained how shock waves are produced in the atmosphere by an aircraft in flight, illustrated by a shadow photograph of a plane flying at Mach 1.4. The plane was not a full-size one but the Dinky which was being used as a more manageable subject. The toy had its undercarriage filed off and was fired from a 17-pounder anti-tank gun at about 1,500 feet per second. *Meccano Magazine* was proud to be able to report that the model flew well at supersonic speed!

Hawker Hunter Fighter – 736

The Dinky drawing of the Hunter was completed in April 1954, between the flight of the first prototype and the pre-production F1 and the 1/190 scale model was released a year later. There are no material changes in the drawing of this one-piece casting, an attractive and accurate model with the standard undercarriage appearing somewhat less obtrusive. The camouflage finish is grey with dark green oversprayed on the top surface and a silvered cockpit. Transfer RAF roundels fit within cast circles on the wings and the tail is decorated with a flash.

P.1B Lightning Fighter – 737

Once again the Dinky was released before the plane went into service. At 1/194 scale, this single casting with a frontal orifice to accept the plastic probe is a fair representation of the original though the 'needle-nose', modelled in plastic, the first use of this material in the Dinky plane range, incorrectly has the probe mounted centrally. The finish is silver with RAF roundels transferred onto the wings and nose and a fin flash. The cockpit is blued. In 1964, the finish was changed to metallic grey and in 1965 the wheels to black-treaded plastic. Sometime during or after 1960, the roundels were changed from transfers to self-adhesive labels. A good model but not a particularly attractive piece, it was in the catalogue for ten years, having the longest run for a post-war plane and overlapping well into the time of the 'Big Plane' range.

DH 110 Sea Vixen Fighter – 738

The original had not flown in service when the Dinky was produced using a name, DH Sea Vixen that is a hybrid; the plane on which it was based, the De Havilland 110 was developed into the *Hawker* Sea Vixen. The only extant drawing dated December 1959, less than a year before the release of the 1/190 scale model, is that for the Royal Navy transfers on the tail booms. It is a smooth two-piece casting with good upper surface detail, the top casting comprising most of the toy with only the lower fuselage and forward undercarriage making up the lower one. Splitting the casting saved metal by allowing the centre box-sectioned fuselage and engine pods to be hollow. The upper casting was painted medium sea grey with the radome finished in gloss black and the cockpit in silver. The lower casting is white. Royal Navy in black is transferred onto the tail booms. The roundels on the wings sit in cast location circles and there should be a roundel either side of the nose. Later these became self-adhesive paper. The Sea Vixen die was sent to India to become a Nicky Toy.

Avro Vulcan Delta Wing Bomber – 749/992

The tale of Dinky's 1/190 scale model of the Vulcan, the drawing of which is dated 20.3.53, based on the first prototype, is intriguing and an insight into the difficulties toy manufacturers can face and how they can try to minimise their losses. At first, it appeared that the Vulcan was a one-off, as the only example known was in a locked glass cabinet at the Meccano factory in Binns Road, Liverpool. Then, when Alan Dimmock, one of the earliest Dinky aeroplane aficionados, wrote to Meccano he had the following reply which he quoted in *Dinky Toys and Modelled Miniatures* and which I repeat because it is still the authentic story of what happened:

'... the Vulcan was originally allotted sales number 703 previously destined for the Herald, but it was eventually at drawing board stage given the number 707. It was then decided that because of the bulk of the model – it measured 6.25″ span by 6″ long – it would be very heavy to cast in mazac, and since at the time there was a severe shortage of the material following the Korean War (we are talking of 1955) the decision was made to cast the model in aluminium. A special machine was produced for this purpose but, unfortunately, the dies were not really suitable for the high temperature involved in aluminium casting, and as a result of attempting to use them for this purpose they were damaged. ...The change (of number) to 749 was made at the time it was decided to make the model in aluminium. We believe this was done to identify it as a non-mazac casting.'

The drawing change is dated 17.6.53. Further correspondence revealed that 'the wing tips were originally very much more pointed and squared-off, but because of the thinness of these extremities and their distance from the main bulk of the model they did not "fill" properly in the mould, which, after one or two shots, was blocked to round off the wingtips'. There is no sign of this on the drawing which shows the tips, which are squared off at right angles, precisely one centimetre long. Whatever was or was not done to the mould, there are several examples with one wingtip more deformed than the other, though it must be remembered that the aluminium could distort if a plane was dropped. The Vulcan was not announced in *Meccano Magazine* but it was available in North America. A *Meccano Bulletin* dated April 1955 published by Meccano Ltd, 675 King St. West, Toronto, Canada, carried the following announcement:

SPECIAL NEW DINKY TOYS to be advertised next:
No. 992 Avro Vulcan Delta Wing Bomber. The latest in Aeroplanes.
A finely finished Jet Model of entirely different design. Every boy will want one at $1.40 retail.

The model was packed in a Supertoys striped box and had also been re-allocated to the supertoy number block, the drawing having been changed from Dinky Toys 749 to Dinky Supertoys 992 on 11.1.55. However this change was not implemented on the model. The letter quoted from above continues to say that 'various stories have been heard of upward of 500 castings being produced before the tools finally became useless and it is the opinion of one who was here at the time that they were all despatched to Canada and that this was the only order ever made...' The last dated reference so far found to the Vulcan is a 1956 Canadian catalogue, ignominiously tucked away amongst 'Models not illustrated': 992 Avro Vulcan Delta Wing Bomber $1.40.

The beautiful, large, one-piece aluminium casting has short stubby undercarriage legs which are fitted with three two-wheel assemblies. Finished in silver with RAF roundels on the wings and smaller ones either side of the cockpit with a red, white and blue flash on either side of the tail as shown on the assembly drawing dated 10.4.53. The Supertoy box is numbered 992 and at least one example has the Meccano date stamp, 1955, inside the lid. A very few (possibly three) mazac examples with shortened wingtips turned up in various tool cabinets in the factory. The whereabouts of these and the examples on display in the managing director's office is not known. There are some white metal versions that have been made for the collector. A half-size model in pewter was made from the original drawing as a souvenir of the Dinky Exhibition in 1983.

ISSUES OF THE LATE 50s AND EARLY 60s

702 DH Comet Jet Airliner 1954–55
183m
'Dinky Toys Comet' under starboard wing, '702' under port.
BOAC livery, white and blue with silver wings and tailplane, white fin.
Window lines and nose decking sprayed on in royal blue.
Cockpit and passenger windows silver.
Registration G-ALYV in black. Gold wheels.
Box: blue and white Supertoy stripes, illustration as plane.
1955: renumbered 999
.

703 Handley Page Herald
Not issued.

706 Vickers Viscount Airliner Air France 1956–57
150mm
'Viscount 706' under starboard wing, 'Made in England Meccano Ltd' under port.
Air France livery, silver with white upper fuselage. Sprayed blue nose decking. Transferred windows with line, 'Air France' and registration in blue with tricolour.
Silver of fuselage shows through for windows.
Tail transfer blue.
Registration F-B on port wing, GNL on starboard in black.
Replaced by 708.
*See also: French Dinky 60E (green-blue transfers)
Registration F-BGNX).*

708 Vickers Viscount Airliner BEA 1957–65
Casting as 706 but number deleted.
BEA livery, silver with white rudder, upper fuselage and elevators.
Nose decking sprayed red. Fuselage transfer with windows in black, red cheat lines, 'British European Airways' on upper fuselage, BEA and the yellow airmail insignia of a crown with a post horn suspended from it, lower rear.
Union Jack and registration on fin.
Wings: 'BEA' in slanting letters and registration G-AOJA.
Plated metal wheels.
Later: metallic grey and white, 'B E A' in upright letters on port wing.
1965 plastic wheels.
See also: Nicky Toys.

715 Bristol 173 Helicopter 1956–62
(Rotor diameter 72mm) Length 86mm
Light blue/green, later turquoise – shades vary.
Cockpit and cabin windows in aluminium, red flash on upper. fuselage, red rotors.
Spurious registration G-AUXR in black.
To 1957: Box has technical information on back.
After 1957: information deleted.

716 Westland-Sikorsky S51 Helicopter 1957–62
(Rotor diameter 72mm) Length 66mm
Dark red with cream rotor pylon. Cockpit silver.
Spurious registration G-ATWX in cream.
Yellow box with and without picture.

734 Supermarine Swift 1955–62
51mm
Medium grey and dark green camouflage on upper surfaces, grey on lower. Cockpit silver.
RAF roundels, oblong rudder markings.

735 Gloster Javelin Delta Wing Fighter 1955–66
83mm
Medium grey and dark green camouflage on upper surface, grey on lower.
RAF wing and tail markings. Smooth wheels until 1965, then black treaded.
See also: Nicky Toys.

736 Hawker Hunter 1955–63
53mm
Medium grey and dark green camouflage on upper surfaces, medium grey below. Cockpit silver.
RAF roundels and tail markings.

737 P.1B Lightning Fighter 1959–68
55mm
Black plastic nose probe. Silver.
RAF roundel transfers on nose and upper wing with red, white and blue markings on tail.
From 1964: metallic silver-grey.
Smooth metal wheels until 1965, then black plastic.
Later: paper roundels.

738 DH 110 Sea Vixen Fighter 1960–65
80mm
Medium sea grey with white lower surfaces. Nose radar painted black. Cockpit silver.
Service roundels transferred on nose and wings.
'Royal Navy' in black on tail booms.
Later: paper roundels.
See also: Nicky Toys.

749 Avro Vulcan Delta Wing Bomber
Catalogued and boxed as 992.

992 Avro Vulcan Delta Wing Bomber 1955–56
156mm
Silver with RAF roundels on wings and nose.
Blue-striped Supertoy box.

997 Caravelle SE210 Airliner 1962–65
180mm
Casting as French Dinky but marked: 'Made in England'.
Air France livery, silver with white upper fuselage.
Blue painted band on nose merges into dark blue (almost green) transfer of side stripe edged with light green, light green triangular windows, white central line.
'Air France' in thicker letters than French Dinky, tricolour, registration below tail all part of decal.
Straight-edged tail flash.
Registration F-BGNY stamped on starboard wing.
Supertoy striped box.
1965: black plastic wheels. Yellow view box.
See: French Dinky 60F.

998 Bristol Britannia Airliner 1959–65
225mm
Canadian Pacific Livery. Silver with white upper fuselage and rudder, cockpit silver, nose radar black.
Transfers: blue line with silver windows and silver interlining surmounted by Canadian Pacific in blue script.
Blue horizontal lines on leading edge of tail fin with 421 and registration. CF-CZA in blue on starboard wing.
Striped Supertoy box with plane in blue.
From 1960: red fuselage and tail lines.
Striped Supertoy box with plane in red.
From c.1964: metallic grey and white.
Yellow box with view.

999 DH Comet Jet Airliner 1955/6–65
Renumbering of 702 but with 'Dinky Supertoys' under starboard wing, '999' under port.
Silver wheels.
BOAC livery as 702, white and blue with silver wings and tailplane, white fin.
Registration G-ALYV. *From 1959/60:* G-ALYX.
Later: blue transfer with white letters etc. on tail.
From 1964: metallic silver-grey wings and tailplane.
Thicker registration letters.
Box: 'Supertoy' stripes, illustration of plane.
Later: red and yellow with view.
See also: Nicky Toys.

Nicky Toys – 'Indian Dinky Toys' *circa* 1968–86

In 1970, the Meccano Factory (by this time owned by Lines Bros.) wrote in the following vein after advertising to buy obsolete Dinkies:

'We are in the process of arranging for Dinky and other Lines Bros. products to be manufactured in other countries where, for various reasons, it is impossible to sell by direct export from here. Accordingly, we arrange to supply tools, either on loan or for payment, and these enable local manufacturers to produce Dinky and other toys which would otherwise not be available in those countries.

'Needless to say, we can only spare tools for obsolete models which is why we wish to obtain samples, because the manufacturers in the foreign countries wished to have samples of the product they were about to manufacture, and although Meccano could provide catalogues and pictures, they did not have any stocks left of some of the articles themselves, hence our reasons for advertising.'

In February 1968 some dies, of which four were aircraft, had already been shipped to S Kumar and Co. trading as Atamco Private Ltd in Calcutta. To protect the Meccano trademark, the toys were to be marked Nicky Toys' and 'Made in India'. 'Dinky and Meccano' should have been deleted from the underside of the wings, but on some types this was done in a rough and ready fashion with 'DIN' being crudely recarved into 'NIC', the 'KY' being untouched. Sometimes, 'Dinky' has been deleted but not replaced. Each model can have a variety of markings. Thus, the Viscount first had a blank in place of the word 'Dinky' which was later filled in with 'NICKY'. The already old dies received a lot more wear. The wheels are usually small, turned aluminium ones but can be black plastic. The quality of the casting ranges from acceptable to poor. Much industrial production in India is done by outworkers in their own homes and the finish of the models reflects this. There are different types of wheel. The decal and sticker printing is obviously done in different places and to different artwork each time and the standard of finish is variable. There are very many differences so the following table gives a general description of those commonly found. The boxes similarly should have been overprinted or reprinted and most have, though some are identical to the Dinky boxes and have been hand altered with a ballpoint pen to transform 'Dinky' into 'Nicky'. Yellow boxes with black and white pictures of actual planes or plain boxes are also found. The catalogue numbers remain the same. A price list, dated June 1979, still features all four castings, but not all were available ex-stock. In 1990, examples were still to be found in shops in India but it is doubtful if manufacturing continues. They are also known amongst collectors as 'Indian Dinkies'.

Viscount Airliner – 708

The casting has an additional non-prototypical raised line on the wings beyond the outside engine and forward of the flaps as if it was intended as a decal location line. It is finished in the 1959–69 BEA livery, redolent of the sixties with its flat expanses of colour: silver with top half of fuselage in white, sprayed red upper and lower wing surfaces, black nose. Some have forward end of engine nascelles sprayed black. Round-headed propeller pins, red four-blade propellers. Transferred black window line with clear windows to allow silver to show through with red BEA square, red square on tail fin, black top to fin with registration, G-AOHL, a genuine registration (of plane named Charles Sturt) on starboard boxed in white, BEA boxed in white on port wing. Later: all stickers – black window stripe with 12 (or incorrectly 13) white windows (or both). Later: as above but without red wing surfaces.

Gloster Javelin – 735

Slight casting differences from Dinky: thickened nose wheel support, four raised blips aft of cockpit deleted. Name bodged to 'NKY TOYS'. RAF colours, silver with RAF roundels with red, white and blue stripes on leading edge of tailfin, or wrapped around leading edge. Camouflaged.

Sea Vixen – 738

Silver with RAF roundels and Royal Navy on tail booms. Also sea grey, RAF roundels with extra outer ring of white, flash on tailplane edged in white. Also silver with Indian Air Force white, orange and green roundels. Early: minute 12mm x 4mm transfer panel with licensee, place of manufacture and 'Prop. of DT trade mark is Mecc. Ltd. L'pool'.

Comet Airliner – 999

Several different shades in the grey to silver band. Transferred blue window line with transparent windows to allow white body to show through. BOAC incorporated into line. Cockpit unsilvered. G-ALYX in black on starboard wing. Later: bright metallic blue and white fuselage sticker with BOAC. Clear sellotape with blue registration on wing. Several different decal printings in colour and configuration.

The Big Planes 1965–79

Despite the success of Dinky Toys, Meccano was in difficulty in the early sixties because of its inability to recoup the costs of the retooling for Hornby Dublo trains in 1959. The losses were such that the firm failed and was taken over by Tri-ang in 1964. In 1965, the planes produced consisted of four airliners including the Viscount and three fighters, all simple but well-finished castings with good transfers, in restrained finishes and approximately related in scale. The new broom of Tri-ang, who had been making brightly-coloured action toys with great success for almost 50 years, began to sweep through the Meccano empire. The first Tri-ang/ Dinky plane was a bright red and white small plane, a Beechcraft Bonanza in 1/78 scale, nearly the same size as the Viscount model. This emphasis on eyecatching decoration and gimmicks characterises the new Big Plane range, which consists of a mixture of private planes, an airliner, historic planes from the WWII, current jet fighters and helicopters in a variety of scales. There does not seem to have been an overall coherent plan for producing the models in this group, unless it was one of 'hedging your bets'. The name 'The Big Planes' was first used in the 1973 catalogue, but it is generally applied to all post 1965 introductions. The Big Planes were exported to France and are to be found in French Dinky catalogues. The same numbers with an 'L' suffix were used.

BOXES

At first all-card boxes were used but, during 1973–74, they gradually changed to a card base with a clear thin plastic lid moulded to retain the models in position. The first bases were white or light blue with black edges. The later ones had light blue bases with dark blue around the edge. The number of different packagings in which a model can be found depends on the production span of the model. Some later issues were always packed in clear-topped boxes. These were difficult for the retailer to display and eventually Meccano invented a hanging system whereby hooks, from which the packaging could be suspended, were slipped into the required position in a corrugated sheet so displaying the flat top and the model inside.

DECALS

Some are paper stickers which tend to discolour and peel off. Some have clear self-adhesive tape stickers. Good quality waterslide transfers were also supplied with some of the military models which could be used to replace some of the stickers or to provide additional decoration.

MARKINGS

The large castings are usually marked with 'Dinky Toys', the catalogue number and the name of the plane.

PROTOTYPES

The authors were given access to a storeroom at Binns Road in 1977 and found a Phantom II in a shade of grey similar to the RAF colours on the Hurricane with greenish white undersurfaces and undercarriage legs. The dark green camouflage is hand applied and the red and blue roundels are from the SEPECAT Jaguar. It most probably dates from 1972/3, and is perhaps a prototype for a Phantom in RAF finish. It was used for the illustration in the 1977 Trade Catalogue. There was also a Bell Helicopter fitted with stretchers. Other similar experimental and unusual finishes exist but are difficult to authenticate. Several oddities appeared around the closure of the factory in 1979/80. Other variations could be produced by building non-standard Dinky Kits.

DINKY KITS

The kits were virtually the same as (six of) the diecast models, but unpainted and unassembled. Small glass tubes of Humbrol paint were supplied and the parts screwed together instead of being rivetted. Transfers were enclosed in the rigid bubble pack enclosed in a cardbook 'book' cover.

PRIVATE PLANES

Beechcraft S35 Bonanza – 710

The Dinky is an attractive 1/77 scale model. The white plastic propeller rotates and the engine cover lifts off to reveal a rudimentary power unit. The catalogue picture shows the registration number to be N5121A but the model always has the number N8695M and 'Beechcraft' in script. The fixed undercarriage stubs have small black wheels usually carrying a witness of a tread. Cost-saving changes from 1971 are detailed in the list. A 1975 casting change, a raised line on the upper surface of the wings, facilitated the positioning of the spray mask for the red band. The colour change was apparently at the request of Beechcraft who had one in such a livery. This last version later also had a new registration number, N4480W.

Beechcraft C55 Baron – 715/US Army T-42A – 712

This is a pretty model in 1/77 scale that has a family resemblance round the window line to the earlier Beechcraft. The '1st Again' gimmick was a simple retractable undercarriage, which clicked firmly into place. The plastic engine covers hid more detailed engines than before and there was a jewelled headlamp in the nose. There are two castings, with good flap detail. Underneath, as part of a four-line engraving, the catalogue number 715 is on a block replacing another number, but why it was changed is not known. Sometime in 1973, the inscription on the undersurface was changed to three lines with the catalogue number deleted to accommodate the introduction of the US Army T-42A, 712, which shared the same casting. This toy was fitted with push-on black plastic wingtip tanks.

Hawker Siddeley Executive Jet – 723/ RAF Dominie – 728

It is a reasonable 1/108 scale model. Its 'first', an opening, bright metal drop-down door complete with stairway, is not the neatest nor was it a true 'first' because the early sixties French/English Dinky Caravelle (60F/997) had demountable stairs. The retractable undercarriage parts are metal. The model lacks grace and there is a strange bottle-glass effect of the thick glazing on the too square fuselage windows. From some angles, the engine pods look too far forward or too low. Their position is dictated by the need to trap the piece securely between upper and lower fuselage castings. The wings are a fourth casting and the whole is a solid toy. The HS125s were used by the RAF under the name of Dominie T.Mk1. The original number, 723, was left under the wing of the RAF Dominie, 728. The metallic blue with green camouflage finish is not authentic.

AIRLINER

The most likely reason that Dinky only produced one airliner is that it was a heavy, expensive casting and that sales were insufficient to keep the type in the catalogue.

Boeing 737 – 717

The Dinky is quite a good 1/186 scale model. The gimmick was an automatic retractable undercarriage operated by a heavy diecast lever, just behind the starboard wing, which detracts from the plane's appearance. Two hefty castings trap the engines between them, the lower fuselage casting extending down underneath the wings to the engines for this purpose.

WORLD WAR II PLANES

A group of fighter planes, fitted with rudimentary pilots, from four of the leading combatants in the Second World War introduced in the late sixties and early seventies were part of the first post-war British nostalgia trip. 'Direct from the epic film *Battle of Britain*' came a Spitfire MkII and a Junkers Ju87B Stuka. The boxes were cardboard emblazoned with action shots of the planes and a Union Jack enveloping an Iron Cross. Three scenes from the film were shown on one side of the boxes with the Stuka coming to a fiery end at the foot of a pylon. The planes were issued with applied paper sticker decals, although some had clear tape decals or even transfers applied. Most had replacement/additional decals supplied on waterslide transfer sheets.

Spitfire MkII – 719, 741, 700, 1042 kit

The casting of this large virtually single-piece 1/65 scale diecasting is very good with plenty of neat panel detail and a smooth surface remarkably free of die split lines. There is a second casting beneath the front fuselage, with name of plane, manufacturer and at the rear wing root the sales number, 719. A plastic piece at the rear hides the battery (not included, Sales no. 035), that powers the 'First Again' motor-driven propeller. The undercarriage legs are individually retractable. The instruction leaflet describes the method of starting the propeller that eliminates the need for disfiguring levers: 'Flick propeller in anti-clockwise direction to start motor. Insert finger into spinning propeller to stop motor. This procedure is completely harmless.' Paper roundels were fitted on the wings, as were clear self-adhesive tape squadron markings. Later the squadron markings come on a separate sheet. In 1978, the battery-powered version was replaced by one without working propeller, on the number, 741. The old sales number was removed and it was soon cast with a circular hole at the wing root. The hole was needed for the last version, Spitfire, Diamond Jubilee of the Royal Air Force, 700. It was a promotional idea about which little is known. The only indication of the origin of this souvenir desk ornament is on the box in very small print '1978 C Unicorn and Dragon/Gilbey Jubilee Collection'. Exactly the same parts are used, but the whole plane is chromed, and the decals are factory-applied. The hole under the fuselage has a bent rod secured with protruding nuts. The rod fits in a hole in the top of a two-piece 'onyx' green plastic plinth. The lower section has a silver sticker, 'Diamond Jubilee of the Royal Air Force'. The upper carries a gold plastic circular wreathed plate with a sticker incorporating the motto of the RAF: *Per Ardua ad Astra*, (Through Travail to the Stars). The box is a splendid, strong, dark blue cardboard affair, with a slip-over acetate lid. The box base holds the ensemble securely. In late 1979 and early 1980, batches appeared in the shops, presumably sold as part of the clearance of Binns Road warehouse stocks. Also available as Dinky Kits, 1042.

Junkers Ju87B Stuka – 721

Dinky modelled in about 1/72 scale, this second *Battle of Britain* film release, a relatively early Ju 87B with a deep underslung radiator, a feature that was reduced in later types. The upper fuselage and the whole of the tail is one casting and the wings and lower fuselage another. Diecast inserts under the wings have the manufacturer's details and trap the separate undercarriage legs in position.

Hawker Hurricane MkIIc – 718, 1041 kit

Dinky produced a good heavy model in 1/65 scale with plenty of surface line and rivet detail. It consisted of one main casting for fuselage, wings, tail, and tail wheel, with a small one for part of the underwing and lower fuselage. The ratchet wheel for the RAT-TAT-TAT gun on the top of the fuselage detracts little from the appearance but the noises are disappointingly unrealistic. Also available as Dinky Kits, 1041.

Messerschmitt Bf 109E – 726, 1044 kit

The model, whose single main upper fuselage, wing and tail including tail wheel casting does not have as much surface detail as previous ones, is in 1/60 scale. The on/off switch for the battery-powered propeller is hidden under the fuselage. The undercarriage legs retract individually. Also available as Dinky Kits, 1044.

P-47 Thunderbolt – 734

In 1/76 scale, the Thunderbolt is constructed from three excellent castings, one for the main smooth upper, one a small under casting which unscrews to give access to the battery compartment as before and, the last one, a great single nose cowl. The clear cockpit bubble is a little large, as is the pilot. The propeller kicks back quite realistically, even when turned with the finger, instead of just going round.

A6M5 Zero-Sen – 739

The Dinky is a fair 1/60 scale model though somewhat on the heavy side with over-thick wing and tail sections. There are two main castings and the motor switch for the kick-back action propeller is underneath.

MODERN JET FIGHTERS

All are fitted with pilot figures and most have hard, black plastic nose cones. The models are fair to good.

Hawker Harrier –
722

Dinky produced the GR1 Harrier Jump Jet in 1/71 scale just after it entered service with the RAF and thereby reaped untold benefits from the enthusiasm amongst the general public engendered by the real thing. The combined action of the undercarriage legs lowering and the jet exhausts swivelling is operated by a lever in a slot along the top of the fuselage.

F-4K Phantom II –
725, 727, 730, 733

This one is 1/89 scale, composed of two big heavy castings, and is more or less accurate depending on the type name. The undercarriage is hand-operated. Plastic bombs slide into a slot up the centre of the lower fuselage compressing a spring. Depressing the lever on the starboard side of the fuselage allows the tension on the spring to release and the missile to pop out. Phantom II F-4K, 725, was in dark blue Royal Navy finish. The US Navy Phantom, 730, is all-over mid grey but the factory ran out of the properly coloured wing in the run up to Christmas 1974 and used the already painted Bundesluftwaffe wing with matt dark grey/green camouflage shading. The pieces screw together so each example requires authentication. The F-4K Phantom II Der Bundesluftwaffe, 733, was specially made for export to Germany. The last production scheme was also for export, US Air Force F-4 Phantom II, 727.

SEPECAT Jaguar
– 731, 1043 kit

Dinky's 1/82 scale model has a wheel configuration (twin nose and single rear wheels) only found on the Jaguar M prototype. The ejector button on the top of the fuselage operates a spring which raises the canopy seat and allows the pilot to eject. The rear undercarriage wheels fold forward manually and then the covers hinge backwards to give a smooth undersurface in flight. Also available as Dinky Kits, 1043.

Panavia MRCA
(Multi-role Combat
Aircraft) – 729

This version in 1/85 scale is not particularly accurate. The lever on top of the fuselage to work the swing wing-cum-undercarriage retraction is relative discreet and hardly detracts from the appearance.

HELICOPTERS

Sea King
Helicopter – 724,
736, 618 part, 1040 kit

Dinky modelled the fuselage in 1/103 scale but used a 1/170 scale rotor. The card inner of the box has a scene of a carrier deck with a Sea King taking off. The motor-powered main rotor is switched on by a lever beneath the craft and is started by flicking the rotor anti-clockwise. The winch for recovering an Apollo Space Capsule is finger-operated by turning the knurled wheel in the starboard side. The diecast door to the battery compartment is in the port side and the battery sits above the winch mechanism. The second version is the Bundesmarine Sea King Helicopter, 736 with Sonar Device. As the the firm was running into its final difficulties, the helicopter, without the motor, was packaged as AEC Artic Transporter with Helicopter, 618. Also available as Dinky Kits, 1040.

Bell Police
Helicopter – 732,
part 299, 303,
M*A*S*H

This one is in 1/60 scale and the rotor is nearly correct in 1/66. There are no gimmicks, its size and delicacy precluding them, but, of course, the rotors go round. The seat-cum-cabin floor-cum-engine is diecast and the lower boom tinplate. The rest is plastic. Because of shortages in the period before Christmas 1974 a red 'Captain Scarlet' was fitted as pilot. 'Police

Accident' notice board and road cones were included in the packaging. It figured in Police Crash Squad, 299 and in Commando Squad, 303. A group of vehicles in M*A*S*H livery was planned but not released. A mock-up of a stretcher-carrying Bell helicopter exists. Some M*A*S*H stickers were applied to olive drab helicopters and these have appeared unboxed on the collectors' circuit.

SPACE SHUTTLE

As the firm was failing, new product was still being designed. The Space Shuttle was released in 1979 a short time before the factory closure but its availability was patchy. It figured in the 1980 Trade Brochure issued at the Earls Court Toy Fair at the end of January. Some time after the factory closed, a quantity said to have been stored in a warehouse came onto the collectors' market. Subsequently, the Shuttle casting with either of the two loads but without the booster assembly turned up in some quantity, in a variety of plastic bags or bubble packaging.

Space Shuttle – 364

Not a very accurate representation of the Shuttle, the two-piece diecast body of the model was fitted with opening payload doors. A card and a plastic kit payload was supplied. Following the example of the Big Planes, replacement transfers were in the impressive blue and red window box. The fuel tank and booster rocket assembly into which the Shuttle's undercarriage legs clip is white plastic.

THE BIG PLANES 1965–79

The descriptions after the names of the planes are mainly from the catalogues.

700 Spitfire Mk II Diamond Jubilee of the RAF (not in catalogue) 1979–79
173mm
Casting of 741 with circular hole at wing root.
Chromed. Black plastic propeller, exhausts, aerial.
Paper stickers: red and blue roundels on wings, flash on tail.
Sellotape squadron markings: A1-roundel-E.
Green plastic plinth with 'Diamond Jubilee of the Royal Air Force'.
Box: square dark blue card with slip-over acetate lid.

710 Beechcraft S35 Bonanza with removable engine cover opening fuselage door 1965–76
133mm
White upper fuselage with red on upper and lower tail surfaces, red lower fuselage and wings with white wingtips.
White plastic propeller, engine cover, red door, two cases, treaded tyres.
Stickers: red and black lines with 'Beechcraft' above and N8695M below.
Colourful card box depicting luggage.
From 1971: plain tyres, no luggage in plane or on packaging, white background box.
From 1972: yellow upper casting with bronze panels, bronze lower casting with yellow wingtips.
Black plastic propeller, engine cover, door.
Box with clear lid.
1975: Casting line added along wing at colour split.
White upper with red tail flaps, dark blue lower with red rear half of wings (Beechcraft livery).
Black propeller, white engine cover.
Late 1975: registration N4480W.

712 US Army T-42A 1972–77
153mm
Casting of 715 with plastic wingtip tanks.
Drab green.
All plastic parts black.
Stickers: 24506 on starboard wing, star-on-bar on port.
Box with clear lid.

715 Beechcraft C55 Baron with retractable undercarriage, removable engine covers, jewelled nose light 1968–76
150mm
Four-line engraving under fuselage.
White with yellow wingtips.
Yellow plastic propellers and engine covers, white undercarriage legs.
Sticker: N555C on fuselage and 'Beechcraft' on tail with black and yellow stripes.
Cardboard box.
From 1969: yellow plastic undercarriage.
From 1971/2: Red with yellow wingtips.
From 1972: three-line engraving.
Box with clear lid.

717 Boeing 737 with automatic retractable undercarriage 1970 – 75
152mm
White with blue tail, white engines, silver cockpit windows, matt black nose.
Stickers: 'Lufthansa' and blue window line, yellow circle with crane on tail.
From 1971: blue engines.
From 1974: box with clear lid.

718 Hawker Hurricane Mk IIc with cannon noise and retractable undercarriage 1972–75
188mm
All over grey with dark green shading on upper surface.
Black plastic propeller exhausts, cannon.
Stickers: paper wing roundels, tail flash.
Separate transfers: squadron markings, QO roundel Y, JX roundel B.
Box with clear lid.
Also as kit 1041.

719 Spitfire MkII, direct from the epic film *Battle of Britain*, with motor-driven propeller and retractable undercarriage 1969– 78
173mm
Cast circles on wings to position roundels.
Green with brown camouflage on upper surfaces, duck egg green on under surfaces.
Black plastic propeller (with yellow tips), exhausts, aerial.
Stickers: paper – red and blue roundels on wings, red, white and blue tail flash; clear tape squadron markings.
Battle of Britain film card box.
From 1972: modification of battery (Mallory Mn 9100) housing.
Transfer squadron markings factory applied.
From 1973: Cast circles on wings removed.
Separate transfers for squadron markings:
A1-roundel -A, -B, -E.
Box with clear lid, no mention of film.
Replaced by 741.

721 Junkers Ju.87B Stuka, direct from the epic film *Battle of Britain* with dropping cap-firing bomb 1969–80
191mm
Service green upper surfaces and undercarriage, duck egg blue on undersurfaces, high gloss yellow nose band and tail fin.
Black plastic propeller with yellow tips.
Stickers: paper crosses on wings; clear tape fin swastika, squadron markings W8+BN, W8+CN, W8+LN.
Battle of Britain film card box.
Later: separate transfers for fin swastika and squadron markings.
From 1972: box with clear lid, no mention of film.
From 1976: yellow plastic propeller.

722 Hawker Harrier, with fully retractable undercarriage linked to swivelling jet exhausts operated by sliding button. Retractable wing tip stabilising wheels 1970–80
108mm
Early catalogue and card box colours not issued.
Metallic blue with green shading on upper (varies), blueish white lower casting.
Black plastic nose probe, wing tip stabilisers.
Stickers: Blue and red roundels as 1977 Cat. not supplied; paper red, white and blue roundels on fuselage sides and wings, tail flash.
Card box.
From 1973: box with clear top.

723 Hawker Siddeley HS125 Executive Jet with diecast opening door-cum-stairway, retractable undercarriage 1970–75
132mm
White upper, yellow lower and wings, metallic blue engines.
Sticker: Red fuselage stripe.
Cardboard box showing 2nd livery.
From 1972/3: White upper, the rest metallic blue.
Black nose triangle.
Box with clear lid.

724 Sea King Helicopter with battery-powered main rotor, finger-operated recovery winch, floating Apollo Space Capsule 1971–79
179mm
White upper casting, metallic blue lower.
Mid-blue plastic rotors, red interior, white capsule.
Stickers: '66' in black.
Separate transfers: replacement 66, 'NAVY', star-on-bar, four capsule recovery.
Card box with scenic interior.
From c.1973: black plastic interior.
From c.1974: blue or black rotors, white or yellow capsule.
Later: box with clear top.
In set 618 in green.
Also as kit 1040.

725 F-4k Phantom II, with spring-fired 'stand off' missile and retractable undercarriage 1972–77
132mm
Ultramarine blue, light blue undersurfaces.
Black plastic nose cone.
Stickers: red, white and blue roundels on fuselage and wingtips, yellow eagle on tail.
Later: smaller roundels.
Separate transfers: ROYAL NAVY, '153' in white, red stars, 'RESCUE' in yellow.
Two white plastic missiles in box with clear lid.

726 Messerschmitt Bf109E, propeller driven by battery-powered motor, retractable undercarriage 1972–75
165mm
Bronze catalogue finish not released.
Desert sand with varying spots of green on upper casting, shiny light blue lower casting and undercarriage.
Brown plastic propeller and aerial.
Paper stickers: black and white crosses on wings.
Separate transfer squadron markings, S9+IS, <+wave, 5+small+, four tailfin swastikas, six pairs shields or roundels.
Box with clear lid.
1975: dark grey-green with yellow nose, rudder and wingtips, or with more than half the wing yellow (liveries of the Yellow Nose Squadrons, the elite of the Luftwaffe).
Also as kit 1044.

727 US Air Force F-4 Phantom II (not in catalogue) 1976–77
132mm
Casting of 725.
Greyish brown with olive green camouflage on upper, pale grey lower, chromed legs.
Stickers: star-on-bar on wingtips.
Yellow plastic missiles in box with clear top dated 1976.

728 RAF Dominie 1972–75
132mm
Casting of 723.
Mid-metallic blue with bright metal door, mid green camouflage.
Stickers: RAF roundels on wings, tail flash registration XG172.
Box with clear lid.

729 Panavia Multi-Role Combat Aircraft with swing-wing linked to retracting undercarriage 1974–75
164mm
Grey with dull green camouflage on upper surfaces.
Stickers: red and blue roundels, tail flashes.
Separate transfers: replacement roundels and flashes, XX610, small triangles, etc.
Box with clear lid.
Also as kit 1045.

730 US Navy Phantom II 1972–75
132mm
Casting of 725.
Mid-grey, white undersurfaces, grey undercarriage legs.
Later: plated legs.
Pre-Xmas 1974 only: wings with matt dark grey/green shading (= wing of 733), plated legs.
Stickers: 'NAVY' on fuselage sides, star-on-bar on port wing, 'AC' on starboard wing and tail fin.
Separate transfers: cat with bomb, '101', 'JET INTAKE', 'USS SARATOGA' above red flash.
Box with clear lid.

731 S E P E C A T Jaguar, with ejecting pilot and retractable undercarriage 1973–75
106mm
Light metallic blue with dull green camouflage on top surfaces, grey underfuselage.
Stickers: small RAF roundels, tail flashes.
Separate transfers: XW514, jaguar (lower case), small symbol.
Spare orange plastic pilot in box with clear top.
Also as kit 1043.

732 Bell Police Helicopter 1974–80
211mm
Blue engine/cockpit floor, white tinplate lower boom.
Orange plastic upper boom and skids, black rotors, blue pilot
Stickers: 'POLICE'.
Grey 'Police Accident' board, two red and white cones.
Helicopter wired down in clear topped box.
Late 1974: black board.
Pre-Xmas 1974 only: red 'Captain Scarlet' pilot.
From c.1975: also red and yellow cones, orange notice board.
1976: clear box top moulded to restrain helicopter.
Some: pilot with facemask from military jets.
Some: red plastic boom.
Also in Set 299.
In Set 303 in green.
1979: green, M*A*S*H sticker, unboxed, not in catalogue.

733 F-4k Phantom II Der Bundesluftwaffe (not in catalogue) 1973–73
132mm
Casting of 725.
Dark grey with matt grey/green camouflage on upper surfaces, legs plated.
Stickers: German crosses on wing tips, flash on tail.
Separate transfers: squadron nos 26 and 35, two replacement wing crosses, roundel, hatch markings.
White plastic missiles in box with clear lid, wording mainly in German, dated 1972.

734 P-47 Thunderbolt, motor driven propeller, retractable undercarriage 1975–78
190mm
Gloss silver with gloss black engine cowling and stripe down centre top of fuselage.
Bright red plastic propeller, bombs, aerial.
Stickers: plasticised star-on-bar on port wing; clear tape 37 star-on-bar on fuselage.
Separate transfers: replacement black stripe and squadron markings, red lighting flashes, identification number, 'Amy Lou'; and yellow and black chequered band for radiator cowl, squadron numbers E star-on-bar LH.
Box with clear lid.

736 Bundesmarine Sea King Helicopter, with battery-powered main rotor, finger-operated recovery winch, sonar device 1973–78
179mm
Casting of 724.
Grey with red engine casing and tail-fin.
Black plastic rotors, interior.
Stickers: black cross in front of rotor, 89-50 on rear fuselage.
Separate transfers: red oblong with 'SAR' in grey, 'MARINE' in black etc.
Yellow sonar device in box with clear lid.

739 A6M5 Zero-Sen, motor driven propeller, retractable undercarriage 1975–78
184mm
Metallic blue-green above, grey lower, engine cowl black.
Red plastic propeller.
Stickers: red plasticised paper roundels; paper 61–131 on tail.
Separate transfers: replacement rising sun roundels, tail no 655–117, yellow leading wing-edge strips, 121 squadron flashes.
Box with clear lid.

741 Spitfire MkII 1978–80
173mm
Casting of 719 but without number and motor-driven propeller.
Finish, decals, box as last issue 719.
Later: circular hole at wing root.

SETS

299 Crash Squad 1979–80
Bell Police Helicopter livery as 732 + 244 Plymouth Police Car, Police Signs and road cones.

303 Commando Squad 1979–80
Bell Helicopter 732, green, ARMY sticker
+ 607 Convoy Army Truck, 667 Armoured Patrol Car.

618 AEC Artic Transporter and Helicopter 1976–80
Sea King Helicopter 724, unmotorised, green, black rotor.
Stickers: ARMY, red cross, Union Jack.
Separate transfers: red crosses, Union Jacks, RESCUE, DANGER

DINKY KITS

1040 Sea King Helicopter 1971–78 Casting of 724
1041 Hawker Hurricane MkIIC 1973–76 Casting of 718
1042 Spitfire MkII 1971–78 Casting of 719
1043 S E P E C A T Jaguar 1974–76 Casting of 731
1044 Messerschmitt Bf109E 1972–75 Casting of 726
1045 M R C A 1975–76 Casting of 729

364 Space Shuttle 1979–80
186mm
Opening payload doors.
White with black under.
Red plastic exhausts, wheels.
Mounted on white plastic booster rocket.
Stickers: cabin windows, Stars and Stripes with United States on sides, flag also on wings and main fuel tank.
Transfers: NASA, UNITED STATES (vertically), Explorer, stars and stripes.
Payload: orange plastic kit 'Orbiter Laboratory Instruments' and card 'Alternative Orbiter Instrument Panel'.
Window box with hanging back card.
After factory closure: Shuttle (no fuel tank etc) as above with either card or kit load packed in plastic packaging.

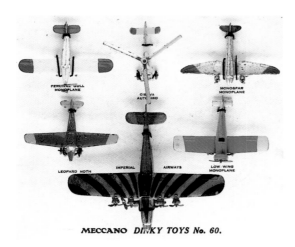

1 The original, very briefly released 60 Set. The planes are mounted 'the other way up' from usual (see the early 60 Set) and the printing on the box lining is different. This set is so unusual that it is though of as 'the first' which is followed by the standard 'early' set

2 The stylish box lid for the original 60 Set. The label on the end is dated in factory code May 1934

3 The early 60 Set: Atalanta with Sunray pattern (127mm), small planes with no registration letters

4 The early 60 Set lid reading 'MECCANO DINKY TOYS'

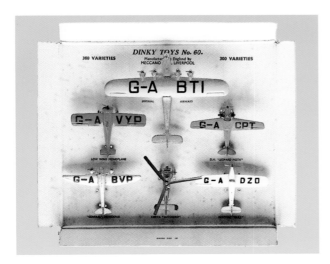

5 The later 60 Set: all planes, except Autogiro, with registration letters

6 The later 60 Set lid reading 'DINKY TOYS Manufactured by MECCANO Ltd'

7 60a Atalanta (127mm): four of the variety of unusual early liveries

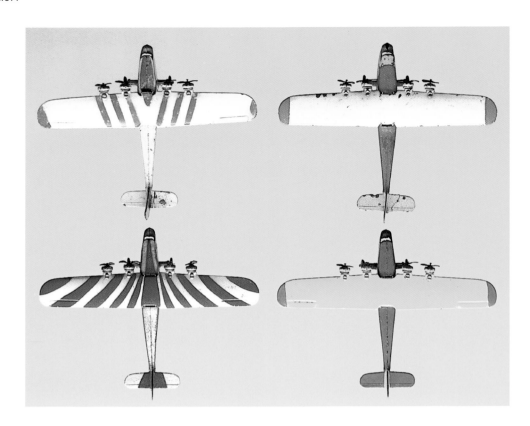

8 60a Atalanta (127mm): four of the variety of unusual later liveries

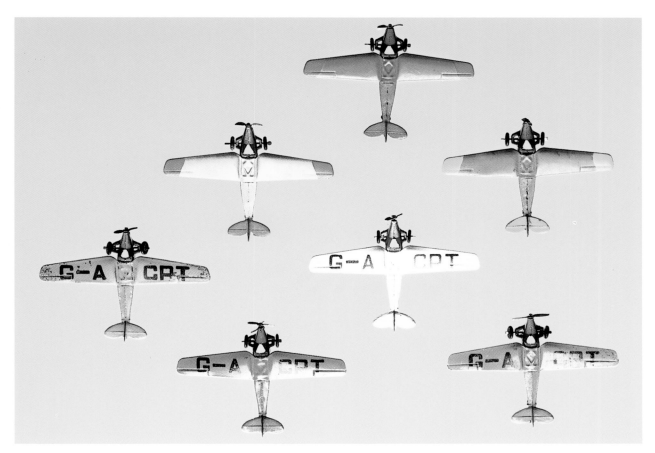

9 60b Leopard Moth (76mm): three early (no letters) and four later liveries

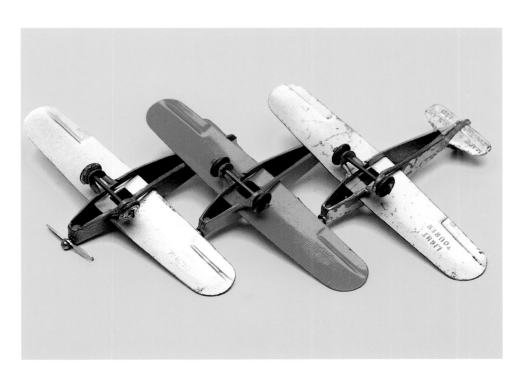

10 60c Percival Gull (76mm) showing successive pre- and post-war underwing stampings: PERCIVAL GULL; PERCIVAL TOURER; LIGHT TOURER

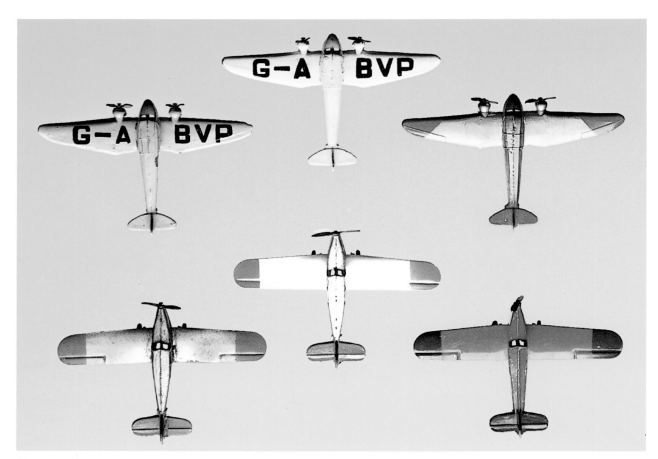

11 *top row:* 60e General Monospar (80mm): one early (no letters) and two later liveries
bottom row: 60c Percival Gull early liveries

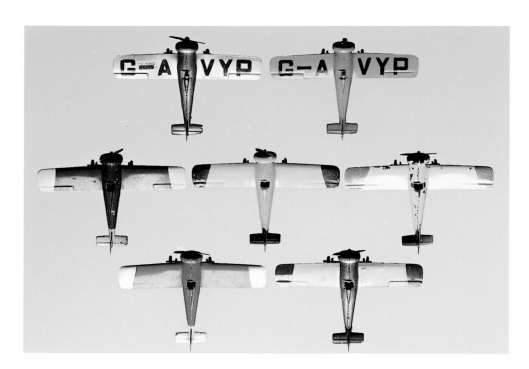

12 60d Low Wing Monoplane (76mm): five early without letters or pilot, two later with both

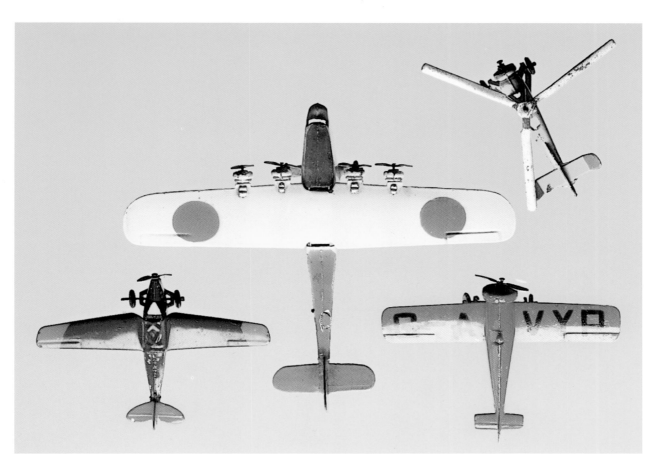

13 Unusual liveries on 60a Atalanta (127mm), 60b Leopard Moth, 60f Cierva Autogiro, 60d Low Wing Monoplane

14 Three 60e General Monospar (80mm)

15 60f Cierva Autogiro (53mm), no pilot green, with pilot blue, with pilot red, 66f Army Co-operation Autogiro, with pilot grey

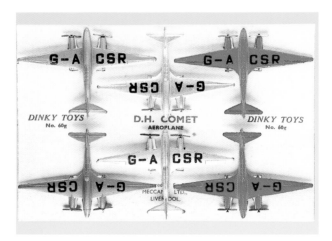

16 60g D.H. Comet (86mm) trade box of 6 with registration G-ACSR

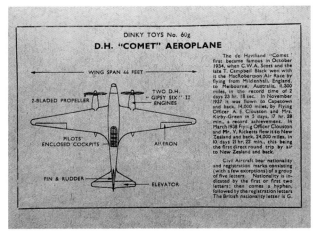

17 Lid of 60g Comet trade box

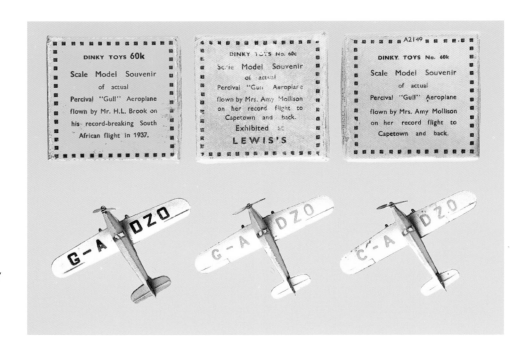

18 60k Percival Gull (76mm) HL Brooks – black registration letters, 60c early special box for Lewis's department store Amy Mollison – blue letters, 60k Amy Mollison with letter error C instead of G.

19 60m Four Engined Flying Boat (126mm): five liveries with spurious registration letters

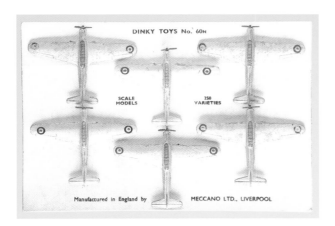

20 60n Fairey Battle Bomber (75mm) trade box of 6

21 Lid of 60n Fairey Battle Bomber trade box

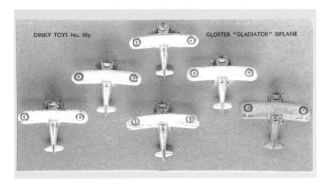

22 60p Gloster Gladiator Biplane (44mm) trade box of 6

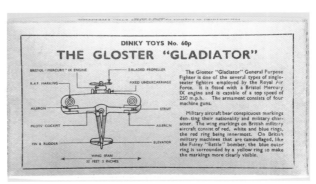

23 Lid of 60p Gloster Gladiator trade box

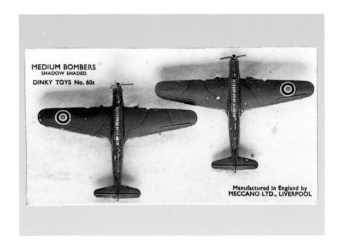

24 60s Medium Bomber (75mm) 'Mirror' Pair

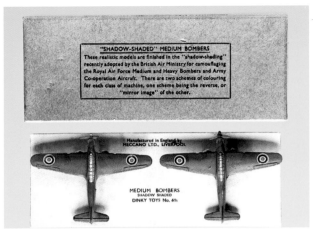

25 60s Medium Bomber (75mm) 'Shadow Shaded' Pair with lid – note that the box layout is different from the 'Mirror' Pair

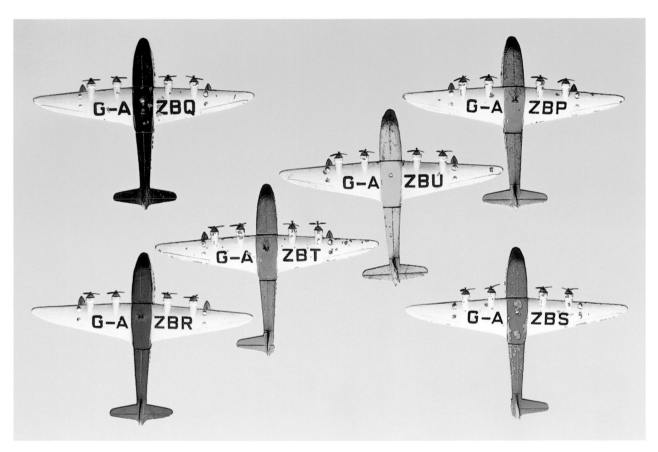

26 A selection of 60x Atlantic Flying Boat (156mm)

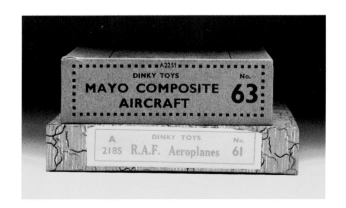

27 61 RAF Aeroplanes set early box with squiggle and dash pattern and plain blue 63 Mayo Composite box lid

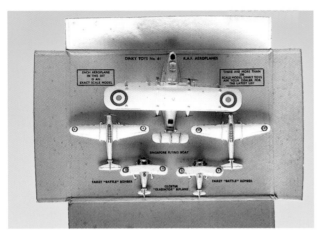

28 61 Set: RAF Aeroplanes: 60h Singapore Flying Boat (126mm), 2 x 60n Fairey Battle Bomber, 2 x 60p Gloster Gladiator

29 60h Singapore Flying Boat showing later simplified hull and earlier keel-shaped nose of hull

30 *Meccano Magazine* advertisement for 'Spitfire Fund' Spitfire, November 1940

31 *Meccano Magazine* advertisement for 'Spitfire Fund' Spitfire, January 1941

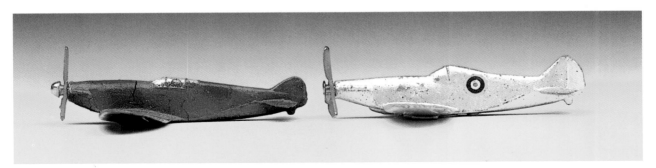

32 Pre-war (camouflaged) and post-war Spitfires (52mm) showing different cockpit areas and fins

33 *left:* 62a Spitfire (52mm), 62e Camouflaged Spitfire; *centre:* 'Spitfire Fund' Spitfire with its box; *right:* 62h Hurricane Camouflaged, 2 x 62s Hurricane with different roundels

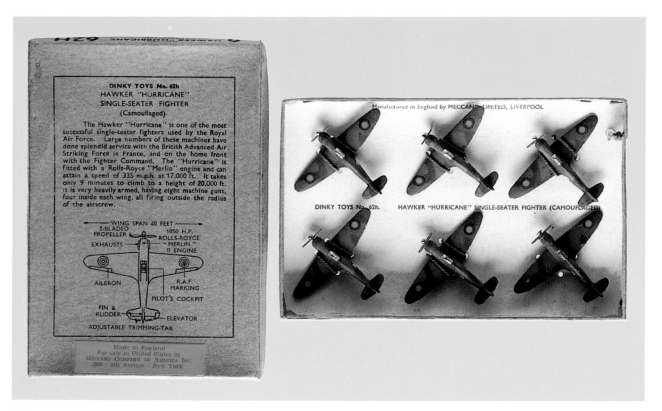

34 Trade box of 62h Camouflaged Hurricane (55mm) with lid

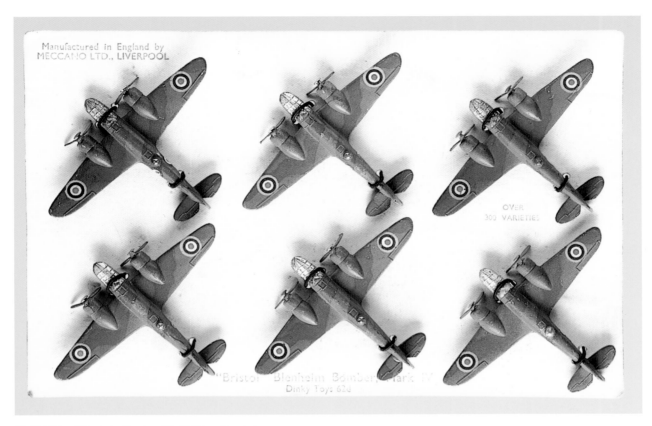

35 62d Bristol Blenheim Bomber Mk IV (78mm) trade box

36 Trade box of 62e Camouflaged Spitfire (52mm) with lid

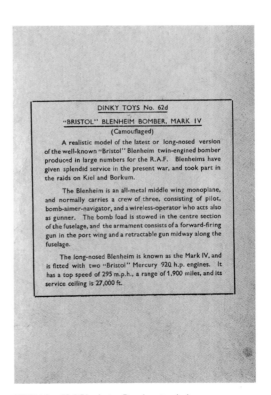

37 Lid for 62d Blenheim Bomber trade box

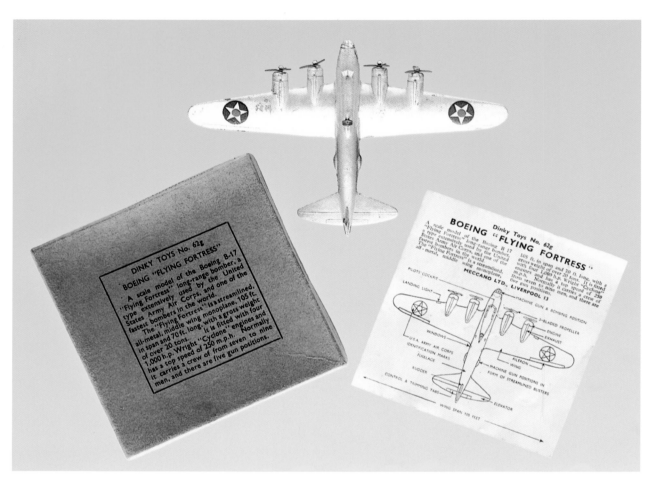

38 62g Boeing Flying Fortress (144mm) with box lid and descriptive leaflet

39 *top*: 62m Airspeed Envoy (91mm), 60g Comet Racer; *bottom*: 62k King's Aeroplane, 62b Blenheim Bomber

40 62n Junkers Ju90 Airliner (160mm), 67a Junkers Ju89 Heavy Bomber

41 The underwing name cartouches of 60n Junkers Ju90 Airliner, 67a Junkers Ju89 Heavy Bomber
and post-war reissue 62y Giant High Speed Monoplane

42 The square and rectangular boxes for 60r Empire Flying Boat

43 60r Empire Flying Boat: later simplified hull, earlier filled in nose of hull

44 Meccano Fund Spitfire Pendant with its box

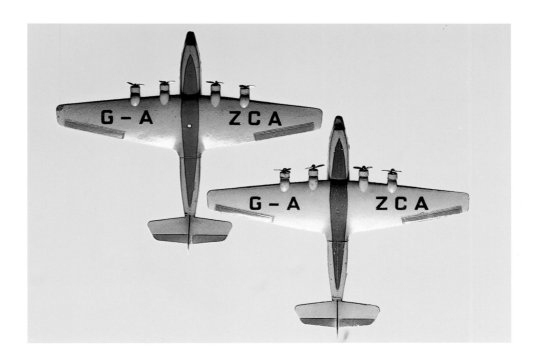

45 Two of the colour
schemes on 62x British
40 Seater Airliner
(173mm)

46 63 Mayo Composite:
Maia Flying Boat (156mm)
carrying Mercury
Seaplane

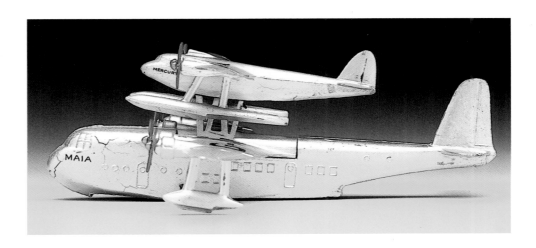

47 63 Mayo Composite:
Maia Flying Boat (156mm)
carrying Mercury
Seaplane

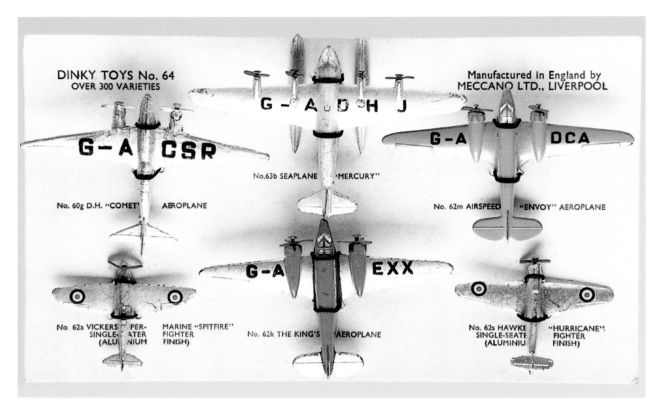

48 64 Presentation Aeroplane Set contains an unusual selection of small planes – the Camouflaged Hurricane has been replaced by a Spitfire (52mm) in silver showing that it is a set made for export

49 The lid for the 64 Set with its US label

50 The leaflet enclosed in the 64 (export) Set giving details of planes

51 Dinky Toy advertisement from *Meccano Magazine*, May 1940

52 65 Presentation Aeroplane Set contains eight of the larger planes (62p Armstrong Whitworth Airliner 173mm)

53 The lid of the 65 Set

55 The leaflet enclosed in the 65 Set giving details of the planes

54 The lid for the 66 set with US export label

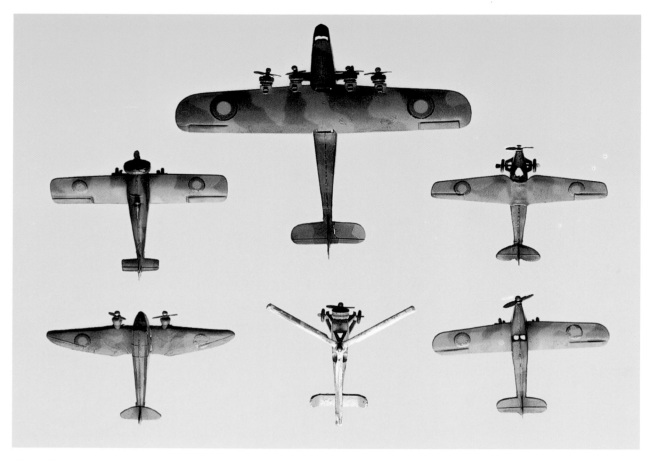

56 The 66 Camouflaged Aeroplanes Set uses the castings of the 60 Set.
top: 66a Heavy Bomber (127mm);
centre: 66d Torpedo Dive Bomber, 66b Dive-Bomber Fighter;
bottom: 66e Medium Bomber, 66f Army Co-operation Autogiro, 66c Two-Seater Fighter

57 *top:* Black and white
shading on underside of
62e Spitfire (52mm);
bottom: Dark camouflage
aircraft 60s Fairey Battle,
68a Ensign Airliner, 62d
Blenheim Bomber

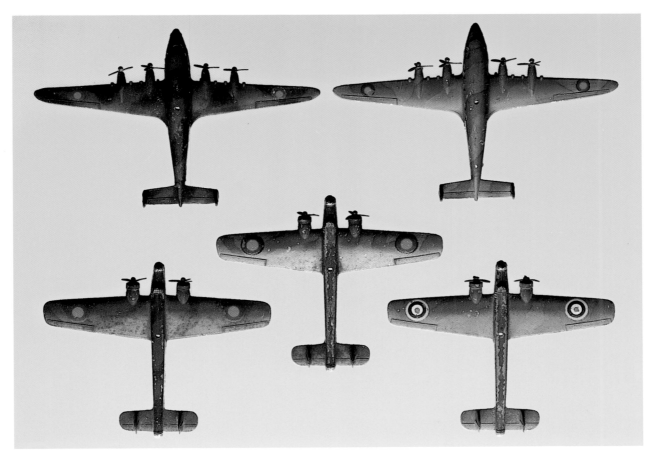

58 *top:* 68b Frobisher (145mm) in dark camouflage and in light;
bottom: 62t Whitley Bomber in dark camouflage, two with different roundels in light camouflage

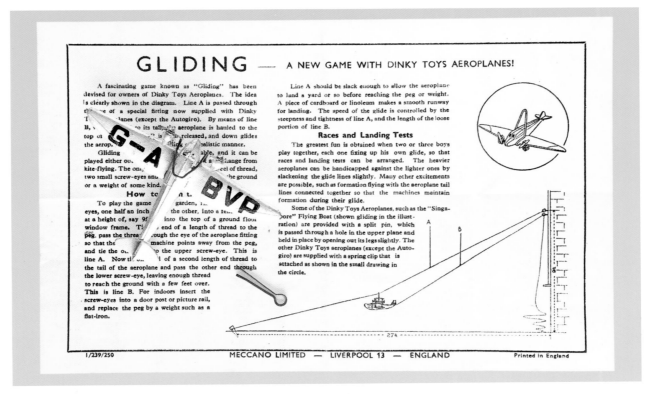

59 Gliding Game leaflet with 60e General Monospar and spare suspension clips

60 *top:* Wooden master for 62g Flying Fortress (144mm), green factory trial colour on 62s Hurricane;
bottom: Wooden master for 62k King's Aeroplane, silver factory trial colour on 62m Envoy

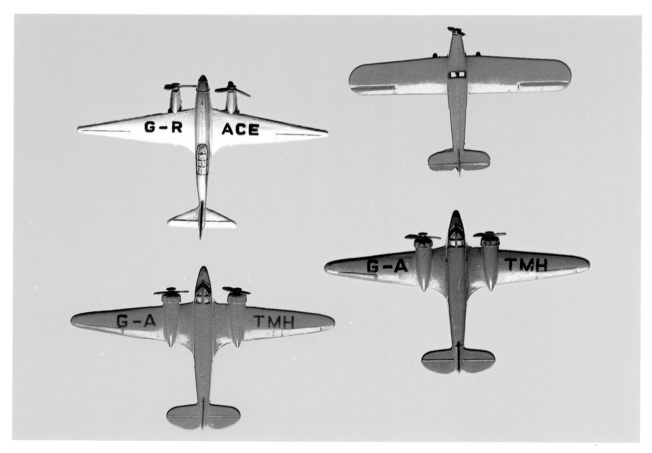

61 *top:* 60g Light Racer (86mm), 60k Light Tourer; *bottom* 2 x 62m Light Transport

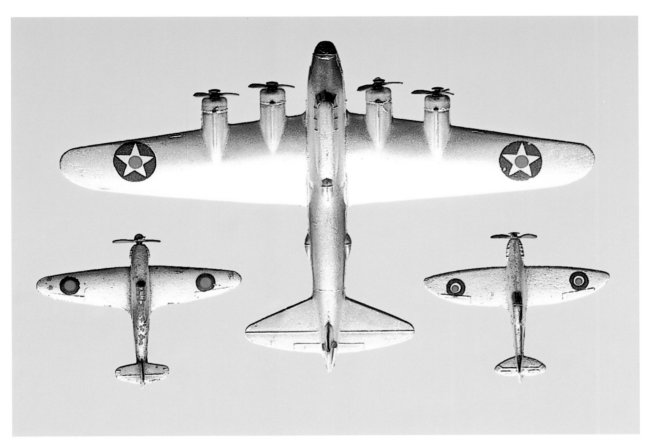

62 *top:* 62g Long Range Bomber (144mm);
bottom: 62s Hurricane, 62a Spitfire (new casting)

63 62p Armstrong Whitworth Airliners (173mm)

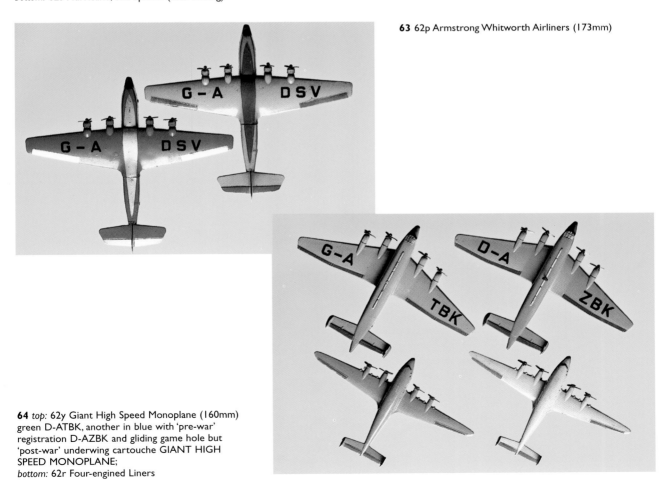

64 *top:* 62y Giant High Speed Monoplane (160mm)
green D-ATBK, another in blue with 'pre-war'
registration D-AZBK and gliding game hole but
'post-war' underwing cartouche GIANT HIGH
SPEED MONOPLANE;
bottom: 62r Four-engined Liners

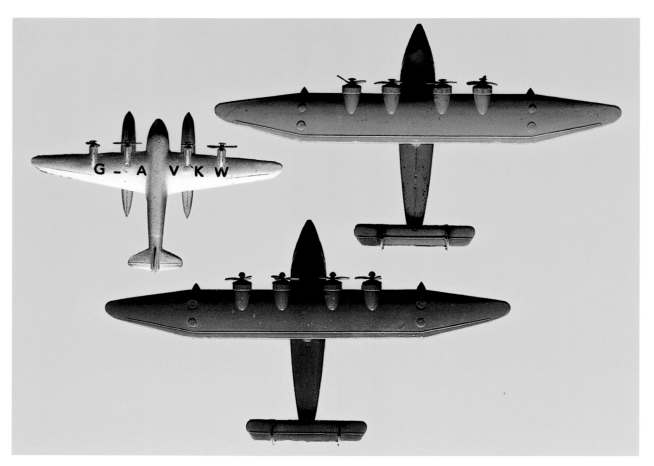

65 63b/700 Seaplane (101mm), 2 x 60w Flying Boat

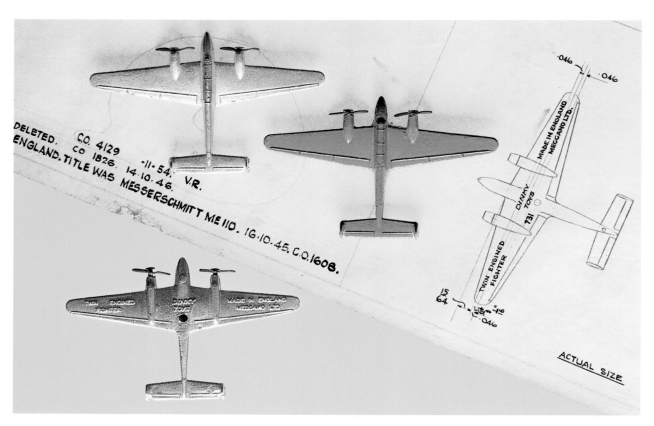

66 70d Twin Engined Fighter (76mm) with unusual blue example on factory drawing showing that the name of the pre-war design for a Messerschmitt Me110 had been changed post-war to Twin Engined Fighter

67 *top:* 70d/731 Twin Engined Fighter (76mm); *centre:* upper 70e/732 Gloster Meteor; *centre:* lower 70b/730 Tempest II
bottom: 70f/733 Shooting Star with blued cockpit cover

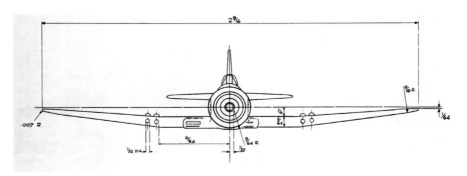

68 Factory drawing of 70b/730
Tempest II (nose on view)

69 70f/733 Shooting Star (61mm)
on factory drawing – drawing
originally dated 2.11.45

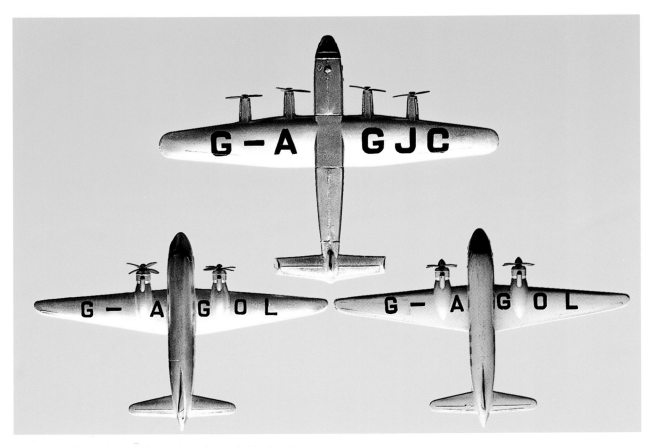

70 *top:* 70a/704 Avro York (160mm), shiny silver with blued cockpit;
bottom: 70c/705 Viking Airliner in silver and grey

71 701 Shetland Flying Boat (236mm)

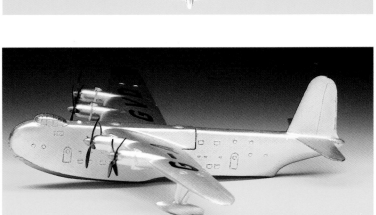

72 Box label for the first Supertoy plane: 701
Shetland Flying Boat

73 701 Shetland Flying Boat (236mm)

74 702 DH Comet Jet Airliner (183mm) (early livery), 999 Comet (later livery)

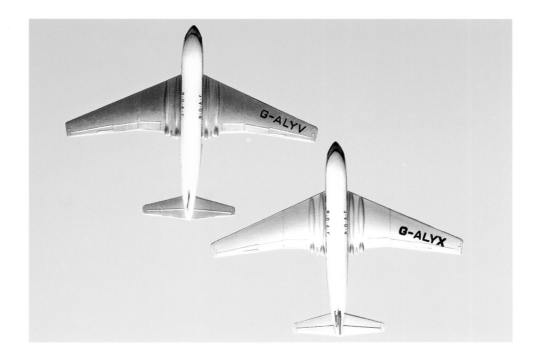

75 999 DH Comet (183mm) blue tail decal (later livery), 702/999 Comet early tail

76 Boxes for 999 Comet, 702 Comet

77 *top:* 708 Vickers
Viscount Airliner
(150mm) (later livery),
708 Viscount (early
livery);
bottom: Dinky 706 Vickers
Viscount, French Dinky
60E Vickers Viscount

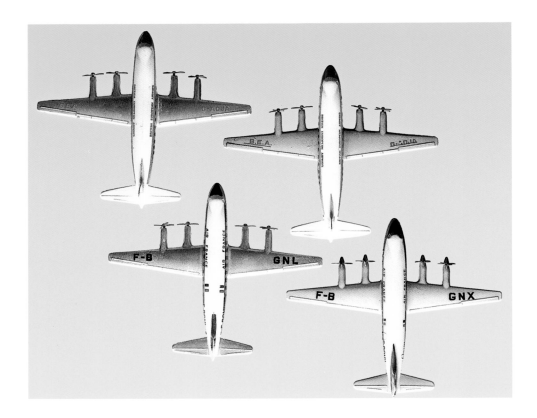

78 Dinky 706 Vickers Viscount (150mm), French Dinky 60E Viscount showing transfer
and undercarriage differences

79 Boxes for Dinky 706 Viscount, French Dinky 60E Viscount, Dinky 708 Viscount B.E.A.

80 Undersides of Dinky
706 Viscount, French
Dinky 60E Viscount

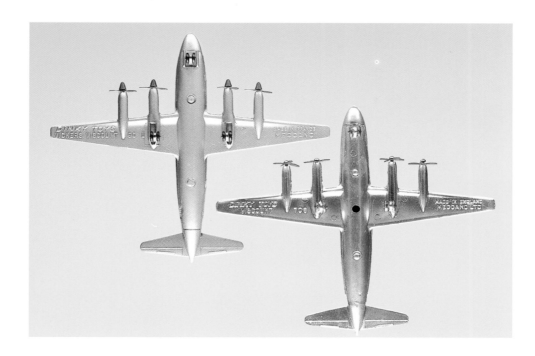

81 Drawing for tail
transfer of Dinky 706
Viscount Air France

MECCANO LTD

| TITLE:— TRANSFERS for VICKERS VISCOUNT (TAIL) (AIR FRANCE) | MEMO Nº 20,531. |

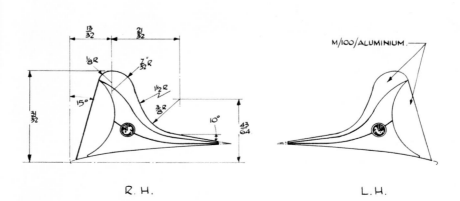

R. H.   L. H.

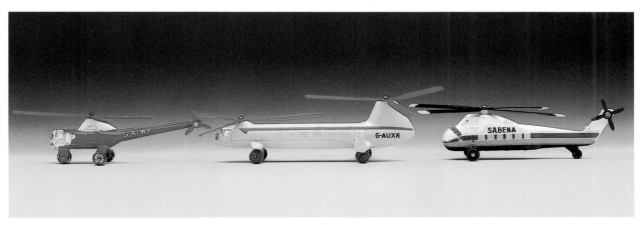

82 Dinky 716 Westland Sikorsky S51 (66mm), 715 Bristol 173, French Dinky 60D/802 Sikorsky S.58

83 *top:* 734 Supermarine Swift (51mm), 736 Hawker Hunter; *bottom:* 735 Gloster Javelin, 737 P.1B Lightning Fighter, 738 Sea Vixen

84 992 Avro Vulcan (156mm) on factory drawing first dated March 1953

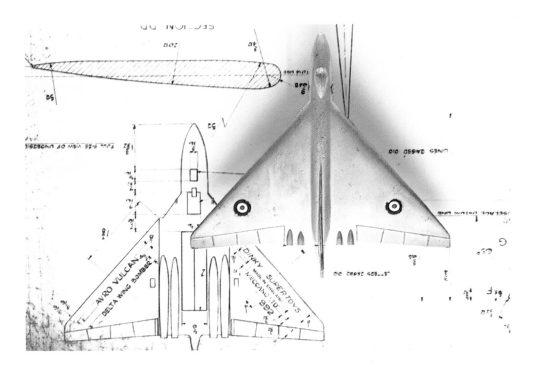

85 734 Supermarine Swift (51mm) on factory drawing dated 24.6.53. Some of the wording on this drawing is in French but there is no evidence that a copy of the drawing was ever sent to the French factory.

86 998 Bristol Britannia (225mm) blue lines and silver wings (early livery), red lines and silver grey wings (later livery)

87 The factory drawing of the transfers for the Bristol Britannia – a change dated 23.5.59 reads 'G.10 red lines were G31 blue, M/100 Alim (aluminium) lines were G50 white'

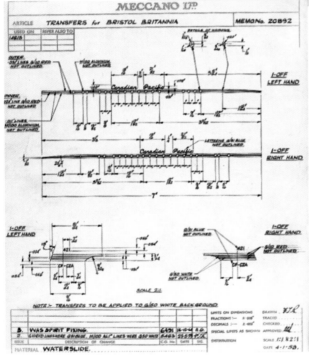

88 Supertoy striped (early) and pictorial 998 Britannia boxes

89 998 Bristol Britannia (225mm) with red (later) livery, blue (early) livery

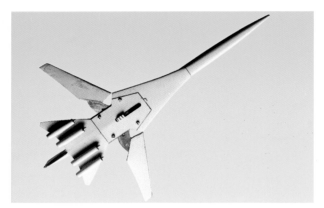

90 Boeing 2707 SST, the USA's supersonic reply to Concorde: prototype for a Dinky Toy designed by Vic Mumby who worked for Meccano between 1961 and 1979 becoming Chief Draughtsman. The die was cut, the number 995 or 996 was allocated, but production was stopped when America cancelled the original. This model was subsequently presented to Vic Mumby. Plan view, wings retracted

91 Boeing 2707 SST prototype, underside, wings opened

92 Boeing SST prototype, side view

93 *top:* Nicky Toys 999 Comet (183mm) (later), 999 Comet still with Dinky logo under wing but marked 'Made in India'

94 *top:* Nicky Toys 708 Viscount (150mm) (silver grey wings), 735 Gloster Javelin; *bottom:* 738 Sea Vixen, 708 Viscount (red wings)

95 Undersides of Nicky Toys Viscounts: 'NICKY TOYS', '(Dinky obliterated) TOYS'

96 700 The RAF Diamond
Jubilee Spitfire (173mm)
with its stand

97 710 Beechcraft Bonanza (133mm) – the three basic liveries

98 710 Beechcraft Bonanza (133mm): different registration numbers on the later red, white and blue version

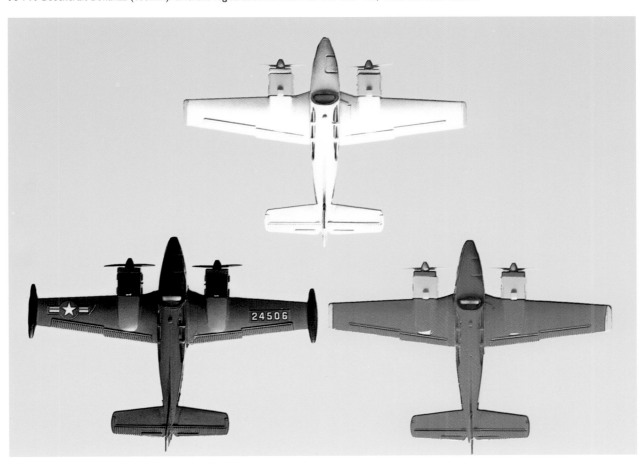

99 *top:* 715 Beechcraft Baron (150mm); *bottom:* 712 US Army T-42A, 715 Beechcraft Baron

100 718 Hawker
Hurricane (188mm) with
box base and decals

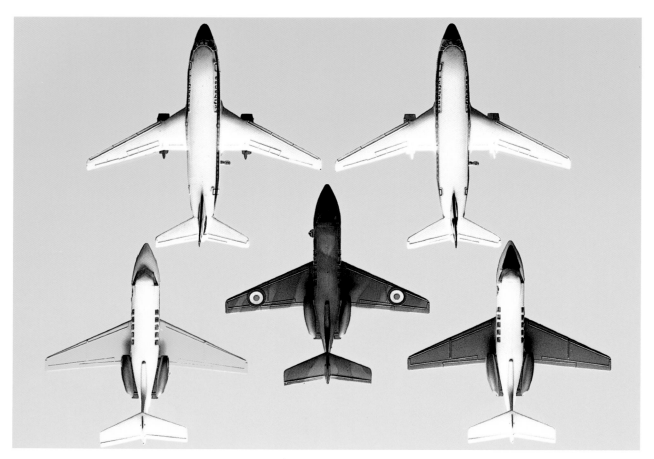

101 *top:* 717 Boeing 737 (152mm) blue engines (later), white engines (early); *centre:* 728 Hawker Siddeley Dominie RAF
bottom: 723 Hawker Siddeley HS125 white and yellow (early), white and metallic blue (later)

102 'Battle of Britain' 721
Stuka (191mm), 719
Spitfire on page from
1970 catalogue

103 724 Sea King Rescue
Helicopter (179mm) with
'Apollo' capsule and box

104 Army Helicopter' from set 618 (179mm), 736 Bundesmarine Sea King Helicopter

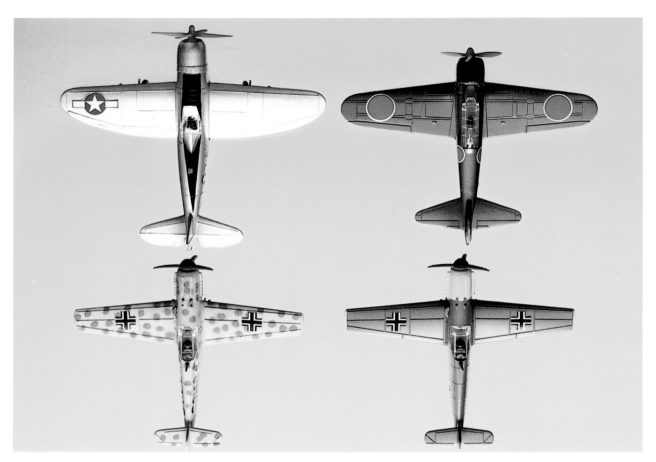

105 *top:* 734 P-47 Thunderbolt (190mm), 739 A6M5 Zero-Sen; *bottom:* 726 Messerschmitt Bf109E desert sand, grey/green

106 *top:* Phantom F-4K II 730 US Navy (132mm), 733 Bundesluftwaffe; *bottom:* 725 Royal Navy, 727 US Air Force

107 725 Phantom in special factory finish on 1977 Trade Catalogue featuring the model

108 722 Hawker Harrier (108mm), 729 Panavia MRCA, 731 SEPECAT Jaguar

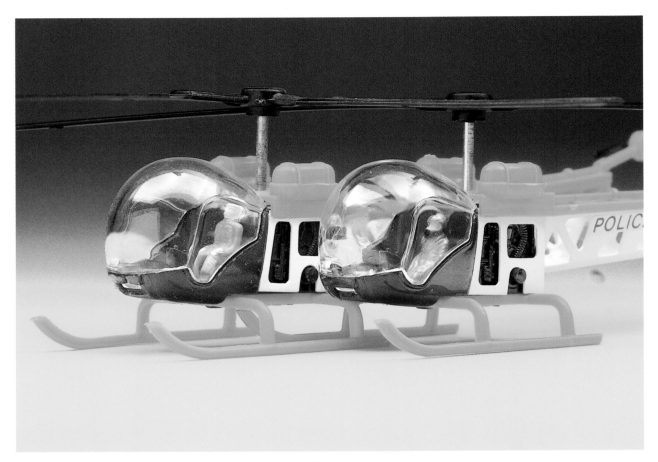

109 732 Bell Police Helicopter (211mm) with usual blue pilot on left, pilot from jets on right

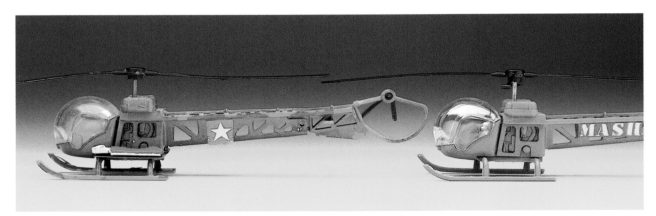

110 Factory mock-up with stretchers for M*A*S*H helicopter (211mm), late production M*A*S*H helicopter (not shown in catalogue)

111 Big Planes advertising streamer

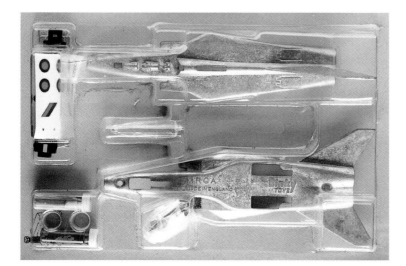

112 Box for Dinky Kit
1045 Panavia MRCA

113 Dinky Kit 1045
Panavia MRCA (164mm)
still in its original
packaging

114 Front of Big Planes single sheet flyer

115 Reverse of Big Planes single sheet flyer

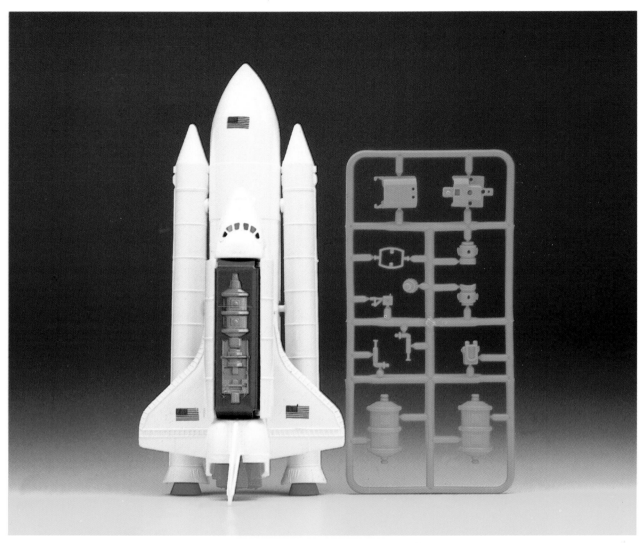

116 364 NASA Space Shuttle (186mm) with Booster Rockets and Satellite

117 The reverse of 364
NASA Space Shuttle box

2 Dinky Toys – French

No sooner had the news of the first flights of Wilbur and Orville Wright crossed the Atlantic than France was gripped with flying madness. As early as 1903, The Aero Club de France, which had been established as a result of balloon mania, offered a prize to anyone who could emulate the new achievements. Enthusiasm was fuelled by the performance of a Wright Flyer at Le Mans in 1908 and huge crowds attended the 1909 Aviation Week at Rheims. Indeed, by the end of 1909, all the main aviation records were held by Frenchmen flying French planes. More by luck than skill or a good plane, it was nevertheless a Frenchman, Blériot, who made the first Channel crossing and secured the £1,000 prize from Lord Northcliffe's *Daily Mail*.

The British Army was equipped with French machines, Blériots, Breguets and Farmans, though some consolation might have been received from the nationality of Henri Farman, an Englishman abroad. At the beginning of 1919, Farman machines modified from bombers established the first airline route from Paris to London and made the inaugural flight from Paris to Brussels. As flying developed, the government, fired by national pride, provided subsidies to no less than eight airlines, each of which had its own sphere of operation to encourage French technical developments, navigational systems, weather forecasting and so on. State aid was extended even further by advancing a certain amount of the purchase price to flying enthusiasts who wanted to buy their own aeroplanes. In 1933, a new subsidy was introduced for those small aeroplanes with engines developing up to 50hp. A group of airframe manufacturers including Breguet, Blériot, Caudron, Farman and Morane had formed the Compagnie des Messageries Aeriennes (CMA) which, in 1933 became Air France. Initially it had a mixed fleet of outdated planes but soon the mainstay became the Wibault-Penhoet 283, a fast three-engined machine. The industry concentrated on standardising equipment and produced planes strictly fitted to Air France requirements resulting in the Dewoitine D338 and Potez 62 in 1936 and the Bloch 220 in 1937. The airline's range extended across the world with the establishment of the China route in the following year. To combat the build-up in technical advancement and quality of the German Air Forces, the French aircraft industry was nationalised in 1937, but this was too late for it to get itself reorganised effectively.

The French toy industry, AR, SR, Mignot responded early on to this enthusiasm by producing charming little diecastings of the early flying machines, but, apart from Solido, there was no indigenous large toy manufacturer capable of producing castings by the thousand for the mass market and Solido, with its more expensive demountable vehicles, played to the more expensive end of the market. Meanwhile, another force in the French industry was developing. Frank Hornby, ever aware of the need to expand his markets, had set up Meccano France SA to act as an importer for the Meccano Construction Sets and Hornby Trains and between 1929 and 1934, a factory had been built at 70-88 ave Henri-Barbusse, Bobigny, on the outskirts of Paris, to complement the offices in the rue Rebeval. The factory and production processes were closely monitored by Binns Road and indeed many of the machines came from Liverpool so that the product was technically indistinguishable from the English. Thus the systems were in place to respond to the pleas of the French child.

> **Advertisement in 1935 French *Meccano Magazine***
>
> '...*S'inspirant de leurs suggestions, Meccano eut l'idée de créer quelques sujets en miniature, exécutés en métal fondu. L'accueil que la jeunesse fit à ces nouveaux jouets fut si chaleureux, si enthousiaste, que bientôt on se vit obligé de donner à leur fabrication une extension prodigieuse: tout le monde s'empressa de profiter des possibilités nouvelles qu'apportaient les petits Dinky Toys pour renouveler, rehausser l'intérêt des modèles et des Trains.*'
>
> '...Inspired by the young people's suggestions, Meccano had the idea of creating some items in miniature, made of cast metal. The reception the youngsters gave these new toys was so warm, so enthusiastic, that soon they were obliged to increase their production enormously: the new opportunities brought by these little Dinky Toys to renew and enhance their interest in [Meccano] models and [Hornby] trains have caught everybody's imagination.'

When Dinky Toys were first produced in 1934, at Bobigny, the models and dies had been approved in England and bore many similarities to English production. Indeed it is difficult to tell some apart, but soon a French identity in the choice of subject began to be established and by the time mazac had been introduced to replace lead and the 22 series cars designed, not only was the product different but there is an distinct French style in the delicacy of the castings and the style of decoration.

An article in the December 1936 French *Meccano Magazine*, entitled 'To what can the success of Dinky Toys be attributed', describes the production process in detail. From photographs and detailed plans, a scale model was made, not in wood as in England, but in plaster which allowed finer surface detail, exactly the same size as the finished toy. Then a mould was made in steel with two or three inserts to create the hollow body. A cast of lead gave a sample which was minutely examined, checked and corrected if necessary. The corrections were transferred to the mould which thus acquires its final form. The casting was automatically ejected on the opening of the mould. The toy was finished by the removal of flash from the joins. The polished casting was then enamelled with automatic paint sprays. The article emphasises that the zinc mixture made for an unbreakable toy. In France this was a most important selling point (over the fragile product from other manufacturers) as was the precision and detail of the modelling.

Indeed, French Dinky advertising puts more emphasis on the accuracy and fidelity of the model than its English parent which emphasised play value. The sales potential of getting children 'hooked' onto a range was grasped and from 1936 the modern-sounding subtitle *Le Jouet du*

Collectionneur, (Toys for the Collector) was added to the catalogue. The latest catalogue is dated September 1940 but production probably stopped before then because after the fall of Paris the factory was turned over to making parts for the German toy company, Märklin. The spirits of the German people were to be maintained during hostilities by keeping the normal range of goods in the shops, for the war was, after all, being fought to benefit the German people. It was 1946 before Dinky Toys were made again and some of the pre-war planes reappeared in the catalogue.

At the outbreak of war, almost all the French aircraft industry was under efficient control so that up to 120 planes a month were being produced but, largely because of non-cooperation, very little new was designed and apart from a few types that survived hostilities, the industry had to start all over again in 1945. The development of new French design types was slow so that Air France had to buy abroad, notably the Lockheed Constellation and then the Vickers Viscount. However, by 1950 the industry was sufficiently reconstructed to design the Caravelle and Mystère. Co-ordination of production was handled by the state controlled SNCA (Sociétés Nationales de Constructions Aeronautiques) which acted as a production facility to assist firms such as Dassault who had design capacity but insufficient factory space.

In 1951, the Paris Meccano office closed and all functions were transferred to Bobigny and it was there that all the post-war planes were made. The whole Meccano Empire came under the control of Tri-ang in 1964 and the name was changed to Meccano-Tri-ang. Eventually, in 1970, because of the escalating value of the Bobigny site, production was transferred to the factory Tri-ang had built in 1959 in Calais, but by this time there was only one plane left in the French Dinky range. Strangely, the country that was so excited about the early developments of flying produced relatively few diecast toy planes pre-war. The post-war production was not great either but in France, Dinky was competing with other French diecast toys, Solido and CIJ and did not manage to achieve the iron grip on the toy market exerted by its parent. By the late 1960s all French Dinky planes had been phased out and replaced by the English Dinky Big Plane range using the same numbers but with an 'L' suffix.

Pre-war production and sets/ Post-war re-issues

Aeroplanes were first introduced into the French Dinky Toy range in 1935, one year after the first English Dinkies had been released. Most are marked: '*Dinky Toys Fab en France Meccano*', but the odd one has '*Fad en France*' instead!

Le Vol Plané: Gliding Game

The French Gliding Game leaflet is an accurate translation of the English Dinky version, the only difference being in the last paragraph which refers to the French toy, the Arc-en-Ciel. The illustration is of a Hanriot with the gliding clip fitted and of the Arc-en-Ciel flying down the string. The smaller planes were flown in a spring clip, the larger with a split-pin that fitted down the oblong gliding game hole. This feature is found on post-war issues as well, though the hole may be flashed over.

PROPELLERS · There does not seem to be any pattern to the fitting of the large or small tinplate propellers which are commonly bright metal (referred to as silver) or red but are also found in black and which are held on with a variety of sizes of pins with domed or flat heads.

DECALS · The registration numbers and later French Air Force roundels were not transfers but were tampo printed. Early roundels were hand-painted. This gives an unevenness to their outline and alignment which looks a little amateurish.

BOXES · Both the pre-war and post-war re-issues were available in mixed sets in presentation boxes or in yellow boxes of six from which the retailer sold individual planes.

NUMBERING · The numbering block 60 was used for all the pre-war issues with the individual items designated by the number followed by a capital letter, rather than the lower case ones used by English Dinky. It was used again in the 1950s for a new group of planes before renumbering to the 800 block in 1959.

THE AEROPLANES

The 60 Set, Le Coffret, Le Coffret Luxe, Avions Coffret Luxe

The title of this set, introduced in 1935 and listed until 1940, varied. The common box is a square one in blue with an illustration of the six planes in the set in circles on the lid, both box and illustration are obviously based on that of the English Dinky 60 Set. An earlier one was coloured purple and gold, and another was brick red with yellow interior with a label, shared with later (including road vehicle) sets, of a boy with his arm raised over three rows of vehicles. The planes were corded down, flying upwards 1,2,2,1, onto a pale green backing card headed 'Meccano Dinky Toys No. 60' in seriffed letters and the position of each plane was labelled with its name. The price of the set was the sum of the prices of the individual units. The set was exported to the UK with a circular label, 60z, stuck over the 60 on the lid. All the small planes in this and the 61 Set are fitted with two undercarriage legs carrying one axle and two small wheels. The attractive and meticulously applied patterns on the toys were based on the sort of decoration that was applied to full-size planes. None of the small planes in either set is marked with its name and they are most easily distinguished by their liveries. The set contained the gliding game leaflet and hooks. An anomaly appears in a December 1939 advertisement. The caption reads: *'Coffret 60 Avions – Elegant coffret réunissant six types d'avions français. Avec attaches et notice pour 'le Vol Plané'* ('An elegant box containing six French planes') but the picture shows the Arc-en-Ciel and Autogiro with the four small planes from the English Dinky 60 Set. There is no evidence that this version was ever issued.

Arc-en-Ciel – 60A

The only one of its kind and christened 'The Rainbow', the Couzinet 70 was piloted by the daredevil adventurer Jean Mermoz on his eventually successful attempt to cross the South Atlantic from St Louis in Senegal to Natal in Brazil in January 1933 in 14hrs 27mins. It was then lengthened and the tail was altered and it made eight regular flights for Air France across the South Atlantic. After further alterations in 1935, it dropped from the scene. Late French catalogues billed it as '*L'Avion du regretté Mermoz*', the 'much-missed' Mermoz, and when it was released in England, the *Meccano Magazine* for March 1938 had it as 'A scale model of the famous French triple-engined monoplane Arc-en-Ciel that made several fine pioneer double crossings of the South Atlantic.' The scale is, in fact 1/220 and it is a delicately elegant model. The thin curved wing casting, complete with undercarriage fairings, nestles into, and is rivetted to, the hollow fuselage/tail casting which incorporates a dummy tail wheel in its fairing. The two large wheels are on individual axles and three large black two-blade propellers are fitted. The detail of the open cockpit windows and nose is very fine. The pretty decoration of a solid undercolour with contrasting angled flashes across the wingtips and along the top of the fuselage is not the Air France livery which featured a rainbow across the fuselage. Sold in the UK as 60az. See also Dewoitine D338, 61A.

Potez 58 – 60B, 61D

One of a plethora of small, very similar planes, typical of French production at the time, the toy has a diecast fuselage with a deep cabin. Three windows run down each side, with the centre one being surrounded by a clearly-outlined door. The splayed undercarriage struts are part of the casting as is the single radial engine. The laterally curved tinplate wing has flap-like projections on the leading edges and a pattern of glazing panes above the cabin. The tinplate clips through the diecasting to secure the wing. A large black two-blade propeller is fitted. The decoration consists of a solid ground colour with a contrasting one applied, through a mask, onto the upper surfaces of the tail plane and fuselage and across part of the wings, a pretty effect that from behind looks like a flattened Y. In a different finish, the same unit was issued as Potez 58 Sanitaire, 61D.

Hanriot Type H180T – 60C, 61E

This is a model of a sesquiplane, an unusual configuration in which additional lift is supplied by small stub wings that double as part of the undercarriage assembly. It consists of a main casting with a single tinplate wing clipped in above the cabin. The straight-edged wings have a neat flap line along their trailing edge. A small black propeller is fitted. The whole is sprayed one colour with the leading edge of the wing and the outside edges of the tail carrying a contrasting stripe. Reliveried, it became Hanriot H180M, 61E, and the casting was used for the Potez 56, 61B.

Breguet Type Corsaire – 60D, also 61C

The single casting consists of fuselage with radial engine and pointed tail. The open triangular cockpits, one behind the other, have streamlining cowls in front and to the rear. The pointed tinplate wing with a delicate pattern of ribs pressed in, slots through and is tabbed to the lower fuselage. The painting pattern is complex using a solid ground colour with a contrasting one on the leading edge of the wings and tail. With the wing ends cropped and a new colour scheme, the pieces were used for the Farman F360, 61C.

Dewoitine Type 500/D 500 Chasseur/ de chasse – 60E, 61F

This small plane was modelled in 1/151 scale and is quite a good representation. The tinplate wing slots through and clips onto the diecast fuselage with its open cockpit and cast-in undercarriage struts. The detail is such that the six exhaust stubs along each cylinder head can be counted. The small two-blade propeller is plated and the two small wheels, in common with those of the rest of the small planes, are on a single axle.

The civilian livery on Dewoitine type D500, 60E, is an overall base colour with flashes of a contrasting colour angling over the wings and on the ends of the tailplane. Exactly the same casting is used for Dewoitine D500 Chasseur (Fighter), alternatively called Dewoitine de chasse, 61F, the military version finished all over in silver with French Air Force roundels of red outer with a blue central dot on the wing tips.

Autogire De La Cierva – 60F

The small casting is not marked and it is probably not possible to distinguish between French and English-made castings, though the cockpit hole tends to be oval not round and the cowling round the motor seems more pronounced. It was also available, possibly at the same time, with a representation of a pilot's head in the cockpit.

The 61 Set, Le Coffret, Le Coffret Luxe, Avions Coffret Luxe

This group of six planes bears much resemblance to the previous set because to start with there are no new castings. Some are modified but others are merely re-liveried. Originally the Dewoitine D338 was a modified Arc-en-Ciel but then a new casting was introduced so that there are two versions of the set. The box was originally purple but the common type is blue with pictures of the planes in circles, exactly the same as the 60 Set. There is a third box, dark green with the standard French Dinky label of a boy calling out joyfully in front of rows of road vehicles. This box contains the new accurate casting of the Dewoitine D338. The green or yellow backing card is headed, in serifed letters, 'Meccano Dinky Toys No. 61'. The planes are corded down into labelled positions flying in formation to bottom left with the leading plane, the Dewoitine, being subtitled 'air france marseille – saigon'. A gliding game leaflet was enclosed. One catalogue claims: *'Une autre serie de modèles d'avions français des plus connus...'* ('Another series of well-known French aeroplanes'), a comment that was a little inaccurate, even at the time when the planes were in production. Sold in the UK as French Aeroplanes, 61z.

Dewoitine D338 – 61A 1st version, 61A 2nd version

The castings of 60A Arc-en-Ciel were fitted with three large turned engine covers and large three-blade propellers. This made for an extremely inaccurate model, except for the engine covers which mimic the full size both in shape and shine. To make the casting look as different as possible from the original a complex colouring pattern was employed: the entire castings were painted the ground colour, silver or gold, and the second colour, green or red was applied to the flattish top of the fuselage, the whole length of the forward and trailing edges of the wings and the flaps at the rear of the tail plane. The catalogues continued to show a drawing of this type after the introduction of the new casting.

This new correct type, with its name cast in under the wing, is a very good, if unglamorous, 1/213 scale casting fitted with two small wheels on short undercarriage legs and prototypical two-blade propellers. The long rows of windows with their thin glazing bars and the cockpit windows are cleanly indented in the casting which has a gliding game hole in the upper fuselage. Normally finished in silver with black registration letters. Also part of the 64 Set, the backing card of which described it as: Ligne Air France Marseilles-Saigon. Sold in the UK as 61az. Re-issued post-war only in the 64 Set.

Potez 56 – 61B

The French Dinky is a poor model in 1/232 scale of this pretty plane. Although the wings are reasonably good, the fuselage has no sign of passenger windows and the tail is quite inaccurate. The fuselage of the Hanriot H180T, with the cast-in stub wings from which protrude the undercarriage legs, has had a low tinplate wing fitted immediately above the stub wings, concealing them. Cast engines with small two-blade propellers are fitted onto the tinplate wings. This pretty toy is finished in a bright colour oversprayed with silver on the top of the fuselage and engines.

Farman F360 – 61C

The casting of 60D Breguet-Corsair was used with the tinplate wings cropped square at the tips, finished in silver with a contrasting top to the fuselage.

Potez 58 Sanitaire – 61D

The deep cabin with doors either side made it suitable as an ambulance plane. Thus the casting and pressing of 60B Potez 58 has been reliveried in overall silver with small red crosses on the wingtips.

Hanriot H180M – 61E

Casting of 60C Hanriot H180T finished in silver.

Dewoitine de Chasse/500 chasseur – 61F

Casting of Dewoitine D500 60E in silver.

The 62 Set, Avions Coffret Luxe – not issued

A mixed set of English and French Dinky Toys were illustrated and priced in a December 1939 catalogue. The planes were shown flying in echelon, 1,3,2 towards the bottom left-hand corner of the box. Another December 1939 catalogue lists the models but does not feature the set. By September 1940, a listing shows 'suspendu' (suspended) instead of a price and, indeed, stocks of the English-made planes except for 62N Junkers Ju90 had by now run out. The set was offered for sale only in France. It has been reported but confirmation and details are required.

Listed as: English Dinky 60R Caledonia, Empire Flying Boat
60W Clipper III, Flying Boat
62P Ensign Air Liner
62N Junkers Ju90
French Dinky 64A Amiot 37
64B Bloch 220
64D Potez 662

The 64 Set, Avions

The set was made up of 61A Dewoitine D338 using the correct second casting and four completely new planes, all single castings with gliding game holes and with their names marked under their starboard wings. The undercarriages consist of a pair of twin lugs protruding from beneath each of the engines retaining medium-size wheels on short axles, as first found on the Dewoitine D338 61A second casting. Packed in a square green box with the standard French Dinky label of a boy calling out joyfully in front of rows of road vehicles some with a separate name label stuck over that of the 61 Set, the five planes are corded down flying in echelon to top left. The dark cream backing card is headed in the usual typescript, 'Meccano Dinky Toys No. 64' and the position of each plane is labelled with its name, number and description. The planes are all silver though there is an unconfirmed report of a set of coloured ones. It was not referred to in the

December 1939 catalogues. A 64 Set is listed in the September 1940 catalogue as 'Air France' Coffret Luxe, the only reference using this name, marked as suspended. The set was re-issued post-war.

Amiot 370 – 64A   *Meccano Magazine* credits their version, probably a one-off, with a 1938 speed record of 249mph and the backing card of the 64 Set describes it as '*Avion militaire de reconnaissance Record mondiale* (world record) *sur 10,000kms*'. Another single casting in about 1/220 scale with the characteristics of this group, name under the starboard wing, gliding hole etc., the plane is fitted with three-blade propellers and is finished in all-over silver with French Air Force roundels applied to the wing tips. Exported to England in 1939, it was numbered 64az and featured in that year's *Meccano Magazine* and in the 1939/40 catalogue. A catalogue of June 1940 lists Amiot avion d'observation, 64AC, in camouflage but this version was not issued. Re-issued post-war in France.

Bloch 220 – 64B   Described on the backing-card of the 64 Set as 'Ligne Air France Paris-Londres', the hollow fuselage casting of the 1/215 scale Dinky is a good model with the angling of the wings beyond the engines being particularly well caught. The window/cockpit detail is accurately represented on the casting. Red three-blade propellers are fitted. The Bloch 220 was exported to England and appeared in the *Meccano Magazine* in 1939 and in the 1939/40 catalogue numbered 64bz. One experimental example without an undercarriage finished in silver with no registration number probably came from Binns Road rather than France. Re-issued post-war in France.

Potez 63 – 64C   Described on the backing card of the 64 Set as '*Avion militaire triplace*' (three-seater) *de défence*', the single-piece model at 1/175 scale is quite good and is fitted with four-blade propellers. Finished in silver with French Air Force roundels. A catalogue entry of June 1940 lists Potez 63 avion de reconnaissance, 64CC, in camouflage but this version was not issued. Re-issued post-war.

Potez 662 – 64D   Recognition features: four-engined low wing pointed nose airliner with twin tail fins. The literature describes it as a fast 12-passenger airliner. Its original Renault engines gave a speed of 240mph, but the later Gnome-Rhone ones slowed it to just over 200mph. The casting has good detail with indented side windows and the usual attributes of this group. Four-bladed propellers are fitted. A catalogue entry of June 1940 lists Potez 662 bombardier, 64DC, in camouflage but this version was not issued. The casting was re-issued post-war. There is a report of a post-war one with the registration F-B GNX, an unlikely version as this is the registration used on the very much later Viscount.

English Dinky toys imported into France

Towards the end of the pre-war period, a selection of the English Dinky Toy planes were imported into France and were included in the catalogues. Whereas French product in the English catalogues was almost invariably designated as being made in France, the following are to be found in the December 1939 catalogue mixed in with French-manufactured toys. The catalogue numbers are the same except that capital letters instead of lower case suffixes are used, but the names are often shortened and simplified and can sound rather quaint in translation. Supplies to France stopped with the outbreak of war and by the September 1940 catalogue all except 62N Junkers were marked as suspended. For further details, see English Dinky Toys *circa* 1939.

60H Singapore Flying Boat
Four-engined flying boat bomber. Aluminium finish

60M The same model in colourful finishes

60R Caledonia
Imperial Airways giant four-engined flying boat. Aluminium finish

60W Clipper III
American four-engined flying boat. Aluminium finish

62K Airspeed Envoy
Private plane of King George VI

62N German transport plane Junkers Ju-90 410km/hr

62P Ensign
Model of the biggest and fastest Imperial Airways plane. Ensign Class

62W Frobisher
Imperial Airways 22-seater airliner

63 Mayo Composite
English piggy-back plane, Mayo, constructed for Atlantic crossing trials

A December 1939 catalogue shows four of the above, 60R Caledonia, 60W Clipper III, 62N Junkers Ju-90, 62P Ensign

Post-war re-issues

Manufacture of French Dinky Toys did not begin again until 1946 and then the start was shaky. The first releases were the planes that constituted the earlier 64 Set, the earliest mention being in the first post-war trade catalogue, though they were, as yet, not available.

Nouveauté – Coffret 64
5 avions assortis
61A Dewoitine 338
64A Amiot 370
64B Bloch 220
64C Potez 63
64D Potez 662

'Le coffret 64 se compose des 4 avions ci-dessus et de l'avion 61A Dewoitine 338, pour lequel nous n'assurerons pas de réassortiment pour le vente séparée.' ('Set 64 is made up of 64A-D and 61A Dewoitine 338, which will not be sold separately.') An approximate price was given.

The text continues: 'We ask you to establish your requirements to the end of the year and to send in your order for delivery as soon as they are available. Actually, we are unable to guarantee fulfilling the whole of your order at once, because we have some difficulties in obtaining supplies in the right quantities. However, we assure you that we will fulfil your order to the very best of our ability. Moreover, the knowledge of your requirements will give us a valuable guide to establishing our manufacturing programme. We thank you in advance and assure you that the motto of Meccano always was and always will be "*Faire l'impossible pour satisfaire sa fidéle clientele*" – (Do the impossible to keep faith with the customer).'

Apart from 61A Dewoitine which was only available in the set, the other planes were also delivered to the retailer in boxes of six. They remained available for about two years.

Post-war issues

MARKINGS
All the post-war French planes are clearly marked under their wings with their name, number, manufacturer and country of origin (as 'Made in France' not '*Fab. en France*' to facilitate exports). The helicopter has the information closely packed on the base. The numbers consist of a 60 number followed by an upper-case letter, and are thus easy to distinguish from the English Dinky numbers which used a lower-case letter. When renumbering took place in 1959, they were all renumbered to the 800 block, the small planes being allocated the first few and the two Supertoy sized ones being given 880 numbers. The Gift Set was renumbered 501, away from the others in the set block.

BOXES
The models were packed in standard yellow boxes, except for the Constellation, Caravelle and Gift Set, all of which were in Supertoy blue and white striped boxes. All have a picture of the plane signed by the artist, J Masse.

DATES
The planes were normally illustrated in the catalogues but towards the end of some of the production runs they were only listed on the flimsy sheets stapled into the centre of the books. The French *Meccano Magazine* of September 1957 has a double-page spread publicising the first five of the planes. After 1968, no French Dinky planes were produced. Those appearing in the catalogues with an 'L' suffix are those imported from the English Dinky 'Big Plane' range.

SCALE
Though there is some discrepancy, they were all stated in the aforementioned publicity to be to 1/190 scale.

WHEELS
There was a certain amount of standardisation of the small parts. The wheels are all a smooth bronzed material and come in two sizes. The small ones are found on all the aeroplanes. They were also used for the nose wheels on the three larger planes which have similar but larger ones for the main undercarriage. The fixed undercarriages, themselves, are more detailed than on most toy planes of the era with the housing being represented open.

PROPELLERS
The large red spinners are common to all the propeller planes though they do have different propellers.

COLOUR | The base colour of all the fixed wing planes is a light silvery grey which can look very different from one model to another particularly when playworn. The cockpit canopies of the military planes are blue.

TRANSFERS | The roundels and tailfin flashes are *l'armée de l'air française*, French Air Force, blue, white and red. Incidentally, it was French planes that first carried identifying roundels. The carrier film of the transfers has discoloured with age and turned yellow, giving a greeny tinge to blue decals. All the detail down each side of the airliners is in one long transfer. The civilian wing registrations, as was the French practice at the time, are split over the two wings, F-B appearing on the port wing with the other three letters on the starboard. There is no split in the registration on the fuselage. Usually, genuine registrations were used, but they belonged to different planes, usually Comets.

PROTOTYPES | The prototypes of 60A Mystère IVA and 60B Vautour were recently found in a Paris toy shop, reputedly bought in from an engineer from Meccano around 1980. They are both solid brass, painted silver, the latter having wing roundels.

BIG PLANES | The English Dinky 'Big Plane' range was imported into France. The English catalogue numbers, with the addition of an 'L' suffix, were used.

THE AEROPLANES

Gift Set – 60, 501 | The Gift Set consists of the group of four planes that were issued in 1957. Some of the Supertoy Gift Set boxes have a label on the corner of the backing card to which the planes are secured, advertising the (French) Dinky Toy Club which was set up in June 1957.

60	Coffret Cadeau Avions	Renumbered 501
60A	Mystère IVA M. Daussault	800
60B	Vautour SNCASO	801
60D	Helicoptère Sikorsky S58	802
60E	Vickers Viscount	803

Mystère IVa M. Dassault – 60A, 800 | The virtually 1/190 scale toy is a neat one-piece casting with surface hatch detail far finer than on comparable English Dinkies. The air intake in the nose is deeply bifurcated and the wing roundel positions are marked on the castings. Painted silver-grey with a blue cockpit, it sports wing roundels and tail fin flash.

Vautour SNCASO – 60B, 801 | The model is an excellent representation with the slight anhedral (droop) of the wings being correctly modelled. The neat single casting has recessed air intakes, roundel locations cast-in and a lovely smooth finish to the surface, allowing for a particularly gleaming silver-grey paint finish. The quadricycle undercarriage has two sets of double wheels under the fuselage and singles below the engines.

Super 'G' Constellation – 60C, 892 | The scale of this accurate and beautiful model is 1/190 and it is made from two castings, one for the fuselage top, nose and tail, and the other for the wings and the undercarriage legs. Large three-blade propellers are fitted. The silver-grey finish has a good depth and almost looks as if it has had a coat of clear lacquer. Puzzlingly, this finish seems to be inaccurate, photographs of the Air France Connies showing the top of the fuselage finished in white. The yellowing of the transfer carrier sheet makes the mid-blue transfer look greeny blue. Slight liberties, like adding wing and tail plane surface detail, have been taken with the lovely drawing of the plane on the lid of the Supertoy box to make it look a bit more like the real thing.

Vickers Viscount – 60E, 803

The toy consists of two castings, the lower of which, unlike the English Dinky, has no spigot hole and is clearly marked with name, number and country of origin. The casting detail is much better and more detailed than that of its English counterpart. The flap lines on trailing edges of wings and tail stand neatly proud of the main casting and oval front and rear door outlines are similarly defined. The wings are gracefully faired into the fuselage. It thus has all the hallmarks of a French Dinky casting. Small four-blade propellers are fitted. The full-length fuselage transfers and the beautiful shark's tail decal on the tail plane with the winged horse with sea serpent's tail logo in the centre, are far superior to those of the English Dinky. The back of the box gives some technical details and an explanation that the Viscount is a four-engined passenger plane, remarkable for its turbo prop engines, which being turbine, not piston powered, give 'smoothness and a total absence of vibrations'. A touch of Gallic exaggeration there!

Sikorsky S58 Helicopter – 60D, 802

The model accurately depicts the wheel arrangement with two small ones on outriggers at the front and the single rear one as part of the solid one-piece 1/196 scale casting. The large four-bladed rotor is of very stiff tinplate and the small four-blade tail rotor is a Viscount propeller. This is a really pretty model and is arguably one of the best helicopters from any toy manufacturer. Another toy firm obviously thought so too as Mont Blanc Vuillerme made a very good plastic copy marketed as 'Jouet Miniluxe Bob and Lily', even ripping off the yellow French Dinky box.

Caravelle SE210 Airliner – 60F, 891, 891B, 891C, 891D

The nose, upper fuselage and tail are one piece and the wings and lower fuselage another. When these are rivetted together the separate engine pod unit is held in place. The front undercarriage leg is part of the lower casting but, in a new manner, with the twin rear legs separate pieces of pressed steel rivetted on. A 'first' was the set of stairs that could be hinged down from beneath the fuselage and held open with a spring. The 1/190 scale model was introduced in 1959 and remained in the catalogue for eight years so that it was the only plane casting that survived after the purchase of Meccano by Tri-ang. To clear up previously published inaccuracies, the casting changes are given in detail. The casting was marked 60F and 'Made in France' under the starboard wing. That same year the range was renumbered and it was allocated 891 in the Supertoy group. The Supertoy striped box sometimes advertising *Escalier Escamotable* (let-down stairs) on a sticker, with full technical details, had this number added to the side but the model was not altered. Before the die was sent to England for the Caravelle to enter the English Dinky range as 997 in 1962, the English number was added to the port wing. 'FRANCE' under the other wing was engraved onto a removable cartouche, as was 'ENGLAND' onto another, so that the correct name for the country of manufacture could be inserted into the die. The only other differences that have been found on the castings are that the separate engine piece on the French Dinky has cone detail within the air intakes as has the early

English Dinky, but the later one has simple indentations and a spigot hole in the centre of the lower fuselage. The Air France transfers are more finely drawn and more accurate than the English ones and have 'Caravelle' in script towards the nose. There are twin small wheels under the nose and four pairs of larger ones below the wing roots held on with tinplate pieces painted the same silver-grey as the casting. In 1961, or perhaps 1960, both dates having been given for the trade order form on which they were listed, three other finishes were released, presumably intended as export versions or perhaps requested by the airlines: Swissair Caravelle, 891B; SAS Caravelle Jet, 891C; Air Algerie Caravelle, 891D. The casting is the first one with '60F' and 'FRANCE' on the main tool and they are packed in Supertoy type boxes with both 60F and the appropriate 891 number printed on the edge. The box lid is covered almost completely with a large red and white label designed by M R Goirand, showing a side view of the plane with the appropriate decoration and the names as above. A small paper label demonstrating the operation of the stairs was enclosed. They are extremely scarce items. All have the same basic paint finish of silver-grey with a white fuselage top. The liveries and registrations are authentic but the split across the wings is on the wrong place on the first two: the Swissair should be HB-ICX and the SAS SE-DAA.

Nord 2501
Noratlas – 804

This, the last French Dinky plane, was released post renumbering. The two castings that make up the 1/190 scale model, a large main one of fuselage top, wings and tail with a much smaller under fuselage insert rivetted on, are beautifully detailed with raised flap lines and indented rear door out-lines. The large glass nose area is particularly neat. There are no roundel location circles on the casting and the three undercarriage legs project from the nose and under the engines. The large, four-blade propellers are particular to this plane. The cockpit can be painted light or dark blue. The specifications printed on the box differ somewhat from those above.

PRE-WAR ISSUES

60 Set/Le Coffret/Coffret luxe/Avions, Coffret Luxe
1935–40
60A, B, C, D, E, F below.

60z French Aeroplanes 1937–40
Number used when 60 Set sold in the UK.

60A L'Arc-en-Ciel 1935–40
135mm
Silver with red trim on top of fuselage and wingtips, gold with deep red, blue or green, or cream with sage green or red.
Three large black two-blade propellers.
See also: 61A

60az Arc-en-Ciel 1937–40
Number used when 60A sold in the UK.

60B Potez 58 1935–40
75mm
Yellow with grey stencilling on upper surfaces, orange with grey, or red with silver.
Large black two-blade propeller.
See also: 61D

60C Hanriot H.180T 1935–40
80mm
Green with white leading edges of wing and outside edges of tail. Green with red, blue with white, or red with silver.
Small black two-blade propeller.
See also: 61B, 61E

60D Breguet Corsaire 1935–40
78mm
Red with green leading edges of wings and tail, silver with red, yellow with red, red with white, or red with yellow.
Large black two-blade propeller.
See also: 61C

60E Dewoitine type D.500 1935–40
80mm
Cream with red ends of tailplane and angled flashes on wingtips, cream with blue, white with blue, or cream with green, small silver two-blade propeller.
See also: 61F

60F Autogire De La Cierva 1935–40
(rotor diameter 72mm) Length 53mm
Without pilot: green with yellow tail tips and rotor, silver with red, gold with blue, cream with red or blue, silver with blue, red with cream tail tips and silver rotor, yellow with green and cream, silver with red and cream, gold with blue and red, lemon yellow with green tail tips and engine cowl and silver rotor.
With pilot: gold with blue tail tips and rotor, green with yellow, red with white, red with cream tail tips and silver rotor, yellow with green and silver, silver-grey with green and silver, blue with white and gold.
Small red two-blade propeller.

61 Set/Le Coffret/Avions, Coffret luxe 1938–39
61A (1st version), 61B, 61C, 61D, 61E, 61F below

1939–40
61A (2nd version), 61B, 61C, 61D, 61E, 61F below

61z French Aeroplanes 1938–39
Number used when 61 Set (1st version) sold in the UK.

61A Dewoitine D338 1938–39
135mm
Casting of 60A L'Arc-en-Ciel with chromed, turned radial engines fitted. Silver with green top of fuselage and leading and trailing edges of wings and trailing edge of tail, silver with red, or gold with red. Also: silver with blue.
Three red three-blade propellers.

61A Dewoitine D338 1939–40
138mm
New casting. Name under wing. silver with no registration, light green with no registration, silver with registration F-ADBF.
Silver propellers.

61az Dewoitine D338 1938–40
Number used when 2nd casting sold in the UK.

61A Dewoitine D338 1946–48
Re-issue of new casting above.
Silver only.

61B Potez 56 1938–40
69mm
Casting of 60C Hanriot H.180T with fuselage with cast engines and low tinplate wing.
Blue, red, yellow or mustard yellow all with silver trim on engines, fuselage top and tail fin.
Two red two-blade propellers.

61C Farman F360 1938–40
70mm
Casting of 60D Breguet Corsaire with clipped wingtips.
Silver with red flash along top of fuselage.
Silver with yellow, or silver with blue. Some with French Air Force roundels.
Three-blade propeller.
Later: large red two-blade propeller.

61D Potez 58 Sanitaire 1938–40
75mm
Casting of 60B.
Silver with red cross, sometimes on a white ground.
Large red two-blade propeller.

61E Hanriot H.180M 1938–40
80mm
Casting of 60C.
Silver, with French Air Force roundels.
Red three-blade propeller or black two-blade propeller.

61F Dewoitine de Chasse/500 Chasseur 1938–40
80mm
Casting of 60E Dewoitine 500.
Silver with French Air Force roundels.
Large silver two-blade propeller.

62 Set /Le Coffret /Avions
Not issued. Listed 1939.

64 Set/Le Coffret /Avions 1939–40
61A (new casting), 64A, B, C, D below.
All planes silver.

64 Set /Le Coffret /Avions 1946–48
Re-issue of above, models in silver.

64A Amiot 370 1939–40
104mm
With gliding hole, name under wing.
Silver with French A.F. roundels (pale green also seen).
Beige, blue, red, pink.

64az Amiot 370 1939–40
Number used when 64A sold in UK.

64A Amiot 370 1946–48
Re-issue of above some with gliding hole flashed over, silver only.

64AC Amiot 370 avion d'observation camouflaged
Not issued.

64B Bloch 220 1939–40
103mm
With gliding hole, name under wing.
Silver, dark red, pale green, cream, light blue, beige.
Registration F-AOHJ.
Two red three-blade propellers.

64bz Bloch 220 1939–40
Number used when sold in the UK.

64B Bloch 220 1946–48
Re-issue of above, silver only.

64C Potez 63 1939–40
91mm
With gliding hole, name under wing.
Silver with French AF roundels.
Blue, red, beige.

64C Potez 63 1946–48
Re-issue of above, silver only.

64CC Potez 63 avion de reconnaissance camouflaged
Not issued.

64D Potez 662 1939–40
103mm
With gliding hole, name under wing.
Silver, red, light blue, yellow.
Registration F-ARAY.

64D Potez 662 1946–48
Re-issue of above, silver only.

64DC Potez 662 bombardier camouflaged
Not issued.

64E Potez 161
Not issued.

64F Leo 47
Not issued.

64G Leo 246
Not issued.

70 Locomotion Moderne Set
Not issued.

POST-WAR ISSUES

60 Coffret Cadeau Avions 1957–60
60A, 60B, 60D, 60E below.
Supertoy box.
Renumbered 501 in 1959.

60A Mystère IVa Marcel Dassault 1957–64
59mm
Silver-grey, blue cockpit.
French Air Force roundels and rudder flash.
Yellow box.
Renumbered 800 in 1959.

60B Vautour SNCASO 1957–64
80mm
Silver-grey, blue cockpit.
French Air Force roundels and rudder flash.
Yellow box.
Renumbered 801 in 1959.

60C Super 'G' Constellation 1956–63
200mm
Silver-grey, blue cockpit.
Air France transfers of white-edged pale blue window line starting with flying seahorse on a white ground with 'AIR FRANCE' in blue above wings, square silver (ground colour) windows.
Super G in red script below line in front of wing, black registration letters superimposed on line towards tail.

Tricolour and Air France on outer tail fins.
Some, darker blue window line.
Registration F-BHBX.
Large three-blade propellers.
Supertoy box.
Renumbered 892 in 1959.

60D Helicoptère Sikorsky S58 1957–62
(rotor diameter 87mm) Length 80mm
White with black under surface.
Sabena transfers, mid-blue stripe with square silver windows and doors over a grey line, 'SABENA' above windows in black.
Black tinplate four-blade rotor with yellow tips.
Black four-blade tail rotor.
Yellow box.
Renumbered 802 in 1959.

60E Vickers Viscount 1957–60
150mm
Air France livery, silver-grey with white upper fuselage, blue triangular nose decking, silver cockpit windows.
Mid-blue transfers with flying seahorse towards the rear of the cockpit, incorporating silver windows, black fuselage registration, with 'AIR FRANCE' in blue and tricolour above windows.
Blue curved tail decoration with flying seahorse.
Registration F-BGNX.
Silver four-blade propellers.
Yellow box.
Renumbered 803 in 1959.

60F Caravelle SE 210 1959–67
180mm
Air France livery, silver with white upper fuselage.
Mid-blue painted band on nose merges into medium blue transfers with white script.
'Caravelle' forward, triangular windows, edge bands.
'AIR FRANCE' in thin letters, tricolour, fuselage registration part of the decal, curved tail flash.
Registration F-BGNY.
Blue striped Supertoy box.
1959: renumbered 891, no numbers on plane, both numbers on box.
Before 1962, when English Dinky released: English Dinky number 997 added to casting, 'FRANCE' now in a cartouche.
See also: English Dinky 997.

501 Coffret Cadeau
Renumbering of 60 Set.
800, 801, 802, 803.

800 Mystère IVa Marcel Dassault
Renumbering of 60A.

801 Vautour SNCASO
Renumbering of 60B.

802 Helicoptère Sikorsky S58
Renumbering of 60D.

803 Vickers Viscount
Renumbering of 60E.

804 Nord 2501 Noratlas 1959–63
171mm
Silver-grey.
Dark or light blue cockpit.
French Air Force roundels on wings and tail booms, flashes on fins. Large four-blade propellers. Yellow box.

891 Caravelle SE 210
Renumbering of 60F (Air France).

891B Swissair Caravelle 1961–61

Casting of 60F

Swissair livery, silver with white fuselage top, original blue nose decking overpainted red.

Red line transfer with windows, logo (arrowheaded plane) in red and 'SWISSAIR' in blue above windows.

Red painted tailfin with white cross transfer.

Registration H-BICX.

Supertoy box numbered 60F and 891B with appropriate red and white label.

891C SAS Caravelle Jet 1961–61

Casting of 60F

SAS livery, silver with white fuselage top. Blue transfer line with red flash towards cockpit, 'SCANDINAVIAN AIRLINE SYSTEM' above windows, three-flag badge behind engines.

'SAS' in blue on tail. Registration S-EDAA.

Supertoy box numbered 60F and 981C with appropriate red and white label.

891D Air Algerie Caravelle 1961–61

Casting of 60F

Air Algerie livery, silver with white fuselage top, red noseband, silver cockpit.

Red line transfer with blue 'AIR ALGERIE' and tricolour above windows, registration above line under tail.

Red and white striped tailfin transfer with Air Algerie in blue.

Registration F-OBNH.

Supertoy box numbered 60F and 981D with appropriate red and white label.

892 Super G Constellation

Renumbering of 60C.

118 The 60 Set with 60A
Arc-en-Ciel (135mm)

119 Box label of the 60
Set with 60z sticker
indicating it was for the
British market

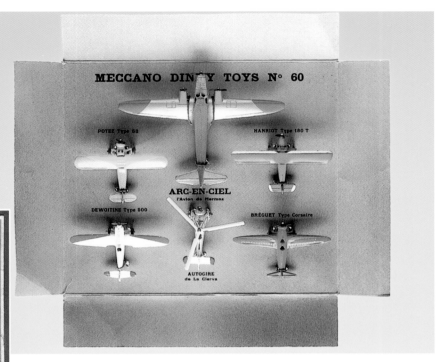

120 The 61 Set with 60A
Arc-en-Ciel (135mm)
modified to 61A
Dewoitine D338

121 Box label of the 61 Set

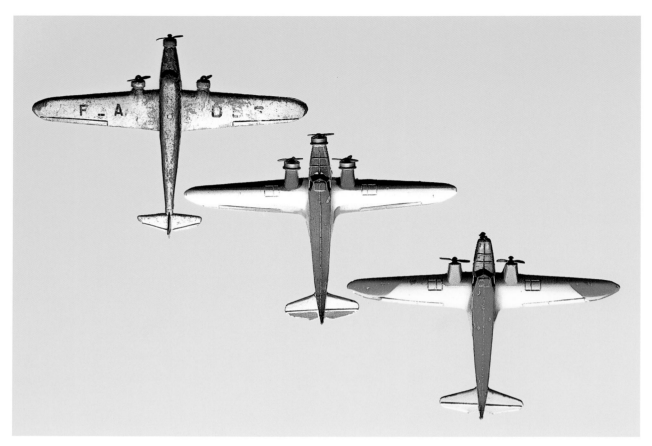

122 *top:* 61A new casting of Dewoitine D338 (138mm);
centre: 61A Arc-en-Ciel modified to Dewoitine D338;
bottom: 60A Arc-en-Ciel

123 The first 61A Dewoitine = Arc-en-Ciel (135mm)
with metal motor rings and the second version showing
the new casting. Note also the differences in the tail shapes

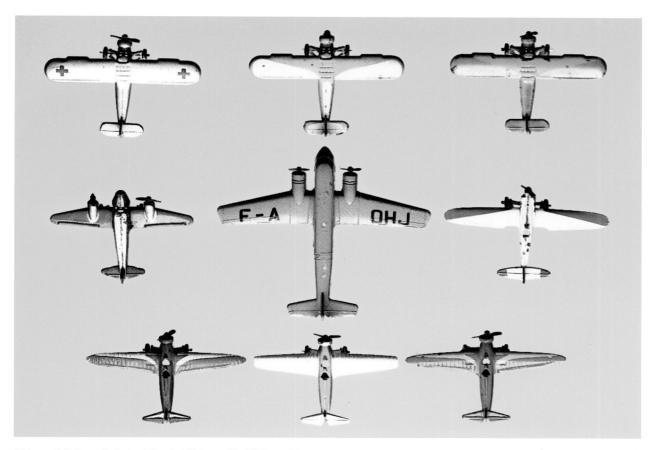

124 *top:* 61D Potez Sanitaire (75mm), 60B Potez 58, 60B Potez 58;
centre: 61B Potez 56, 64B Bloch 220, 60E Dewoitine 500;
bottom: 3 x 60D Breguet Corsaire

125 The 64 Set with new casting of 61A Dewoitine D338 (138mm)

126 Lid of the 64 Set

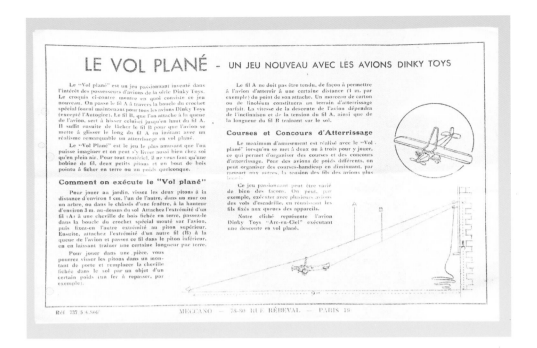

127 Le Vol Plané (flying game) leaflet

128 *top:* 60C/892 Constellation Super G (200mm); *bottom:* 60B/801 Vautour, 60A/800 Mystère IVa

129 60C/892 Lockheed Super Constellation (200mm)

130 *top:* 804 Nord Noratlas (171mm); *bottom:* Dinky 997 Caravelle SE210, French Dinky 60F/891 Caravelle SE210

131 Dinky Caravelle (180mm), French Dinky Caravelle showing the differences in the decals

132 Caravelle Swissair, Air Algerie

133 Caravelle Air France, SAS

134 *top:* Caravelle (180mm): Swissair, Air Algerie; *bottom:* SAS

135 Caravelle boxes
French Dinky, Dinky

136 Box for SAS Caravelle: those for Swissair and Air Algerie are
similar

137 French *Meccano Magazine* cover, No.1 October 1953

3 The world by country

Many of the plane names in this section have been expanded beyond those given by the manufacturer to enable the planes to be more easily identified. They are usually indexed by the name given by the toy manufacturer, so when looking for a particular aeroplane check under the parts of the name eg DC10 and Douglas DC10, A-10 Thunderbolt and Thunderbolt A-10.

ARGENTINA	**Antex**
AUSTRALIA AND NEW ZEALAND	**Micromodels** (including Majormodels), **Tink-E-Toys**
CANADA	**London Toy**
CHINA	See Hong Kong
DENMARK	**Bento, Birk, Blue Sun, Micro, Mollberg, Tekno**
EASTERN EUROPE	**Jotek** (Czech), **Pogus, Metalbox, Russian Models**
FRANCE	**Aluvac** (see Solido), **AR, CIJ, Cofalu, French Dinky** (see separate section), **Gulliver, LR, Majorette, Metallix, Mignot, Pennytoys** (SR and Unidentified) **Quiralu, RM, Sijam, Solido, SR** (see Pennytoys)
GERMANY	**Gescha** (GS), **Märklin, Revell** (see US), **Schuco** and **Schuco Piccolo, Siku, NZG** (see Introduction)
GREECE	**Pilaz, Polfi**
HONG KONG AND CHINA	**Bachmann** (see Lintoy dies), **Benkson Pocket Money Toys, BiPlane, China Light Industrial Product** (see Road Tough), **Corgi** (see Lintoy dies), **Diecast Miniature** (see Novelties), **DTC Super Wings** (see Super Wings), **Dynafighter** (Master Diecast metal), **Edocar** (see Road Tough), **Ertl** (see Lintoy dies), **Fast Lane** (see Dyna-Flites, USA), **Fast Wing** (see Playart Fast Wing), **Fighter Aircraft** (see Toyway), **Flight-of-a-Gun, Flyers** (see Lintoy dies and Road Champs Flyers, USA), **Freda, Home Toys, Imperial, Jet Fighters** (see Home Toys), **Lintoy, Lintoy dies, M** and **Mandarin, Mail Box Series** (see USA), **Manley** (see Road Tough), **Mini Dyna Fighter, Mini Fast Wing** (see Playart Fast Wing), **Miniplanes** (see Mandarin), **Mini-planes, Mini Prop Classics** (see Imperial), **Novelties, Playart Fast Wing, Playmakers** (see Miniplanes), **Racing Champions, Road Champ Flyers** (see Lintoy dies and USA), **Road Tough, SkyBirds** (see Racing Champions), **SkyTomica** (see Lintoy dies), **Sky Wings** (see Home Toys), **Soma, Steel Screamers** (see Imperial), **Super Wings, Tins' Toys Super Wings** (see Super Wings), **Tintoys, Tomica** (see Lintoy dies), **Toy Way** (see also Edison, Italy), **UDC, Victory Force** (see Imperial), **Wild Wings** (see Home Toys, Mandarin, Cragstan Wild Wings, USA), **Wintech** (see Racing Champions), **Wondrie Metal Products, Woolworths** (see Lintoy dies), **WT** (see Tintoys), **YDC** (see Lintoy dies), **Zee Toys** (see also USA), **Zylmex** (see USA)
INDIA	**Maxwell Mini, Milton, Nicky Toys** (see Dinky)

ITALY	**Aviva, Edison Air Lines** (Pyranglo/Toy Way UK), **Mercury, Polistil/Politoys**
JAPAN	**ATC, Bandai Robomachines, Diapet Yonezawa, Edai Grip Technica Flight, Linemar, Mattel-Bandai** (see Bandai), **MiniAir** (Modern Toy), **Nakajima** (NKJ), **Tomica/Tomy, Superwings**
SPAIN	**Guisval, Joal, Mira, Nacoral, Pilen, PlayMe**
UK	**Acorn Toy, Barrett and Sons** (see Taylor & Barrett), **Britains, Cap Bombs, Casting Moulds, Charbens, Corgi, Corgi/Lintoy** (see Lintoy dies Hong Kong), **Crescent, Dinky** (see separate section), **Dyson, Johillco, Kay** (see Taylor & Barrett), **Lone Star DCMT, Mascots, Matchbox Skybusters, Pyranglo** (see Edison Airline, Italy), **RAF Benevolent Fund/Tonka Polistil/Kellogg's, Segal, Skybirds, Taylor & Barrett, Timpo, Toymaker Casting moulds** (see Casting Moulds), **Toyway** (see Edison Airline, Italy), **Tremo**
USA	**Aero Mini, Air Command** (see Dyna-Flites), **Bachmann, Barclay, Best Toy** (see Kansas Toy), **Casting Moulds** (see Introduction), **Cast Iron** (see Introduction), **Cragstan Wild Wings,** 'Dime Store' (see Introduction), **Dyna-Flites, Erie, Ertl, Fairymark** (see also Lincoln Toys NZ), **Frankonia** (see Mail Box Series), **Gabriel** (see Hubley), **Goodee-Toy** (Excel), **Hobby Room** (see Dyna-Flites), **Home Manufacturing Co** (see Casting Moulds, Introduction), **Hot Wings** (see Dyna-Flites), **Hubley Kiddie Toy, Kansas Toy, Kiddie Toy** (see Hubley), **Mail Box Series** (Frankonia), **Midgetoy, MT, Modern Toy** (see Dyna-Flites), **Renwal, Revell, Road Champ Flyers, Slush cast toys** (see Introduction), **Tootsietoys, Unidentified** (see Introduction), **Wings** (see Dyna-Flites), **Zylmex, Zee Toys** (Intex) (see Dyna-Flites).

Argentina

ANTEX

DC10
90mm. 'Varig' in box for Boeing 737

F7-U3 Cutlas Reported.

Australia and New Zealand
Micromodels (inc. Majormodels), **Tink-E-Toys**

MICROMODELS 1952–61

Made by Goodwood (Aust) Productions Pty Ltd, JA Brent and Co., the bold initials GB being used for the catalogue numbers. The name related trademark was a micrometer. Many of the dies went to New Zealand in 1956 and were used by Lincoln Industries/Toys whose trademark incorporates a drawing of Abraham Lincoln! The Airport Set (NZ) does not contain a plane! All road vehicles except:

GB24 (Aust) } Vickers Viscount
4329 (NZ)
158mm
Upper casting, top half of fuselage and tailfin, has 'Trans-Australia Airlines TAA' in script above the windows. Lower casting has 'TAA' cast on the upper port wing, VH-TVA on the upper starboard, 'VICKERS' and 'VISCOUNT', below. 'MICRO MODELS' below fuselage. Plug in diecast undercarriage legs with black rubber wheels. Diecast four-blade propellers. White fuselage top with name picked out in red, blue waistline, the rest is silver.

MAJORMODELS

Larger models produced by the same manufacturers. The Navy Fighter is the same as the Hubley and die is the same as that used by Fairymark (probably USA) and was probably bought from them as the Lincoln castings have been made using a worn die.

4100 Navy (Folding Wing) Fighter, Vought 4-FU Corsair
222mm
Wings painted red with silver star and roundel edge, the rest silver.

TINK-E-TOYS New Zealand

Fairey Battle Bomber Copy of Dinky 60s.

Canada

LONDONTOY c.1948–52

A mixed range of diecast toys, mainly road vehicles, marked 'LONDONTOY', catalogue number, 'Made in Canada', name of plane. Much wartime RAF training was done in Canada.

No.11 Hawker Hurricane
116mm
Single poor casting with Hurricane shaped wings. Propeller boss plugs into flat nose.
Metal wheels.
Mid blue. Red, white and blue RAF roundel transfers on wings.

Denmark
Bento, Birk, Blue Sun, Micro, Mollberg, Tekno
The odd plane or two were made by a few companies including possibly a one-piece diecast Ju-52, but Denmark is famed for the Tekno range.

BENTO 1930s

Heavy metal with roundels cast on wings, indistinctly marked below. Perspex disc propellers.

Seaplane (sim. Comet racer)
59mm
Separate floats under fuselage. Silver, red in roundels.

Single engined biplane
48m
Lower wing much shorter than upper.

BIRK

1 Australiensflyver
120mm
Metallic green cast fuselage with high grey tinplate wing. Rubber wheels.

BLUE SUN 1950s

Boeing B.17 Bomber
123mm. 1/257
One main hollow mazac casting with separate nose cone and plug-in engine faces, marked under tail 'BLUE-SUN DENMARK', four red three-blade propellers. Grey with blue wingtips, blue with orange or orange with grey, star-on-bar paper stickers. Oblong blue box with plane flying past a smiling sun, circular wooden stand, both labelled 'BLUE SUN Legetoj'.

MICRO

Biplane
70mm
Lead. Gold, DDL.

MOLLBERG c. 1960

May or may not be marked 'Mollberg Made in Denmark' on the separate base. The box is like an aircraft hangar and carries name and country of manufacturer.

Sikorsky S55 Helicopter with floats or wheels
Length 100mm. 1/130
All diecast with one main, beautifully detailed, casting pierced for the several windows with much overscale rivet detail. Separate two-blade stabiliser and three-blade rotor, each of the blades being riveted realistically within the rotor head. White with red cross at the tail stem, olive drab with US star-on-bar transfer at the tail stem or grey with 'SPERRY CROSCOPE COMPANY SPORT SKY SB-55' in red on a clear ground.

TEKNO 1944–69

The history of this important firm is complicated and there are no good internal records available. They have made a wide variety of toy vehicles which have only recently been satisfactorily documented. They have always issued many painting and decal variations on each casting. When the factory closed, batches of original decals for the Danish Super Sabre, Super Mystère and DC-7c Sabena fuselage were found and have been available on the collectors' market. They only made 10 aeroplane castings but these differ so greatly that they have been grouped into four sections. Introduction dates are tentative, but the 1965 and 1969 (year of the founder's death) last catalogue appearance dates are firm.

WWII Fighters and Bombers
They have Tekno, Denmark, catalogue number and name cast below the wings. The undercarriage legs, fitted with small metal wheels on individual axles, are part of the casting and descend from underneath the wings. The three-blade propellers are tinplate. The box for 401 has a lift-off lid with 'DANSK LEGETOJ' (Danish Toy) in red printing in diamond patterns on fawn card. The catalogue number is stamped on in black. The Flying Fortress and the Blenheim were both also made by Dinky. Though marked BB-1, the Blenheim is a hybrid with the long nose of the Mk IV but without the step in the glazing.

Air Ambulance: S.A.I. KZ IV
It consists of three large castings: upper fuselage with pierced windows and tail with very small tail wheel, marked Nr 488 Tekno Danmark, forward under-fuselage and wings, rear underfuselage. Wheels in spats. Two-blade cast props. The boxes are either a large version of the Fighter/Bomber box or have lift-off lids with a label on top.

Airliners
They both consist of three castings: upper fuselage and tailfin, forward and rear lower fuselage with tailplane, wings with centre lower fuselage, marked with plane name, 'Tekno' and 'Made in Denmark'. The undercarriages retract. There is a clear plastic insert for cockpit windows. These good models have white upper and silver lower castings. The plane-shaped boxes are moulded plastic, green with a clear lid. The plane name, number, 'Tekno' and 'Made in Denmark' are moulded on the base.

Jet fighters
Usually two smooth main castings, marked with plane name, Tekno and Denmark, plug together behind the wings, with a slot-in tail, rivetted missile pods and retracting undercarriages with single wheels, fitted with clear plastic canopies. Good models of planes that were also modelled by Dinky, Solido etc. The standard boxes have 'Tekno Jet-Plane' on their blue and red hinged lids which half fold up to display the plane sitting on an insert with a cloud pattern on a sky blue ground. A label on the end gives details of the plane and the scale as 1/125.

WWII FIGHTERS AND BOMBERS

401 Flyvende Fœstning, Flying Fortress 1946–65
143mm. 1/221
Two castings: upper fuselage including tail; lower fuselage including nose and wings.
Small propellers, usually red, some black.
White: Red Cross (red cross on white circle or white cross on red) on wings and fin.
Silver: RAF – red, white, blue roundels on wings, flash on fin. US – red centred white star on blue roundels, flash on fin. Sweden – three yellow crowns on yellow edged blue roundel on wings and fin. Denmark – cream centred red roundels, flag on fin. USSR – red star in white roundel on wings and fin.
Very dark grey/black with green and brown camouflage: RAF, Denmark.
Silver upper casting, orange lower: RAF, US, OY-DDL in black on silver across wings, Danish flag on fin,
Blue or silver upper casting, orange/red lower: RAF, OY-DDL, Chrome, no decals.

402 Bombeflyver BB1, Bristol Blenheim 1946–65
91mm. 1/188
Single casting marked 'BB-1'. Small propellers. Camouflage: Denmark, Sweden.
White with red crosses. Silver: RAF, US, Sweden. Yellow or red: RAF.

403 Jager DSB-1, Douglas Dauntless SBD-1 1946–65
87mm. 1/145
Single casting marked 'DSB-1'. Large propeller.
Camouflage, blue (several shades): US, RAF, red crosses.
White with red crosses,
Silver: RAF, US, Denmark, Sweden. Red: RAF.

AIR AMBULANCES

488 Ambulanceflyver/Zonen Ambulanceflyver, Ambulance Plane 1944–65
201mm. approx. 1/80
White, metallic blue or silver with OY-DIZ in black on wings and fuselage sides, 'ZONEN' on nose.
White with OY-DZU, red cross roundels, '1939–1949' and Zonen logo on tailfin.

488x Transportflyver, Transport Plane 1944–65
Silver. Blue fuselage, silver wings. Red with silver wings.
All: OY-DDL, Danish flag on tailfins. Chrome, no decals.

AIRLINERS

765 Douglas DC-7c 1958-1967
193mm. 1/201
Cast four-blade propellers secured by push-fit tubes (one spare in box).

SAS 1958–67
SK SAS (fictional) registration in blue across wings above and below. Blue or lilac line with seats showing though windows with 'SCANDINAVIAN' above and 'SAS' + three coats of arms at rear, blue triangle and 'VIKING' on nose, 'SAS' in blue, '7c' in red on tail.

SABENA 1958–65
OO-SAB in black on starboard wing, dark blue nose and cheat line with delicate letters 'BELGIAN World AIRLINES', DC-7c, OO-SAB incorporated, 'SABENA' and flag above, blue tail with elongated white S, badge. 'SABENA' in black under centre wings.

SWISSAIR 1958–67
HB-IBK above and below starboard wing, red cheat line with 'SWISSAIR' above in blue, blue triangle on nose, red upper tailfin with white cross.

KLM 1958–65
PH-DSJ in red above and thicker above containing 'THE FLYING DUTCHMAN' on port side, 'DE VLIEGENDA HOLLANDER' on the other, 'KLM' in red behind cabin windows. Tail: striped diagonally in light and dark blue with 'KLM' and crown in red in white circle; also: white with red, white, blue blocks at trailing edge with crown, 'PH KONINKLIKE LUCHVAART MY HOLLAND' alongside in black.

ALITALIA 1958–59
I-DUVA in blue above and below wing, ALI logo on fuselage sides and wings, two thick blue lines with three thin green between, red/white/green tail with '7c' and I-DUVA in white.

SUDFLUG 1964–64
D-ABAC above and below wings in black, light blue/mid blue cheat lines with 'SUDFLUG' in blue above, tail with seven horizontal blue lines with white circle and Sudflug logo. German market only.

766 SE-210 Caravelle 1959–69
169mm. 1/203
Three main castings with rear engines trapped, tailplane slotted in. The main undercarriage has ingenious centre-hung doors, lowering rear steps. White upper, silver lower.

AIR FRANCE 1959–67
FB-EHL authentic decals and tail flash.

SAS 1959–69
OY KRA in very dark blue across upper and lower wings. 'SCANDINAVIAN' and registration no. above blue cheat line. 'SCANDINAVIAN AIRLINES SYSTEM' and reg. no. above red over blue cheat line, 'SAS' in very dark blue on tailfin and on stripe on engine pods, coats of arms behind engines.

SWISSAIR 1959–69
HB-ICW on wing, 'SWISSAIR' in red along each side, red tailfin with white cross.

JET FIGHTERS

785 Hawker Hunter 1955–67
82mm. 1/126
Third casting: plug in nose retains nose wheel, no missiles.
Silver. Red, white and pale blue (RAF) roundels above and below wings and on fuselage, flash on tail, WT 557 in black under each wing.

786 MiG-15 1955–67
78mm. 1/129
Gloss olive green or red. White edged red stars on upper and lower wings, rear fuselage and tailfin. '117' in black edged in white on nose.

787 Super Sabre F100 1957–69
85mm. 1/139
Third casting: tailplane rivetted under exhaust.
Silver. 'USAF' on starboard wing, star-on-bar on port, both reversed below, star-on-bar either side of nose, FW-761 in black on fuselage sides, 'US AIR FORCE 25761' on tailfin, or yellow centred red roundels on wings, Danish flag on tailfin, 'YZ-R' on fuselage.

788 Super Mystère B-2 1958–69
80mm. 1/125
Silver. Red line along sides, blue, white, red French roundels on upper and lower wings and rear fuselage, flash on fin, 01 in black below cockpit, or Danish Air Force roundels.

Eastern Europe

Jotek (Czech), **Metalbox** (Czech), **Pogus** (Czech),
Russian Models

JOTEK Czechoslovakia, 1992

Helicopter, toylike
Blue with a white plastic rotor, black plastic wheels.
White decal with 'RENDORSEG'.

METALBOX Czechoslovakia, 1992

Cessna N402CW
1/70 Blue upper, white lower casting, 'MILITARY'.

POGUS Czechoslovakia, 1989

Aircraft
100mm. Marked on the underside with 'POGUS' in a diamond.

RUSSIAN MODELS

In the late 1980s, a range of diecast models of
Russian planes in 1/72 scale, Yaks, Ilyushin
etc. began to appear. They seem to be too
delicate and detailed to have been made as
toys but, mysteriously, they do not seem to
have been exported officially, coming out in
small quantities from 'collectors'. Known
variously as Saratov, Kazan, Kiev or Radon,
they are not within the scope of the book.

AVIATION 1970s

Seven crude single castings, 45-75mm, each
marked below with the plane type, above with
stars on the wings, finished in silver, contained
in a brown card box with a three-colour label
bearing the word 'Aviation' in cyrillic letters.
They are also found in boxes with road
vehicles. Bombers Tu24, M50, Airliners Il62,
Tu144, Fighters Yak25, Su11, Jet fighter Su7.

France

Aluvac (see Solido), **AR, CIJ, Cofalu, Gulliver** (see
Introduction), **LR, Majorette, Metallix, Mignot,
Pennytoys** (SR and Unidentified), **Quiralu, RM,
Sijam, Solido, SR** (see Pennytoys)

INTRODUCTION

The French took to aeroplanes with great
enthusiasm and toy aeroplanes were made as
bric-a-brac and no doubt sold as souvenirs at
the many airshows. Even the earliest ones from
SR are readily identifiable models. There are
several small makes, whose origins are
virtually untraceable. Unusually, French
manufacturers in the 1930s made toys in
aluminium, some of which can be traced to
particular firms. After the war, there were
crude aluminium toys such as a DC3 with a
wire undercarriage cast in and an 85mm span
Lockheed P38 Lightning embossed with US
stars (possibly made by Gulliver). Their love of
flight is however, better demonstrated by the
attractive ranges of French Dinky, Solido etc
which are highly regarded by collectors even if
often difficult to find.

AR 1930s–1940s

AR made cheap toys, mainly road vehicles, in
lead and tin, whose quality ranged from poor
to quite good.

Spirit of St Louis
126mm span of oblong tinplate wing.
110mm length of lead fuselage including tail.
Tinplate propeller. Wheels solid metal, cast hubs with white
rubber tyres or thin composition discs, the two front ones
on a single axle, the tail wheel half within the open fuselage.
There are two versions:
Marked 'AR FRANCE' on port fuselage. Fuselage extends down
to axle position to give room for optional clockwork motor.
Both sides – circular keyhole behind axle and slot in front for
motor tab, also tab recess concealed by wheel. Wing rivetted
to top of fuselage.
Marked 'FRANCE' up inside fuselage. Fuselage extended to axle
position by undercarriage struts. Inside top of fuselage cut
out under wing which is soldered on.
Silver.

Autogiro
Fuselage of Spirit of St Louis fitted with tinplate three-blade
rotor. The clockwork motor powers both wheels and rotor.
Red, cream rotor.

Blériot XI
104mm. Tin wing, lead fuselage.

CIJ 1959–c.1965

CIJ, Compagnie Industrielle du Jouet, had made a wide range of large scale tinplate road vehicles before they turned their attention to diecasting. To celebrate the recently signed Treaty of Rome, they used the name Europarc in advertising. All are excellent quality single castings with 'Made in France' and the plane name cast below. All have the CIJ logo cast underneath except for the smallest, the Norécrin which has it on the upper wing. Some of the larger have the scale 1/300 cast in. All except the two smallest have fixed wheel assemblies rivetted on. Most are fitted with small bright bun-shaped dumb-bell wheels. Tinplate propellers with big spinners. The decoration is partly sprayed and partly transfer. Usually the boxes are standard, blue and yellow with a plan view of the plane on the top, but the planes with airline liveries have special boxes. Some even came in pre-printed plastic bags, eg 1/10 Caravelle. There was available a triangular wooden stand with a steel pin on which to mount the planes and a plastic airport play-sheet with wooden buildings. Many of the very pretty models were also made in comparable quality by Solido.

1/1 Fouga CM170R 1959–65
65mm. 1/174
Stubs for undercarriage.
Silver, blue cockpit and tip tanks, French Air Force roundels on wings.
Also seen in light grey, French roundels.

1/2 Norécrin 1959–65
61mm. 1/165
No undercarriage.
White with diagonal blue bands and tips on wings.

1/10 Caravelle SE210 1959–61
114mm. 1/301
'CARAVELLE' and all windows embossed.
Brass wheels on undercarriage crimped into undernose and wing lugs.
White upper, silver lower separated by blue sprayed window line including engines, name blocked out in silver.
Also hybrid between 1/10 and 1/20.

1/11 Douglas DC7 1959–65
118mm. 1/303
Marked 'Douglas DC 7'.
Four three-blade propellers. Nose-wheel assembly rivetted on, two undercarriage legs incorrectly angled back for stability crimped into holes under wings.
White. Blue cockpit windows, square passenger windows, red line along side, blue 'D7C' on tail.

1/12 Noratlas 1959–65
107mm. 1/304
Two three-blade propellers. Nose wheel cast in, two undercarriage legs rivetted under wings.

Silver with white fuselage top, blue cockpit windows. French AF roundels on wings, flashes on each side of fins.

1/14 Breguet Deux Ponts (Two-deck) 1959–65
142mm. 1/302
Four three-blade propellers. Nose wheel rivetted on, undercarriage legs crimped under wings.
Silver with white top including upper tail surfaces. Blue windows and line with 'Air France' and winged horse logo.

1/15 Boeing 707 1960–61
136mm. 1/293
Undercarriage crimped into slots.
White with silver-blue engine pods. Blue square windows, red lining on sides and tailfin.

1/16 DC6 UAT 1960–65
Casting of 1/11 DC7 with 'DC 7' removed.
White upper including tail-fin, silver lower including wings and tail plane.
'UAT' in yellow, AEROMARITIME in blue above very dark blue over yellow line with blue windows superimposed, 'UAT' on tail, F-B GTX in black across wings.
White box with blue printing.

1/20 Caravelle Air France 1961–65
Casting of 1/10, with embossing removed, 'Ech.:1/300' added underneath.
Undercarriage: bun-shaped wheels on tinplate carriers.
White upper including engines and tail, silver lower.
'AIR FRANCE' in blue above blue line with white windows.
Later: with black windows and tail stripe.

1/20(1) Caravelle Air Maroc 1961–63
Casting of 1/20
White upper, silver lower. 'Royal Air Maroc' (and in Arabic) above green over red line with white window circles, star describing a circle on tail. Multicoloured box.

1/30 Boeing 707 Air France 1961–65
Casting of 1/15 with 'Ech.: 1/300' added.
White upper, silver lower. 'AIR FRANCE' above blue/white/blue line on sides, 'BOEING 707 INTERCONTINENTAL' in red below line and with arrow on tailfin.

COFALU 1940s

The ending of the name indicates that production was in aluminium.

P-38 Lightning
Brown, silver, grey or blue with French roundels and flashes. Separate propellers.

Bell P-39 Airacobra
100mm. Silver

LR 1930s

Le Rapide (LR) made one-piece hollow lead castings of reasonable quality. The plane is marked 'L.R.' up inside the cabin roof and 'FRANCE' up inside the fuselage.

French Trimotor
130mm
Two small lead wheels on a wire axle. Two-blade propellers. All red with silver face to propeller blades. Paper French Air Force roundels.

MAJORETTE Late 1970s–present day

Majorette, 69140 Rillieux, established in 1966, initially manufactured diecast road vehicles in 1/50 scale. In their Lyon factories, they became extremely prolific, specialising in toy vehicles made to fit packaging of a specific length for which they supplied dispensers to toyshops, supermarkets and small general stores. Strong clear plastic boxes were followed by clear moulded plastic tops heat welded to a white pre-formed plastic base. Later, larger models were packed in clear plastic shells strengthened by being slipped into card hanging packs, and bubble packs were also used. Majorette have always been interested in high sales and have no compunction about changing packaging or toy decoration and adding new gimmicks to improve sales. Decals: some transfers but usually clear tape stickers, superceded by tampo printing. Helicopters with diecast upper cockpit and boom and plastic underneath, lower boom and tail were added to the range in the 1980s. Casting were made in such quantities that there is a significant deterioration in quality over the years. Planes, diecast upper with plastic lower, were added in the early 1990s.

SERIES 800 AIRPORT 1992

A new diecast Airport Series 800 was launched in 1992, to compete with Matchbox Skybusters. All are marked with Majorette and carry the name of the plane, plus TM (Trademark) on the Boeings. Five different models were released in 1992. Each plane consists of two generally good castings: upper fuselage and tailfin; lower fuselage, wings and tailplane. The engines and undercarriage legs are cast in, the flap control mechanism is modelled and there is panel and flap detail on the upper surfaces. The wheels are small black plastic dumb-bells. The paint is a hard gloss and the high quality decals are a mixture of tampo printing and plastic tape stickers. Majorette announced 'Specials: Airline liveries not included in the standard range can be produced, with airline approval of course, for special orders. An alternative personalised box can also be specified in place of the blistercard to facilitate sales on board aircraft.' They are bubble-packed in a single blister to a black, red and yellow card depicting an airliner taking off into the sunset. The back of the card carries illustrations of the range. The scales vary from 1/558 to 1/421!

In 1993, the Ideal Loisirs Group acquired both Majorette and Solido and said they intended that they should keep their separate identities.

SERIES 300 – models/packaging nominally 16cm long, 1/70 scale

371 Gazelle
135mm from nose to tail.
Black plastic rotor, exhaust, skids, chrome engine.
Red upper, white lower, green glazing, 'SECURITE CIVILE' in white on black on cockpit side.
White upper, red lower, brown glazing, 'RESCUE' in blue.
All red, brown glazing, 'SOS POMPIERS SOS' in black on white.
All khaki, with decal sheet of red crosses, '7' etc. (1990).
Red plastic rotor, exhaust, skids.
All white, blue glazing, 'CROIX ROUGE' in black with red cross.
White upper, blue lower, blue glazing, 'PRESIDENT' in black with red box line.
Blue plastic rotor, exhaust, skids.
White upper, blue lower, 'POLICE' in blue.
White upper, red lower, 'Caisse d'Epargne' (Savings Bank). (1993).

SETS
601 Low loader and helicopter, 'RESCUE' above.
922 Grand Prix Set with same helicopter.
960 Fire Rescue Set with helicopter, 'RESCUE' above.

322 Helicopter
Black four-blade plastic rotor. White upper, red lower, blue glazing, 'COAST GUARD', star-on-bar in blue, badge on red. Post 1988.

SERIES 3000, Super Movers
3043 Bell Agusta
Length nominally 29cm, 1/60 scale
200mm from nose to tail.
White rotor, chromed exhausts, undercarriage.
Mustard upper, green lower, blue glazing, white 'ALPES SECOURS' and banding.
Brick red rotor. With or without orange plastic skids, road cones etc.
Dark blue upper, white lower, 'POLICE' in blue on white and red stripe.
White upper, blue lower, 'POLICE' as above.
Also reported 'Ewing Oil Co Dallas USA'.

SETS
935 Emergency Rescue with helicopter, white upper, blue lower, 'Police' above. 1987.
3094 Helicopter Transporter with Agusta, red prop, all black 'TURBO COPTER' and stripes in red with white flash. 1987.

SERIES 2380, Sonic Flashers – Air Force with variable engine sound. 1990.

2381 Helicopter with machine gun
140mm
Plastic upper, metal lower. Black plastic propellers, missiles, skids, red light on roof, revolving rotor.
Dark blue upper, white lower, 'POLICE' in white with badge.

2382 Helicopter with missile launcher
Sand, 'USAF' in black with star-on-bar.

2383 Helicopter with machine gun
'COASTGUARD' as above.

2385 F-15 with cannon
91mm. Metallised silver, blue cockpit. 'US AIR FORCE' in black on fuselage, 'USAF' on starboard wing, star-on-bar on port.

2386 F-15 rapid firing
Black, 'BLACK EAGLE' in red on fuselage with gold eagles on wings.

2387 F-15 rapid firing
White, '62' in purple with red and purple stripes on wings.

2360 Helicopter
2360 with eight different sounds and eight buttons on side of toy to produce them.
195mm.
Metal upper, plastic lower.
Black plastic rotor blades, skids.
Dark green, black 'TURBO COPTER', or white and red 'COASTGUARD'.

SERIES 800 AIRPORT 1992

801 Boeing 747/400
107mm. 1/558
White. 'AIR FRANCE' in blue, blue and red stripes on tail with EC star circle.
White upper, silver lower. 'CATHAY PACIFIC' in red with green window line and tail stripes with Union Jack on tail.
'THAI'.

802 Airbus A300
91mm. 1/493
All white. 'SINGAPORE AIRLINES' window stripe and tail in blue with gold band below and stylised bird tail logo. A310 on decal is incorrect as the A310 has a new wing.
'Alitalia'.
'Swissair'.

803 Boeing 767
103mm. 1/462
White upper, silver lower. 'AIR CANADA', tail and window line in red with dark red band below. White maple leaf in circle on tail.
'JAL'.

804 Douglas MD80 (Super DC9)
78mm. 1/421
White. 'Alitalia' in black on fuselage and wings, green window line, green and red 'A' tail logo.
'SCANDINAVIAN'.

805 Douglas DC10
101mm. 1/499
White. 'IBERIA' on red, orange and yellow stripe curving up over top of fuselage behind cockpit, 'IB' on tail.

METALLIX 1930s

Metallix used aluminium for their one-piece castings which are marked with the plane name, 'ECHELLE 100' (scale), 'METALLIX' and 'FABRIQUE EN FRANCE' under the wings. They are fitted with tinplate propellers and finished with French Air Force roundel transfers.

Breguet 690 C3
150mm
Three-blade propellers, wheels on individual axles.
Red with silver wingtips and cockpit, silver and blue, red and green camouflage.

Morane Saulnier 406
Three-blade propeller. Red with silver.

MIGNOT 1939

Known for its tin and lead toy soldiers and aeroplane in the 1920s, Mignot produced a diecast Dewoitine 500 in 1939.

PENNYTOYS: SR AND UNMARKED 1910–35

Small toys produced for sale at about one Penny, of a very variable quality, were made by several small companies in Paris. The best were made in engraved metal moulds and cast in a lead alloy hardened with antimony and tin. The intricate castings are normally one piece with additional spoked wheels and two-blade propeller. SR was a partnership of Simon and Rivollet and their product was high quality, often with a bronzed or silvered look. Many were marked 'SR', had 'France' or 'Déposé' or both, or 'Made in France', up inside the fuselage. It is often not possible, however, to identify the manufacturer especially if the piece is painted grey. There is a great similarity between the Tootsietoy Bleriot and the SR/unidentified one and there is much controversy over who copied whom. The French one has many more hatch markings on the wings than the Tootsietoy.

Blériot XI
58mm
Paddle-shaped propeller blades.
Fine chord ribs with very fine hatchings or feather pattern wings, with or without paper French Air Force roundels.

Breguet I Biplane
42mm. Paddle-shaped blades.

Farman Biplane 1919
74mm
Two castings, narrow blades.

Morane Saulnier 1914
69mm
Narrow blades, scalloped trailing edges or without scalloped edges, with solid wheels.

Rumpler Taube 1910
65mm. Paddle-shaped blades. The tinplate wing is on the wrong way round!

QUIRALU 1930s

A two-piece twin-engined bomber, probably a Bloch 200 1934, which has an enormous glazed snout, marked 'Quiralu' faintly under the wing, in aluminium, fitted with two-blade tinplate propellers.

Bloch 200 Bomber
198mm. 1/113. Grey.

RM

RM manufactured in aluminium.

1 Spitfire 65mm
3 Boeing B29
4 Lockheed P-38
6 Curtiss XP55

SIJAM

Boeing 747
85mm. Air France.

MiG-21
105mm. Green, red or light blue.

SOLIDO 1932–82

'Amusants, Instructifs, Incassable et Français' (Entertaining, instructive, unbreakable and French.)

Solido slogan

Ferdinand de Vazeilles claimed, somewhat inaccurately, that he had set up the first pressure diecasting factory in Paris in 1919, having seen the machines in London, and that he virtually invented the French diecast toy industry. However, his factory was making toys for other firms before October 1932 when he took out a patent for unassembled constructional toys built by means of spigots, screws and pins. These would make a recognisable model, say of a car, which could be easily changed into another by the substitution of a few parts.

In 1925, de Vazeilles had travelled to the States and signed a deal with the American Aluminium Company. The first name on his product relevant to the toy production of his firm that also made gear boxes etc for the motor vehicle industry was Aluvac, ALUminium VAzeilles Croissant (an associate). It is found on the first 'car' made in 1932, a promotional item in the shape of a spark plug. There is also a plane in polished mazac, marked 'ALUVAC' in a rectangle up inside the hollow fuselage. The model appears to be a hybrid, with the appearance of a twin-engine heavy bomber (span 185mm). It has a long cockpit with bubble behind and a large rounded tail – perhaps a demonstration piece to show the versatility of his machines. A factory, Etablissement Solivac, especially to demonstrate that the new pressure diecasting technology was suitable for the toy industry had been set up at Nanterre. In 1937, production was moved to Ivry-la-Bataille in Normandy when de Vazeilles decided to concentrate on toys and gave up the other sides of the business to associates.

The tradename Solido (*solide* in French means 'strong', 'reliable' or 'trustworthy') was not registered until 1934, though it had been used on the castings for some time. The 1935 catalogue stated that the latest new Solido was the Amphibie, a kit that would make a car, a boat or a plane. This was followed by a kit that made several types of plane. After the War, production restarted with this one and it was joined by a more complex set. Jean (Ferdinand's son) was responsible for the more realistic production from 1948. 1954 and 1955 saw the introduction of two supposedly more modern planes the 'Shooting Stars', the second of which had plastic wings. The company also had a dabble with balsa wood planes propelled by Jetex fuel and later with plastic kits. The main range of diecasts, in 1/150 and 1/300 scale, was released in 1955 and dropped in 1960. An attractive group of larger scale, brightly coloured helicopters was in production from 1978 to 1992. In May 1993, Solido and Majorette were both taken over by the Ideal Loisirs Group.

CONSTRUCTIONAL PLANES 1933–56/7

> 'From an aeroplane, you make a boat and of the boat a car; at the end of the sequence, the child puts an aeroplane back in the box!'
>
> *Le Temps* 1934 (translation)

In common with the rest of the Solido toys, this group were all assembled with hexagonal headed bolts. Spanners were supplied in the sets. The name 'Solido' is embossed up inside the fuselage but not on the other pieces. The parts were banded down onto a plain blue backing card with cotton tape. The boxes were also usually blue with a cream or yellow label with black and red printing covering the lid: 1933 – the lid features a boy kneeling; 1935 – two children; 1938 – a boy holding up a bus and a plane; 1939/40 – a boy astride a road. The built-up items were available separately and so were all the individual pieces. The prices quoted to clarify easily confused products are from the 1935 catalogue.

1945–c.1958

After the War the Avion M1, now fitted with black rubber wheels, was re-issued. It was not available in chrome. It was now said to make six 'avions de tourisme ou d'acrobaties' but there are no more parts in the kit than before. This plane was joined by two others, records of which occur as early as 1943 though production did not get going in earnest until 1949. One is described as Avion de chasse 'Loocked' or 'Lookeed' (sic) which looks like a cross between a twin-boom Lockheed P-38 and a Crusader; the other has a slim fuselage with multilight cockpit. Though given, internally, individual numbers, they were not available separately. The set is said to be able to make 12 different planes but it seems that the twin-boom plane could only produce two of these, one with wheels and one with floats, with all the others being permutations of the 2 tails, three engines and floats or wheels on the other. The combination of the two sets is said to make 18 planes. The boxes are blue or yellow with a silver label, with 'Solido' and other wording in red, in the centre of the lid.

1954–1958

The next plane used parts from the long-lived Avion 1. Called 'Shooting Star', it has a diecast fuselage resembling the Lockheed F-80 Shooting Star. The second used the same fuselage but has plastic 45deg swept wings making it more of a model of the Republic F-84F Thunderstreak, but no more attractive. There is a retractable nose wheel and undercarriage legs, straight on the first type and angled on the second to fold up out of sight under the wing. They are held together with the construction set hexagonal headed bolts. They are fitted with a mazac pilot painted black with a diecast helmet under a clear plastic canopy except in sets in which it carries Leduc 021. Approximately 1/72 scale.

SOLIDO MAQUETTE – DIECAST PLANES

1955 was the start of 'modern' toy production, fine, scale (*maquette* = scale model), diecast models replacing the crude but charming bolt together kit sets (above). Solido announced 12 aeroplane castings late in that year and spread the other 13 over the following four years but they could not have sold well because they were last in the 1960 catalogue but available in shops for some years after. The planes were said to represent 'Aviation Mondiale', World Aviation, four countries being represented, France, Britain, USA and USSR. The French selection included some obscure planes. Five of the group were also modelled at the same time by French and English Dinky.

CASTINGS — They were claimed to be 'incassables', unbreakable. The majority are single solid castings with orifices hollowed out and are light and very sturdy. The airliners and the Breguet Alizé are made up of two pieces. Most are marked 'Solido' in script and have the name of the plane in block capitals. The larger planes may have scale and 'Made in France' as well. This attribution was also added to some of the castings after the first issue eg Super Sabre and Baroudeur. Usually wire undercarriage legs were cast in. These were turned over at the ends after being fitted with small brass wheels. The airliners and the Breguet Alizé had sturdier undercarriages with dumb-bell wheels.

SCALE — They were stated to be 'rigoureusement à l'échelle', strictly to a scale of 1/150 with the three airliners in 1/300. The first claim is a little inaccurate. Some 1955 issues, Morane Saulnier, Super Cigale and the helicopters did not have the scale cast in, but the others had it under the wing. The rotors of the helicopters are virtually in scale with the machines.

COLOUR AND DECALS — Most are finished in a matt silver grey with blued cockpit covers but later production can be quite bright silver with no blueing. Metallic blue types have silver glazing. The colour is over the whole of the toy, wheels included. Decals are transfers. As the backing film of some of the decals yellows it tends to turn blue into green. There are very few variations in decoration, the majority of the models having a single colour/decal finish. The star-on-bar US transfer should be on the port wing but occasionally it is found incorrectly on the starboard.

BOXES — The larger models are packed individually in plain yellow square boxes with the description stamped on one end of the lid. The smaller ones, strung down with flat white paper tape, are packed in blue, some faded to grey, or yellow, boxes of six. From 1957, all boxes were yellow. The top has a silver label with, in red, 'Solido Maquette (in script) AVIONS DE COLLECTIONS MADE IN FRANCE'. There is a label on the end of the box to identify the contents. Sometimes a small square deep box with the planes stacked vertically separated by card was used. The flat set boxes are blue or yellow with a similar label on the lid.

CATALOGUES — Catalogues are scarce and the models were not allocated numbers in them. Once introduced, the planes remained in production until their last appearance in the 1959 catalogue. The 1960 catalogue which appeared in October has an airliner on the cover and is almost identical to the 1958 and 1959 catalogues but it omits the words 'Avions Miniatures de Collection'. The line drawings of the planes are merely sketches and some are misleading: the Sikorsky S.55 was issued with floats not wheels; the Super-Constellation did not have wingtip tanks. Some of the wingspans given in the 1955 catalogue are incorrect. A concertina-fold catalogue was packed in some of the boxes. A leaflet that is to be found in some 100 Series car boxes depicting a USAF X15 is advertising a plastic kit that was not released.

ACCESSORIES — The 1956 catalogue advertised a control tower, hangar and runway of which only the runway was released. It consists of two pieces of card glued together to form, when opened, an area 21x27cm with a runway printed diagonally across. It fitted inside a gift set box.

PROMOTIONALS — The Air France versions of the Caravelle were sold as toys, the other very scarce liveries, eight different airlines plus Sud-Aviation were promotional give-aways to passengers.

DIECAST PLANES 1955–60

Because Solido did not put catalogue numbers on models, boxes, or catalogues, this group are listed in alphabetical order. The numbers are from internal Solido records. Once introduced, the planes remained in production until their last appearance in the 1959 catalogue. Some wingspans given in the catalogues are slightly innacurate.

HELICOPTERS 1979–92

Sketches of Gazelle helicopters first appeared in the 1979 New Items catalogue. After the release of a Gazelle and an Alouette featured in the 1980/81 catalogue, castings in a variety of liveries were sporadically available. Liveries first shown in early catalogues, are also featured as 'New' later, e.g. the (Gazelle) Europ Assist 1980 and 1985. The Alouette III Gendarmerie was allocated three different numbers at different times. Several were in the catalogue for only one year and there are some short production promotional issues. The last catalogue to feature helicopters, 1992, also included four, marked 'New' but not released. There were, at times, quality problems such as missing small parts or decal sheets.

DECALS — Some examples have the decals already applied, others have an additional decal sheet.

BOXES — Bulky window boxes, 1980 in black, 1982 all-over blue, 1986 with a blue ray pattern, superceded in 1989 by ones decorated with white clouds on a blue sky with the word 'helicopters' in the shape of one. The boxes are not usually numbered. The helicopters are secured to the cardboard bases with large plastic discs held to the castings with a long screw.

Aérospatiale SA 319B Alouette — The model is 1/56 scale though it is marked 1/55 on the plastic tail piece. The other markings on the toy, 'Solido', 'Alouette 3', 'Made in France' are also confined to this piece. There are two good castings, the split being longitudinal, held together by two phillips screws.

Aérospatiale SA 431/342 Gazelle — The 1/56 scale model is constructed like the Alouette. The plastic tail plane is marked '1/55' and '2/79', the month and year of its design. The plastic under section carrying the skids is marked 'Solido', 'Made in France' and 'Gazelle'.

Aérospatiale AS 332 Super Puma — The construction is as before and the markings of this excellent 1/82 scale model are beneath the rotor blades and read: 'Solido Made in France 09/88' (design date) '1/80 Puma AS 332'.

CONSTRUCTIONAL PLANES 1933–39/40

M1 and 2 Amphibie (price Fr75) 1933–39
(M1 has plane built, M2 has car built)
Makes a car or boat or plane with the propeller fitting below the radiator.
Finished in various colours including chrome.

Plane from Amphibie (price Fr45)
Consists of seven pieces from the set plus wheels and bolts.

M100 Avion – four transformations (price Fr30) 1935
Makes:
1 High wing monoplane with undercarriage
2 High wing seaplane with underpan and floats
3 Biplane with undercarriage
4 Biplane with underpan and floats.
162mm with the chromed or lacquered propeller fitting at the top of the nose. Many minor casting variations.
Cast wheel centres with white tyres.
Fuselage: early in chrome, then light blue, cream, light grey, dark red, metallic colours: blue, brown, green, late in brown and green camouflage, with contrasting wings in the above plus a few other colours.
Re-issued post-war.

M100 High wing monoplane with undercarriage
(price Frs15)
Non-construction version of first type in Avion set above.

1945–c.1958

A1 Avion 1 1946
Re-issue of Avion Model 100 but with black rubber wheels.
Briefly black then red or blue with fawn/cream or silver wings.

142/3/4 Avion 2 1949
Slim fuselage plane with choice of two tails. Initially black then red, silver, light green, bronzed or white parts.

145 Avion Lookeed 1949
Red and silver.

A2 Set (coffret) 1949
Avion 2 and Lookeed in one box.

A3 Avion 3 1949
All three planes in one box.

1954-58

146A Avion V Shooting Star 1954
160mm
Straight metal wings from Avion 1.
Light blue, dark blue, light grey, dark grey. French roundels.

146B Avion V Shooting Star 1955–58
140mm
Swept plastic wings with tip tanks.
Single or two-tone light grey, silver, light blue, dark blue, dark grey, metallic blue.
(Also photographed in Jouets Solido, Azema in sets with 16 and 21 vehicles, in set with all three previous planes, in set with Avion 2 and Lookeed + wings from Avion 1)
French roundels.
Also available in sets with 1955–diecast planes.

DIECAST PLANES 1955–60

183 Aquilon (Aquillon on model) 1958
89mm. 1/143
Dark blue. French AF roundels. Individual box.

173 Baroudeur with launching trolley 1956
67mm. 1/142
With or without 'Made in France'.
Silver with dark green trolley (not wheels). French AF roundels. Individual box.

186 Breguet Alizé 1959
104mm. 1/150
Two castings: fuselage including tail; wings and underfuselage. Wire support below tail. Cream four-blade tinplate propeller.
Dark blue. French Navy decals (roundel with anchor superimposed) on wings, 'alizé' on nose, tail flash. Individual box.

176 Caravelle 1956
114mm. 1/300
Two castings: fuselage including tail; wings and underfuselage.
Painted dumb-bell wheels on nose strut, double on each main undercarriage strut.
Silver with white 'roof' area or light metallic blue and white. 'AIR FRANCE'. Silver with white promotionals: Air Algérie, Air Maroc, Alitalia, Finnair (thick or thin letters), SAS, Sud Aviation, Swissair (white cross on red tail), United, Varig (thick or thin letters). Individual boxes.

180 Convair XFY1 Vertical 1957
51mm. 1/165
Silver main casting with additional black propeller separator and nose cone with two black (some silver) tinplate three-blade propellers.
US star-on-bar on port wing, starboard wing blank, or with 'USAF' or with 'NAVY', incorrectly with star-on-bar.

185 Etendard IV 1959
64mm. 1/147
Dark blue. French Navy roundel – with anchor superimposed. Individual box.

179 Fairey Delta FD2 1957
53mm. 1/154
Silver. RAF roundels.

164 Fouga Magister C.M.170 1955
75mm without tip tanks replaced by 77mm with tip tanks, 1/157. Silver, with or without blued cockpit, all-over light blue, or light blue with dark blue cockpit and tip tanks. Large, later small, French AF roundels.

171 Hawker Hunter 1956
68mm. 1/148
Dark or light green on grey camouflage on upper surfaces.
RAF roundels.

174 Javelin 1956
104mm. 1/153
Light or dark green on light grey, dark green on dark grey camouflage on upper surfaces, also vague green on dark grey.
Blued canopy. RAF roundels on wings, some with small roundels on nose.

167 Leduc 021 1955
78mm. 1/152
Wire skids only (not separate wheels).
Silver usually with, sometimes without, blue band round nose. Also green.

170 MiG-15 1956
78mm length 1/147, span 1/138
Early not marked 'Made in France'.
White, white glazing. Russian stars on wings, some also on side of nose.

182 Morane Saulnier Paris 760 1957
67mm. 1/151
Silver. French AF roundels.

163 Mystère IVA 1955
73mm. 1/139
Early: not marked 'Made in France'.
Silver. French AF roundels.

169 Sikorsky S.55 Helicopter
(with floats, not wheels as catalogue) 1955
85mm long 1/153
Some marked 'Solido France' on right hand side of web between tail and rear cabin. Floats – a separate casting. Tinplate three-blade main, two-blade tail rotors. All-over silver or green. Also reported in grey-blue and dark blue. French AF roundels. Individual box.

Sikorsky S.55 Sanitaire (as above) 1956
All-over silver or white.
Red cross on red edged white square on port fuselage.

165 Skyray (Douglas F4D-1) 1955
65mm. 1/157
Silver, with or without blued cockpit. US star-on-bar on port wing. 1956 Dark blue. 'NAVY' on starboard, US star-on-bar on port wing.

177 Super-Cigale de tourisme 1956
62mm. 1/161
No casting markings. Transfer beneath port wing: 'Solido SUPER CIGALE'.
Blue, light blue, yellow, light yellow, orange-yellow including two-blade tinplate propeller with silver screen and cabin roof window.
Super-Cigale Sanitaire 1956
White. Red cross on red edged white square on starboard wing.

125 Super-Constellation 1956
151mm. 1/302
Two castings with fuselage split between the wings and the tail. Black dumb-bell wheels. Tinplate four-blade propellers. Silver or light metallic blue. US flag and 'TRANS WORLD AIRLINES' in red above blue windows above red line ending in 'TWA'. 'TWA' in red on wings. 1959 Raised cast windows. Silver blue with white top of fuselage, or silver with white or all silver blue. 'TWA' in red to rear of windows and on wings. Individual box.

184 Super-Mystère B2 1958
69mm. 1/140
Silver. French AF roundels. Early with long red arrow along fuselage.

186 Super-Sabre F100 (North American F-100D) 1955
72mm. 1/166
With or without indented nose intake. With or without 'Made in France'. Silver, with or without blued cockpit. US star-on-bar on port wing, 'USAF' on starboard.

172 Thunderjet (Republic F-84G) 1956
75mm. 1/148
Silver. US star-on-bar on port wing, with or without 'USAF' on starboard.

178 Trident 1956
49mm. 1/165
Marked 'France'. Silver. French roundels.

187 Tupolev Tu-104 1959
120mm. 1/285
Two castings: fuselage including tail; wings, engines and underfuselage. Dumb-bell wheels on formed tinplate brackets under wings. White. 'Aeroflot' in cyrillic letters in blue with blue windows over red line and (cyrillic registration of prototype) CCCP-H5400. Individual box.

166 Vautour 1955
100mm. 1/144
Silver with blued or silver cockpit. Small French roundels.

181 Vertol/Piasecki H.21 Helicopter 1957
105mm long. 1/152
Name, door and three windows cast on sides of casting.
Two black three-blade tinplate rotors.
181 A Vertol H-21 cast on.
181 B Piaseki (sic) H-21 cast on. Silver, screen, door and three cast windows blued, with or without two extra blued windows or green with screen, door and three cast windows silvered. French roundels on rear fuselage. Also seen with RAF roundels on Vertol version.

GIFT SETS

Two sets containing the larger scale early plane.

5 Aircraft
Shooting Star Swept Wing Fighter (diecast and plastic) without cockpit glazing and pilot but with Leduc 021, Fouga Magister without wingtip tanks, Mystère IV, Skyray in silver.

8 Aircraft
Shooting Star Swept Wing Fighter (diecast and plastic) as above with Leduc 021, Fouga Magister, Mystère IV, Sikorsky S-55, Skyray, Super Sabre, Vautour.

Two sets consisting only of 1/150 and 1/300 diecast planes.

5 Aircraft
Fairey Delta, Hawker Hunter, Sikorsky S-55, Super-Constellation, Trident.

9 Aircraft
Baradour, Caravelle, Javelin, Hawker Hunter, MiG-15, Super Cigale, Super-Constellation, Thunderjet, Trident.

Other sets may also exist.

HELICOPTERS 1979–92
The dates are introduction or reintroduction dates

381 Gazelle Helicopter
Shown as new in 1979. Catalogue shows it red and white with aerospatiale decal. See 3810.

381b Gazelle Gendarmerie
Shown as new in 1979. (See 3811)

3810 Gazelle Europ Assistance 1980 and 1985
175mm
Rigid black three-blade rotor. White. 'europ assistance' on boom in orange, orange tailfin decal.

3811 Gazelle Gendarmerie 1980
Dark blue. 'GENDARMERIE' in white on boom, white tailfin decal.

3814 Alouette III Securité Civile 1980 and 1985
170mm
Rigid black three-blade rotor, white plastic tail plane, rotor guard and rotor.
Red, blue glazing. Blue, white, red and yellow roundel.
Additional decals: 'SECURITE CIVILE', F-ZBAH (some catalogues F-ZBAG).

3817 Alouette III Air Secours 1986
White. 'AIR SECOURS INTERNATIONAL' on boom, logo on cabin.
Promotional issue in white box.

Alouette III Air Zermatt 1986
Red. 'AIR ZERMATT' HB-XDA – thick letters on decal.
1987 thin letters tampo. Promotional model.

Alouette III Rega 1987
Red. 'SCHWEIZERISCHE RETTUNGSFLUGWACHT, REGA, HB-XFM'.
Box with over-sticker.

3815 Gazelle lance missiles 1980 and 1985
Light coloured plastic clip on missile pods.
Khaki and white camouflage.
1988 Military green, clear glazing.

3816 Alouette III Gendarmerie 1985
Dark blue. 'GENDARMERIE' in white on boom.
See also 3819, 3827.

Alouette III Le Grand Raid 1985
White. 'LE CAP TERRE DE FEU'. Box with details of the TV game.

Alouette III Carabinieri 1986
Dark blue. 'CARABINIERI' on boom in white.
Issued for Italian market.

Alouette III Brest Marine 1987
Dark blue. '804 MARINE' on boom, roundel with anchor on rear cabin. Special box.

3819 Gazelle Gendarmerie 1986
Dark blue. 'GENDARMERIE' in white on boom.
(See also 3816, 3827) 'CARABINIERI'. 'POLIZIA'.

3820 Alouette III 1987
Number given to 3814 when in Coffret Montagne (Mountain Set).

3820 Alouette III Privé 1987
Black. Yellow to red stripes on cabin and boom.

3822 Gazelle Civile 1988
Yellow, clear glazing. 'PHI' in black on rear cockpit, black on fin with reg. nos. and 'Gazelle'

3823 Alouette III JBL Gendarmerie 1989
Dark blue, blue glazing. 'JBL GENDARMERIE' and roundel on rear cabin.

3823 Alouette III Liasons Aéroport 1991
White, blue glazing. Dark blue and green decal on cabin top.
Additional decals: green and blue line with 'F-BZAH LIASONS AEROPORTS'.

Alouette III OAMTC 1989
Yellow. Red cross, 'OAMTC', 'NOTRUF 144' on cabin, Christophorus OE.NOE on boom. Austrian market.

3824 Puma AS 332 militaire 1989
185mm
Military green, smoked glazing. 'armée de TERRE' on boom, roundel on doors.

3825 Puma AS 332 civile 1989
Red, clear glazing.
'SECURITE CIVILE' on stripe on fuselage.
1989: some models released without decals.
1992: 'SUPER PUMA AS 332' in white on door.

3827 Gazelle Gendarmerie 1991
Dark blue. 'GENDARMERIE' in white on boom.
(See also 3816, 3827)

In 1992 catalogue, but not issued.

3828 Cougaras AS 532
3829 Gazelle HOT
3830 Agusta A109 K2
3830 Agusta A109 CM

SETS

7015 Coffret Montagne (Mountain Set) 1986
Two vehicles (slight variations over the years) and 3820 Alouette 'Air Secours' white with yellow fin.

7028 Coffret Gendarmerie 1989
Two vehicles and Alouette III Gendarmerie

7033 Le Grand Raid 1985
Five vehicles and Alouette III, white, Le Cap Terre de Feu.

7035 Coffret Aéroport de Paris 1988
Three vehicles and 3823 Alouette Liasons Aéroports.

Germany

Gescha (GS), **Märklin**, **Schuco**, **Schuco Piccolo**, **Siku**

Germany is renowned for making very accurate models of planes, some of which were intended to be toys. Wiking, one of the best known ranges, making plastic recognition models, falls outside the scope of the book. Siku first issued a range in plastic which should also have been excluded but, because they are an excellent group of toys, they are listed at the end. When Schuco failed, their small range of toy planes was continued by Schabak who enlarged the production and marketed them as models. Thus Schabak is not included. NZG, who major on the production of model earthmoving equipment, made one plane in the 1980s, a lovely 1/100 scale model of a 1931 Lockheed Orion in red and white Swissair livery (138mm span). Again, this must be regarded as a model. Herpa, a new range, are also models.

GESCHA (GS) 1930s

The only known plane is marked 'D.R.G.M.' (Deutsches-Reichs-Gebranchs-Muster), indicating that the design had been registered, 'Made in Germany', and with the trademark, a difficult to decipher elongated 'gs'. The toy is a cap-bomb with a plunger in the nose connected to a striker with a thick spring between it and a bar across the fuselage. Behind the wings, the fuselage, decorated with a lightning flash, is open. It may have inspired the Crescent Comet Racer, which, though very similar, is not from the same die.

Comet Racer
98mm. Single casting – wheels housed in fairings, later cast in wheels. Two-blade tinplate propeller. Silver, some with red rudder.

MÄRKLIN 1939–40

Better known for their tinplate trains, Märklin also made several groups of diecast road vehicles, but only one plane, a Dornier Wal Seaplane.

5524 Hydravion
120mm. Silver

SCHUCO AND SCHUCO PICCOLO 1956–76

The name, Schuco, is derived from Schreyer Und Co. (Heinrich Mueller and Heinrich Schreyer) which was established in 1912 in Nurnberg, though Schreyer, a businessman, left the firm, not believing in Germany's ability to recover economically. Mueller, who had worked with Bing as a sample maker and technical designer, was joined by Adolf Kahn, a businessman, and made a group of ingenious mechanical tinplate cars and other toys in the 1930s. Mueller died in 1958, by which time diecast toys were being released. Schuco went bankrupt in 1976 after a massive fire and the dies for the diecast planes were taken over by Schabak. Some merely had their name amended but others were completely revamped. They continued the number series but removed the name Schuco from underneath the fuselages. Later production is marked Schabak. The Schabak marketing is aimed at the collector, many of the boxes being marked 'Sammel-Modelle' (Collector's Model), 'Sammelbox', or 'Souvenir-Modelle'. Whilst they are no doubt played with by children and are inexpensive, the Schabak range does not fall within the scope of this book. A casting of a Lufthansa Boeing 727 with the same dimensions as the Schuco but with panel and flap detail on the wings, packed in a grey Schuco-type box marked 'Lufthansa Europa Jet', was made by Lintoy in the 1970s, presumably around the time that Schabak took over the dies.

SCHUCO PICCOLO 1956–66

In the flimsy Piccolo catalogues, four one-piece diecast planes with heavy undercarriage legs, fitted with very large rubber tyred turned wheels, were illustrated with line drawings. They are marked under wings: starboard - 'Schuco', model number, 'Int. Pat. Pdg'; port - model name, 'Made in Western Germany'. The decals are transfers. The small red boxes are individual to each plane but have a drawing of all four on one side. The 1/200 scale models make no pretence to be anything other than toys.

SCHUCO MICRO-JET

The Piccolo planes were also released in a larger size, said to be 1/100 scale, fitted with a clockwork motor. Two castings were used with the split below the waistline. A knurled nob on the side controls the front wheel (black rubber tyre) steering. There is a lever to disengage the motor from the wheels. Black rubber shock absorbing noses were fitted to protect furniture. The grey rubber rear tyres are marked 'Schuco Cord'. The colours and (larger) decals are the same as Piccolo. As models they are rather ugly but as toys they have charm. The square boxes are either blue with Schuco repeated along a black band along the edge or are red and yellow with a blue band. They are decorated with a drawings of the planes with 'speed swirls'.

SCHUCO 1966–76

Despite being marked 'Piccolo', the Ju 52 is better regarded as being a pair with the Junkers F-13 bracketing the rest of the Schuco in age as the Ju 52 was the first to be produced and the F-13 was the last in 1976. They are both finely detailed two-piece castings with realistic corrugated ribbing, turned brass wheels and tinplate two-blade propellers. The 1930s Lufthansa livery was all-over silver, with black registration letters on transfers on the wings.

AIRLINERS c.1965–76

The first group of planes were numbered 784/. The one- or two-piece 1/600 scale diecastings with fixed undercarriages and dumb-bell wheels, were marked with plane name and catalogue number. All were shown in Lufthansa livery in the catalogue. A few of the early castings have 'LUFTHANSA' cast under the wing suggesting that they were perhaps initially made for the airline. They were all later given 335 numbers, which are found on the boxes but the castings were not re-engraved. Some of the catalogues are not dated but the 1966 issue used the figures 784/1 and /2, with 784/3 marked as new. 784/1 to 384/5 were renumbered 335 785 to 335 789.

Subsequently all the catalogue numbers are prefixed by 335. All have fixed undercarriages with dumb-bell wheels. All are marked 'Schuco', 'Made in Germany' and have the plane name and catalogue number on the lower surfaces. The castings are accurate, the finishes authentic and well applied. Very large transfers were used and each casting was usually painted a single colour. Thus a one-piece casting in a livery with a colour split at the cheat line would have the whole casting painted silver and all of the upper fuselage covered by a coloured transfer. Except where specified in the list the livery remains the same as the first one described. Very attractive models, all were still in the catalogue in the early 1970s, the last one 797 Iljushin IL-62 being released in 1974.

The boxes are finely presented, usually silver or white, showing the aircraft silhouette and type and the airline logo. Others boxes are printed in the airline's colours:

Alitalia – green
Pan-Am, Air France – blue
Czech – orange and red
KLM – light and dark blue
Swissair – red

SCHUCO PICCOLO 1956–66

780 Thunderjet, USA
53mm
Silver with blued canopy or red with silver.
Star-on-bar on port wing, 'Schuco' in trademark script on starboard, red on silver planes, gold on red.

781 Magister 170R, Frankreich
60mm. Finish as above

782 Super Sabre F100, USA
53mm. Finish as above

783 Douglas F4D-1, USA
45mm. Finish as above
Re-issued in the 1980s: heavy castings with the Schuco name removed, finished in silver with star-on-bar decals. No marking on the planes but the blue and white boxes are printed with 'Made in Germany' .

SCHUCO MICRO-JET

1030 Thunderjet
1031 Magister 170R
1032 Super Sabre F100 110mm
1033 Douglas F4D-1
Re-issued in 1987 by Nutz, the new castings do not fit together so well, and the previously rubber parts are now plastic. 1031 – red, 1030, 1032, 1033 – silver grey.

SCHUCO 1966–76

784 Junkers Ju 52
74mm. 1/403
Marked 'Schuco Piccolo'. 'D-A' on port 'DOM' on starboard wing. The box is numbered 335 784.

335 779 Junkers F13
70mm. 1/253
Marked 'Schuco'. D1 on both wings.
Small pale grey box.

AIRLINERS c.1965–76

784/1, 785 Boeing 737
46mm
Early: stub for front wheel, 'LUFTHANSA' cast under wing, decals: 'Lufthansa' only on white tailfin.
'Lufthansa', white upper fuselage, dark blue window line and tailfin, blue crane on yellow circle on tailfin.

784/2, 786 Boeing 727
60mm
Early: slim engines with holes for air intakes, 'LUFTHANSA' cast under wing, decals: 'Lufthansa' only on white tailfin.
'AIR FRANCE', dark blue window line, arrow head on tail.
'Condor', white upper fuselage, silver lower, wings, tailplane and lower half of engines, yellow upper engines and tail, dark blue window line.
'Lufthansa'. 'PAN AMERICAN', white upper fuselage, mid-blue cheat line, globe logo on tail.
'TAP', also found in bubble pack.

784/3, 787 Boeing 707
76mm
Early: 'LUFTHANSA' cast under wing, decals: 'Lufthansa' in bold lettering in centre of fuselage, white fin with 'Lufthansa', later blue fin with crane.
'Air France', arrow head on tail.
'Condor'. 'Lufthansa'. 'PAN AMERICAN'. 'TAP'.

784/4 788 Boeing 747
80mm. 1/750 (cat says 1/729).

Single casting. 'Condor'. 'KLM': blue upper fuselage. 'Swissair'. 'Lufthansa', some marked so on underside of casting. 'BOAC'.

784/5 789 Supersonic (Concorde)
54cm span, 115mm long. (cat says 1/587)
Plane name blanked out. 'AIR FRANCE', dark blue window line, arrow head on tail. 'BOAC'. 'Lufthansa'.
c.1976: 122mm long casting numbered 335 789, named 'Concorde', internal lines within flaps in Schuco box. Later Air France livery of blue, white and red lines. F-BVFA on tail.

790 DC8
78mm
'Alitalia'. 'KLM', white upper fuselage. 'KLM', blue upper fuselage in catalogue, dark blue window line with silver windows, thin white line below white tail.
'UTA'. 'Swissair'.

790 DC8-63 (stretched DC8)
78mm (fuselage length 93mm)
'KLM', light blue upper fuselage, registration letters PH-DTJ towards tail.
'Swissair', in blue over red window line, red tail top with white cross. (DC8 or DC8-62 on box.)

791 DC9-30
47mm
'Alitalia', silver with white tail, green fuselage stripe.
'KLM', white upper fuselage, also found in bubble pack
'KLM', blue upper fuselage, white engines and tail.
'Swissair'.

792 DC10
78mm
'Alitalia'. 'KLM', white upper fuselage, registration letters PH-DTJ. 'Lufthansa'. PAN AM. Swissair. UTA.

793 Boeing 747
100mm. Two castings.
Air France, red and blue lines on tail.
Alitalia. BOAC. Condor. KLM, white upper fuselage. KLM, blue upper fuselage. Lufthansa. 'Lufthansa Cargo' above cheat line. Olympic Airways. Pan Am, white upper casting, silver lower. 'PAN AM' in black with blue window line and world logo on tail. Swissair. TAP.
'VIASA' in orange either side of 'VENEZUELA' in blue above blue window line all on white upper, orange tailfin.

794 Lear Jet
53mm
Marked '25B' under body. White with yellow flash. Marked '36' under body. White black windows, orange flash. Also (one off?) gold plated, marked 'Lear-Jet 36', 'Made in Germany' under body.

795 Airbus A300B
76m
'AIR FRANCE' arrow head on tail. 'AIR FRANCE' red and blue lines on tail. Lufthansa.

796 Boeing 747 Freightliner
Appears to be catalogue number only as the plane used is 793.

797 Iljushin IL-62 issued 1974
73mm
Two castings: main fuselage and wings, tail and rear engines.
'CZECHOSLOVAK AIRLINES'. Silver. Orange lettering and window line with black cockpit windows on a white transfer for the whole of the upper fuselage, 'OK JET' on tail fin.

KLM Set 785
Four planes in square window box: DC8, DC9, DC10, Boeing 747.

SIKU 1985–present day

In 1965, Siku, D-5880 Ludenscheid, West Germany, substituted diecast for the plastic that they had used for aeroplanes and cars. (The 1/250 scale planes, being plastic, are not strictly within the scope of this book, but are of a similar style and quality to the diecasts covered and are therefore listed at the end of this section.) Thereafter, they produced high quality road vehicles, with interesting and varied transfers in 1/55 scale. Though, usually, excellent models, the range has always been produced as toys. The boxes, at first all card and later with windows, are a distinctive purple with pink, purple and yellow stripes, the colours lightening and becoming shaded over the years.

HELICOPTERS 1985 – PRESENT DAY

In 1985, the first helicopter of the Siku (later Siku Super Serie) was produced, claiming to be to the standard 1/55 scale. The make of the helicopters is not marked on the models (but is incorporated in some decals) or the packaging, though some technical details are given.

MBB BO105 (Messerschmitt-Bolkow-Blohm)

The scale of the model is 1/50, with the rotor slightly small at 1/55. The model, 170mm in overall length, consists of two main diecastings, one for each side, marked SIKU on the engine housing. Two diecast doors at the rear of the bulbous body open to reveal the plastic interior with a stretcher held in slots. The four blades of the main rotor, which fold two fore and two aft, two-bladed stabiliser and skids are usually grey plastic. The skids were fragile and were strengthened in 1988 by the addition of material along most of the top edge. The plastic tail plane is in the colour of the boom. The decals are stickers. 175mm long.

MBB/Kawasaki BK117

The 1/56 scale model is contructed as above but has no identification markings except for part numbers on the inside of the castings. The rotors are the same. It has large plastic floats and tail-fin. The decals are tampo printed. 175mm long.

AIRLINERS 1993 – PRESENT DAY

The new range of 1/500 scale airliners is accurate and features some of the latest versions. They consist of two castings (upper fuselage including tailplane and wings with under fuselage) and, innovatively, a coloured plastic tailfin. The castings are marked with 'Siku', the plane name, catalogue number and CE Eurologo. Black plastic wheel units. The paint is good quality and the tampo printing so clear that the plane names can be read. They were mainly not released in the liveries shown in the first catalogue. The planes are held secured in a preformed clear bubble and the packaging colours are the same as those for the helicopters.

SIKU CLUB 1990 – PRESENT DAY

'Matchbox' sized miniatures introduced in 1990. Cleanly cast, chunky die-castings, some not particularly accurate but attractive sturdy toys. Black plastic wheels and small parts. The A320 Airbus is a good two-piece casting with self-coloured plastic tailfin (see: Siku Airliners). Marked with 'SIKU' and catalogue number. Good paintwork and tampo printing. Bubble-packed.

PLASTIC SIKU 1/250 SCALE c.1960–63

1960 catalogue: 'SIKU-aero models are toys and educational aids of a uniform scale of 1:250. Design true to model, rolling metal wheels, rotating propellers and rotors etc. Distinctive marks of many airlines by coloured foils and hand painting'. The details below, including wingspan, are mostly (up to F27) taken from the 1960 catalogue.

HELICOPTERS 1985–PRESENT DAY

3719 Ford Cargo with Helicopter (MBB BO105) 1985
Yellow. 'ADAC' in black, red cross on fuselage.

2222/2231/2531 Polizei Helicopter (MBB BO105) 1986
White upper fuselage and boom, green lower, red doors.
Badge and 'POLIZEI' in white on lower fuselage, D-HNWE in
black on boom, red and green stripes on tail rotor mount.

2222 Fire Rescue Helicopter (MBB BO105) 1987
Yellow upper, white lower.
'METRO-DADE, FIRE-RESCUE' in red above and below green stripe
with badge on fuselage. 'AIR RESCUE ONE' in red on tail rotor
mount, one in white on green on pylon, one in yellow
underneath.

2224 Feuerwehr Helicopter (MBB BO105) 1990
Red. 'FEUERWEHR' in white on lower fuselage, D-STHN in
white on boom. 'BO 105' on white background on tail rotor
mount, red flash on tailfins.

2222 Rijkspolitie Helicopter (MBB BO105) 1993
Mid blue with dark blue doors.
Dark blue and white side sticker with 'RIJKSPOLITIE' and badge
in white on blue part. White band along tail with
PH-RPS registration. Made for Dutch market.

2228 ADAC Helicopter (BK117) 1993
Yellow. ADAC, D-HLTB on body, red cross on tail.

2614 Helicopter with floats, Katastrophenschutz
(BK117) 1993
Orange, with blue plastic floats, finned tail-plane.
KATASTROPHENSCHUTZ (lit: defence against disaster), D-HGSL
tampo'd in black.

2222 Polis Helicopter (MBB BO105) 1993
White. Blue and yellow stripe on lower fuselage broken by
'POLIS' in blue, coat of arms above. SE-HPD in blue on tail
boom, flag on pylon. Made for Swedish market.

2222 Sécurité Civil Helicopter (MBB BO105) 1993
Red. 'SECURITE CIVIL' in white, roundel on cabin DI on boom.
Made for French Market.

2224 Sussex Police Helicopter (MBB BO105) 1993
White with mid-blue doors. 'SUSSEX POLICE', chequers, bands,
tail in mid-blue, G-PASX in white. Made for UK market.

2224 Rega Helicopter (MBB BO105) 1993
Red. White oblong with winged cross Rega Schweizerische
Rettungsflugwacht. HB-XGT, white cross on tail. Made for
Swiss market.

AIRLINERS 1993–PRESENT DAY

1719 Boeing 767-200
96mm
White, grey under engines, yellow tail. 'Condor' in black.

1720 Lockheed TriStar L-1011-500
102mm
Red upper including tail with white window line, silver lower
and wings. LTU remains white on the tail.

1926 Boeing 747-400
130mm
White with light grey under, dark blue tail.
'Lufthansa' in blue, grey windows, yellow crane logo on tail.

1927 Airbus A340-200
124mm
White, grey under and engines, dark blue tail.
'Lufthansa' in blue with yellow logo on tail.

SIKU CLUB 1990–PRESENT DAY

0807 Helicopter 1990
White, green lower fuselage. 'POLIZEI' in green.

0831 Helicopter 1993
ADAC

0832 Helicopter 1993
FEUERWEHR

0817 Space Shuttle 1991
48mm. 'United States'

0830 Airbus 320 1993
70mm
White, grey under and engines, dark blue plastic tail.
'Lufthansa' with tail logo.

PLASTIC SIKU 1/250 SCALE c.1960–63

F1 Sud-Aviation Caravelle
137mm. (a and b as per Siku catalogue)
a Air France
b SAS (Scandinavian Airlines System)

F2 Vertol (Piasecki) YH-16A
94mm long.
a US Air Force

F3 Boeing 707 Intercontinental
173mm
a Pan American
b Sabena

F4 Lockheed L 1649 A Super-Star-Constellation
182mm
a Lufthansa
b Air France

F5 De Havilland Comet 4
139mm
a BOAC (British Overseas Airways Corp.)
b BEA (British European Airways)

F6 Dornier Do 27
48mm
a Sanitätsflugzeug – with wheels
b Schwimmerflugzeug – with floats

F7 Tupolew Tu 104
146mm
a Aero-Flot (Soviet-Union)

F8 Cessna 310
44mm
a Reiseflugzeug.
Later: Red Cross

F9 Douglas DC-7 Seven Seas
153mm
a Swissair
b KLM (Royal Dutch Airlines)

F10 F 100 Super Sabre
44mm
a US Air Force

F11 Lockheed F 104 Starfighter
27mm
a Bundeswehr
b US Air Force

F12 Convair 440 Metropolitan
127mm
a Lufthansa
b Alitalia (Linee Aeree Italiane)

F13 Convair B 58 Hustler
59mm
a US Air Force

F14 Sikorski S 58
80mm long
a Sabena

F15 Nord 2501 Noratlas
129mm
a Bundeswehr
b UAT (Union Aeromaritime de transport)

F16 Fokker F 27 Friendship
115mm
a Philippine Air Force
b Aer Lingus Teoranta (Ireland)

F17 Viscount 814
114mm
a Lufthansa
b TCA (Trans-Canada-Airlines)

F18 Lockheed L-188 Electra
123mm
a KLM (Royal Dutch Airlines)
b AA (American Airlines)

F19 Douglas DC-8
167mm
a Swissair
b United Air Lines Inc.

F20 Fairey Rotodyne
72mm long
a mit Werkskennzeichen

F21 Martin P 6 M-2 Seamaster
122mm
a US Navy

F22 Convair CV-880
146mm
a TWA (Trans World Airlines Inc.)
b Delta Airlines Inc.

F23 X-15 (Bell)
27mm
a US Air Force

F24 Segelflugzeug (glider)
68mm. Scheibe Zugvogel III

F25 Fiat G-91
34mm
a Bundeswehr
b Ital. Luftwaffe

F26 F 105 Thunderchief
43mm
a US Air Force

F27 Boeing B-52 Stratofortress
225mm
a US Air Force

F28 Lockheed U2
NASA

F29 Sikorsky Turbine Helicopter

F30 Lightning F1
RAF

F31 Mirage IIIA
French Air Force

F32 Breguet 1150 Atlantic
NATO

F32a WV-2 Warning Star (with radar saucer)
US Navy

F33 MiG 21
Soviet Air Force

F34 SAAB 35a
Swedish Air Force

In addition, a selection of airport buildings and vehicles, F200-F216, and a paper airport plan F217.

Greece
Pilaz, Polfi

PILAZ: The Sovereigns of the Sky

Variable quality castings, marked with Pilaz trademark, 'Made in Greece', the name of the plane and catalogue number. Plastic undercarriages with soft rubber wheels. The boxes are based on the Matchbox Skybuster window boxes and have four of possibly the entire range on the back. Decals are self-adhesive tape.

51A Concorde
61mm. Single casting.
Silver. 'Lufthansa' in blue and yellow or spurious Air France decals.

52A Tornado
70mm. Two castings.
Mid-metallic blue. USAF and star-on-bar or spurious Greek Air Force markings on wings and tailfin.

Boeing 747

Lockheed Lightning P-38
Blue

POLFI TOYS Mid 1980s

Small single castings marked 'Polfi Toys' with plastic wheels or skids, bubble-packed onto card. Decals are paper stickers.

Concorde
43mm. White, Air France stickers.

Bell 222 Helicopter
82mm long. Olive, Greek Air Force roundels.

Hong Kong and China

Bachmann (see Lintoy dies), **Benkson Pocket Money Toys**, **BiPlane**, **China Light Industrial Product** (see Road Tough), **Corgi** (see Lintoy dies), **Die-cast Miniature** (see Novelties), **DTC Super Wings** (see Super Wings), **Dynafighter** (Master Diecast metal), **Edocar** (see Road Tough), **Ertl** (see Lintoy dies), **Fast Lane** (see Dyna-Flites, USA), **Fast Wing** (see Playart Fast Wing), **Fighter Aircraft** (see Toyway), **Flight-of-a-Gun**, **Flyers** (see Lintoy dies and Road Champs Flyers, USA), **Freda**, **Home Toys**, **Imperial**, **Jet Fighters** (see Home Toys), **Lintoy**, **Lintoy dies**, **M and Mandarin**, **Mail Box Series** (see USA), **Manley** (see Road Tough), **Mini Dyna Fighter**, **Mini Fast Wing** (see Playart Fast Wing), **Miniplanes** (see Mandarin), **Mini-planes**, **Mini Prop Classics** (see Imperial), **Novelties**, **Playart Fast Wing**, **Playmakers** (see Miniplanes), **Racing Champions**, **Road Champ Flyers** (see Lintoy dies and USA), **Road Tough**, **SkyBirds** (see Racing Champions), **SkyTomica** (see Lintoy dies), **Sky Wings** (see Home Toys), **Soma**, **Steel Screamers** (see Imperial), **Super Wings**, **Tins' Toys Super Wings** (see Super Wings), **Tintoys**, **Tomica** (see Lintoy dies), **Toy Way** (see also Edison, Italy), **UDC**, **Victory Force** (see Imperial), **Wild Wings** (see Home Toys, Mandarin, Cragstan Wild Wings, USA), **Wintech** (see Racing Champions), **Wondrie Metal Products**, **Woolworths** (see Lintoy dies), **WT** (see Tintoys), **YDC** (see Lintoy dies), **Zee Toys** (see also USA), **Zylmex** (see USA)

Many unmarked castings and ones from unknown manufacturers were made in Hong Kong in the 1970s and 1980s. Some of the toys are 'rip-offs' of marked ranges. Making cheap moulds, as well as quality ones, was well within the technology that had developed. A model could be copied very poorly, using the rough dimensions and concept of the original, probably two-piece, toy to make a single casting, or quite well but without the identifying wording of the original. If a die broke or was not casting properly, it was just as likely that a previously produced good casting would be used as the master, rather than that the original drawing be consulted, for the pantographed die.

Some toys were produced for major toy manufacturers in other countries, for instance helicopters by Lintoy for Corgi. Some were made as independent ranges. Some were factored to anyone who wanted to market a particular range. e.g. Lintoy planes. Some were only boxed in sets. Some were packed in counter sales dispensers and sold loose, often in seaside novelty shops. As one moves down the list, the quality tends to diminish as do the manufacturers' markings.

By the mid-80s, production of similar items was moving to China's coastal economic zones near Hong Kong. Whole ranges moved, some of very good quality, such as Ertl, and others of lesser quality, such as Dyna-Flites and Mandarin. A whole variety of poor to good castings were made, some, such as a baby pink Shuttle (50mm) with speed wheels, being quite amusing. Other parts of the Far East were also tried, Singapore in particular making poor castings in the late Seventies, while Macau and Thailand were favoured by Matchbox. The same unmarked toy can be found decorated and packaged by several different marketers with different range names, often varying from country to country. These are grouped together as far as possible but, because the original manufacturer is not known, the name to which they are cross-referenced may have no special significance. New and re-issued ranges are contantly emerging but in 1994 the EC set quotas for the import of toys from China. These various uncertainties have made this section difficult to tabulate, but the information that is included is firm.

BENKSON POCKET MONEY TOYS Hong Kong

Diecast Fighter Planes: Small one- or two-piece castings marked with plane name, catalogue number and 'Made in Hong Kong' (obliterated on some). Bubble-packaging marked 'Hong Kong'. Brass dumb-bell wheels.

601 Sopwith Biplane
72mm. Metallic blue, Italian roundels.

602 R.E.8 Biplane
71mm. Red, British roundels.

603

604 Junkers J10
72mm. Silver, German roundels.

BIPLANE China c.1990

Diecast body and lower wing, plastic upper wing. The lower wing span varies between 60 and 70mm and the casting is marked with an abbreviated plane name and 'Made in China'.

601 P-12E Boeing – US
 S.E.5A – British
 JN-4D – US
 T-17 Boeing – US

DYNAFIGHTER China

Eight fighter planes with pull-back action in one box, cat. no. 3008. Marked 'Master Diecast Metal'. Quality poor. c.1990.

FLIGHT-OF-A-GUN
Hong Kong late 1980s

602: four fighters approx 100mm long, diecast uppers, plastic lowers, soft black plastic nosecones, that are fired across the floor by an orange plastic handgun on a key clip.

Phantom (metallic brown), SEPECAT Jaguar (silver), Northrop F-5E Tiger 2 (metallic blue), General Dynamics F-16A (metallic green).

FREDA China

Home Toys/Sky Wings Airliners were made from the early 1990s in China, available individually bubble-packed. There is no country of origin marked on the planes. The finish and tampo printing are as good as the originals. (See Home Toys for list.)

HOME TOYS Hong Kong

The logo uses the two words of the title in the shape of a car with the two Os as the wheels. The fighters are to a much larger scale than the airliners. Both have blank cartouches on the underneath of their fuselages and presumably were originated for different manufacturers. There is no manufacturer's name, but catalogue number and plane name are found on the underneath surfaces. The wheels are plastic, the main axle being made of thin wire for 'Fast free wheeling action'. The tampo printing of the reasonably accurate liveries ranges from excellent to poor. Available 1990/1. Originated after 1982 when the Boeing 767 was first used. c.1990 production moved to China. The castings were re-issued with some new liveries bubble packed as Freda.

Wild Wings or Sky Wings
The two-piece airliner castings are made to a size, the wingspan ranging from 85 to 90mm, with fairly accurate flaps and other details on their wing and tail upper surfaces. White upper fuselage and tailfin, silver lower fuselage, wings and tail plane. The airliners are packed in sets of five in a display box.

8811 Set of five of the following Airliners:

F801 Boeing 747 American, Singapore Airlines

F802 A300 Airbus Alitalia, Swissair

F003 Boeing 767 Lufthansa, United

F804 Douglas DC10 KLM, Japan Air Lines, Cathay Pacific

F805 Boeing 727 Delta, Air France

F806 Lockheed Tristar Northwest Orient, Cathay Pacific

Jet Fighters were bubble-packed individually onto card. The nose and lower fuselage, with integral missiles, are plastic. The fighters are a much larger scale than the airliners at 68 and 72mm.

F807 F-16
Light/dark green camouflage, USA.
Light/dark brown camouflage, USAF
Grey with red wings, USAF

F808 F-18 Hornet
Light/dark green camouflage, USA.
Light/dark brown camouflage, USAF
Grey with red and blue arrow display team markings

IMPERIAL DIE-CAST China

Packed for the USA, labelled 'Light Sound Action', the castings of Wondrie Metal Products have their grey plastic housing marked 'Made in China' and the missiles fitted with lights. Pressing down on the wheels activates the 'dual action fighter-bomber sounds' of firing missiles etc. and flashes exhaust or muzzle lights. The Space Shuttle makes blast-off sounds. Bubble-packed onto card backing numbered 771, 1989.

Scale given as 1/175
F-16 Fighter Gold and black camouflage
F-5A Freedom Black, star-on-bar, F-5A stickers
A-4F Skyhawk Silver, green, white and red roundels
F-4E Phantom II Olive and brown camouflage

Scale given as 1/370
Space Shuttle   'United States'

Imperial Die-cast Toy Corporation registered in Los Angeles, California in 1989 marketed Steel Screamers and Mini Prop Classics made in China. Clearly engraved, one-piece castings between 35 and 40mm long, bubble-packed onto card in sets. Easily recognisable attractive caricatures with good paintwork and tampo printing. Bubble-packed onto card numbered 8100C.

Mini Prop Classics
P-51 Mustang USA, P-38 Lightning USA, Corsair USA, Zero Japan, ME 109 Messerschmitt Germany.

Steel Screamers
Boeing 747 USA, F-19 Stealth USA, Concorde Air France, F-14A Tomcat, B1 Bomber USA, A-10 Thunderbolt 2 USA, F-15 Fighter USA, FA-18 Hornet USA, F-4E Phantom II USA, TU-26 Backfire USSR.

Victory Force
The military Steel Screamers are also used in bubble-packed sets consisting of a plane, a plastic boat and a road vehicle. No.7984.

LINTOY c.1970–1983

The name Lintoy derives from that of the proprietor of South Asia Industries (HK) Ltd and the South Asia Diecasting Co Ltd of Hong Kong, Peter Lin. They are best known for the range of planes that they marketed under the name Lintoy and sold to others to market under their names.

Presumably at the time that Schuco went out of business and the dies were taken over by Schabak, a Boeing 727 with the same dimensions as the Schuco and packed in a grey box marked 'Lufthansa Europa Jet' was made by Lintoy for Lufthansa. There are four castings: fuselage, wings, tail and engines. The upper and lower wing surfaces have panel and flap detail and the model is marked 'Boeing 727 Lintoy, Made in Hong Kong'. The bright dumb-bell wheels are as Schuco.

Lufthansa Europa Jet Boeing 727
60mm
Silver with dark blue tail engine and tail.
Transfer for white upper fuselage with blue windows, yellow disc with crane on tail.

LINTOY DIES Hong Kong, Singapore, China, 1970–90

Corgi, Bachmann, Ertl, Flyers, Lintoy, SkyTomica, Road Champ Flyers (see also USA), **Tomica** (see SkyTomica), **Woolworths** (see Flyers), **YDC** (see Flyers)

Most of the castings covered in this section were originally made in Hong Kong by Lintoy, but they are commonly found in Corgi packaging. The best documentation is in Corgi catalogues. Thus, though strictly, the section should start with Lintoy, it begins with the most accessible range, Corgi. At first all of the castings were marked 'LINTOY, Made in Hong Kong', plane name, and the quality was excellent. If they were subsequently made in Singapore, the country of origin was usually deleted. These castings are of lower quality and it seems that at least some of the dies were withdrawn from there and returned to Hong Kong. In the early 1980s they were available in South Asia. When they were issued as Flyers and made in China, the country of origin was removed as was the name Lintoy. Some of the castings changed over the years: see comparative table at the end of the section. They were at first packed in square clear-topped boxes, but most of the later ranges were bubble-packed. The issues are covered in approximate date, not alphabetical, order starting with the most prominent range, Corgi.

CORGI/LINTOY PLANES 1972–80

Corgi who had started making diecast cars in 1956 had no history of making planes, though the parent company, Mettoy, had produced many tinplate ones in preceding decades. But Dinky was marketing Big Planes, Matchbox was launching Skybusters and Corgi was tempted to join in. They were obviously rather wary of the sales potential of planes because they chose not to manufacture most of the models themselves. In this, they made a wise decision because sales were always rather disappointing.

CASTINGS   The main group of Corgi planes are castings made by Lintoy in Hong Kong. Once out of the packaging it is usually not possible to distinguish between a Lintoy marketed in the Corgi range and one which was sold under another brand name. The markings on the underfuselage are: 'LINTOY, Made in Hong Kong', plane name. Some of the mid-term ones were made in Singapore and had had 'Hong Kong' erased. The airliners usually consist of three excellent castings (though the Singapore versions are not to the same standard) with good flap detail: upper fuselage and tail; lower fuselage and tailplane; wings with part under-fuselage. Cockpit windows are pierced. As the dies wore, the casting of the cockpit windows became raggy, the two castings tend to 'gap' at the front and the engines distort as they are pushed onto the pylons. The two-piece casting of the others is usually split horizontally along the fuselage just above or below the wings. Some have 'working control surfaces', usually plastic wing flaps, which don't really enhance the toys. Other have moveable tail planes. The cast planes are joined by a round bar which is concealed between the upper and lower fuselage castings. When the toy is new there is just enough friction to enable the tail plane to be set in position.

WHEELS   The airliners and modern jets have undercarriages that are retractable and fitted with small metal dumb-bell wheels. Historic planes have larger wheels.

DECALS AND COLOURS   The decals are stickers, usually on clear plastic tape, that normally adhere well, though the glue on small decals tends to dry out and they fall off. There is an excellent hard, usually gloss, paint finish. All the planes except some of the airliners were issued in two colours for the whole of the catalogue life of the toys. The decoration is often exactly that found on those packaged as Lintoy and as Bachmann/Lintoy. Some castings, the Learjet, Lockheed TriStar, Douglas DC8 and DC9, did not appear in the catalogues and judging by the number of Canadian liveries, they may have been made made for the Canadian market. Canadian liveries are found on other airliners and there are special schemes on the Pipers. Many of the boxes have French wording.

DATES   When the range was first featured in the Corgi Catalogue in 1973, there were eight planes in all. The 1974 catalogue came out rather late in the year and has, marked as 'new', the Vickers Supermarine Spitfire in camouflaged finish only, cat. no. 1317, and four new airliners, including Concorde, which is marked 'SUPERSONIC JET'. This and the Spitfire which was also released in silver, cat. no. 1321, are scarce as Corgi promptly dropped the entire plane range. The catalogues are not a good guide: the liveries illustrated are not accurate; there are no aircraft in the 1975 catalogue which did not appear till midsummer; though some were released in 1978, they did not feature in the catalogue until 1979. None of the castings were issued again by Corgi until 1978. The 1979 catalogue shows new airliners and Concorde, a new casting in a larger scale made in Great Britain by Corgi. The three Lintoys were marked 'available UK only' but the restriction was removed in the 1980 catalogue. Then Corgi abandoned Lintoy planes.

The following statistics are from *The Great Book of Corgi*: In 1972, 'Each aircraft in the new 1300 series sold in approximately equal quantities' of about 30,000 in a poor trading year. The following year, when Corgi made the best profit before tax to date, the original batch that were released in 1972 sold from 18,000 to 24,000 per item and the 1973 additions from 25,000 to 47,000. Their popularity began to wane and in 1974, though the Boeing 747 casting sold 39,000, the rest only scored 9,000 to 26,000. In 1975, 'Aircraft had all but died'. No figures are given for sales between 1978 and 1980 when some of the airliners were re-introduced, according to the catalogue, mainly for the UK market. The dates in the list are taken from Corgi records.

BOXES   The packaging is standard Lintoy consisting of clear square rigid box tops with card bases representing a cloudy sky. The toys are held securely and well displayed. Initially, the planes were wired down to a thin stiff clear acetate sheet with copper wire which tends to damage the paint finish. Later, the planes were bubbled down onto the card. All the boxes are marked on the underneath 'Made by Lintoy in Hong Kong for the Mettoy Co. Ltd.' There are five types of printing on the yellow base of the box.

1 All text, providing technical specifications of the plane, copyright 1972.

2 Part text accompanied by blueprint side and plan views of the plane, copyright 1973.

3 Side and plan views only with captions in English and French, marked 'Made by Lintoy in Singapore . . .' with the address Kallang Basin, PO Box 668 Singapore 9133, copyright 1973. The card is cut so that it can protrude from the lid enabling the pack to be hung on a dispenser.

4 Part text, part blueprint, as 2. but marked 'Made by Lintoy in Singapore . . .' with that address, copyright 1975.

5 Side and plan views only with captions in English and French, the address of Lintoy in Hong Kong, PO Box 6526, Tsim Sha Tsui Post Office, copyright 1977, with the card cut enabling it to be hung on a dispenser.

Some issues can be found in boxes that considerably predate their release.

SCALES There is a wide discrepancy in scales as the castings have been made to fit the boxes.

ERRORS The name of the plane was sometimes prefixed with the country of origin of the decoration and Corgi made a mistake. The 'Danish' Saab 35X Draken has Swedish markings as well as being a Swedish plane. I have dropped the references to the country. There are some number inconsistencies as well. The Wardair Boeing 747 is found in boxes numbered 1315 and 1323; the CP Air in 1322 or 1323; an Air Canada in a box numbered 1326 or with the number blocked out. The P-51D Mustang and Me410 are said to have moveable control surfaces but, apart from a few early Mustangs, they do not. The Zero-Sen is incorrectly given the mark A6M5 on the casting: it is an A6M2. The Grumman is incorrectly referred to as the F-11A: it is an F11F-1 as marked on the casting.

The dates are taken from Corgi records.
Wingspans: (see table)
Unless a change is noted, the sticker information applies to all colour schemes.

1301 Piper Cherokee Arrow (moveable plastic flaps) 1972–74
All white. Dark blue sticker flashes on wings, registration N2864A in black on rear fuselage.
White plastic propeller, red interior or yellow upper fuselage and tail fin, white lower fuselage and wings. Black sticker triangles on nose and top of fuselage. Yellow propeller.

1302 Piper Navajo (moveable plastic flaps) 1972–75
Yellow upper fuselage and tail, white lower fuselage wing and tailplane. Registration N9219Y in black on rear fuselage, sticker band round engines matches upper fuselage colour.
Yellow plastic fold-down undercarriage, white or yellow propellers, interior as Cherokee; or red and white.
Later: maroon and white, or orange and white. White or yellow propellers.

1303 Lockheed F-104A Starfighter 1972–75
Silver, or dark green and dark sand semi-matt camouflage.
Luftwaffe iron crosses on wings and either side cockpit.

1304 MiG-21 P.F (moveable metal tailplane) 1972–75
High gloss silver, or high gloss dark blue.
Red and white star with hammer and sickle in centre on wings and tailfin, 57 on nose. Brown or black plastic missiles.

1305 Grumman F11F-1 Tiger (moveable metal tailplane) 1972–75
With small wing fillet on upper casting, thick bar on tailplane, or whole of wing on lower casting, thin bar on tailplane.
Silver, red plastic exhausts, or blue, yellow exhausts.
'Blue Angels', 'NAVY' on fuselage sides, 4 on tail, all in yellow, star in roundel on wings. Black plastic missiles.

1306 North American P-51D Mustang (with, later without, moveable plastic flaps) 1972–74
Vertical split in fuselage casting.
Silver, or mid grey with dark green camouflage.
71, star, 'US NAVY' on fuselage, star on wings.
Black plastic four blade propeller, bombs.

1307 Saab 35X Draken 1972–75
Silver, or semi-matt grey with dark green camouflage.
Swedish markings: three yellow crowns on a blue roundel with a yellow edge on wings and tailfin, crown and 9 on nose.
Black plastic missiles.

1308 BAC (or SEPECAT) Jaguar (moveable plastic flaps) 1972–74
Silver, silver flaps, red plastic air intakes;
or dark green with sand camouflage, dark green flaps, air intakes.
RAF roundels on wings and nose, flash and W8268 on tail fin.

1309 Sud Aviation Concorde 1973–74
White, with dark blue metal droop snoot.
'BOAC' in gold with 'Concorde' above on dark blue cheat line, registration on line G-BOAC at rear of fuselage and on port wing, Union Jack above doors, Speedbird on dark blue tail sticker.

1310 Boeing 707B 1973–75
No plane name on casting.
White upper fuselage and tailfin, silver lower fuselage and wing, 'AIR FRANCE' and 'BOEING 707B' in blue above blue window line, blue arrowhead on tail, black windows.

1311 Messerschmitt Me410 1973–75
Silver, or light grey with light brown camouflage.
F6 and K on rear fuselage, iron crosses on wings.
Black plastic three-blade propeller, nose cannon, machine guns.

1312 Boeing 727 1973–75
White upper fuselage and high tail, silver lower fuselage, wings and engines, Red window line with 'TWA' above, reg. N727TW in black, 'TWA' and stars and stripes on tail.
1973–75 White and silver as above, 'AIR CANADA' in black above red window line, red tail with white maple leaf.
Also: 'Made in Singapore'.

1313 Zero-Sen A6M2 incorrectly marked A6M5 1973–75
Silver, black cowl, or metallic green with silver under, black cowl.
Red sun emblems on wings and rear fuselage, V-103 in black on tail.
Black plastic three-blade propeller.

1315 Boeing 747 Jumbo 1974–75
Made in Hong Kong, later Singapore.
White upper fuselage and tailfin, silver lower fuselage, wings and tailplane.
'PANAM', N743PA in black above blue window line. Panam globe in blue and US flag on tail.
1974–75 White and silver as above. 'WARDAIR' in blue above blue line and windows, red flash along fuselage from leading edge of wing and up tail.
Also numbered 1323.
1978–80 White and silver as above.
'British airways' and line of windows in blue, part Union Jack on tail.
(See also 1322, 1323, 1326.)

1316 McDonnell Douglas F-4E Phantom II 1976–75
Silver, red plastic air intakes or dark green with sand camouflage, matt white undersurface, with black plastic intakes. Star-on-bar on wings, on fuselage at rear wing root joined by red line. Black plastic rockets.

1317 Lockheed TriStar 1978–80
White upper fuselage and tail, silver lower and wings.
'AIR CANADA' in black above red window line, red tail with white maple leaf.
Also: Made in Singapore.
1978–80 White and silver as above.
'AIR FRANCE', line and arrowhead on tail in blue.

1318 Douglas DC9 1978–80
White upper fuselage and tail fin, silver lower, wings.
'AIR CANADA' in black above red window line, red tailfin with white maple leaf.
1978-1980 White and silver as above.
Scandinavian.
Also: Made in Singapore.

1319 Douglas DC8 1978–80
Casting of Boeing 707 with radio probe on top of fin removed.
White upper fuselage, silver lower fuselage and wings.
'AIR CANADA' in black above red window line, red tailfin with white maple leaf.
Also: Made in Singapore.

1320 Vickers VC10 1978–80
White upper fuselage, dark blue lower, silver wings.
'British airways', red tailplane, part Union Jack on tail.
Made in Singapore as above but silver under fuselage.

1321 Vickers Supermarine Spitfire 1974–75
Catalogue: grey with dark green camouflage – not issued.
Sand with dark brown camouflage, or silver.
Also: Made in Singapore.
RAF roundel with thin yellow band on rear fuselage, red and blue roundel on wings, flash on tail. YT roundel 'L' on rear fuselage, red and blue roundel on wings, flash on tail.

1322 Boeing 747 1978–80
Silver, orange top of fuselage and tail outlined in red.
Canadian Pacific registration C-FCRA 'Empress of Asia'
Also numbered 1323. Also: Made in Singapore.

1323 Boeing 747 1978–80
Wardair. Number used also for CP Air 1322.
Also: Made in Singapore.

1324 Lear Jet 1978–80
Fold down door/stair.
White.
Made in Singapore (no country of origin on casting).
Green stripe with red edges on fuselage sides and wingtip tanks, red Canadian flag above green registration C-GPDZ.

1325 Douglas DC10 1978–80
White upper fuselage and tailplane, other castings silver.
'SWISSAIR' in blue above red window line, red tail fin with white cross.
Also seen with 'American' decals as below (incorrect paint scheme).
1978-1980 Silver. 'American' in red above blue, white and red line, 'AA' on tail.
Made in Singapore.

1326 Boeing 747 1978–80
White upper, silver lower.
'AIR CANADA' in black above red window line, red tail with white maple leaf.
Also made in Singapore with casting detail finishing at rear wing edge.
1978–80 'British airways' as 1315 above. Made in Singapore.

LINTOY

Quite apart from their own range of planes which they packed for sale by many companies across the world, Lintoy made helicopters for Corgi and additional castings for Ertl including Ertl 1513 Nasa Boeing 747 and Shuttle Enterprise as well as cars for Dinky. There is a DC10 Jetliner 90mm long (usual length 140mm). In the 1980s, many Lintoys with boxes printed in French, turned up in Canada. There are no catalogue numbers on the box, square with clear rigid top with the card liner marked 'LINTOY' or 'CIVIL AIRCRAFT' (some of which contains fighters). The card, yellow for the earlier issues, orange for later ones, had details of the plane printed on. Models marked 'LINTOY, Made in Hong Kong', name of plane (unless noted in the list).

Details are as Corgi unless noted below.
(See table at end of section for castings made in Singapore.)

3501 F-104A Starfighter As Corgi

3502 DB7 Boston Havoc
Olive drab with brown shading on upper surfaces or, olive drab with variable chocolate brown and sand camouflage on upper surfaces, blue on lower. TH and RAF roundel on fuselage. W8268 and flash or roundel on tailfin. Roundels on wings.

3503 P-47D Thunderbolt (with moveable plastic wing and tail flaps)
Fuselage castings split vertically, separate wing piece, no plane name on casting. Black plastic four-blade propeller, drop tanks and bomb. Matt paint with rough surface finish, dull grey with dark geen camouflage on upper surface. Star-on-bar stickers on wings and rear fuselage.
(Without moveable flaps) Fuselage casting split horizontally, with plane name on casting. Gloss olive green. Star-on-bar on wings, 'QIOC' in white on sides, 'Zombie' in yellow on engine cowl sides.

3504 North American P-51D Mustang
Red plastic propeller, black bombs.
Dark green with light green and brown camouflage, light blue under.
Stars in roundels on wings, 'US Navy star 71' on fuselage sides.

3505 Messerschmitt Me262
Solid heavy castings with separate jet engines. Black plastic bombs.
1 Smooth nose, straight trailing edge on tailplane, two-wheel retracting undercarriage with stub under tail.
2 Nostril nose, trailing edge of tailplane notched in centre, tricycle retracting undercarriage.
Colours:
1 Silver.
2 Light green on white camouflage on fuselage, dark green and very dark green on wings and tailplane.
Decals:
1 F6+K on fuselage and iron cross on wings (as Me410).
2 Iron cross on wing and with X on fuselage, swastika on tail.

3506 Boeing 707
White upper fuselage and tail, silver lower fuselage and wings.
'DELTA' in blue above blue window line with red stripe, triangle/arrow motif on stripe and tail, or 'AIR FRANCE' as Corgi, or 'SOUTH AFRICAN AIRWAYS/SUID AFRIKAANSE LUGDIENS', orange tail.

3507 Saab 35X Draken
Silver or rough finish paint dull grey with dark geen camouflage on upper surface.

3508 MiG-21 PF As Corgi.

3509 Messerschmitt Me410
White with green and black camouflage on upper surfaces, F6+WK on rear fuselage, iron crosses on wings.

3510 BAC (or SEPECAT) Jaguar As Corgi

3511 Grumman F11F-1 Tiger As Corgi

3512 Douglas DC8
'UNITED', N2073U

3513 De Havilland DH 88 Comet Racer
Dark metallic blue. White plastic moveable flap section, white two-blade propeller, clear canopy and nose. Dark blue wing sticker edged in white. Registration G-A CSS. Incorrect livery for registration.

3514 Piper Cherokee Arrow
Yellow – as Corgi

3515 Piper Navajo
Maroon and white, or orange and white.

3519 Zero-Sen A6M2 (A6M5) As Corgi
Information on back of box is correct for A6M2.

3520 Gates Lear Jet As Corgi

3571 Boeing 747
Blue and silver, KLM, registration PH-BUJ.
White and silver, 'JAPAN AIRLINES, JA 8102' on wing, crane on tail, or
'Pan American'. 'South African Airways'.

3572 Concorde
White with light blue window line.
'British airways', representation of part Union Jack on tail, or white with light and dark blue line.
'EASTERN' in dark blue, or white upper, silver lower.
'JAPAN AIR LINES' in blue above red and blue line, JA8041 on wings, 'JAL' on tail.

3573 Lockheed TriStar
White upper, silver lower.
'AIR FRANCE', arrow on tail as Corgi.

3574 Boeing 727
Blue upper, sea green lower, silver wings, fuselage, engines, tail plane.
'BRANIFF INTERNATIONAL' and window line in white. 'BI' and green flash on tail pylon.
'South African Airways'.

3575 Douglas DC9
'Air Canada', 'Swissair', 'TWA', 'Eastern'.
Some in bubble packs.

3576 Douglas DC10
White fuselage, silver wings. 'UNITED', 'AIR FRANCE'.

3577 McDonnell Douglas F-4E Phantom II As Corgi

3578 Supermarine Spitfire MkII
Sand with dark green camouflage, matt white under.
YT roundel L on fuselage and other stickers as Corgi.

3579 Vickers VC10
'British airways'

Set contains: 747, 727, 707 in South African Airways livery, the box is decorated with the emblems of United, JAL, Lufthansa, American Airlines.

SKYTOMICA/LINTOY 1973–78

Castings, marked 'LINTOY, Made in Hong Kong', plane name, were issued in Japan as SkyTomica at the same time as they were being sold by Corgi. The castings are the same apart from minor differences on the engine pods. Tomica also used 'Tomy' as a trade name. The planes rest on a preformed undertray within the bubble-packaging. Some of the airliners were decorated with Japanese liveries (otherwise see Corgi and Lintoy colours). SuperWings, made by Tomica in a larger scale were introduced in 1978 (see Japan – Tomica).

1 Starfighter F-104A 1973–77

2 Boston Havoc 1973–77

3 P-47D Thunderbolt 1973–77

4 P-51D Mustang 1973–77

5 Boeing 707 1973–78

6 Concorde 1973–78 'British airways'

7 Saab 35X Draken 1973–77

8 MiG-21 PF 1973–77

9 Messerschmitt Me410 1973–77

10 Jaguar 1973–77

11 Douglas DC8 1973–78
White upper, silver lower.
Japan Airlines: red sun, 'JAL', one in blue on port wing, JA 8041 and sun on starboard.

12 Boeing 747 Jumbo 1973–78

13 Zero-Sen A6M2 (A6M5) 1974–77

14 Phantom II 1974–77

15 Lockheed TriStar 1974–78
White upper fuselage, silver lower and wings.
Blue windows and stripe along top of fuselage, tail engine and tail.
'ALL NIPPON AIRWAYS' and three Japanese characters in black on white of fuselage, company logo on tail on tail, JA 8501 in black on port wing, orange sun on starboard.

16 Lear Jet 1974–77

17 Douglas DC9 1974–78

18 Grumman F11F-1 1974–77

Gift Set 1977
Five small airport vehicles with Lockheed TriStar All Nippon Airways.

Gift Set 1977–78
The same five small airport vehicles with Lockheed TriStar All Nippon Airways and Boeing 747.

BACHMANN/LINTOY 1972–75

Bachmann Bros Inc of Philadelphia, better known for their 'Mini Planes', excellently detailed small plastic planes, marketed 22 of the Lintoy range. The packaging, an adaptation of the square clear plastic box which incorporated a header card is marked 'BACHMANN/LINTOY SUPER METAL Mini-Planes' and is the only range to acknowledge Lintoy so openly. The underneath of the packaging carries a 'blueprint' and details of the plane. The decoration is as Corgi unless noted. The full catalogue number has the format 3501:200, but the boxes carry the last two digits only. They were made in Hong Kong, or, with cruder engine pods, in Singapore.

All airliners, except Concorde had white upper casting and silver lower.

01 Starfighter F-104A
Military green and light blue camouflage.

02 Boston Havoc
Military green and light blue camouflage.

03 P-47D Thunderbolt
Olive and grey.

04 P-51D Mustang
Camouflaged and blue.

05 Messerschmitt Me262 (nostril nose)
Dark green, light green over white camouflage as Lintoy.

06 Boeing 707 'TWA'

07 Saab 35X Draken
Smooth satin grey and green camouflage.

08 MiG-21 P.F. Silver

09 Messerschmitt Me410
Military green and white.

10 Jaguar
Brown and green camouflage as Corgi.

11 Grumman F11F-1 Royal blue

12 Douglas DC8 – casting of **3506 Boeing 707** 'United'

13 Comet Racer Dark blue

14 Piper Cherokee
Yellow upper casting, white lower.

15 Piper Navajo
Yellow upper casting, white lower.

71 Boeing 747 'Pan Am' as Corgi.

72 Concorde
White, 'British airways', as Lintoy.

73 Lockheed TriStar
'Delta' or 'AIR FRANCE'.

74 Boeing 727 'TWA' as Corgi

75 Douglas DC9 'TWA'

76 Douglas DC10 'AIR FRANCE'

77 Phantom II
Camouflaged

ERTL/LINTOY c.1975–79 and c.1981–84

Ertl packed 18 of the Lintoy castings, marked Lintoy etc, as before and made first in Hong Kong and later in Singapore, in three series, Commercial, Military and World War II. They were first advertised on the packaging, an oblong card with the bubble in the shape of the plane, as 'Planes of the World' and then 'Airplanes'. The back of the card lists others in the range and gives details of the plane. The casting quality is not so fine in later production. The decals which are self-adhesive tape with a clear background differ slightly over the years. All three assortments were last listed, but not pictured, in the 1984 catalogue. Decoration as Corgi and Lintoy unless noted below.

All airliners, except where noted have white upper castings, and silver, later metallic silver, lower castings.

1510 COMMERCIAL AIRLINE ASSORTMENT

1476 Boeing 707
DC8 casting – no radio probe. Silver, 'American'
1477 Douglas DC10 'United', 'AIR FRANCE'
1478 Boeing 747 'Pan Am'
1479 Lockheed TriStar L-1011 'TRANS WORLD', 'AIR FRANCE'
1480 Douglas DC9 'Eastern'
1481 Boeing 727
Two-tone blue, 'Braniff International'

1511 MILITARY PLANE ASSORTMENT

Jaguar
Phantom II F-4E
1488 Grumman F11F-1 'Blue Angels'
1489 Starfighter F-104A
Light blue and olive camouflage, crosses and JA+204 on sides.
1490 Saab 35X Draken
1491 MiG-21 PF

1512 WORLD WAR II ASSORTMENT

P-47D Thunderbolt
Boston Havoc
P-51D Mustang
Spitfire MkII
Messerschmitt Me262
Zero-Sen A6M2 (A6M5)

Lintoy modified their 747 casting which became Ertl 1513 Nasa Boeing 747 and Shuttle Enterprise (see Ertl).

FLYERS – China
ROAD CHAMPS FLYERS – USA
1980–? /1988–present day

Most of the castings began as standard Lintoy ones, but are of lower quality and the words 'Lintoy' and 'Made in Hong Kong' have been removed from under wing and replaced by 'Made in China' paper stickers. The retracting undercarriage and nose wheels are made in black plastic as are the other plastic parts. The often poor quality colour schemes are simplified and the decals are stickers. Bubble-packed with part of range on the back of the pack. Road Champs Inc., Harrison, New Jersey, USA hold the copyright from 1988 as indicated on backing card. These are better quality marked with 'Road Champs, Made in China' and part of the plane name. The undercarriages are fixed and there is more variety in the decoration schemes. In about 1991, Road Champs dropped some of the old castings and new ones were introduced.

FLYERS/LINTOY

Decoration simplified Lintoy or Corgi unless listed.
Livery also in Woolworths (USA) packaging marked (W) in the tables.
Also packaged for YDC, York, Penn 17402 marked (YDC) in the tables.
Also, later, spurious liveries (see Road Champs Flyers)

6201 COMMERCIAL AIRCRAFT

Picture of airport on backing card.

Douglas DC8 – casting of Boeing 707 Air Canada (YDC).
Boeing 707 (new wing with integral engines, eventually all new die) Pan Am (YDC), Delta (W)
Douglas DC9 Swissair (YDC)
Douglas DC10 United (YDC, (W), American
Boeing 747 Pan Am (YDC), United (W)
Boeing 727 Swissair (YDC), TWA, Pan Am (W)

6202 WWII FIGHTERS

Picture of dog fight on backing card.

P-47D Thunderbolt
Not Lintoy die (see Road Champs Flyers in the USA section).

Messerschmitt Me410
Dark green, white upper fuselage.
White on grey iron crosses, black on grey swastika.

MkII Spitfire Fighter
Dark green. YT roundel I on fuselage.

Zero Fighter
Olive drab. Orange, white rising sun roundels.

DB7 Boston Havoc
Green and sand camouflage.

P-51D Mustang Fighter
US Navy Star-on-bar on fuselage, star on wings on card.

6203/6203A COMBAT JETS ('A' indicates colour change).

Three planes in formation on backing card.

F104 Starfighter
Silver, JA iron cross 2DA on fuselage, iron cross on wings in blue and white on grey.

F-4 Phantom
Green and sand camouflage. Star-on-bar on wings and rear fuselage with red fuselage stripe. (W).

MiG-21
72mm – not the Lintoy die.
Metallic light blue. Red star edged with yellow on wings. (W).

Messerschmitt Me262 (with nostrils)
Shades of green with shades of sand upper fuselage.
White on grey iron cross on wings, ditto with red 'X' on fuselage.

F104 Starfighter   US livery? (W).

BAC Jaguar
Green with sand camouflage. RAF roundels on wings, flash on tail. (W).

Grumman G-11A Tiger
Metallic light blue. Star-on-bar on wings.

ROAD CHAMPS FLYERS

Marked 'Road Champs' under fuselage or wing. Red or blue backing card marked 'Copyright 1988'. For full details of the Airliners, WWII Fighters and Combat Jets which are not Lintoy castings see Road Champs Flyers in the USA section. The P-47D Thunderbolt is from the later Lintoy die. A special packaging was produced for Woolworths.

6201 AIRLINERS
White upper casting, metallised silver lower.

Boeing 747   United, Pan Am

Douglas DC9   Delta, TWA, Swissair

Airbus A310 (not Lintoy)   Eastern

Boeing 727   Continental, TWA, Peoplexpress, Swissair

Douglas DC10   American, United

Boeing 707 (all new die)   Delta, Air Canada, Pan Am

Douglas DC8 (Boeing 707 die)   Air Canada

Comparative table – Lintoy, Bachmann, Corgi, Ertl, Flyers, Road Champs, Skytomica

Airbus A310 (not Lintoy), Road Champs Flyers

Boeing 707, Bachmann   113mm 1/384
Boeing 707B, Corgi
Boeing 707, Ertl
Boeing 707, Flyers–new wing with integral engines, eventually all new die
Boeing 707, Lintoy
Boeing 707 (all new die), Road Champs Flyers
Boeing 707, SkyTomica

Boeing 727, Bachmann   99mm 1/332
Boeing 727, Corgi
Boeing 727, Ertl
Boeing 727, Flyers
Boeing 727, Lintoy – some made in Singapore
Boeing 727, Road Champs Flyers

Boeing 747, Bachmann   130mm 1/458
Boeing 747, Corgi
Boeing 747, Ertl – also with extra tail fences and supports for Space Shuttle.
Boeing 747, Flyers
Boeing 747, Lintoy – some made in Singapore
Boeing 747, Road Champs Flyers
Boeing 747, SkyTomica

Boston Havoc, Bachmann   132mm 1/141
Boston Havoc, Ertl
Boston Havoc, Flyers
Boston Havoc, Lintoy
Boston Havoc, SkyTomica

Comet Racer, Bachmann   125mm 1/107
Comet Racer, Lintoy

Concorde, Bachmann   73mm span 1/350, length 1/393
Concorde, Corgi
Concorde, Lintoy
Concorde, SkyTomica

Douglas DC8, Bachmann – used Boeing 707 die (see above)
Douglas DC8, Corgi   118mm 1/393
Douglas DC8, Flyers
Douglas DC8, Lintoy
Douglas DC8 (Boeing 707 all new die), Road Champs Flyers
Douglas DC8, SkyTomica

Douglas DC9, Bachmann   102mm 1/280
Douglas DC9, Corgi
Douglas DC9, Ertl
Douglas DC9, Flyers
Douglas DC9, Lintoy – some made in Singapore
Douglas DC9, Road Champs Flyers
Douglas DC9, SkyTomica

Douglas DC10, Bachmann   114mm if DC10-10 1/415, if DC10-30 1/442
Douglas DC10, Corgi
Douglas DC10, Ertl

Douglas DC10, Flyers
Douglas DC10, Lintoy – some made in Singapore
Douglas DC10, Road Champs Flyers

Grumman F11F-1, Bachmann 99mm 1/97
Grumman F11F-1, Corgi
Grumman F11F-1, Ertl
Grumman F11F-1, Flyers
Grumman F11F-1, Lintoy
Die 1: Has upper fuselage with slight wing fillet incorporated. One front rivet. Thick bar between tail and fin.
Die 2: Modification of 1. Die has whole of wing on lower casting giving neater fit. Rivetted nose and tail. Thin bar between tail and fin.
Grumman F11F-1, SkyTomica

Jaguar, Bachmann 80mm 1/106
Jaguar, Corgi
Jaguar, Ertl
Jaguar, Flyers – die has two extra rivets
Jaguar, Lintoy
Jaguar, SkyTomica

Lear Jet, Corgi 115mm 1/104
Lear Jet, Lintoy – made in Singapore
Lear Jet, SkyTomica

Lockheed TriStar, Bachmann 117mm 1/411
Lockheed TriStar, Corgi
Lockheed TriStar, Ertl
Lockheed TriStar, Lintoy – some made in Singapore
Lockheed TriStar, SkyTomica

Messerschmitt Me262, Bachmann 132mm 1/95
Messerschmitt Me262, Ertl – some made in Singapore
Messerschmitt Me262, Flyers
Messerschmitt Me262, Lintoy
Die 1: Tailplane rear edge straight, no nosewheel.
Die 2: Tailplane rear edge notched at fuselage. Nostrils on nose. Tricycle undercarriage. Missiles to rear.

Messerschmitt Me410, Bachmann 135mm 1/121
Messerschmitt Me410, Corgi
Messerschmitt Me410, Flyers
Messerschmitt Me410, Lintoy – some made in Singapore
Messerschmitt Me410, SkyTomica

MiG-21 (not the Lintoy die), Flyers
MiG-21 P.F., Bachmann 69mm 1/110
MiG-21 P.F., Corgi
MiG-21 P.F., Ertl
MiG-21 P.F., Lintoy
MiG-21 P.F., SkyTomica

Nasa Boeing 747 and Shuttle Enterprise, Ertl

P-47D Thunderbolt, Bachmann 126mm 1/114
P-47D Thunderbolt, Ertl – some made in Singapore
P-47D Thunderbolt (fuselage with horizontal split), Flyers
P-47D Thunderbolt, Lintoy – fuselage with vertical split
P-47D Thunderbolt (casting as Flyers), Road Champs Flyers
P-47D Thunderbolt, SkyTomica

P-51D Mustang, Bachmann 133mm 1/85
P-51D Mustang, Corgi – early with moveable plastic flaps
P-51D Mustang, Ertl – some made in Singapore
P-51D Mustang, Flyers
P-51D Mustang, Lintoy
P-51D Mustang, SkyTomica

Phantom II, Bachmann 84mm 1/139
Phantom II, Corgi
Phantom II, Ertl
Phantom II, Flyers – detail fitting changes

Phantom II, Lintoy
Phantom II, SkyTomica

Piper Cherokee, Bachmann 131mm 1/70
Piper Cherokee, Corgi
Piper Cherokee, Lintoy

Piper Navajo, Bachmann 150mm 1/83
Piper Navajo, Corgi
Piper Navajo, Lintoy

Saab 35X Draken, Bachmann 92mm 1/102
Saab 35X Draken, Corgi
Saab 35X Draken, Ertl
Saab 35X Draken, Lintoy – different missile fin lengths
Saab 35X Draken, SkyTomica

Spitfire, Corgi 136mm 1/82
Spitfire, Ertl
Spitfire, Flyers
Spitfire, Lintoy – some made in Singapore

Starfighter F-104A, Bachmann 63mm span 1/106, length 1/124
Starfighter F-104A, Corgi
Starfighter F-104A, Ertl –- some made in Singapore
Starfighter F-104A, Flyers – extra rivet
Starfighter F-104A, Lintoy – canopy clear or blue
Starfighter F-104A, SkyTomica

Vickers VC10, Corgi 122mm 1/356
Vickers VC10, Lintoy – some made in Singapore

Zero-Sen A6M2 (A6M5), Corgi 133mm 1/75
Zero-Sen A6M2 (A6M5), Ertl
Zero-Sen A6M2 (A6M5), Flyers
Zero-Sen A6M2 (A6M5), Lintoy
Zero-Sen A6M2 (A6M5), SkyTomica

M & MANDARIN 1970s and 1980s

M – Mandarin Miniplanes, Hong Kong

Models marked with 'M' in a circle. Probably an early bubble-packaging announces three groups (prefix AA, BB, DD) as 'Gold medal collector series' with 'Permanent landing carriage'. There is no country of origin on the packaging or on the castings, so are most likely to be from Hong Kong some time before 1980. The castings which fit the packing are of average quality. The decals are stickers. Small parts are usually black plastic and missiles are chromed.

Mandarin Industrial Corporation Pte Ltd, Singapore

Bubble-packaging marked 'Wild Wings' on the face lists seven groups on the reverse, numbered 1101, 1102 etc.

Despite the similarity between the larger scale Mandarin products and Cragstan, and the shared use of the name Wild Wings, the two ranges do not share the same dies. Mandarin has one-piece solid fuselages, not two-piece hollow construction. The wing stagger and detail lines differ considerably between the two manufacturers. The quality of Mandarin is well below that of Cragstan.

AA-101 AND 1101

Fokker E 111
88mm
Mid green/black camouflage, iron cross black on white squares on wings, fuselage, tailfin.

Albatros D111
Red, iron cross cut outs on wings and fusealge sides and on white on tail fin.

Nieuport 17
89mm
Grey, blue chevron on upper wing, '74' and shooting star on fuselage sides.

Sopwith Camel
92mm
Sand. Large RAF roundels on wings, fuselage, tail flash, red V on wings.

BB-202 AND 1103

Junkers JU-8
Sand. Swastika on tail, F2+K on fuselage, black and white cross on wings.

North American Mitchell
92mm
Sand and muddy green. RAF roundels on wings and fuselage, flashes on tail fins.

Lightning P-38

Mitsubishi 'Betty'
94mm
Olive green. Sun roundels on wings, fuselage, yellow flash along leading edges of wings.

DD-404 AND 1102

Mirage 4A
46mm
Dark green with darker green camouflage. French roundels on wings and fuselage, flash on tail.

Thunderchief F-105
45mm
Light sand with brown camouflage. Star-on-bar on port wing and fuselage, USAF starboard.

3 Phantom F-41C (actually F-4K)
60mm
Grey with green camouflage. RAF roundels on wings, fuselage and tail.

MiG-21C
44mm
White. Red stars on wings.

1104

B-29 Superfortress
Lancaster Mk 1
Focke-Wulf FW200
Nakajima G8N1 'Renzen'

1105

Boeing 747
Boeing 727
Vickers VC-10
Douglas DC-10

1106

Cobra Copter
Alouette
Jolly Green Giant
AH-1G Bell Huey Cobra

1107

Supersonic Concorde
Jumbo Airbus
Boeing 737
Boeing 707

M

A similar, larger range of fairly good, two-piece castings. Black plastic small parts or tinplate wing struts. Plastic piece between wheel struts into which axles plug. Similar to Cragstan. The name 'Wheeler' appears on some packaging. Made in Hong Kong and Singapore.

Black plastic small parts. Heavy casting, marked 'M' in circle, name of plane, model number, 'Made in Hong Kong'. Paper sticker decals, some self-adhesive tape.

In around 1990 came the Imperial Toy Company Shuttle whose cast upper was fitted with a black plastic housing, incorporating exhausts and nose wheel support, for the pull back/let go motor. The underside marked 'W.22 1/370 Space Shuttle (Pull Back) Made in China'. Bubble-packed onto card.

A-01 Sopwith Triplane
115mm
Cream with green camouflage. 'BLACK MARIA'.

A-02 Fokker DR1
Red

A-03 Forch CR-42
107mm
Yellow. 'SWEDISH AIR'

A-04 Roland C-11 Biplane
105mm
Dark green, orange upper surface of tail plane.

A-06 SE-5 Scout
105mm
Light grey.

A-07 Sopwith Camel
115mm
Cream with brown camouflage. RAF roundels, red V on wings.

A-08 Fokker F-7
106mm
White. Black on white iron crosses on upper and lower wings, black band on rear fuselage.

B-09 PLZ P-11c (Polish)
Yellow.

B-11 Grumman F8-F2 Bearcat

B-12 Junkers Ju-87D Stuka
Green.

B-14 Zero
Grey.

B-15 Spitfire Camouflaged.

B-29 DC9

C-20 SR71 Interceptor YF12A Dark green/red.

C-21 North American X15 Black.

C-23 F.111

C-24 F.86 Sabre

C-25 Starfighter F.104

C-34 MiG 21

D-27 Boeing 747 Pan Am

D-29 Boeing 727

E-30 Bell Cobra Copter Grey, green.

E-31 Sikorsky Skycrane Orange and white.

E-32 Alouette Helicopter Blue, 'Police'.

Boeing SST

Convair B-58 Hustler

P.51 Mustang

Buccaneer

W.22 Space Shuttle 'United States'

MINI DYNA FIGHTER China 1991

With pull-back action, 4 x 45mm span, diecast uppers, bubble-packed onto card: F-15, F-16, F-19, EFA Mk2.

MINI-PLANES OR PLAYMAKERS Hong Kong

Bubble packaging marked 'Mini-Planes, diecast scale model', some also 'Free wheeling'. The range is also found packaged as Playmakers. Casting marked with catalogue number, plane name and 'Made in Hong Kong'.

301 Boeing 72 Pan Am

302 Boeing 747 Japan Air Lines

303 Boeing 707 Japan Air Lines, Cathay Pacific, Continental

304 Concorde
47mm
Air France with arrow on tail

305 DC-10
75mm
TWA, Lufthansa, British Airways

306 L-1011 TriStar Delta, Lufthansa

307 Boeing 707
Air France with arrow on tail, Pan Am, Piedmont.

308 Vickers VC10
82mm
United, Eastern, Delta, white with red and blue stickers 'VC-10'.

NOVELTIES 1980–present day

Die-cast Miniature made in Hong Kong

9643A-D F-16 Pencil Sharpener
70mm
Two castings, the upper deeply engraved and the lower enclosing a pencil sharpener. Metallised silver top, red lower. Star-on-bar sticker on wings. F-16 and stars and stripes on tail. Attractive.

Biplane Pencil Sharpener
Details similar to above. Bronze antique finish. Unattractive.

PLAYART FAST WING Hong Kong

Bubble-packed onto card printed in sunburst colours with the wording on the front in English and French. The wording on the back, in English only reads: '7545/7546 4 Die-cast metal planes with/without stand'. The models are one- or two-piece neat castings with good surface detail. They are marked 'Playart' 'Made in Hong Kong' and with the name and catalogue number and have a circular indentation in the centre to take the point of the stand. They are usually painted one colour with good quality decals usually printed on clear sticky tape. The undercarriages are usually fixed and have large bright turned dumb-bell wheels. The canopies are blued plastic and the propellers and other small parts are black plastic. The three-piece, grey plastic stand and the assembly instructions are packed below the plane. The wingspans vary between 100mm and 115mm and the scale is given on the list on the reverse of the backing card.

7400 IL-2M3 Stormovik
115mm. 1/122
Olive drab or sand yellow. Russian lettering 'chalayevtsy' on fuselage. Yellow edged red star on wings and tailfin.

7401 AW Seahawk (Hawker Sea Hawk manufactured by Armstrong Whitworth)
110mm. 1/108
Olive drab. XE395 in black and RAF roundel on each wing. 'A' on tailfin.

7402 Jet Provost T.Mk.3
1/108. Olive green. XM346.

7403 Fairey Battle
118mm. 1/137
Olive green or pale grey green (later with retractable undercarriage).

7404 North American P51B Mustang (actuallly P-51B)
115mm. 1/108
Olive drab. Black and white D-day stripes round wings with blue and white star-on-bar on tips. Black and white stripes with blue and white star-on-bar superimposed round rear fuselage.

7405 Junkers JU 87B (Stuka)
1/108. Olive green, SZ-FS.

7406 Lockheed Lightning P-38J
1/130. Olive green, square and triangle.

7407 Chance Vought F4V-ID Corsair
1/108. Olive green, silver cowl.

7408 Messerschmitt BF-110-D
1/137. Olive green, SF + CM.

7409 Hurricane IV
1/108. Olive green, FJ-C. Red propellers. Retractable undercarriage.

7410 Messerschmitt ME-410
120mm. 1/137
Grey or olive green. White-edged black crosses above and below wings. Yellow band round fuselage.

7411 Grumman Wildcat VI
1/108. Olive green with silver cowl.

7412 Boeing 747
1/508
A British Airways
B Japan Airlines
C Pan American Airways
D Swiss Airways
Transamerica

7413 Grumman Wildcat VI 1924
1/108. Olive drab with yellow cowl.

7414 Boeing 707
1/408. Pan American Airways

7415 Boeing 727
1/331
A Lufthansa Airways
B United Airways

7416 Supermarine Spitfire Mk II
115mm. 1/100
Olive drab. YQ roundel 'T' in white on fuselage with yellow band. Roundels above and below wings, tail flash.

7417 Mitsubishi Type-Zero 'Zeke'
1/90. Olive green

4718 Henschel HS 123 1/108

7419 Fiat C.R.42 1/108

7420 Concorde
1/446
A British Airways
B Air France

7421 Lockheed Tristar
1/446
A All Nippon Airways
B Air Canada

7422 Boeing Clipper (Flying Boat)
121mm. 1/380
White upper, blue lower. NC18605, US flag below cockpit.

7423 DC-8 Super 61
1/475. United Airways

7424 Vickers VC-10
1/420. British Airways

7425 DC-10
1/460
A Swiss Airways
B American Airways

7426 MiG-21PF 1/137

7740 Bell Jet Helicopter
A later addition that is not on all of the backing cards.
R Forest Patrol
F Fire Fighter
P Police Patrol
M US Army 1/120

7574 Set containing two airport vehicles and
Boeing 747 British Airways
Boeing 707 Pan Am
Lockheed TriStar Air Canada

Playart 7600 Series – Mini Fast Wings
Retractable wheels
P-38
P-51
Fairey Battle
Stormovik

RACING CHAMPIONS
China, 1992–present day

The bubble-packaging of these good quality diecast planes is marked 'SkyBirds' and 'Wintech Collectors Series'. The two-piece castings, split horizontally, are marked 'C 1992 RACING CHAMPIONS', the plane name and 'Made in China'. The two pieces are rivetted together and trap a simple diecast retractable undercarriage fitted with black plastic wheels. The cockpit covers and small parts are hard black plastic. The paint finishes are good quality and the decals are mostly tampo. The reverse of the backing card is printed in full colour with three ranges: historic prop fighters; modern combat jets; and helicopters.

HISTORIC PROP FIGHTERS

Mustang P-51D
130mm
Green-grey. White on blue star-on-bar on both wings, registration AX-G.

Mitsubishi Zero
Stuka JU 87G-1
Tiger Shark P-40B
Corsair F4U-4
Spitfire

MODERN JET FIGHTERS

F-4 Phantom II
MiG-37B Ferret-E
F-14 Tomcat
B-1B Bomber
F-16 Falcon
Hawker Harrier
SR-71 Blackbird
A-10 Thunderbolt II
F-19 Stealth
MiG-29 Fulcrum
F-15 Eagle
F/A-18 (actually **F-18A**) **Hornet**

HELICOPTERS

SV-3 Super Cruiser Two liveries
Bell AH-1W Super Cobra Two liveries
Mil Mi-24 Hind Gunship Two liveries
Hughes AH-64A Apache Two liveries

ROAD TOUGH
Hong Kong and China, 1980s and 1990s

A selection of small-scale castings of (mainly road) emergency vehicles which were initially made in Hong Kong in the 1980s with the production moving to China *c.*1990. The quality varies, the better quality usually being tampo printed and the poorer having stickers. The manufacture of some is credited to the China National Light Industrial Products I/E Corp, Donguan City, Guandong, China. Some of the castings, including the helicopter, figure also as Zee Toys. Zee was at one point a Zylmex brand name (see Dyna-Flites USA). There are many sets in a variety of sizes.

Hughes 369 Helicopter
Two-piece diecast, black or white plastic parts, no identification marks, 90mm including bubble nose.

Examples of sets:

Zee Toys (tampo printing)
Highway Patrol: Helicopter in black 'Highway Patrol' with three vehicles.

Road Tough (tampo printing)
Highway Patrol: Helicopter in white, red cross 'Rescue' in black plus three vehicles. The same set as Zee Toys above.
Emergency Force Highway Patrol: two Helicopters in white, one with red cross 'Rescue' in red; one with badge 'Highway Patrol' in black, and eight vehicles.
Emergency Force Fire Rescue: two Helicopters, one in white as above, one in red with Fire Department Badge and eight vehicles.
Emergency Force Military: two Helicopters in dark green with yellow camouflage with six other vehicles.

China National Light Industrial Products (stickers)
Chips Special Squadron Highway Patrol: Helicopter in black 'Police' in white and three vehicles.

Manley (tampo printing)
Registered in the US. Product made in China similar to Road Tough Sets including the Hughes 369 Helicopter in 'Rescue' livery.

Made in Hong Kong (no manufacturer named) crude versions of Hughes 369 Helicopter and other vehicles with poor stickers.

Edocar (China – 1993)
Ambulance Team Action Set includes a Hughes 369 Helicopter in white 'DOCTOR'.

SOMA China, late 80s

Micro Jets: small size (70–75mm long) modern jet aircraft. One-piece diecast, upper incorporating nose wheel support fitted with plastic housing for the 'pull'n go' motor, marked '1988 Soma Made in China'. Clear plastic cockpit bubble. Nose wheel turned metal, rear wheels gripping rubber. Nicely tampo printed in blue and silver, white with red and blue markings or desert sand and brown camouflage with USAF and star-on-bar markings. Bubble-packed in sets onto card printed with an aircraft carrier scene with cardboard aircraft carrier deck playmat enclosed. Sets of three planes with moulded plastic launch pads to hold the motor wound, a set of six (No 2967) without and a set of three planes on a plastic aircraft carrier (No 333). The packaging is most attractive.

Planes: **F5, F15, F16, F18, Mirage** and an attempt at **Stealth Bomber**.

SUPER WINGS (TINS' TOYS OR DCT) Hong Kong, early 1970s

Each plane 9.5–11.5cm long (as annouced on the bubble packaging) consists of two castings of variable quality and accuracy, fitted with black plastic dumb-bell wheels. The toys are marked with the name of the plane and the catalogue number. There are paper or adhesive tape stickers. The range is pictured on the back of the card.

T243 Boeing 727 TWA

T244 Boeing 737 Pan Am

T245 Boeing 747 Lufthansa, Pan Am

T246 DC10 SAS

T247 DC8 Swissair

T248 Concorde
53mm. Air France with arrow on tail

T249 Starfighter F104 German Air Force

T250 Phantom
64mm. Silver. US Air Force

Vickers Super VC-10 BOAC

TINTOYS Hong Kong, early 1970s

The well detailed castings are marked with a catalogue number prefixed 'W.T.', the name of plane and 'Hong Kong', but not with 'Tintoys' which appears on the bubble packaging. The castings are usually two large pieces with other smaller ones e.g. engines and tailfin on VC-10, positionable tailplane on MiG-21. Bright metal dumb-bell wheels on plug-in plastic undercarriages. Decals are usually on clear self-adhesive tape. The scales vary considerably.

W.T.207 Vickers VC-10
133mm
White fuselage, silver wings, engine. Dark blue BOAC decals.

W.T.208 Boeing 747
133mm
White fuselage, silver wings, tailplane. Dark blue Pan Am decals.

W.T.209 Boeing 727
133mm
White fuselage, silver wings, engines. Red JAL decals.

W.T.210 DC-10
129mm
White fuselage, silver wings, tailplane. Red Swissair decals. Green Alitalia decals.

W.T.215 F-105

W.T.216 F-4EJ Phantom II
78mm
Orange. RAF roundels, XR.

W.T.217 F-106A Delta Dart
72mm
White, USAF, red stripes on fin.

W.T.218 F-5A Freedom Fighter
71mm
Silver/black camouflage, Korean livery.

W.T.219 MiG-15
100mm
Light grey, red stars, 346 on nose.

W.T.220 A-4F Skyhawk
80mm
Brown/green camouflage, Italian roundels.

W.T.221 F-104J

W.T.222 MiG-21
71mm
Silver. 17569 in red on nose, yellow, red and black GDR markings on wings and tailfin. Plastic missiles.

HELICOPTERS

W.T.601 PK108 Westland Lynx
Army camouflage green and dark brown.

W.T.602 Sikorsky H-19 Rescue
Two-tone green camouflage.

W.T.603 Sikorsky H-19 Seaking
Navy

W.T.604 H-16 Turbojet
Green, Royal Navy

TOYWAY China, early 1990s

Registered in England, Toyway imported excellent quality reproductions of Edison Air Lines, Italy. But by 1993, they were selling 'Fighter Aircraft', bubble-packed, extremely bad castings fitted with black plastic undercarriages, poor quality paint and stickers. The first four of the list may be old Flyers dies.

F-4 Phantom, MiG 21, BAC Jaguar, Grumman G-11A Tiger

F-16
90mm. White, Thunderbirds Display Team.

F-18 Blue Angels Display Team

UDC Hong Kong

HELICOPTERS: length 100mm (excluding rotor)

Hughes 500
Olive green, red cross.
Black, Police or Highway Patrol.
White, Ambulance, red cross.

Bell 206 JetRanger
Yellow, Air Taxi.
Light green, US Star.

WONDRIE METAL PRODUCTS MFG CO LTD Hong Kong, China, 1980s and 1990s

Hong Kong production consisted of one-piece hollow fuselage castings of a standard size (approximately 100mm long) fitted with a grey plastic housing incorporating the nose wheel support and underwing missiles. Plastic clip-in canopies. Free wheel types had catalogue numbers 201–4, Pull Backs 2011–2014.

In the early 1990s, Wondrie made in China counter display boxes of Puma helicopters in assorted colours. The two-piece 90mm long diecasts with plastic motor housing have a 'pull back – let go' action. Marked with the catalogue number and 'China', they have good paint finishes and tampo printing.

1984–85

F-16 Fighter
Mid-metallic blue, 'USAF', F-16 decals

F-5A Freedom
Dark blue, Star-on-bar, F-5A decals

A-4F Skyhawk
Silver, green, white and red roundels

F-4E J Phantom II
Gold, white star on blue circle

W33 Puma Helicopter
Yellow, blue and green diagonal stripe.
Olive drab, 'S152 USAF' in silver.
White, 'Police P131' in blue.
Red, 'Rescue F18' in white.

ZYLMEX Hong Kong

Zylmex was a Hong Kong trademark but it was aquired by Intex of California and the castings were marked and marketed as Zee Toys. Subsequently, the range was added to. To give a coherent picture, the details are included in the USA section under Dyna-Flites.

India

Maxwell, Milton, Nicky (see Dinky)
India is not known either for the originality or the quality of its toy production, much of which was made and finished by outworkers in the back alleys of Calcutta. It was intended for the domestic market.

MAXWELL MINI 1970–90

Maxwell, Calcutta, made a low quality but sturdy range of diecast vehicles with no identification marks. Brightly coloured boxes depict the planes in action. The Boeing 747 has the salient features of the same size Schuco and is most probably a 'rip-off'.

539 Boeing 747 Lufthansa
99mm
Two-piece casting. White upper, metallic grey lower.

545 BOAC (sic) Boeing 747
Casting as above. White upper, dark blue lower. 'British airways'.

456 Boeing 747 Swissair
Casting as above.

557 Boeing 747 Air India
Casting and colouring as 539. AIR-INDIA in English and Hindi, in red.

541 MiG
70mm
Two-piece casting with fixed undercarriage. Blue with red stars on wings and red cross on white ground on tail.

542 Mirage (Miraj)
Red or blue. Indian Air Force markings.

573 Douglas Navy Skyhawk
Blue and white.

MILTON 1970–80

Morgan Milton Private Ltd of Calcutta traded in the 1970s as Milton Mini Toys or Mini Model Toys. Their spelling was not consistent and even their name was rendered as Miltan. A catalogue states, amongst paragraphs of flowery prose, that 'We are working for the betterment and improvement of India's Toy Industry . . .'! Unfortunately, production standards did not keep up with the sentiment. Their warplanes are very poor with large plastic wheels. The Concorde is a crude copy of the Corgi with the same configuration and fixing of the underfuselage-cum-engine casting. The wording reads 'CONCORDE A MILTON PRODUCT' The waterslide transfers are dark blue and caricature the Corgi Air France decals. Even the stand and its Concorde sticker mimic Corgi. The yellow and blue box copies more than the colours and dimensions: the picture is similar; the 'Working Droop Nose' illustrative drawing is the same; the wording is identical.

339 Concorde
85mm
Copy of Corgi. White, Air France.

358 IAF Gnat
Silver. Orange and green Indian Air Force flashes on tail.

359 Hunter
Silver. Decals as 358.

318 Caravelle SE210 (Super Mini Jet Plane)
127mm. Fixed undercarriage. White upper fuselage, silver grey lower and wings, 'INDIAN AIRLINES' on port side, and in Indian script on starboard, VT-DPO on rear sides and under wings, black cheat line, later blue.

Italy

Aviva, Edison Airlines (and Pyranglo/Toy Way UK), Mercury, Polistil/Politoys

While most diecast planes were made post-war, it is possible that some were made earlier. A low wing, humped, solid lead tri-motor with wings and engines like an SM73 and a tail like a Savoia Marchetti 83 has been seen. 130mm span. The cast-in wire undercarriage legs are fitted with small lead wheels. The two-blade propeller are small. Cream with Italian registration.

AVIVA (HASBRO)

72039/2 Snoopy plane
Yellow/chrome. High wing, tiny three-blade propeller. Span approximately 3.5in.

EDISON AIRLINES AND PYRANGLO/TOY WAY
1970, 1991–present day

There has always been great enthusiasm for flying in Italy and for the use of planes in war, the first air raid (1911) being the Italian attack on Turkish lines in Libya in the Italo/Turkish War.

Three series, a careful selection of important early planes with high quality, accurate multiple castings, were issued in the order below, the first two being available by spring 1971. They are marked under the fuselage 'Made in Italy by Edison Giocattoli SpA', with plane name and '1:72' for most of the series, but 1:84 for 1202 and 1204. The biplane castings usually consist of three pieces: fuselage and tail; lower wing with undercarriage; upper wing. Engine covers and other intricate small parts, machine guns, windscreens etc. are in variously coloured plastic. The machine guns and plastic tail fins swivel. The wheels are plastic and with separate tyres. Often the upper and lower wing surfaces are painted different colours as are the cockpits. The decals are, mainly, paper stickers which tend to peel. The Grumman Gulfhawk was not issued.

The range, Edison Air Line HF, is packed in irregularly octagonal plastic boxes with a deep lid. The bases have the plane names cast in them and pegs to locate the rear of the fuselage. The edges of a shaped card base which announces that the models have been made with the cooperation of the aeronautical industries that manufactured the planes facilitate an interference fit between the base and lid. A leaflet describing each range, the covers printed with different views, fits between the card and plastic bases. In the early issues, between the base and the leaflet of the Italian Sky series were two 'stamps' depicting that plane. You kept the coloured one and stuck the black and white version onto a card. If, having bought all four in the range and completed the card, you returned it to Edison, 50019 Sesto Fiorentino, Italy before 30 April 1972, you would receive a publication with the history of the planes in the series, become a member of the Edison Air Club and receive a membership card and your name would be entered in a grand draw in which 'hundreds of fabulous prizes' would be won every four months. Later, just called Edison Air Line, they were in small square card boxes with an angled window which listed the other planes on the back in four languages and had details of the planes on the sides.

Five of the biplanes and the triplane, the simpler castings, were reissued in 1991 as WORLD WAR I BIPLANES, by Pyranglo, Letchworth UK. Later, the Pyranglo name was replaced by Toy Way, the markings being on the 'Made in China' bubble-packing. The castings have had 'Made in Italy' removed and the quality is virtually that of the originals. The finish is similar except that the cockpits are not painted in a contrasting colour and there are shade changes on some plastic parts. There are slight decal changes.

1001–1004 and 1101–1104 were also available as sets in cardboard boxes with flip-up lids with an illustration of an air battle on the inside.

HEROES' WINGS

1001 RAF SE 5a 1917
112mm
Sage green fuselage and upper surfaces, cream lower, red seat.
Red plastic engine block, buff propeller. Royal Flying Corps roundels on wings and fuselage, rudder stripes, A8898 on tail.

1002 Fokker Dr I 1917
100mm
Red
White plastic cowl and tailfin, red tail plane, black propeller. Black on white iron crosses on wings, fuselage and tailfin.

1003 Spad S XIII 1917
113mm
Dark sage green, red side panels and seat, grey undersurfaces.
US white, blue and red roundels on wings, stripes on tail. Hat in ring and one emblem on blue on fuselage: American Expeditionary Force Squadron Serial No. PU 145.

1004 Macchi Nieuport II 'Bébé' 1916
103m
Silver grey. Blue plastic engine cowl.
Red, white and green Italian roundels on wings, stripes on tail, roundel and prancing horse on white on fuselage.

ITALIAN SKY: ACES OF WORLD WAR I

1101 Ansaldo A.1 Balilla 1917
106mm
Greenish yellow. Black plastic parts.
Italian red, white and green roundels on wings, stripes on tailfin, A1 18878 and roundel on red on fuselage

1102 Aviatik D.1 Berg 1917
109mm
Maroon fuselage and upper surfaces, cream undersurfaces and seat.
Maroon plastic moveable flaps, white engine cover, black propeller. Black on white iron crosses on wings, black on yellow on tailfin, red 'T' on white on fuselage.

1103 Ansaldo Sopwith Baby 1916
108mm
White fuselage and float legs, red wings.
Blue plastic engine cowl ring, rear float and lower part of front floats. Italian roundels on wings, stripes on tail, roundel N 2079 on fuselage.

1104 Hansa-Brandenburg D.1 'Spinne' 1916
117mm
Dark metallic blue with yellow undercarriage, red seat.
Yellow plastic engine cover, tailfin. Black on white iron crosses on wings, black cross on tail, three diamond and cross label on fuselage.

RECORDS IN THE SKY

1201 Supermarine S.5 1927
112mm
Wings and float legs, upper fuselage silver, lower fuselage and tail red, engine and floats dark metallic blue (seven separate castings).
Red plastic wing flaps, silver propeller, tail flaps. Wire wing stay.
'4' on wing, fuselage, stripes on tail.

1202 Macchi Castoldi MC72 1932
113mm
Red. Silver grey plastic double propellers, wing flaps, upper float sections, lower floats and rear fuselage, red fuselage side panel and tail flaps. Wire float stay. 'M.C.72' on fuselage, tail stripes.

1203 Gee Bee Super Sportster 1933
105mm
Yellow. Red plastic engine cowling, black wing and tail flaps, lifting cockpit, wheel spat sides.
Black '7' on port wing, NR77V on starboard, red '7' on fuselage in front of cockpit, pterodactyl behind.

1204 Grumman Gulfhawk 1936. Not issued.

A POKER OF ACES

Planned but not released:
1301 North American P51 Mustang
1302 Mitsubishi A6M Zero-Sen
1303 Messerschmitt BF109E
1304 Supermarine Spitfire II

PYRANGLO/TOY WAY – UK
1991–present day

'WORLD WAR I BIPLANES' are re-issues of some of the Edison by Pyranglo, Letchworth UK, later Toy Way in 1991. The bubble-pack is marked 'Made in China' and the castings are identical to those of Edison except that 'Made in Italy' has been removed from the lower casting. Some of the colours of plastic parts have been changed but the metal parts are the same colours, except that the seats have not been touched in. There are slight decal changes. Unusually for re-issues, the quality is virtually that of the originals.

RAF SE 5
Sage green with cream lower surfaces. Dark red plastic engine cover and propeller. (RAF standing for Royal Aircraft Factory.)

Fokker Dr-1
Red. As Edison.

Spad S XIII
Dark sage green including seat, darker red side panels. Darker blue plastic cowl.

Ansaldo Balilla
Greenish yellow. Larger Italian roundels, no tail stripes, roundel N2079 on white on fuselage sides.

Aviatic Berg
Maroon including seat, cream undersurfaces. Red propeller and flaps.

Hansa-Brandenburg
Dark metallic blue including seat. Lighter yellow plastic parts.

MERCURY 1953–1966

Mercury were making diecast toys before World War II and quickly got back into production afterwards, turning their attention to aeroplanes in about 1953 and producing them all within three or four years. They had all been deleted by 1966. All but three are single castings and are marked with the plane name, catalogue number, 'Made in Italy' and the Mercury logo of the name across a cog wheel. There is very little surface detail on the early ones but the later models have finely cast cockpit bars etc. Reflecting the general shortage of mazac at the time, some of the bigger castings are in aluminium. The models are, on the whole good though the Mystère wings do not have a dramatic enough sweep and the MiG-19 does not seem to be a model of anything. The Lockheed F.90 and Republic XF91 Thunderceptor were experimental planes. The Vampire is a model of the Venom. It is an important range because most of the planes have not been made by any other toy manufacturer and, where they have, eg Tootsietoy, the Mercury is a better model. The very small wheels are usually mounted on wires cast into the body and bent at right angles. Some have casting pegs to represent nose wheels. The three- or four-bladed propellers are usually unpainted stamped aluminium. The decoration is very plain with only a variety of air force transfers employed, which have creamy coloured bands where white or clear should have been used. The small planes were packed either flat or vertically in boxes of six held in place by their undercarriages being pushed through a card insert. The large planes had dull grey boxes printed in dark blue with the name of the plane, catalogue number and Mercury logo.

DATES
The only firm dates that can be found from the mainly undated catalogues is that all castings were still in production in 1960 but had been deleted by 1965 except for the silver Fiat G.212 which was dropped in 1966.

PAINT AND DECALS
All models are finished in silver, the roundels and USSR stars are on both wings and either side of the rear fuselage, the US star-on-bar is on port wing and rear fuselage sides, unless otherwise stated.

401 Fiat G 59
59mm. 1/201
Four-blade propeller
Also: green, cream, red Italian roundels.

402 Fiat G 212
145mm. 1/202
Two castings rivetted together: upper fuselage including nose and tail; lower including wings. Three-blade propellers. Italian roundels.

402A Fiat G 212 (Croce Rosso)
Casting of 402.
White. Red crosses on wings and tail.

403 Fiat G 80
55mm. 1/21
Tricycle undercarriage. Italian roundels.

404 Vampire (actually a Venom)
63mm. 1/200
Two wheels and a nose skid. Italian roundels.

405 Lockheed F.90
62mm. US star-on-bar.

406 Avro 707A
51mm. 1/204
RAF red, white and blue roundels on wings.

407 Comet DH106 (Comet 1)
138mm. 1/253
Aluminium with cast-in square windows.
RAF roundels on wings.

408 Mystère (I or II)
60mm. 1/194
French blue, white and red roundels.

409 Missile
27mm
With or without star-on-bar on port wing.

410 Sabre F 86 (error in catalogue: F 84)
51mm. 1/221
Star-on-bar.

411 Piaggio P 148
54mm. 1/206
Two-blade tinplate propeller, two undercarriage wheels.
Italian roundels.

412 MIG 15
50mm. 1/201
White. USSR red stars.

413 XF92A Convair
46mm. 1/207
Star-on-bar on both wings.

414 Piaggio 136
66mm. 1/205
Wing tip floats a push fit on stalks down from wings.
Two small two-blade tinplate propellers. Italian roundels.

415 Boeing B 50 (actually a model of a B-29)
172mm. 1/25
Aluminium with cockpit glazing engraved on die.
Four-blade propellers. Star-on-bar.

416 Convair RB 36 E
234mm. 1/300
Aluminium with cockpit windows cast in, jet engine pods cramped under wings.
Large double wheels on three axles on cast straight legs.
Six four-blade propellers. Star-on-bar.

417 Sikorsky S 55
62mm long. 1/208
Star-on-bar on sides of rear fuselage.

418 Boeing B47 Stratojet
140mm. 1/252
Aluminium with four engine pods pressed under wings.
Cockpit bubble painted blue. Star-on-bar.

419 Douglas D558-2 Skyrocket
41mm
White. Black plastic nose probe. Star-on-bar.

420 MIG 19
50mm. USSR stars.

421 Convair XFY-1 Vertical Riser
47mm. 1/175
Landing wheels moulded in, two three-blade cast propellers.
Cockpit painted blue. Star-on-bar on port wing.

422 Cutlass F7U-3
58mm. 1/203
Cockpit windows moulded in. Silver with light blue nose or mid-blue with silver mid and front cockpit windows.
Star-on-bar on port wing and either side of cockpit.

423 Corsair F4U-5N
61mm. 1/205
Four-blade propeller. Mid-blue, silver cockpit, some with red missile tips. Star-on-bar.

424 Lockheed F94C Starfire
66mm. 1/196
Casting marked 'LOCKEED', with or without small fin at rear of wingtip tanks. Star-on-bar.

425 Lightning P38
79mm. 1/200
Cockpit glazing bars cast in. Three-blade propellers.
Early: bent wire 'nose wheel', later, cast peg.
Mid-blue with silver cockpit. Star-on-bar on port wing.

426 Republic XF.91
48mm. 1/197
Missiles crimped on under wing.
Silver with red nose and dark blue flash on top of fuselage.
Star-on-bar.

SETS

400A Box of 8 assorted planes
Avro 707
Convair B36
MiG-15
Sabre F.86
Mystère
Lockheed F.90
Two Missiles

400B Box of 7 assorted planes (catalogues say 7, contents actually 8)
Fiat G.80
Avro 707
Comet
Mystère
Piaggio P.148
Piaggio P.136
Two Missiles

400 Box of 8 assorted planes
Lockheed F.90
Sabre F.86
Fiat G.80
Avro 707
Comet
Mystère
Two Missiles

400C Box of 14 assorted planes
Fiat G.212
Fiat G.59
Fiat G.80
Vampire
Lockheed F.90
Avro 707
Comet
Mystère
Piaggio P.148
Convair XF92A
Piaggio P.136
Convair B36
Two Missiles

POLISTIL/POLITOYS 1973, c.1976

Politoys were advertised as 'made in Italy by Polistil' and, in 1973 made a range of Walt Disney toys supposedly in 1/32 scale including W7 Donald Duck's Plane in red and blue.

A range of diecasts, six single castings, followed by another six, was released in the mid-seventies. They are all modern jet fighters, the most up-to-date being the Northrop F-5A which first entered service in 1974. They were made to fit the Tricolore (green, red and white) boxes and stated to be 1/125 to 1/297 scale (span 42-56mm). They are marked with the logo, catalogue number, 'Made in Italy' and name of plane. There are dumb-bell wheels and a cockpit glazing piece. The decals are paper or clear tape stickers. Most have red plastic missiles on a sprue clipped under the casting.

AZ-1 Phantom F4K
Green and yellow camouflage, RAF roundels.

AZ-2 Starfighter F-104
Green/green camouflage, 'US AIR FORCE' in white.

AZ-3 Mirage 4A
Grey or brown/green camouflage, French Air Force roundels.

AZ-4 MiG-21C
Chrome or olive green, red stars.

AZ-5 F-105 Thunderchief
Sand, US decals.

AZ-6 Hustler B58
Chrome, US decals.

AZ-7 Hawker Harrier
Green, RAF roundels.

AZ-8 Northrop F-5A
Green, USAF.

AZ-9 Fiat G.91Y
Dark blue, Italian roundels.

AZ-10 Saab 37
Grey, Swedish crown roundels.

AZ-11 McDonnell-Douglas Skyhawk
Grey, USAF in black.

AZ-12 MiG-23 (actually a MiG-25)
Chrome, red stars.

Japan
ATC, Bandai Robomachines, Diapet Yonezawa, Dieca Hobby, Edai Grip Technica Flight, Linemar, Mattel Bandai (see Bandai)**, MiniAir** (Modern Toy)**, Nakajima, Tomica/Tomy SuperWings**

There were virtually no diecast toys made before the war. There are some that remind one forcibly of SR from France, both in thinness of metal, surface detailing and 'gold' finish, but I do not know of any planes. Post-war production is very varied but is usually large scale and very well finished and not in the catalogue for very long. Many were supplied with stands for display or labelled 'Collector Model' but it is difficult to decide whether this was meant to be taken literally. There is also the occasional novelty such as a plane-shaped cigarette lighter.

ATC 1962

In the first ATC catalogue two planes are shown:

401 Zero Se 127mm

402 DC-8 152mm

BANDAI ROBOMACHINES AND MATTEL-BANDAI
1980 and 1985–present day

These ingenious toys, a mixture of diecast and plastic parts, which transformed themselves with cunningly devised manipulation, from vehicles to space creatures and back took the toy market by storm in 1985 and became a craze. A non-transforming space precursor was made by Mattel-Bandai in about 1980. The Shogun Series contained PA74 Gorenger Varidorn Vertilift, span open 143mm, diecast body in red and black, plastic wing, red, yellow, blue and white.

Usually sold to the retailer in assortments bubble-packed onto card, the 1985 catalogue contained the following. The first word is the name of the plane, the one after the oblique (if there is one) is the Robo name. Shuttle 82mm long.

RM-03 Jet
RM-04 Helicopter
RM-14 Space Shuttle
RM-19 Harrier/Royal T
RM-25 F-15 Eagle/Leader
RM-31 Cessna/Water Walk
RM-39 Zero Fighter
RM-40 Kaman Battle Copter
RM-41 Apache Helicopter/Sky Gun
RM-42 Battle Helicopter/Carry-all
RM-45 Blackbird
RM-47 A-10 Fairchild
RM-49 F-16 Jet Fighter

DIAPET

Diapet is a brand name of Yonezawa whose trademark is 'Y' in a five-petalled flower. Pictured with stands in the 1979 catalogue only:

J1 Mikoyan MiG-25 1/170
J2 Grumman F-14 Tomcat 1/143

DIECA HOBBY

Battery-powered diecast planes, supplied with decal sheets and bombs, packed in square boxes with clear plastic lids.

Me.109E 160mm
P-51D Mustang 160mm
Mitsubishi A6M5

EDAI GRIP TECHNICA FLIGHT 1970s

The trademark of Edai Grip is a 'G' incorporating an arrow head in a square. They made a small group of planes using the brand name Technica Flight. The 1/88 scale fighters have two main, big, chunky, but smooth, castings, with tampo printing. There is a pilot seated in the opening cockpit, with that and the opening engine cover being operated by an inconspicuous rod on top of the fuselage. The undercarriage is fixed. A selection of missiles and a stand are contained in the polystyrene inner of the window box.

TF2 F-15 Eagle
150mm
White with red white and blue Thunderbirds markings with 1776–1976 Centennial marking.

F-16A
White with blue 'camouflage' markings, or red, white and blue with '76' stripes.

Also illustrated in catalogue:

F14A
Harrier
Boeing 747
Space Shuttle

LINEMAR 1950s

Several small aeroplanes, a helicopter, delta wing plane, airliner etc, 2-3cm long, are corded down with cars, tanks, etc, onto a chequered board. Made for Marx for export to the US. Also individually boxed in sliding tray boxes:

93 Boeing P-26A
95 Curtiss Hawk P6E Biplane
98 Douglas M-2 Biplane

MINIAIR (MODERN TOY) 1976–80

It is difficult to say whether MiniAir, made by the Masudaya Corporation, trademark 'MT' for Modern Toy in a diamond, were intended as toys or not. The quality of the three-piece casting, with tampo printing on the upper fuselage and stickers on the wings is very good, between that of Ertl and Aero Mini. Masudaya had been casting Aero Mini and selling them in Japan without an agreement. The retracting undercarriages lack detail. The planes are marked only 'TM JAPAN' and the boxes are printed with the plane type etc. The plane and its stand rest in preformed polystyrene.

4554 Boeing 747-200B 1976
171mm. 1/370
Japan Air Lines JA-8102
Pan Am

4556 BAC/Aérospatial Concorde 2 1976
116mm. 1/240
British airways G-BBDG
British airways with incorrect blue upper on tail flag.
Air France F-BVFA.

4759 Boeing 747-SR 1980
171mm. 1/370
With P&W engines (angular) or with RR engines (bulbous).
All Nippon Airways JA8133.

4765 Lockheed TriStar L-1011 1980
170mm. 1/250
All Nippon Airways JA-8501

NAKAJIMA

A group of models, consisting of two large castings marked 'NKJ MODEL PLANE' and the plane name, with plastic parts, opening translucent blue cockpit canopies, black exhausts, white bomb clips, are fitted with batteries to power whining jet noises operated by a peg protruding from the centre top of the fuselage. The metal undercarriage legs retract. The multicoloured masked painting is very fine and the additional decoration consists of clear tape stickers.

Packed, complete with bombs, rockets and stand, in a card box with an illustration of the plane.

F-4 (Phantom)
134mm. 1/87
White with red and blue stripes on nose, wingtips and tail. 'US AIR FORCE' and star-on-bar on sides, '3' in a circle of stars on the fin.

F-14A (Tomcat)
122mm with wings folded in. 1/96
Grey upper castings, white lower. Grey plastic swing wings. '115', star-on-bar and red design below cockpit, star-on-bar on port wing, NK and animal head on tailfins.

F-15A (Eagle)
134mm. 1/97
Light blue with red triangular flashes on all leading edges. F-15 USAF etc below cockpit and on tailfins, USAF on starboard, star-on-bar on port wing.

F-16A
139mm. 1/70
Red, white and blue lengthwise stripes.
US AIR FORCE and star-on-bar on upper body, USAF, star-on-bar on wings, 'General Dynamics F-16' on fin.

TOMICA/TOMY SUPERWINGS
1978–present day

The first planes marketed by Tomica or Tomy, both names being used on toys and in catalogues at the same time, were called SkyTomica. They are castings from the Lintoy stable and are detailed under Corgi/Lintoy.

The 1977 catalogue has two sets containing SkyTomica Boeing 747 and TriStar, but with box art of the two much more detailed SuperWings that were introduced the following year. By 1980, three modern fighters had joined the group but they were soon dropped. Both liveries of All Nippon Airways seem to have been in production at the same time. Very much later, the second livery of Japan Air Lines, JAL initials only was released. The high quality, detailed castings are marked with 'Japan', both 'Tomica' and 'Tomy', the catalogue number, the name of the plane, the scale and copyright date. The upper fuselage is finished with very high quality tampo printing and the wings have stickers. They are fitted with fully detailed retracting undercarriages with small dumb-bell wheels and are supplied with a two-piece black plastic stand. The fighters have plastic bombs and rockets. The window boxes for the individual planes are simple, purple and yellow with the appropriate airline logo sticker on them. Some of the fighters were sold in pictorial card boxes. The planes nest in preformed polystyrene. The set boxes are brighter with good illustrations of the airliners in them. The 1980 catalogue labels a picture of two versions of both airliners and one each of the fighters with a series of numbers, but these are a key to the photograph and not the catalogue number which is cast into the model.

1 Boeing 747 1978
128mm. 1/415 scale
Japan Air Lines JA8108 (old livery)
All Nippon Airways JA8190 (old livery)
Alitalia. Later: JAL (new livery)

2 TriStar L-1011 1978
144mm. 1/366
All Nippon Airways JA8501 (old livery).
All Nippon Airways JA8501 (new livery)
British airways
Air Canada

F-15 Eagle 1979–82
1/100. Blue, red and white stripes on wings.

F-16A Falcon 1979–82
1/100. Red, white and blue, US AIR FORCE.

F-14A Grumman Tomcat 1980–82
White, US star-on-bar on port wing.

SETS

The sets which figure in the catalogues for the listed years all contain four small airport vehicles.
1978, 1980, 1983 with Boeing 747 JAPAN AIR LINES
1983 with TriStar All Nippon Airways
c.1990 with Boeing 747 JAL (new livery)

Dandy: Tomica also made a range of Matchbox sized toys:

19 Twin-rotor helicopter
1977 White upper, yellow lower.
1980 White upper, red lower.
1983 Blue upper, white lower.

Spain

Guisval, Joal, Mira, Nacoral, Pilen, PlayMe

GUISVAL 1980–present day

Based in Alicante, Guisval made a range of road vehicles mainly for the domestic market but turned their attention to helicopters in the early 1980s. In the early 1990s, they marketed Super Dyna-Flites under their own brand name (see USA).

75 Aérospatiale Puma Helicopter
80mm long
Brown, white numbers 001, 14 either side of red, yellow, red Spanish roundel on tail boom or silver, with winged anchor 'MARINA'.

78 Bell 47 'Icona' Helicopter

81 Hughes OH-6A 'Safari Jungla' Helicopter

82 Bell 47 'Aero Club' Helicopter

MBB BO105 Helicopter
Dark green, US Army, desert livery, US Army or blue 'Alpino'.

JOAL COMPACT 1994–present day

Joal, whose original and recently re-equipped factory is in Alicante, began production in 1968 using existing dies purchased from Tekno, Mercury etc. but later changed to using their own tools to make model construction equipment, diggers etc. By 1994, the factory had new 'fully ecological' paint equipment which produced superb gleaming paint finishes on nicely detailed very smooth castings. A helicopter was introduced in several colour schemes with good quality sticker decals, though some of the wording is odd: 'widely by patents and patent' and 'Marks Tradeare world throughou'! The large castings are split horizontally but with doglegs and secured with cross-headed screws. The base is embossed with the trademark 'JOAL' superimposed over a shield. The undercarriage struts are chromed and fitted with black plastic wheels. The nosewheel is steerable. Two black rotor blades are supplied separately in the expanded polystyrene inner packaging of the good quality window boxes. Clear glazing and detailed interior with chairs and a table.

182 Agusta Helicopter 1994
217mm
Metallised silver upper, metallised dark grey lower. 'POSTE' in white and arrow white and red band, registration EH-KLF on another band on tail boom and on tailfin.

From Rescue Set:
Agusta Helicopter 1994
Casting as 182, all red.
'RESCUE' in white between yellow stripes along fuselage behind doors. Registration NH-90 in white above and on tail and wording as text. 'SAR' in black on orange square on door.

Augusta Helicopter 1994
Casting as 182, all red. 'REGA' (Switzerland).

MIRA 1980–present day

These sturdy toyish castings have pierced windows and are marked with 'MIRA' on a band across an oval cartouche making it rather difficult to read, 'Made in Spain', the catalogue number and plane name. The colour split co-incides with casting splits. They are fitted with bun-shaped bright metal dumb-bell wheels. Issued in the 1990s in window boxes (CE Eurologo) with strange colours and stickers eg HS-125 on a Concorde.

351 Tornado Red

353 Ejecutive (Executive) Jet (HS 125)
112mm
White upper fuselage, red lower fuselage with wings and engine tail piece, 'AIRLINES' F-SV4270 across wings.

355 Gloster Gladiator
Red upper fuselage with remainder white.

357 P-38 Lightning
Silver, yellow decals with blue, white and red roundels. PT roundel 38 on tail plane. Sand with dark sand shading. Metallic blue.

359 Skyhawk White and blue

361 Boeing 747
94mm
White upper, metallic blue lower, AIR FRANCE B-747 AIR-F. White upper, silver lower, Iberia, M-362, IB-YES.

363 Concorde
White, Airlines G-AYBH, HS-125.

365 Cessna
95mm
Maroon upper fuselage, white lower and wings. AM-72 in black on wings.

There is also a range, ref 594, of eight small (50-70mm) unmarked one-piece castings, hollow uder the fuselage, painted in bright colours with colourful stickers. Black plastic dumb-bell wheels: six jet fighters, Executive Jet, Concorde, Jumbo Jet.

NACORAL

Bell Huey Cobra Helicopter
190mm long. Green, USA 3472321

PILEN 1970s and 1980s

Pilen made an interesting selection of aircraft, several not otherwise modelled. The good quality, usually, single castings bear a reasonable likeness to the original, and are marked 'Pilen SA, Made in Spain', plane name and catalogue number. Mostly the casting is marked with an even number eg 700 Messerschmitt and the catalogue shows two different liveries one on 700 and one on 701. Occasionally, a casting is marked with the odd number. The span of the planes is 60–95mm and the length of the helicopters is 90–100mm. Dumb-bell wheels fit on stubs from the main casting. Decals are good transfers. Black plastic propellers. Bubble-packed. A multi-plane display card was available for shops. In 1976, Pilen issued a Concorde, a rip-off of the Corgi casting complete with stand but with a metal droop snoot. Advertised in the old Air France livery but it had a green stripe along the window line and a red tail fin.

M700 Messerschmitt (ME 109)
Khaki green, 7 and cross on fuselage, cross on wings, or Spanish Air Force roundels.

M701
Dark sand with grey camouflage, F1+FH on fuselage, cross on wings.

M702 Zero
Pale metallic blue, red rising sun on wings, dark blue bands round rear of fuselage, or spurious red/black/yellow fan style roundels.

M703
Khaki green, rising suns, white and yellow veed band round rear fuselage.

M704 Lear Jet 36
White with orange engines and tail fin (separate casting), 'aero taxi' across wings.

M705
White with blue tail.

M706 Boeing 707
White, yellow to red bands, Iberia.

M707
White, Lufthansa livery.

M708 Cessna 402
White lower casting, metallic blue upper, AP708 on wing.

M709
Green lower, white upper, 'foto-cine estudios' across wing.

M710 Cessna 210
Yellow wing and lower casting, white upper fuselage, AR710 and stripes on wing.

M711
Red wing and lower casting with white, 'ICONA' AP711 across wings.

M712 C-101 Aviojet
White, Spanish roundels and two-tone blue stripes on wings.

M713
Silver with grey shading, 'MARINES' FA-989 across wings.

M714 Super Mirage 4000
White, French roundels.

M715
Silver, French roundels.

M716 Fokker-VFW F27 (Friendship)
Red. US flags on yellow decal across wings.

M717
Matt sand with grey shading, roundel on bar on wings.

The later helicopters have blue or red plastic underpanels, marked with the name and catalogue number, and matching plastic rotors. The glazing is bottle green. Scales are variable e.g. 901 (90mm long) is 1/108, 905 (95mm) is 1/135.

901 Gazelle SA-341
Orange. '10' in white roundel on blue flash.
Green, RAF roundels.
Blue base with skids.

903 Huey-Cobra
Royal blue. Red blob decal under cockpit with yellow flashes along fuselage.
Fawn/grey camouflage, RAF roundels.
Red base with skids.

905 Sikorsky H19
Dark red. Yellow and black diagonal stripes on fuselage, 'Safari' on boom. White, red cross. Blue base with floats.

907 JetRanger
Yellow, dark blue flashes.
Light blue, 'Policia'.
Blue base with skids.

909 Boeing UH-H6
Blue, 'ARMY' in black, 'F28' in red circle.
Light maroon or fawn/grey camouflage, US.
Red base with undercarriage legs.

911 Hughes OH6A
Blue with red flashes, '7' in black circle.
Orange 'Rescue', '257'.
Red base with skids.

PLAYME 1960s–1970s

The factory was located in Beniparrell, Valencia. The planes usually consist of a single casting with a wingspan between 110 and 120mm, to fit the box, not to scale. Most are marked 'PlayMe', but not with catalogue number or plane name. Later, some have '*F do En Espana*' (Made in Spain). The early versions of some have folding undercarriages; later they were fixed. The wheels are frequently cast solid but may be black plastic as are the propellers and rotor blades. Some have a wire spring between the wheels. The decals are simple transfers. Many are fitted with the red, yellow, red roundel used in Spain between 1928–31 and from 1939. There is a wide divergence in accuracy and charm across the range which includes some models neglected by other manufacturers.

The boxes have of a clear plastic square base and slip over lid with card backing carrying a product list on the underneath and an airfield scene (one with a river, the other with a tall building) to show behind the plane. The edge of the card which fits between the two plastic pieces to hold them together is printed with the contents. The plane is secured to the plastic base with elastic string. The range first listed 101–120 with information in Spanish about the plane printed on the box. The list increased to 101–125 and the notes, often idiosyncratic and fiercely patriotic, were on a separate flimsy leaflet in several languages. One example reads 'Autogiro "La Cierva" Juan de la Cierva born in Murcia (Spain) 1895. The rotor is the true source of propulsive lift and also acts as a speed regulator whether advancing or descending, and there is even the case where the suspension coefficient, within very flexible limits, proportionally increases the angle of attack, and avoids the dreaded "stall" where the plane loses lift and falls. Through all the successive innovations of aircraft carried out, the autogiro remains an invention unparalleled by any of those existing.' The later box is of card with a clear window. The plane is secured to a separate backing card showing a named picture of the plane. Listed on the back of the box were 15 items from nos. 105-128. However the range was not confined to this as models not on the list are found in this packaging.

101 RAF SE 5 Scout Biplane

102 Sopwith Camel Biplane

103 Messerschmitt

104 Spad XIII Biplane

105 Spitfire VII

118mm
1960s production: folding undercarriage, bright blue with red white and bright blue roundels on wings and fuselage.
1970s: fixed undercarriage, metallic blue.

106 North American P-51 Mustang

107 Japanese Zero (Mitsubishi A6M)

108 Fokker D7 Biplane

109 Lockheed F104 Starfighter
53mm. Dark green. Star-on-bar stickers on wing.
Early: folding undercarriage. Later: fixed.

110 General Dynamics F111 Swing Wing
Early: folding undercarriage. Later: fixed.

111 Republic F105-D Thunderchief

112 North American F86 Sabre Jet

113 Dassault Mirage IIIC
70mm. Dark green or metallic green. White-edged French red, white and blue roundels on wings and fuselage behind cockpit.

114 Douglas Super DC-8

115 Boeing 747 Jumbo
100mm. No markings on casting. White. 'IBERIA' and window line in red, 'IB' on yellow roundel on tail.

116 McDonnell F-4 Phantom

117 Stuka Ju87 Bomber
114mm. Silver grey, black crosses on wings and fuselage.

118 Autogiro 'La Cierva'
76mm long
Dark silver grey, Spanish roundels on forward fuselage.

119 Dornier Wal Seaplane
119mm. Two main castings with no markings. Silver grey. Spanish roundels on wings and nose.

120 Junkers Ju52 Airliner
116mm. Mid olive green, red, black and white window transfers, iron crosses on wings and fuselage. A 1/250 scale model, with the correct proportions but omitting the distinctive corrugations of the surfaces.

121 Piper Tri-pacer

122 Fiat CR-32 'Chirri'
112mm. Dark green, Spanish roundels on upper wing and fuselage sides.

123 Polikarpov I-16 'Rata'
114mm. Folding undercarriage. Silver, Spanish roundels on wings and fuselage sides.

124 Casa C-212 'Aviocar'
115mm. Two castings. Circular windows pierced through upper casting. Brown. Spanish roundels on wings and rear fuselage.

125 Helicopter Bell 'Huey Cobra'
125mm. Yellow, 'USAF' and star-on-bar on each side.

126 Douglas F-15 Eagle

127 Casa C-101 Aviojet (Trainer)

128 Douglas DC10

UK toy manufacturers – excluding Dinky Toys

Acorn Toy, **Barrett & Sons** (see Taylor & Barrett), **Britains**, **Cap Bombs**, **Casting Moulds**, **Charbens**, **Corgi**, **Corgi/Lintoy** (see Lintoy dies Hong Kong) **Crescent**, **Dyson**, **Johillco**, **Kay** (see Taylor & Barrett), **Lone Star DCMT**, **Mascots**, **Matchbox Skybusters**, **Pyranglo** (see Edison Airline, Italy), **RAF Benevolent Fund/Tonka Polistil/Kellogg's**, **Segal**, **Skybirds**, **Taylor & Barrett**, **Timpo**, **Toymaker Casting moulds** (see Casting Moulds), **Toyway** (see Edison Airline, Italy), **Tremo**

For 45 of the 85 years of this century's production of toy planes, Dinky Toys were being made. All the other UK manufacture should be seen against the rise and fall of this great firm.

ACORN 1945–50

The unpainted one-piece mazac casting with good detail is marked 'Acorn Toy Co Ltd Made in England'. There are stubs to represent the undercarriage.

Hurricane 56mm

BRITAINS LTD 1931–40

Britains, the oldest British toy maker who, from 1893 had been famed for its range of fine hollowcast lead soldiers, had promised to make aircraft as early as 1919 but it was 1931 before the first was released, the square-winged monoplane, in RAF and US markings. They were all listed in the final 1940 catalogue, and not re-issued post-war.

Comper Swift – 433, 434, (1521), 435, 436, (1325)

It does seem that the early planes had squared-off wings as the first Britains but later the wing tips were curved and the tail rounded at the top. The tail of the toy was not modified when the wings were. The nose of the fuselage was initially pointed with small engine pots. This was replaced by one showing heavy exposed engine cylinders.

The Swift was not made in biplane form. The toys are recognisably Comper Swifts, though the tail fin is not correct. The hollowcast lead fuselage of the toy incorporates solid undercarriage flaps and a tailskid, and is marked underneath 'MADE IN ENGLAND BY BRITAINS LTD LONDON'. The cockpit is cast open with a seat for the separate pilot (seated with outstretched right arm and kitted out in a brown or white flying suit) which was supplied with the toy. The wings and tail are made of thick tinplate. The forward edge of the wing is folded to secure the thick wire wingstrut which passes through holes in the undercarriage flaps and holds the front of the wing in place. The centre of the wing is rivetted to flanges sticking out from the fuselage. There are two flanges at the rear of the fuselage to which are rivetted the tail fin and plane. The toy can be suspended from a cord by securing the ends to the loop on nose and the hole in tailfin.

FIRST CASTING

The first casting was of a plane with straight-edged square-tipped wings. The pointed nose of the fuselage was modelled with engine pots and the 55mm two-bladed propeller was part of a conical spinner. The thick wire axle was fitted with metal wheels. Painted silver with a brown propeller with nose cone, the plane was decorated with paper RAF roundels above and below the wings and on the fuselage sides. The tailfin was painted with a red, white and blue flash.

SECOND CASTING The second casting which replaced the first has a large exposed six-cylinder radial engine at the front fitted with a two-blade propeller with no nose cone. There are two extra rivet heads on each side of the undercarriage just below the fuselage. The wing has both leading and trailing edges angled and the tips are rounded. The lead wheel hubs are fitted with white tyres. Finished in silver with a brown propeller. The roundels are transfers. Tailfin as before.

BIPLANE The biplane uses the second casting of the monoplane fuselage with additional wings below, fitted onto the rivet pegs on the undercarriage. The upper wing is raised from the mountings for the wing of the monoplane on a cast lead bridge that fits over the rivets on the fuselage to position it above the pilot's view line. Lead struts are fitted towards the outer wing ends to hold the upper and lower wings apart.

In their 'Armies of the World' series, Britains released the same toys in US colours, finished in dark green, with paper stickers, blue centre to white star in a red circle, fixed above and below the wingtips. Tailflash as RAF.

BOXES For both UK and US liveries:

1st box square-winged monoplane: 'AIRCRAFT SERIES' scrolled. Plane shown with square wingtips.

2nd box rounded-winged monoplane and biplane: 'AIRCRAFT SERIES' straight. Plane shown with rounded tips and incorrect rounded tail.

The bottom of the boxes make into a hangar. 'The Hangar . . . is made by reforming the specially designed box in which the Aeroplane is contained; it is a rigid structure when set up and is entirely self contained . . . To erect, pull out tabs, raise roof to shape, insert tabs to keep roof in position'.

Autogiro – 1392, 1413, 1899 This beautiful model of the Cierva Autogiro consists of a hollowcast lead fuselage (with legs), not marked Britains. The tinplate tailfin is cast in and the tin tail plane added. The lead struts for the rotor are a separate piece. The standard pilot reaches up to the control lever of the 'non-flying' (no pulley wheel) military version. The civilian type has a rotor unit with pulley wheel covered by a bell housing which is unpainted. Also unpainted is the radial engine, which is fitted with a brown two-blade propeller, first with and then without nose cone. The long tinplate rotor blades are removeable. The tailfin has a small hole in which to locate the hook for the rear pulley wheel (fitted to civilian type only). A coil of wire was supplied to fly it down. To quote from the attractively illustrated lid of the box of the blue civilian autogiro: 'Stretch tightly between any two points . . . the coil of wire provided, fastening one end *slightly* higher than the other, then unhook the wire at the higher end and thread it through the Autogiro so that the two pulley wheels be free to run smoothly along it. The machine should now run gracefully to the lower point with the blades rotating most realistically.' There was a warning to keep oil clear of the rubber friction drive which linked the pulley wheel to the bell housing. Wheels were originally all cast, but later were fitted with white rubber tyres.

An example, fitted with a contrate gear and pinion connecting the propeller shaft to the rotor via a shaft fitted in place of the pulley, is probably a factory experiment.

BOXES   The civilian autogiro with wire and rear pulley was packed flat in a box 28cm x 17cm, a blue line drawing and instructions on the lid. The military UK and US versions (with control lever) are packed in red or brown oblong cardboard boxes with lift-off lid decorated with a label (as the road vehicles).

Short R.24/31 Knuckleduster – 1520   The very scarce bakelite and tinplate model of this prototype flying boat appears to be accurate. There is a machine gunner in the rear cockpit. A wire carrying a small wheel was strung between engines, and there was a wheel centre tail so it could 'fly' down a cord when the 'propellers realistically revolve'.

BOX   A brown lift-off lid type with paper label carrying details of plane and photo of the real thing over the coast.

FIGURES   Britains also made high quality figures, the best with moveable arms and very detailed painting. They were usually sold in sets. The post-war numbers start at 2001. Some were boxed individually in the so-called Picture Packs. There are also anti-aircraft and defence figures and vehicles including barrage baloons.

433 Monoplane (square, later rounded wingtips) 1931
Square 225mm, rounded 215mm. Silver with RAF roundels.

434 Monoplane with Pilot, Hangar and six Aircraftsmen (square, later rounded wingtips) 1932
As above plus
One 330 Officer in short coat
One 331 Officer in overcoat
One 332 Aviator in short coat
One 333 Aviator in Sidcot suit
Two 334 Privates in peak caps

435 Monoplane, with Pilot, Hangar (square later rounded wingtips) 1931
Dark green plane with US star on roundel.

436 Monoplane, with Pilot, Hangar, and six Aircraftsmen 1932
US finish as above.

1521 Biplane with Pilot and Hangar, rounded wings only 225mm. UK livery as above.

1325 Biplane with Pilot and Hangar
US finish as above.

1392 Direct Control Autogiro C30 1935
142mm long excluding propeller.
Blue with white stripe, registration G-ACIN.

1413 Army Co-operation Autogiro
As above, but with control lever. Khaki/brown with RAF roundels.

1899 Army Air Corps Autogiro with Pilot 1935
US finish of 1413.

1520 Short Monoplane Flying Boat 1935
300mm
Mid-blue bakelite fuselage, thick tinplate wings, silver twin-boom tail.
RAF roundels on wingtips and fuselage sides, flahes on fins.
Separate silver engines (two), blue floats.

FIGURES

240 Royal Air Force Personnel 8 pieces
330 Officer in short coat 8 pieces
331 Officer in overcoat 8 pieces
332 Aviator in short coat 8 pieces
333 Aviator in Sidcot Suit 8 pieces
334 Privates in peak cap 8 pieces
1527 Royal Air Force Band 12 pieces
1758 Firefighters of the RAF (asbestos suits) 8 pieces
1894 Pilots of the RAF in full flying kits and WAAFs 6 + 2 pieces
1904 (US) Army Air Corps Officers and Men 8 pieces
1905 (US) Army Air Corps Pilots, Officers and Men 16 pieces
1906 RAF Pilots, Ground Staff and Fire Fighters 16 pieces

2011 22 piece set including: Airman in short jacket
Officer (RAF Regiment)
Bren Gunner x 6 (RAF Regiment)
Men with slung rifles x 6 (RAF Regiment)
Firefighters x 2
Airman in greatcoat
Pilots in flying suit x 2
Despatch rider on motorcycle
WRAF
Airman with flight plans

2073 Royal Air Force Marching at the Slope 8 pieces

Picture Packs
1018B RAF Commodore
WRAF
Pilot
Bren Gunner
Officer
Man with slung rifle

CAP BOMBS

Various plane-shaped cap toys, unmarked and made from unpainted mazac, 5–6cm long and 3–4cm across the wings were available particularly in the 1950s. A toy gun cap was placed between the nose cone and the main body of the toy, the two pieces being secured by rubber bands. When dropped from a height onto the nose, the cap would bang.

CASTING MOULDS 1940s

Because of the shortage of toys and the restictions in the use of materials, during and immediately after the Second World War, there was a trade in moulds which were used to produce toys using scrap materials, such as lead. H. Buckley of Scarborough advertised moulds of hard aluminium alloy including 215 Zeppelin, 25 Whitley Bomber, 88 Spitfire. G. Rhead of Twickenham had a range that overlapped (in soldiers) with Buckley's and an obvious copy of the Crescent HMS *Eagle* aircraft carrier (the core for casting it hollow was extra). He also had three small planes on one mould, one of which was for the loose Cresent planes sold with their carrriers. A further manufacturer illustrated planes from a 'Flying Fortress with a 5 1/2in (140mm) wingspan with four movable propellors' to a 50mm Spitfire and a selection of propellers. The dies were not particularly cheap and were on the whole quite good so that a small manufacturer could produce reasonable quality product. A four-engined bomber is included in a set with six airmen, the box marked 'Weaver Toys made in Eire' in 1949. An unknown manufacturer made a solid lead bomber (118mm) marked 'Blenheim Bomber Made in England' from a casting mould and finished it in camouflage with ordinary or high visibility roundels. There were also

moulds available for pilots etc. Their use was however beyond the skill of many youngsters with the result that unidentifiable blobs abound.

CHARBENS 1950s

Charbens and Co Ltd, Andover Yard, 219 Hornsey Road, London N7, made lead slush and diecast toys from 1929 including copying many of the Tootsietoy road vehicles and perhaps making a copy of their Autogiro. The name was created from the first names of Charles and Ben Reid, the founders. Some toys are marked 'CHARBENS' or 'CHARBENS AND CO. LONDON' and 'MADE IN ENGLAND' but others have no markings and it is quite likely that some of the planes which are unidentified were actually made by Charbens. After the War, production resumed and mazac was later used but planes produced only into the 1950s did not figure largely amongst their products. Charbens ceased trading in 1980. Although their figure dies still exist, all the plane and road vehicle dies were scrapped.

Fighter (Hurricane?)
90mm
One-piece solid lead casting with stub undercarriage, a poor model somewhat between Hurricane and Spitfire. Marked 'CHARBENS & Co. LONDON' under starboard wing. 8mm two-blade tin propeller. Light blue, red.

Blenheim IV Bomber
114mm
One-piece hollow fuselage relatively crude lead casting, marked 'CHARBENS' under port wing. Khaki, silver canopy.

CORGI 1969–91

Mettoy was set up to make tinplate toys in 1934 in England by Philipp Ullmann assisted by Arthur Katz who had left Bing in Germany at the beginning of the Nazi regime. Having dabbled in diecasting after the war and recognising the buoyancy of the market for Dinkies and Matchbox, Mettoy established Corgi to make a range of diecast vehicles in 1956.

Corgi had no history of making planes, though Mettoy, had produced many tinplate ones in preceding decades. When the development of the new supersonic jet passenger plane excited so much interest, Corgi, always looking for new product, sought to cash in on it and produced a model of Concorde in 1969. They were tempted to increase the range but were rather wary of the sales potential of planes and chose not to manufacture the models themselves. Instead they liaised with Lintoy in Hong Kong and had some of the Lintoy range manufactured, decorated and packed in Hong Kong for sale as Corgis. All of these castings are marked Lintoy and full details can be found in Lintoy dies, Hong Kong. In this, they made a wise decision because sales were always rather disappointing. The collaboration with Lintoy proved satisfactory from a technical point of view, and when a range of helicopters was introduced in 1975 they were initially made in Hong Kong by Lintoy specifically for Corgi. Corgi Cubs, castings with no undercuts and no windows, were introduced in 1977. R205 was a helicopter. The range did not figure in retail catalogues.

The helicopters were produced at a time when boys were gradually losing interest in diecast toys and production quantities were reducing, even though initially profitability remained good. In 1980, however, poor trading, high interest rates and a strong pound priced the toys out of export markets and Mettoy made the first trading loss since 1971.

There were huge stocks of all sorts of Corgis sitting unsold in the warehouse in 1983 as a result of the depression that since 1980 had forced virtually the whole of the British toy industry to the wall. In October 1983, the Mettoy Group, Corgi's parent company failed and the future of Corgi, a potentially profitable section, was in jeopardy. A management buyout, assisted by others including the Welsh Office, was organised and by the end of March 1984 Corgi and the factory at Fforestfach, Swansea, had been bought from the receiver. The packaging style was revamped. A Corgi Collectors Club with a magazine was set up and some models were only available through the Club. In 1989, Corgi was sold to Mattel to give improved access to US distribution. Production was moved to China and the Swansea plant was closed. At the end of 1990 production was bought back from Mattel by two of the former Corgi management. The head office was then located in Leicester.

CONCORDE

BAC-Sud Aviation Concorde – 650, 651, 652, 653

There are two distinct Concorde castings: the Lintoy – see Corgi/Lintoy; and the casting marked 'Corgi Toys'. The scale of the span of the Corgi is 1/304 and that of the length is 1/328 but this does not detract from the look of the toy.

DATES | The 1969 catalogue (Copyright 1968) showed no planes but the BOAC Concorde 650 is on the cover of a fold-out leaflet 'The Fantastic World of Corgi Toys', copyright 1969. The Air France Concorde 651 was advertised in France in 1969 but does not feature in the UK catalogue until 1971/2. Though they were in the 1972 catalogue some factory records appear to indicate that 1971 was the last year of production. Utilising the same casting and with either a blue or a white nose, Japan Air 652 and Air Canada 653 do not feature in any catalogue and were apparently only sold in Japan and Canada respectively. The next appearance of 650 and 651 was 1976. Both numbers had new liveries. British Airways had replaced the BOAC and there was a new Air France livery. The plane was re-liveried in 1987, in the new British Airways style with a coat of arms on the tail. After Corgi was taken over by Mattel, the die was sent to China. This casting is marked 'Made in China'.

CASTINGS | There are three castings: main fuselage and tailfin; wings; underfuselage marked 'Concorde', 'Corgi Toys', 'Made in Gt. Britain', engines and fixed rear undercarriage legs. The front undercarriage is grey plastic, later black, and the plastic wheels are black or grey. Early models lost their wheels easily until the undercarriage was redesigned. All have a plastic 'droop snoot'. When the toy was re-introduced in 1984, the plastic used on the 'droop snoot' is often in a softer more translucent polythene. Then, for safety, the nose was blunted and a warning was printed on the backing card. The first issue has the four exhaust stubs in black plastic, subsequent ones having white.

DECALS | The decals are paper stickers. From the mid-80s the width of the white bands on the plasticised tail decals varies from batch to batch becoming more even.

STAND | A black painted triangular metal stand, the first issue usually with a ribbed top, later usually with a smooth top, decorated with a dark metallic blue sticker printed with 'Concorde' in gold was supplied in the box. Towards the end of UK production, Concorde re-appeared without a stand on its own and in Airport Sets with a selection of Corgi Juniors.

BOXES | The first issue have yellow and blue oblong card boxes with a folded corrugated interlining with one basic printing and a star to indicate the livery. The correct number is on the end of the box. The overseas versions come in the standard box with printed paper stickers, name and number, over the pre-printed information. The second issue has window boxes which feature the livery of the toy enclosed. These were replaced by the standard Corgi window box with an orange-shading-to-yellow window surround. Later, the box was dark blue.

SALES | There are no accurate sales figures for Concorde as the records for 1969 were lost, but it seems as if the BOAC version sold in the region of 200,000.

HELICOPTERS

As early as November 1972, the economics of having a large diecast Corgi model tooled and manufactured in Hong Kong were being assessed and by 1975 Corgi-inspired product was being made on Lintoy production lines in Hong Kong.

CASTINGS   The helicopter castings fit together with great ingenuity. The first designs were made of two large fine pieces. The whole of the tail and up to half of the rear boom is cast integrally with one of the sides. The skids and fins are cast into the appropriate parts. The join is a very neat match. When the two sides are screwed or rivetted together, the cog wheel for the 'flick-spin' rotor, any other working mechanism and the cockpit glazing are trapped in place. The later JetRanger helicopter is also made in two pieces, normally plus a small winch or rocket firing casting, but this time the split is round the waistline. The dies probably came back to Britain in 1978 as the Marks & Spencer 'Wings' helicopter and the JetRangers have their rotor, with a blades marked 'Made in Gt Britain'. Nearly all the helicopters have action features, the commonest of which is the 'flick-spin' rotor, operated by a relatively unobtrusive cog wheel geared to the rotor. Some of the rotor blades are weighted with metal studs at their tips.

MARKINGS   Most of the castings are not marked 'Corgi'. The underneath of one of the rotor blades is however inscribed with 'CORGI PATS APPLIED FOR MADE IN HONG KONG', or later, 'MADE IN GT BRITAIN' and the make of the helicopter. When the Marks & Spencers versions were issued 'CORGI' was removed from the blades. Late issues of the JetRangers are fitted with this type as well.

DECALS   The castings are decorated with stickers some of which adhere better than others. One is usually positioned over the recess for the Phillips screw which holds the toy together. The last JetRangers were tampo printed.

BOXES   The toys were always packed in a window box with the helicopter rubber banded down to a, usually, yellow, piece of stiff card. The colours of the boxes changed through the years. A greenish-brown surround to the coloured stripes was followed by black and then by very dark blue. The JetRangers are packed in a modification of this box with some having a headercard and an illustration of the helicopter in action. The enlarged area was particularly suitable for publicity for the films that featured the machines. After 1982, the boxes became all over blue, or red for some of the sets.

MARKETING   Corgi were always very keen to obtain maximum publicity for their film and TV related products, timing their launch carefully – for instance to coincide with a film premier – and making full use of the material to which they had acquired the rights by producing eye-catching packaging featuring the appropriate action hero. An internal memo states: 'Another PR success we had last week was the illustration of Corgi C921 Police Helicopter in Womans Weekly, a top national magazine which has a circulation of 1,709,000.' To maximise their sales receipts some items, eg the Batcopter Set, were released to mail order firms and subsequently to the public before the individual items were made available.

SALES   More than 4 million helicopters were made. Top seller was the Hughes with well over 2 million being cast, 50% of which were Batcopters. Over 1 million JetRangers were made, the vast majority TV and film related. 158,000 Spidercopter, 400,000 Bell AH-16a, over 350,000 Sikorsky Skycranes and over 150,000 Bell 205s were produced.

The first illustration does not always show the correct or usual decoration scheme. The name in the catalogue is not always the same as that on the packaging so I have included the name of the full size machine. Corgi prefixed individual items and gift sets with 'C' but to differentiate them I have used 'GS' for the latter.

All the helicopters were withdrawn in 1982. The reconstituted Corgi released export versions of the JetRanger and in 1990 one for the UK plus a special issue Unipart JetRanger.

Bell AH-1G – C920, GS17

The fine and well-detailed casting is a fair model in 1/104 scale. The rocket under the nose is fired by pressing the red plastic catch on the underside. The Bell AH-1G was used in the Military Gift Set, GS17, of which there are two versions.

Hughes 369 – 921, GS18, GS20, 9212, 9214, 9216, 9921, 925, GS40, M & S Set

The Corgi is quite a good model in 1/51 scale. The four-blade rotor, some of which have studs on the rotor tips, fold up fore and aft to pack flatter. Usually it and the tail rotor are dark blue. The winch string with its bright metal hook comes down from the centre belly through a nick in one edge. The castings of the struts and vertical tail fins were thickened in turn between 1977 and 1979. The first issue was Police, 921, which also featured in the Emergency Services Gift Sets, GS18 and GS20. A batch of four export only versions were released: two Police, Politie, 9212 for the Dutch market [22,000] and Polizei, 9921, for the German [55,000]; a yellow ADAC, 9214, for Germany [50,000]; and the red Swiss Air Rescue, 9216, for Switzerland [36,000]. The Batcopter, 925, which was not a model of the 'real' Batcopter was issued after the release of the Batman Gift Set. GS40. The seat with a hole for Batman was occasionally used in the other Hughes. A silver version was packaged for Marks & Spencer (see that section).

Sikorsky CH-54A Skycrane – 922, 923

The 1/142 scale model is a fair representation and was issued in two versions, the Casualty Skycrane, 922 and the US Army Skycrane, 923.

Bell 205 Rescue Helicopter – 924 JetRanger 206B

The Corgi is 1/91 scale. Late production shows die wear: cracks in screen pillars and badly fitting doors.

Helicopter – 926, 927, 929, 930, 931, GS19, GS21, GS77, Export GS1412, GS54, GS65, M & S Sets

The Corgi basic model in 1/63 scale could be fitted with features, a winch with a hook operated by a knurled wheel, or a rocket launcher fitted with two rockets fired by pressing stubby levers, or floats. There are two main castings, the split being nearly horizontal following the line of the underpan which slopes up towards the rear of the body. The lower has either a pair of skids cast on or spread legs on which large angular plastic floats were fitted. A coloured 'line' is created along the join by extending the plastic moulding that is the five-seater interior to act like jam in a sandwich. For all the issues, except the M & S version, before 1982 the main rotor was marked 'CORGI MADE IN GT BRITAIN BELL JETRANGER 206B'. Subsequently, the name CORGI was removed. The cockpit glazing changed from amber to clear in 1982. The Stromberg Helicopter, 926, from the James Bond Film sold 250,000. The Chopper Squad JetRanger, 927, has the base with spread legs and is marked PPC 1978 for Paramount Pictures Corporation. Its decoration is much simplified from the original [195,000 sold]. The Daily Planet Jetcopter, 929, is also included in the Superman Gift Set, GS21. Together they sold about 165,000. The Drax JetRanger,

930, bears quite a close resemblance to the one in the James Bond film, Moonraker [157,000]. Utilising the same base as the Chopper Squad machine but with no markings, the Police JetRanger, 931, [20,000] which was also in the Emergency Gift Set, GS19, [40,000] were the last to be produced before Mettoy went into receivership. JetRangers had also been packaged for Marks & Spencer (see that section). After the management buyout of Corgi, small quantities of this toy without features were made, mainly for export and packaged with a road vehicle. The Swiss Police Set, GS1412, [5,000] and the Rega Set, GS54, [1,500] were made for Switzerland but some of the latter were available in the UK. The Redningssett, GS65, was made for Norway. A Polis appeared in a Swedish Set, 73/1. A set containing a Saab 9000/Helicopter, GS77 appeared on the UK market in Police livery. A promotional JetRanger was made for Unipart in 1991.

Coincidentally, a Director of Unipart was also a Director of Corgi which accounts for the short production run of 1,200, 100 being reserved for the Corgi Club. For three years Fox FM sent a helicopter aloft to monitor traffic movements and provide traffic news for the Oxford area. Unipart sponsored it for an hour a day and it appeared at airshows.

The Spidercopter, 928, also in the Spiderman Gift Set, GS23, [total 158,000] is copyright of the Marvel Comics Group and features a blue scorpion-shaped body with red plastic spider legs undercarriage and a webby rotor.

NIPPER AIRCRAFT

The Tipsy Nipper Aircraft was originally designed by a Belgian, Mr Tips. Corgi's toy consists of a diecast fuselage 92mm long with a plastic demountable wing/cockpit unit and a similarly coloured plastic 2-blade prop. The plane always comes on a trailer and in a set. A version was made for Marks & Spencer.

CORGI FOR MARKS & SPENCER

For Christmas 1978, Corgi packed a selection of its existing castings for Marks & Spencer under the St. Michael brand name. The name, Corgi, was removed from the toys and they were finished in special liveries. The following year, another group were released. They were all only available in flagship stores. There were two liveries on the sets containing the Nipper plane and helicopters. The 'Wings' Hughes 369 helicopter and road vehicles were finished in silver and decorated with stickers reading 'WINGS flying club' and with a multicoloured W logo. The rotors are red without studs though the box shows them in blue. The black plane with white wings has 'Blackbird' in white script on the plane fuselage. The 'Spindrift' Sets were mainly bright yellow, the JetRanger helicopter being dark green above the waistline. The sticker on the rear cabin is a white S in a white bordered dark blue oval. The bright red or blue window boxes are eyecatching and attractive and have more impact than the brown that was initially suggested. Various other liveries and sets were proposed. They include the Hughes in white with Traffic Control decals and in silver green in a different colour scheme in the Wings Flying Club Set. Unfortunately, as a letter from their Archivist states, '. . . no trace remains of the Department that bought the Corgi Toys sold in our stores. At Marks & Spencer we pride ourselves on our successful efforts to keep paperwork to a minimum and to destroy records no longer needed.'

SPACE SHUTTLE

Film related models came to be introduced at a press launch co-inciding with the press preview of the film at the Odeon Leicester Square, at one of which a mounted James Bond 007 Space Shuttle was presented to the Duke of Edinburgh.

CORGI JUNIORS

Corgi Juniors were made in Great Britain and, apart from the larger sets, were bubble packed onto backing cards. Some names have been adapted to make it clear which casting the toy is based on. All dimensions are in lengths.

CONCORDE

C650 BAC-Sud Concorde 1969–72
85mm (190mm long)
White upper castings and wings, silver lower. Dark blue droop snoot.
Dark metallic blue window line with silver windows and 'Concorde BOAC' in gold behind the cockpit, dark metallic blue tail sticker with Speedbird in gold.
Also, perhaps first issue: cream upper casting, pale gold, less accurate Speedbird.

C650 British Airways Concorde 1976–87
Bright white finish. White droop snoot. Blue line with white windows, Speedbird, 'British airways', G-BBDG below line, part Union Jack on tailfin.

C650/1 British Airways Concorde 1987–91
Tampo printed red line along fuselage below dark blue windows, 'British airways' in dark blue beneath line. Part flag on tail: two dark blue sections, the upper with a white coat of arms, and a red line.

C651 BAC-Sud Concorde 1969–72
White droop snoot. Blue window line with white windows, 'Concorde' behind cockpit, French flag and 'AIR FRANCE' above line, blue arrow head along leading edge and base of tail fin.

C651 Air France Concorde 1976–83
A line of square blue windows ending with F-BVFA, 'AIR FRANCE' below the line, blue and white with red diagonal stripes on tail.

C652 BAC-Sud Concorde 1970–71
Blue or white droop snoot. Red window line, red circular crane logo behind cabin on dark blue line and on tailfin. 'JAPAN AIR LINES' in blue above windows, line below.

C653 BAC-Sud Concorde 1970–71
Blue or white droop snoot. Red window line with white windows, maple leaf, 'AIR CANADA' in blue above it, red tail fin sticker with white maple leaf and 'Concorde' in blue.

91835 Concorde British Airways 1992-
Made in China.

SETS

Sets not listed in the catalogues came out with some frequency after 1984.

J3125 Airport 1984–85
Four Corgi Juniors (Police helicopter, tanker, bus, van or four helicopters, red, blue, yellow, white) and Concorde 'British Airways'.

J3125/1 Airport 1988–89
Four Corgi Juniors (van, taxi, bus, minibus) and Concorde 'British airways'.

J3219/1 Airport 1990–91
Corgi (Yorkie) truck, three Corgi Juniors (taxi, van, minibus), a cut-out play scene and Concorde 'British Airways'.

HELICOPTERS 1975–93

The dates up to 1982 are those given in *The Great Book of Corgi*.

C920 Bell AH-1G Fires rockets (1 fitted, 10 on sprue), flick-spin rotor 1975–80
130mm long
Two-blade dark green rotor with bright metal ends, two-blade tail rotor.
Dark green and sand US Army camouflage.
Star-on-bar below cockpit, 'US ARMY A-26' stencilled in white along tail boom.

C921 Hughes 369 Police Flick-spin rotor and winch 1975–80
143mm long
1977–79 Skid struts thickened with web, then vertical tail fins, thickened, smoothed and squared off.
Four-blade dark blue rotor, two-blade tail rotor, red cog wheels and interior.
White. G-BBXF in black on boom, 'POLICE' in black over blue bordered red flash on waistline, metallised sticker with 'POLICE' and two spotlights on belly.

C9212 Politie – Dutch Police. (Not available in UK) 1979
Casting etc of 921, but metal studs on rotor tips.
White, with red keel. 'POLITIE' in black on boom, blue and red horizontal bands below window, RP007 in black on rear cabin, silver spotlamp sticker with 'POLITIE' in white below belly, red and blue bands on tail plane.

C9214 ADAC (Not available in UK) 1979
Casting etc as 921. Yellow. D-HFFM in black on boom, 'ADAC' above clipped starburst in white on red, logo of shield with Bavarian eagle in white and red on cabin, 'ADAC' in black and starburst on belly.

C9216 Swiss Air Rescue (Not in UK catalogue, nor available in UK) 1979
Casting etc as 921. Red. HB-XEE in boom in white, 'SWISS AIR RESCUE RETTUNGSFLUGWACHT' and winged red cross on circular dark blue and white logo on cabin.

C921 Polizei – German Police (Not available in UK)
1979
Casting etc as 921 but metal studs on rotor tips.
White, dark blue lower cabin and skids.
D-HBSI on boom in blue, 'POLIZEI' in white with red or orange band at waistline, spotlight decal with 'Polizei'.

C922 Sikorsky CH-54A Skycrane Casualty Helicopter
1975–78. 160mm long
Flick-spin rotor and detachable opening pod.
Six-blade black main rotor, four-blade tail rotor.
Red body, white plastic pod, yellow intakes/exhausts.
Red crosses on copter and pod, N998H in black on tail boom, '3' on pod.

C923 US Army Skycrane Helicopter 1975–78
Casting etc as 922.
Olive drab body and pod, yellow band round boom, red intakes/exhausts.
Red Cross stickers, 'US ARMY' in black on the yellow, pod has 'ARMY' in white.

C924 Bell 205 Rescue Helicopter with opening doors
1976–79
150mm long
Black two-blade main rotor, four-blade tail rotor, yellow plastic tubular floats, red interior.
Blue. Later red. N428 in white on cabin sides, yellow and black danger zone stripes on boom, 'RESCUE' in black on floats.
1979–80
Orange. Black rotor and floats.
'RESCUE 01' in white on black band above N857 in black on cabin sides, narrow yellow and black danger zone stripes on boom, yellow and black stripes above white Air Sea 'RESCUE' on floats.

C925 Batcopter 1976–81
Casting as 921 but orange plastic batwing rotors, seat with hole for blue Batman.
Black. Thin Bat and BATMAN decals in yellow and red.

C926 Stromberg Helicopter James Bond 007, from
The Spy Who Loved Me
1978–80
156 mm long
Two working rocket launchers (10 rockets on sprue)
Yellow. Two-blade main and tail rotors, tail stabilizer, amber glazing.
Cast rocket pod marked 'STROMBERG'S COPTER'. All black, yellow 'line' extended by yellow edged decal with fish logo.

C927 Chopper Squad JetRanger Helicopter Surf Rescue 1978–80
Long spin rotor and working winch.
Upper casting as 926, base, marked PPC 1978, with angled legs fitted with plastic square section floats.
Catalogue colour: orange with black detail and white plastic parts.
White plastic parts. Mid metallic blue with white engine section, silver line.
'Surf' in blue on white, 'Rescue' in white on blue sticker on rear of cabin. 'CHOPPER SQUAD' in orange on floats.

C928 Spiderman Spidercopter. 1979–82
142mm long
Flicking tongue and eye shutter mechanism
Blue body marked *c*.1979 'MCG' (Marvel Comic Group).
Black plastic spider rotor, red plastic legs for undercarriage.

C929 Daily Planet Jetcopter 1979–80
Superman–DC Comics Inc. Rocket firing.
Casting as 926, but rocket pod marked 'CORGI'.
White plastic parts. Red with white engine section, chrome 'line'.
Red 'DAILY PLANET' on white sticker behind the doors.

C930 James Bond 007 Drax JetRanger Rocket Firing Helicopter 1979–80
Casting as 929.
Yellow plastic parts. All white, yellow 'line'.
Yellow 'DRAX ENTERPRISE CORPORATION – MOONRAKER' encircling roundel. 'DRAX AIRLINES' in black on roof.

C931 JetRanger Helicopter, Rescue with Winch 1980
Casting as 927 but no markings.
Red plastic parts including floats. All white, red 'line'.
'POLICE in white on red band on rear of cabin. 'RESCUE' in black on white band on floats.

Unipart JetRanger 1981
Casting as 926 no action features, clear glazing.
White plastic parts. White, blue floats.
'UNIPART in white on blue band on rear of cockpit, in blue on nose, FOX FM below windows, G-ROGR in blue on boom.

GIFT SETS

GS17 Military Gift Set 1975–77
German Tiger Tank, Saladin Armoured Car and 920 Bell AH-1G Helicopter.
1977–80 Contains: German King Tiger Tank, Saladin Armoured Car and 920 Bell AH-1G.

GS18 Emergency Services Gift Set 1975–78
Police Cortina GXL, Range Rover Ambulance, warning signs and 921 Hughes Police Helicopter

GS19 Emergency Gift Set 1980–82
Rover Police Car, Policeman, bollards, warning signs and 931 Jet Ranger Police Helicopter

GS20 Emergency Services Gift Set 1978–80
Jaguar Police Car, Range Rover Ambulance, stretcher bearers, warning signs and 921 Hughes Police Helicopter

GS21 Superman Gift Set 1980–82
Two vehicles and 929 Daily Planet Helicopter

GS23 Spiderman Gift Set 1980–82
Two vehicles and 928 Spidercopter

GS40 Batman Gift Set 1977–80
Batcar, Batboat and 925 Batcopter

GS1412 Swiss Police Set 1986
Export but some remained at factory closure.
Range Rover and JetRanger casting as 926 without working features, clear glazing.
White plastic parts. Red upper, white lower, black 'line'.
'POLIZEI' in white on rear cabin, HB-XCU on boom.

GS54 REGA Set 1986
For Switzerland but some available in UK.
Merc Bonna Ambulance 'SANITATSKORPS ZURICH' and JetRanger as in GS1412 but black plastic parts.
All red, white 'line'. Red winged cross on white oblong on rear of cabin, HB-XGY in white on boom.

GS65 Redningssett 1988 For Norway.
Ford Transit Ambulance Norwegian Red Cross and JetRanger as in GS1412.
Red upper, white lower, black 'line'.
Blue and white winged roundel 'NORWEGIAN AIR AMBULANCE NORSK LUFTAMBULANSE' on rear of cabin, LN-OSH in white on boom.

GS72 Nordsk Luftambulanse Set 1988
Catalogue photo shows CG65 Redningsset.

GS73/1, 92800 Swedish Polis Set 1988–93 (1987 catalogue black and white)
Ford Transit 'Ambulans',
Volvo 740 'Polis' and JetRanger as GS1412.
White with blue, yellow and white line with 'POLIS' superimposed, SE-HLP on boom.
Renumbered 92800 in 1992 when production moved to China. Decals now tampo.

GS77 Saab 9000/Helicopter 1990
Saab 9000 Police and JetRanger as GS1412.
White plastic parts.
White with engine/gearbox unit dark blue, black 'line'.
'POLICE' tampo in blue.

NIPPER AIRCRAFT

GS19 Land Rover and Nipper Aircraft on Trailer 1972–77
Landrover, trailer and plane with orange fuselage and yellow.
Later (c.1976) white wing. '23' on port, G-ATXZ on starboard wing.

GS49 Flying Club Set 1978–80
Jeep, trailer and plane with dark metallic blue fuselage and white wing.
Bluebird in script on fuselage, 'CORGI FLYING CLUB' on starboard wing, twisted wing logo on port.

CORGI FOR MARKS & SPENCER

8001 Wings Flying Team 1978
Lotus Elite with trailer and Tipsy Nipper Aircraft.
Orange fuselage with white wing.

8101 Wings Flying School 1978
Landrover with trailer, and Tipsy Nipper Aircraft, black fuselage with white wing, and Hughes 369 Helicopter.

8401 Wings Flying Club 1978
Lotus Elite, Landrover with trailer, two Nipper Aircraft, one orange, one black both with white wings, and Hughes 369 Helicopter, silver.
(A factory mock-up of this set contained in a plain white box went through a Christies Auction in 1992. It contained the standard Police versions of the Landrover and Hughes helicopter.)

8103 Spindrift Power Boat Racing 1979
Ferrari Daytona, Powerboat and JetRanger with winch and floats.

8403 Spindrift Power Boat Rescue 1979
Ferrari Daytona, Powerboat, Massey Ferguson Tractor with small boat on trailer, Inflatable and JetRanger with winch and floats.

8801 Spindrift Helicopter 1979
JetRanger with winch and floats only.

SPACE SHUTTLE

C648 NASA Space Shuttle 1980–83
Casting of 649. White. United States and flag stickers.

C649 James Bond 007 Space Shuttle, 1979–82
102mm
Retractable undercarriage, opening doors, satellite with hinged solar panels.
White cast upper, black plastic lower.
Early: with yellow plastic recovery arm.
Yellow flashes with '6' and Drax logo on wings and tail, yellow diagonal bands on doors, 'MOONRAKER' in black on side.

GS22 James Bond Gift Set 1980–82
Aston, Esprit and Moonraker Space Shuttle.

CORGI JUNIORS

E3 Stromberg's JetRanger (James Bond) 1978–79
Casting of E63. Black. Yellow plastic skids. Blue fish logo on yellow sticker on rear cab.

E5 NASA Shuttle Enterprise 1980–83
71mm
Opening plastic hatches, gold interior, retractable undercarriage. White upper, black under. Union flag, US stickers.
Renumbered J1.

E6 Daily Planet JetRanger (Superman) 1979–80
Casting of E63. Red. White plastic skids. 'DAILY PLANET' in red on white stickers on rear body.

E34 Sting Army Helicopter (based on Sud-Aviation SO-1221 Djinn) 1975–78
74mm
Dark green. Black plastic skids. 'ARMY' in white on boom.

E35 Airbus Helicopter (based on Boeing CH-47 Vertol) 1978–79
Blue (78 cat), orange. Black plastic wheels. 'AIRBUS' in black, white line.

E40 Redcross Helicopter 1977–79
Casting of E35 Airbus. Military green with red cross.

E41 James Bond Moonraker Space Shuttle 1979–81
Casting of E5. White. Orange stickers with '6' and Drax logo on either wing.

E46 Helicopter (non-prototypical) 1977–83
White. Blue plastic skids.
Stickers: 'POLICE' in blue below blue-edged red stripe.
Also blue, red etc no stickers.
Available in sets only 1984–

E63 Chopper Squad Surf Rescue JetRanger 1977–80
78mm
Dark metallic blue. White plastic floats. Blue 'Surf', white 'Rescue' on white and blue sticker on rear body. (1978 yellow, 'Surf Rescue' in black.)

E73 Drax JetRanger (James Bond Moonraker) 1979–80
Casting of E63.
White. Yellow plastic skids. Yellow windows, also clear.

E75 Spidercopter 1978–84
Casting of E34 Sting.
Metallic blue. Black plastic web rotor, red spider's legs undercarriage. Spider labels on bubble cabin sides.

E78 Batcopter 1977–81
Casting of E46.
Black. Red plastic skids, batwing rotor.
Stickers: yellow 'BATMAN' on red bat logo.

E79 Olive Oyl's Aeroplane 1980–83
67mm
Yellow cast upper, black plastic lower. Olive Oyl waving.
Olive and Popeye stickers on wings.

E83 Goodyear Blimp 1980–81
78mm
Silver. Red and blue plastic fins. Stickers: 'GOODYEAR' in blue on white part, 'CORGI' in orange on black.

E98 JetRanger Police Helicopter 1980–81
Casting of E63.
White. Red plastic floats.
'POLICE' in white on blue edged red band.

J1 NASA Shuttle 1984
Renumbering of E5.

TWINPACKS

E2503 1978–80
Police Rover and E98 JetRanger Police

E2505 1979–80
Daily Planet Van and E6 Daily Planet JetRanger

E2508 1980–82
Popeye's Paddlewagon and E79 Olive Oyl's Aeroplane

E2511 1975–78
Scoutcar and E34 Sting Army Helicopter

E2512 (Blake's 7) 1979–81/2
Star Ship Liberator and E5 Space Shuttle

E2521 1980–81
E41 James Bond Space Shuttle and E73 Drax JetRanger

E2527 1978–79
Kojak Buick and E46 Helicopter, metallic mid-blue, white plastic skids. Stickers: City of New York Police.

E2529 1978–79
James Bond Lotus and E3 Stromberg's JetRanger

E2530 1978–79
Rescue Range Rover and E46 Police Helicopter

E2538 1982
Starfighter and Space Shuttle

TRIPLEPACKS

E2601 Batman Triple Pack 1977–79
Batcar, boat and E78 Batcopter

E2602 Emergency Pack
Two vehicles and Police Helicopter

SETS

E3021 Crimefighters Set 1982–83
Four vehicles (Batmobile, 007 Lotus, Kojak's Buick, Starsky and Hutch Torino), and E75 Spidercopter and E78 Batcopter 1982–83 007 Lotus, Starsky and Hutch Torino, 007 Aston, Starfighter and E41 Drax Space Shuttle.

E3026 Emergency Gift Set 1977–78
Six vehicles and casting of E34 Sting Helicopter in white with blue plastic skids. 'POLICE' in black on boom.

E3029 Military Gift Set 1977–79
Five vehicles, gun, figures and E40 Airbus Helicopter, khaki

E3030 James Bond *The Spy Who Loved Me* Gift Set 1976–79
Four vehicles and E3 Stromberg's Jet Ranger

E3080 Batman Set 1980–82
Four vehicles and E 78 Batcopter

E3081 Superman Set 1980–83
Four vehicles and E6 Daily Planet Helicopter

E3082 James Bond Set 1980–81
Three vehicles, E41 James Bond Shuttle and E73 Drax Helicopter

E3084 Cartoon Characters 1980–82
Four cartoon vehicles and E79 Olive Oyl's Plane

E310 Fire Gift Set 1980–81
Five vehicles, figures and E98 Jet Ranger Police Helicopter

SUPER SETS

Each consists of three models and a board building.

E2521 Army Casualty Set 1980
Landrover and E34 Red Cross Helicopter

E3013 Emergency Rescue Set 1980
E34 Sting helicopter in white with blue plastic skids. 'POLICE' in black on boom.

E3052 Police Set 1978–80
E46 Police Helicopter

POST 1984 SETS

Contents of sets vary. Helicopter (E46) not available separately.
Unnumbered cards: Helicopters–red, blue, black, blue 'Police'.

J3125 Airport Set
Corgi Concorde and four helicopters – red, blue, yellow, white.

J3140 Police 1984
Three vehicles and Police Helicopter

J3140 Police 1988
Two vehicles and Police Helicopter

J3141 Royal Mail 1988
Two vehicles and red helicopter

J3184 Datapost Despatch Centre Royal Mail 1988
Five vehicles and red helicopter

J3189 British Telecom Services 1989
Five vehicles and yellow helicopter

BACKING CARDS CUT IN SHAPE OF FIGURES

J3177 Policeman Card 1988
Three vehicles and Police helicopter

J3179 Postman Card 1988
Three vehicles and red helicopter

CRESCENT 1940–c.1955

The Crescent Toy Co Ltd was set up in 1922 by A Schneider and H and A Eagles to make toy soldiers, munition pieces, etc, using a crescent moon as their logo possibly because they established themselves in De Beauvoir Crescent, just north of Liverpool Street Station, before moving out to Fountayne Road, Tottenham N15. They moulded the hollowcast toys by hand using brass or hard steel 'nutcracker' moulds which were kept just below the temperature of liquid lead. Once the piece had a sufficient wall thickness, the surplus was poured off. When it was cool, flash was removed by barrelling. Later, injection casting machines were used for the production of zinc alloy solid models. After granodising in an acid bath, a method of ensuring that the paint would adhere to the metal, the toys were painted, dried off under infra red and then hand detailed. Their 1940 catalogue announced they were 'diecasting to the trade'. After the war, they resumed production using lead and mazac, later moving to Cwmcarn near Newport, South Wales. They also marketed DCMT product to the trade before being bought out by Lone Star. Selling to the retailer, not advertising to the public, their catalogues show 'Best' (corded down) and '2nd Finish' (loose in divisions) qualities and they listed many sets.

The 1940 catalogue showed very angular lead one-piece castings, marked 'CRESCENT TOYS MADE IN ENGLAND' under wing or tail, two- or three-blade tinplate propellers, usually with thick undercarriage stubs terminating in a small section of wheel. The Bombing Plane is a recognisable Comet Racer which has many similarities to the Gescha (Germany) Racer, but they are not from the same die.

A38 'Hurricane' Fighter Plane
57mm. Bare metal. Re-issued post-war.

D372 Bombing Plane
94mm
Some with rotating brass wheels. Brown and green camouflage, khaki or light blue with paper RAF roundels. Re-issued post-war as FC179.

SETS

K663 North Sea Patrol
Two figures and Bombing Plane

O/2 Air Force Set
2nd finish with four figures and two 'Hurricanes'

Q/2 Air Force Set
Best finish with four figures and two 'Hurricanes'

U/2 Air Force Set
Best finish with nine figures, three 'Hurricanes' and two Bombing Planes

NN667 Aircraft Carrier Eagle with three detached planes, span 18mm
(See also Casting Moulds.)
Later: Aircraft Carrier Victorious with three detached planes.

1946 catalogue, usually single-piece fine diecastings marked 'CRESCENT MADE IN ENGLAND'. Stubs for undercarriage, no propellers.

FC38 Spitfire (clipped wing)
50mm. Metallic dark blue, yellow.

FC89 Mosquito
61mm. Red.

FC90 Lightning
53mm. Lead with high domed cockpit, unmarked. Grey/green, red, yellow, brown with cockpit in contrasting colour.

FC372 Lightning
120mm
Light blue, green, red, yellow, brown or black. Red dot in white star in circle on port wing 'USAF' on starboard, or white star in blue circle on wingtips.

FC179 Khaki Bomber
Re-issue of D372 Bombing Plane, lead.

'Hurricane'
Re-issue of A38 'Hurricane', lead.

SETS

FC663 = K663
Two figures and Bombing Plane

1948 catalogue lists a variety of sets from a 14-piece set containing three 'Hurricanes' and 11 other pieces, to ones double the size.

Figures

Small light blue figures:
Man with gun ⎫
Officer saluting ⎬ Dan Dare figures recoloured
Officer marching ⎭
Officer in flying jacket with documents
Airman with landing bats
Man with peaked cap at the slope
Officer in greatcoat
Seated machine gunner
Radio operator

Dark blue figures:
Man in forage cap with slung rifle
Officer with forage cap
Officer with baton
Pilot with leather helmet and gauntlets
Ground crew (mechanic) with petrol can

Khaki/brown figures
Pilot in flying coat (tall)
Pilot with flight plans
US Airman at the slope above recoloured
Pilot with map case

DYSON 1930s

A shadowy firm, Dyson are known for making toys that are virtually copies of those from larger firms. Their full imprint is BRITISH MADE DYSON in bold square-cut letters.

Biplane

Their copy of the Tootsietoy Aerodawn extended right down to the registration on the cabin side, UX 214, but is marked 'BRITISH MADE' inside fuselage. All the lines are less fine than on the original and the lead casting is poor round the radial engine. Two tinplate wings and the propeller are fitted in the same manner as Tootsie.

Autogiro

This is a copy in mazac of the Tootsietoy Autogiro fitted with a tinplate wing and four-blade rotor. The tailplanes have been modified to enable the use of a simpler die. The fuselage lines are proud not engraved and the whole casting is thinner with more flash. There are no markings. Large lead propeller and wheels fitted with white rubber tyres.

Ford Trimotor

Another Tootsietoy copy marked 'BRITISH MADE DYSON' up inside the fuselage. The detail lines on the casting are raised, not indented.

Biplane
95mm
Copy of Tootsietoy Aerodawn with added lower wing.
Silver, mid-green: small (purple) metal wheels.

Autogiro
113mm
Mazac copy of Tootsietoy Autogiro.
Lime green with yellow rotor.

Trimotor
133mm
Copy of Tootsietoy Ford Trimotor.
Lime green with flat-faced 'Toosietoy' wheels and white rubber tyres.

JOHILLCO 1930s

Johillco was the trade mark of John Hill and Co who traded from 1906 to 1956, setting up business in London but later moving to Burnley. One of the members of the firm was F H Wood who had learnt his trade at the Britains' factory. Much of their product mirrored Britains – soldiers, animals, etc. The planes were produced before the war.

Airship R80

The Johillco is a fairly accurate 1/1895 scale model featuring the streamlining and the open observation port on the top of the envelope.

The airship is found in boxed sets with pilot and ground crew figures and a twin-engined bomber, which was not listed individually. It may have been a bought-in tinplate item with a wingspan of approximately 120mm.

DC2

The toy consists of a lead fuselage with a tinplate wing. The bar between the axle supports is marked 'JOHILLCO ENGLAND' and is rivetted through the wing to flanges projecting from the fuselage sides. The wing and tail shapes are correct for the DC2 but the wing has the flaps marked on the leading edge. It is fitted with a two-blade lead propeller in the nose. The DC2 is a twin-engined airliner but this seems to be the only cast toy that is based on the DC2, the forerunner of the vastly more successful DC3.

267B Airship
86mm
Hollowcast lead unmarked. Silver.

Airliner
133mm
Lead fuselage with low tinplate wing. Blue, red or green.

SETS

34/81 Three bombers, 10 figures and two airships.
38/81 Three bombers, 10 figures, three military vehicles.
48/81 Three bombers, 10 figures, five military vehicles.
68/2 Three bombers, 10 figures, one tank, four cavalry, seven infantry and two airships.

FIGURES

267MC RAF Mechanic	WAAF marching
267PC Pilot in brown or white	Pilot running to plane
267RC RAF Rigger	Airman in battledress

LONE STAR 2.5.0 SERIES
Late 1950s–early 1960s

Lone Star Products, from 1950 a division of DCMT (Diecasting Machine Tools Ltd) set up by A R Mills and S H Ambridge in Palmers Green, fulfilled two functions. First, they served to show the scope and quality of the castings that could be made on DCMT machines; second, they constituted a useful product diversification. The firm existed from 1939 until 1983 when it was taken over by a German manufacturer who retained the name. The five planes were made in the late 1950s. The 250 Aircraft of the World, so named for their 1/250 scale, consist of two smooth main diecastings: upper fuselage with nose and tail; lower fuselage and wing. The Boeing 707 has separate diecast engines. The undercarriages are simple projections from the casting and are fitted with large dumb-bell wheels. These excellent models are marked 'LONE STAR 250 SERIES', and have the name and details of plane on the lower casting. The fit of the castings and the fineness of the lettering providing a superb example of what could be made on DCMT machines. Some of the details are a little inaccurate: the length quoted of the Boeing 707 is that of the first version, the 707-120 whereas scale and other details relate to the 707-320 or -420; (see also Comet). Some, Boeing 707, Britannia and Comet 4 at least, were given a good enamelled silver grey and white paint finish and decorated with excellent waterslide transfers. All were also available finished in silver with instructions for painting and applying the transfers. The lid of the attractive square boxes have a general colour picture of the 707 on the top and the others, one on each of the four sides. The lid of the box is stamped with the plane name and the bottom has a circular sticker carrying the name. A shop display card for the 'TWO-FIVE-O' series, which was labelled for the Bristol Britannia, encouraged the purchaser to join up and acquire the badge, a winged shield emblazoned with 'SKY CADET CORPS' and '2-5-O SERIES'.

250 AIRCRAFT OF THE WORLD

Boeing 707
171mm
Two engines rivetted on each wing.
Cast details: 'ENGINES ROLLS-ROYCE CONWAY TURBO-JET. ALL UP WEIGHT 295,000 LBS. length 144' 4". SPAN 142' 5". CRUISING SPEED 585 MPH. RANGE 5,125 MILES'.
Available fully finished: White upper fuselage and tailfin, silver-grey lower, wings and tailplane.
Transfers: light blue cheat line with silver windows. PANAM globe in blue on tail. Registration PAN-AM.

Bristol Britannia
175mm
Four large tinplate propellers.
Cast details: 'ENGINES BRISTOL PROTEUS TURBO-PROP. ALL UP WEIGHT 185,000 LBS. LENGTH 124' 3". SPAN 142' 3". RANGE 4,600 MILES. CRUISING SPEED 357–415 MPH'.
Available fully finished: White upper, silver-grey lower, dark blue nose. Transfers: Dark blue window line with thin red line above and 'BRITISH AND COMMONWEALTH', Britannia and flag on tail. Registration G-BCSC.

Caravelle
137mm
Rear engine casting held in position between upper and lower castings.
Cast details: 'ENGINES ROLLSROYCE AVON. ALL UP WEIGHT 94,000 LBS. SPAN 112' 6". LENGTH 105'. RANGE 1,500 MILES. CRUISING SPEED 510 MPH'.
Finishing instructions: Paint upper fuselage and tailfin white. Transfers: 'SCANDINAVIAN AIRLINE SYSTEM' in blue above red over blue window line. SAS on tailfin. Registration SE-SAS.

Comet 4
138mm
Cast details: 'ALL UP WEIGHT 158,000 LBS. LENGTH 116' 6". ENGINES ROLLS-ROYCE AVON. RANGE 4,800 MILES. SPAN 114' 10". CRUISING SPEED 485MPH'.
Available fully finished: White upper half of fuselage and tailfin, silver-grey lower.
Transfers: 'BOAC' above dark blue window line with round silver windows. Speedbird on tail. Registration G-BOAC.

Vickers Viscount (801)
114mm
Four small tinplate propellers.
Cast details: 'ROLLSROYCE DART TURBO-PROP. ALL UP WEIGHT 76,500 LBS. SPAN 94'. LENGTH 85' 8". RANGE 1,380 MILES. CRUISING SPEED 360 MPH'.
Finishing details: paint fin and cockpit roof white, the rest of the upper casting green.
Transfers: 'AER LINGUS VISCOUNT' in white above white window line. Green shamrock, flag on tail. Registration: EI-EARL.

MASCOTS

Particularly in the 1930s in England, there was a boyish passion for fixing aeroplane mascots to the handlebars of a bicycle. Many of these had oversize propellers which whirled satisfyingly in the breeze. Most of these high quality diecastings were imported, often from France. They can normally be identified by the presence of a screw thread or spigot for attaching them to the bike.

MATCHBOX SKYBUSTERS 1973–93

(Range still in production)

Technical details such as colour split remain the same until a change is specified.

Introduction dates are the 'toy' year of introduction of the casting.

1973–76 The prefix SP was used instead of SB.

1981–82 Some US catalogue numbers are found in the form 08-01-xx where xx is the standard SB number.

1983 No Skybusters listed in the trade or retail catalogue. All list entries should be read with this hiatus in mind.

c.1983 The casting centre was moved from England to Macau. The underwing wording was changed to suit.

Usually a colour scheme was dropped when a new one was introduced.

The scales quoted are those given in an early catalogue.

From 1990, the casting centre was moved from Macau to Thailand. The underwing wording was changed to suit. Subsequently, casting was moved to China. None of the China castings are included in the list.

From about 1988, some castings that had been dropped from the main catalogue were still available in sets.

SB1 Learjet 1973–91
81mm
Cream upper fuselage and tail, white lower fuselage and wings. D-ILDE.
Yellow and white. Lemon and white. All red, 'DATAPOST'.
Purple and white, 'FEDERAL EXPRESS'.
White, 'QX' '-press'. White, 'USAF', US issue.
White and yellow, G-JCB. In G3 JCB Set only.
'Colourchange': white, 'USAF'. White, 'DHL'.

SB1 US issue of SB6, with an accompanying change

SB2 Corsair A7D 1973–84
84mm. 1/140
Dark green upper fuselage and wings, white lower fuselage and tail fins, US star-on-bar.
Light metallic blue and white. Dark metallic blue and white.

Corsair Crusader 1988–90
Beige, green, brown and white soft edge camouflage, 'USAF'. US issue.
'Colourchange': livery as above.

SB2 US issue of SB22

SB3 A300B Airbus 1973–79
90mm
White upper fuselage, silver wings and lower fuselage.
SP3 with wire axles: 'AIR FRANCE.
Lower casting modified for plastic undercarriage: 'AIR FRANCE'.
White and silver, 'Lufthansa'.
White and silver, 'DELTA'.

SB3 NASA Space Shuttle 1979–post 1993
100mm
White upper including wings and tail and grey lower, 'NASA'.
White and silver grey lower. White and black lower.

SB3 US issue of SB6

SB4 Mirage F1 1973–91
54mm. 1/132
Metallic red, red, white, blue and yellow roundels.
Orange upper including wings and tail, brown lower, '122-18' and red and yellow roundels.
White, blue diagonal tips to wings, tail fin and plane, 'Marines'.
Yellow, red with blue chord stripes, 'VAQ 132'. US issue.
'Colourchange': livery as above.
Blue with red and white flashes.

SB4 US issue of SB24

SB5 Starfighter F104 1973–81
52mm. 1/128
White upper fuselage wings and tail, silver grey lower fuselage, Canadian insignia.
Red and silver grey, Canadian insignia.

SB5 US issue of SB27

SB6 MIG 21 1973–81
57mm. 1/125
Blue upper fuselage, wings and tail, white lower fuselage, star in circle or white edged star.

Re-issue 1988–post 1993. Frosted silver, red stars. US issue.
Black with wide yellow lightning flashes. US issue.
'Colourchange': livery as immediately above.

SB6 US issue of SB15

SB7 Junkers 87D 1973–81
99mm. 1/138
Metallic green. Small/large black on white crosses on wings.
Black upper, sand and brown camouflage on lower, black crosses.
Gold plated for Souvenir Range.

Re-issue 1987-post 1993. As above.

SB7 US issue of SB2

SB8 Spitfire 1973–81
102mm. 1/108
Dark brown upper fuselage and tail, gold lower fuselage and wings.
Metallic green and gold. Gold or silver plated. Souvenir Range.
Brown upper, sand and brown camouflage on lower, RAF roundels.

Re-issue 1987–88. As above but made in Macau.

SB8 US issue of SB27

SB9 Cessna 402 1973–89
103mm.
Metallic green and white. Red and green stripes on top of engine covers.
Orange and dark green stripes. Pea green and white.
Metallic green and white, red bands, N7873Q.
Brown and beige, blue and brown lateral striping, N402CW.
White and red, 'DHL'. Blue and yellow, S7-402.

SB9 US issue of SB4

SB10 Boeing 747 1973–post 1993
94mm
White upper fuselage and tail fin, dark blue lower fuselage wings and tail plane, 'BOAC'.
White and gold plated, 'BOAC'. Souvenir range.
White and high gloss dark blue, 'British airways'.
White and silver plated, 'British airways'. Souvenir range.
White and silver grey, 'QANTAS'.
White and dark blue, 'UNITED STATES OF AMERICA'.
White and silver, 'UNITED STATES OF AMERICA'.
White and silver grey, 'MEA' (Middle East Airlines).
White and dark blue, 'British'. In Japanese and Australian catalogues.
White and silver, 'CATHAY PACIFIC'.
White and silver grey, 'Lufthansa'.
White and silver, 'PAN AM'.
White and silver, 'British Caledonian'.
White and silver grey, 'ANA'. In Japanese cat. only.
All white, 'Virgin'. Only in GS6 Virgin Airways Set and in SB150 X3 Set.
Mid-blue and silver, 'KLM'.
Green upper, white lower, grey wings and tailplane, 'AER LINGUS'.
White and grey, Lufthansa.
White and silver, 'EL AL'.
White and silver, 'SOUTH AFRICAN'.
White and silver, 'OLYMPIC'.
White and silver, 'SAUDIA'.

SB10 US issue of SB1

SB11 Alpha Jet 1973–88
88mm. 1/105
Red upper fuselage and tail fin, white lower fuselage, tailplane and wings, white edged black iron crosses.
Blue upper and red lower, white and red stripes.
White upper and red lower, red wingtips, 'AT 39'.
All blue, red and white flashes on tail, '162'.

SB11 US issue of SB24

SB12 Douglas Skyhawk A-4F 1973–79
71mm. 1/118 scale.
Dark blue upper fuselage and tail, white lower fuselage and wings, 'Navy'.
'MARINES'.

SB12 Pitts Special 1980–91
93mm
Red upper fuselage and tail fin, white lower fuselage, tail plane and wings, red chequers. Metallic green and white, red sunray.
White upper fuselage and upper wing, blue lower fuselage and lower wing, 'MATCHBOX'. Red, 'Fly Virgin'. Red, 'Red Rebels Aerobatics'.

SB12 Mission Chopper 1988
MB57 issued as a Skybuster. US only.
Olive main body and dark cream tail boom, 'ARMY'.

SB13 DC-10 1973–post 1993
93mm
White upper fuselage, rear engine and tailfin, red lower fuselage, wings and tailplane, 'SWISSAIR'.
White and silver grey, 'UNITED'.
White and silver grey, 'SWISSAIR'.
White, dark blue diagonal over tail engine 'UTA'. White, 'THAI'. Silver, 'aeromexico'. Silver, 'AMERICAN'. Light blue upper, silver lower, white tailfin, 'KLM'. White, 'JAL'. White and silver, 'SABENA'.
White, 'SCANDINAVIAN'

SB14 Cessna 210 1973–81
101mm
Orange upper fuselage and tailfin, white lower fuselage, tail plane and separate high wing, orange and black lateral stripes. Orange and brown chord stripes, N94209.

SB15 Phantom F4E 1973–81
73mm. 1/162
Metallic red upper fuselage and tail, white lower fuselage and wings, RAF.

Re-issue 1987–post 1993
Metallic red.
Grey. Orange tail and rays on wings, 'MARINES'. US issue.
'Colourchange': livery as above.

SB16 Corsair F4U 1973–81
100mm. 1/122
Metallic blue, US star-on-bar on wings, 'NAVY'.
US star-on-bar on port wing, 'NAVY' on starboard.
Orange.

Re-issue 1987 Light orange.

SB17 Ramrod 1976–81
99mm
Not based on a prototype. Red upper fuselage and tail, white lower fuselage and wings.

SB18 Wildwind 1977–81
99mm
Not based on a prototype. Lime green upper fuselage, tail fin and wings, white lower fuselage and tail plane. 'Wild Wings' sticker decals.

Re-issue 1987 As above but with tampo printing.

SB19 Piper Comanche 1977–88
104mm.
Red upper fuselage and tail, yellow lower fuselage and wings, N246P.
White, 'XP' (Express Parcels livery).
Tan and dark blue, 'COMMANCHE'.

SB20 Helicopter (Bell 222) 1977–84
101mm (length) Olive green, 'ARMY'.
White upper fuselage and pale blue lower, 'COAST GUARD'.
White and red, 'POLICE'.

SB21 Lightning 1978–81
75mm
Olive upper fuselage, wings and tailfin, grey lower, red and blue roundels.
Silver and grey. Silver.

SB22 Tornado (MRCA) 1978
69mm
Light grey and white camouflage, iron crosses.
Dark grey and light grey and white camouflage, iron crosses.
Grey and white, RAF. White and red, RAF.
Grey and white, RAF. US issue.
'Colourchange': livery of above.

SB23 Supersonic Jet/Airliner/Concorde/Air France Jet
1978–post 1993
60mm
White, 'AIR FRANCE', L-EJDA.
'AIR FRANCE', registration letters deleted.
'SINGAPORE AIRLINES'.
'AIR FRANCE', red and blue outlining to wings, no registration letters.
'SUPERSONIC AIRLINER', G-BSAA
'BRITISH AIRWAYS'. 'Heinz 57'

SB24 F16 Fighter 1979
114mm
White upper fuselage and tail, red lower fuselage and wings, 'US AIR FORCE' on fuselage.
White and red, no fuselage decal.

F16A Red and white, 'UNITED STATES AIR FORCE' Thunderbirds Air Demonstration Squadron. US issue.
White and black, stylised pattern of a Thunderbird, 'USAF'.
Pale blue, pale grey and white soft edge camouflage bands, white lower, 'US AIR FORCE'. US issue.
'Colourchange': livery of above.

SB25 Helicopter 1979–post 1993
105mm
Casting of SB20. Yellow, 'RESCUE', RAF.
White, 'LOS ANGELES CITY FIRE DEPARTMENT'. From US *Code Red* TV Series.
Dark blue and white, 'AIR-AID'. Dark blue, 'RAF RESCUE'.
White, 'SHELL'.
White upper, red lower, '007' decals.
In *Licence to Kill* Set.

SB26 Cessna 210 Float Plane 1982–90
101mm
Red upper fuselage and tail and separate wing, white lower fuselage, N264H.
Black and white, C210F. Red, 'FIRE'. White, '007' decals.
In *Licence to Kill* Set.

B27 Harrier Jet 1982–post 1993
70mm
White upper fuselage, wings and tail, red lower, 'MARINES', US flag on tail.
Casting modified to remove US flag from tail.
Light grey and very light grey soft edge camouflage and white, RAF.
Metallic dark blue and white, 'ROYAL NAVY'.

Marine Harrier
Light grey, dark grey soft edge camouflage and white, 'MARINES'. US issue.
'Colourchange': livery as above.

SB28 A300 Airbus 1982–post 1993
90mm
Casting of SB3 A300B Airbus. White upper fuselage and tail, silver lower fuselage and wings, 'Lufthansa'.
White, 'ALITALIA'. White, 'AIR FRANCE'. Mid-blue and silver, 'KOREAN AIR'. White and silver, 'IBERIA'.
White with metallised grey wings and tailplane, 'SWISSAIR'. Swiss issue in red and white box.
White, 'AIR MALTA'. White, 'AIR INTER'. Silver, 'EASTERN'.

SB29 Lockheed SR-71 Blackbird 1990–91
71mm
Satin black, 'US AIR FORCE'.

SB30 Grumman F-14 Tomcat 1990–post 1993
74mm
Grey upper fuselage (with blue) and tail including fins, white lower fuselage and tail planes, 'NAVY'.

SB31 Boeing 747-400 1990–post 1993
94mm
White upper fuselage and tail fin, metallised grey lower fuselage and tailplane, 'CATHAY PACIFIC'. in red with green lining, green bands on tail.
Grey and dark blue,'BRITISH AIRWAYS'.
White and silver, 'SINGAPORE AIRLINES'.
White and grey, 'LUFTHANSA'. White and silver, 'LUFTHANSA'

SB32 Fairchild A-10 Thunderbolt 1990
104mm
Dark green and dark grey camouflage, WR 255.

SB33 Bell JetRanger Helicopter 1990/91–post 1993
106mm (length)
White body, blue engine housing, orange fuselage, 'SKY-RANGER'.

SB34 Lockheed C-130 Hercules 1990–post 1993
110mm
White, 'USCG' (US Coast Guards).

SB35 Mil Mi-24 Hind-D Helicopter 1990–post 1993
112mm (length)
Brown and tan camouflage on upper fuselage, outriggers and tail, grey lower fuselage, red star.

SB36 Lockheed F-117A Stealth Fighter 1990–post 1993
92mm
Matt grey, 'USAF'. White – in Graffic Traffic Sets.

SB37 Hawk Trainer MK 1A 1991–post 1993
92mm
Red, Red Arrows RAF Display Team livery. Part of proceeds of sales donated to RAF Benevolent Fund.
1992 promotion on Kellogg's Frostie packet.

SB38 BAe 146 1992–post 1993
87mm
White, with grey underfuselage, 'DAN-AIR'.
White, 'THAI'.

SB39 Stearman PT17 Kaydett 1991–post 1993
108mm
Yellow, 'Crunchie'. 1991 – promotional for Cadbury's Crunchie based on biplane used by Crunchie Flying Circus Display Team, purple promotional box.
White – in Graffic Traffic Set.
1992 White, 'Circus Circus', red and yellow on upper wing, trailing edges of wing and tail plane.
1992 only in Set MC804.

SB40 Boeing 737.300 1992–post 1993
82mm
White upper, blue lower, silver tail and wing, 'Britannia'.
Blue and silver, 'KLM'.

SKYBUSTER SETS

Sets have frequently been available. To begin with, they were composed of groups of aeroplanes in the same colours as those found in the individual boxes. Subsequently, sets were composed of a mixture of Skybusters and Matchbox 75s/Miniatures, usually road vehicles. Only the planes are included in the listing. The sets usually had a decoration theme e.g. Virgin Airways. The planes in these liveries may or may not have been available in the standard range at the same time. Some of the sets were special issues only available in one or two countries. The listing is in year of issue, not catalogue number, order. The models are packed in oblong, later squarish, boxes with a clear window or windows in the top in the top or in bubble packs. In 1982, 1983 there were no Skybuster Gift Sets in trade or retail catalogues.

G10 Thunder Jets 1976–78
SB2 Corsair A7D, SB4 Mirage F1, SB5 Starfighter F104, SB12 Douglas Skyhawk A4F.

G16 Sky Giants 1978
SB3 A300B Airbus 'Lufthansa', SB3 A300B Airbus 'AIR FRANCE', SB10 Boeing 747 'British airways', SB13 DC10 'Swissair'.

G7 Emergency Set 1979–81
75s etc + SB25 Helicopter 'RESCUE'.

G8 Thunder Jets 1979–81
SB5 Starfighter, SB21 Lightning, SB22 Tornado, SB24 F16.

G18 Sky Giants 1979–81
SB10 Boeing 747 'British airways', SB13 DC10 'SWISSAIR', SB13 DC10 'UNITED, SB23 Concorde 'AIR FRANCE'.

Collect 1800 1984
Convoy, Miniatures + SB3 NASA Space Shuttle. Only in Japanese catalogue.

CY NASA Countdown Gift Set 1984
2 Convoy, Miniatures 75s/miniatures + SB3 NASA Space Shuttle.
Only in US catalogue.

G3 JCB World Beaters in Action 1987
Miniatures including MB75 Helicopter + SB1 Learjet 'JCB'. Not in catalogue. Available on collectors' market.

G5 Federal Express Set 1987
Miniatures + SB1 Learjet 'FEDERAL EXPRESS'. Not in UK catalogue.

G6 Virgin Airways Set 1987
Miniatures including MB75 Helicopter + SB10 Boeing 747 'VIRGIN'.
Not in UK catalogue.

G10 Pan Am Set 1988
Miniatures + SB10 Boeing 747 'PAN AM'. Not in UK catalogue.

G11 Lufthansa Set 1988
Miniatures + SB28 A300B Airbus 'Lufthansa'. Not in UK catalogue.

C11 Japanese Airport Set 1988
Miniatures, Playmat + SB10 Boeing 747 'All Nippon Airways' + SB28 A300B Airbus 'AIR FRANCE'.

SB150 (SB808) Sets/Skybuster x3
All packs consisted of two MB75 + one Skybuster. All bubble packs on blue grid card. Packed for Tesco 1988. Otherwise available 1990. Liveries as described by the title.

150 NASA Set SB3 NASA Space Shuttle
150 Virgin Airways Set SB10 Boeing 747
150 Federal Express Set SB1 Lear Jet
150 Fire Rescue Set SB26 Cessna + MB75 Helicopter
150 Royal Navy Set SB27 Harrier + MB57 Helicopter
150 XP Express Parcels Set SB19 Piper Commanche
150 British Airways Set 1991 SB23 Supersonic Airliner

Available 1990 with labelling in French. (nos 225, 6, 7)
150 Air France Set SB23 Supersonic Airliner
150 Virgin Airways Set as item 2 above
150 Lufthansa Set SB10 Boeing 747

Dogfight Selected 'adversaries' from the special US liveries repackaged in twin-packs, rigid bubble packs. Available 1988.
1 SB7 Corsair Crusader (UK SB2) + SB9 Mirage F1 (UK SB4)
2 SB3 Mig 21 (UK SB6) + SB4 F16A (UK SB24)
3 SB1 Mig 21 (UK SB6) + SB6 Phantom (UK SB15)

Colourchange 1989
'Four for the price of two' blister packs consisting of two Colourchange Skybusters with two similar Miniatures.

James Bond, Licence to Kill Set for Woolworths 1989
Two Miniatures + SB26 Cessna Float Plane in white, red and black 007 livery
SB20 Helicopter ditto.

MC (Motorcity) Sets.
First issue 1990 but see 1991 below.

Battle of Britain/Kellogg's 1990
Kellogg's commissioned a Spitfire from Tonka-Polistil. Demand was so great that at the end of the run a quantity had to be ordered from Matchbox.

SB8 Spitfire
Made in Thailand, light metallic gold, tampo printed green camouflage with red and blue roundels on top of the wings.

Airport Packs Announced 1991
Released in Germany and other parts of mainland Europe.

SB810 Alitalia Set SB28 A300 Airbus
SB811 KLM Set SB13 DC10
SB812 SAS Set SB13 DC10
SB813 Lufthansa Set SB31 Boeing 747-400

MC (Motorcity) Sets.
Introduced with a single set in 1990, they come in a wide variety of sizes with a wide mixture of planes, vehicles and sometimes, plastic buildings. The catalogue illustrations tend to include additional models not sold in the set but this is not always stated. The sets were usually available for two or more years.

MC17 British Airways Gift Set 1990
Three Miniatures + SB23 Concorde + SB31 Boeing 747-400

MC15 Fire Set 1991
Four Miniatures, one Convoy + SB26 Cessna Float Plane

MC150 Motorcity Airport 1991
Hangar, runway, car park playmat only

MC804 Circus Circus 1992
Five Miniatures, one Convoy, cardboard cut-out circus tents
+ SB39 Stearman Biplane

Graffic Traffic 1991
All vehicles in the packs are finished in white. The packs
contain decals and brightly coloured waterproof pens for
decorating the toys.

GF140 Seven vehicle set 1991. SB36 Stealth

GF150 Two vehicle set 1992. SB39 Stearman Biplane

Red Arrows Sets 1992
Part of the proceeds of the sale of of the sets donated to the
RAF Benevolent Fund.

CY108 Hawk Trainer with low loader 1992
One Convoy + SB37 Hawk Trainer

MC24 Red Arrows Set 1992
Two Miniatures and MB75 Helicopter + two SB37 Hawk
Trainers

MC160 Squadron HQ 1992
Playmat, plastic building + two SB 37 Hawk Trainers

Boots The Chemist 1992
Skybusters and Miniatures packaged in own brand packaging.

Twinpack 1992
SB23 Supersonic Airliner AIR FRANCE
SB37 Boeing 737-400 Cathay Pacific

Airport Playset 1992
Two Miniatures + SB23 Supersonic Airliner AIR FRANCE +
SB37 Boeing 737-400 Cathay Pacific

MATCHBOX 75s/MINIATURES
1977–92

Matchbox '75s' or '1-75s' was the group of
models that made Lesney its fame and
fortune. In the first 25 years of production the
toys were all automotive and thereafter, planes
have not figured largely. In 1983, with the
change of ownership, the name was changed
to 'Miniatures' and production moved to
Macau. By 1985 facilities in China were used.
The information on the base includes the
catalogue number, name of model and place of
manufacture. All the toys were made to fit the
box so that the jets have folding wings and
the Mission Helicopter has a plug-in tail
boom. All are fitted with small black wheels.
The plastic parts, rotors, skids, engines, varied
from black to white to grey or chromed over
the colour schemes. Only the introduction
dates of the sets are given. Their availability
was typically two to three years. The scale of
the models is small and their features greatly

exaggerated. At the time of writing the range
is still in production.

The aeroplanes

Seasprite Helicopter – MB75s. In 1986, the
mould was leased to Bulgaria with Matchbox
supplying the wheels. Marked 'Made in
Bulgaria' and bubble-packed it was available
in a large range of colours.

Helicopter – MB75. It is not a model but a
generic toy, produced in many colour variants.
The main versions are listed.

Mission Helicopter – MB57. Featured in the
television series *Blue Thunder*. Casting also
used for SB12 Mission Chopper.

The listing includes versions only available in sets.

MB75 Seasprite Helicopter 1977–81
74mm (length)
White with red base, 'Rescue'.
1986 Made in Bulgaria. Mid-metallic green upper, orange
lower, and in other colours. Bubble-pack.

MB2 S2 Jet 1981–85
60mm.
Black upper fuselage and tail, yellow lower fuselage and
plastic wings.
Blue upper, white lower, 'VIPER'.

Re-issue in Commando range 1989
Olive green, beige patterning.

MB27 Swing Wing Jet 1981–86
Red upper fuselage and tail fins, white lower fuselage and
wings, 'JET' and 'SET'.

Re-issue in Commando range 1989
Black, yellow pattern.

MB75 Helicopter 1982
76mm (length)
White upper fuselage, orange plastic lower, 'MBTV NEWS'.
White upper fuselage, black lower, 'POLICE'.
Silver upper, orange lower, '600'.
White upper, orange lower, 'RESCUE'.
White upper with red tail fin, black lower, 'RESCUE'.
White upper, red lower, 'FIRE DEPT'.
Black, 'AIRCAR'.
White upper, orange lower, 'NASA'.
White upper, red base, Japanese characters.
White upper, yellow lower, 'JCB'.
White upper, red lower, 'Virgin'.
White upper, light yellow lower, 'FIRE DEPT'.
Red upper, white lower, 'AEROBATIC TEAM'.
Red upper, white lower, 'FIRE DEPT'.
White upper with orange tail, black lower, 'RESCUE'.
White upper, yellow lower, '123456' (My First Matchbox)
Red upper, white lower, 'ROYAL AIR FORCE'.

MB57 Mission Helicopter 1985
95mm including detachable tail boom.
Dark blue, red and white patches. Red body, 'SHERRIF'.
In Army livery as SB12 US issue.
In 'NAVY' Rescue livery in SB150 Royal Navy Set.
Red upper, 'REBELS'.
Black with yellow pattern. In Commando range.
White, dark grey lower body, 'POLICE'.

Commando: A range of recolours and re-issues divided into two armies, 'Strike Team' in olive green and 'Dagger Force' in black. A variety of packs including bubble packs and small sets were available in the US and Europe. Listed in separate leaflet, not main catalogue.
Strike Team: MB2 S2 Jet
Dagger Force: MB27 Swing Wing Jet, MB57 Mission Helicopter

75S/MINIATURES GIFT SETS

ACTION PACKS

G7 Emergency Action Pack 1983
Vehicles etc + MB75 Helicopter 'POLICE'.

C6 Collect 1100 (Japanese cat.) 1984
MB 75s + MB77 (UK MB75) Helicopter 'POLICE'.

G3 JCB World Beaters in Action 1988
MB75 Helicopter (See Skybusters Set G3)

G6 Virgin Airways Se 1988
MB75 Helicopter (See Skybusters Set G6)

CONVOY SETS

CY11 Helicopter Transporter 1983
Convoy Low Loader + MB75 Helicopter '600'.
1985: Convoy + MB75 Helicopter 'AIRCAR'.

CY201 Fire Rescue Set 1985
Convoy + MB75 Helicopter 'FIRE DEPT'.

CY202 Police Set 1985
Convoy + MB75 Helicopter 'RESCUE'.

CY204 NASA Set 1986
Convoy, Miniature + MB75 Helicopter 'NASA'.

CY804 Fire Set 1991
Convoy, Miniature + MB75 'FIRE'.

TEAM CONVOY

TC6 Rescue Set 1988
Convoy + MB75 Helicopter 'RESCUE'.

MINIATURES THEME PACKS

MP103 Airport Fire Set 1988
Two Miniatures + MB75 Helicopter 'FIRE DEPT'

MOTORCITY GIFT SETS

MC12 Aerobatic Team 1988
Convoy Aircraft Transporter + MB57 Mission Helicopter 'RED REBELS', MB75 'AEROBATIC TEAM'.

MC13 Police 1988
Convoy, Miniatures + MB 75 'RESCUE'.

EMERGENCY

EM71 Action Police 1992
Two Miniatures, Convoy Low Loader + MB57 'POLICE'.

EM75 Action Fire 1992
Four Miniatures, one Convoy + MB75 'RESCUE'.

EM90 30 Piece Carry Pack 1992 including: MB57, MB75 as above.

RAF BENEVOLENT FUND/ TONKA POLISTIL/KELLOGG'S
1990–

In the summer of 1990, to celebrate the 50th Anniversary of the Battle of Britain and to support the Royal Air Force Benevolent Fund's 'Reach for the Sky' Appeal, Kellogg's carried an offer on the back of Cornflakes packets. Eight tokens plus a small amount for postage secured a Spitfire, a Hurricane or a card model Airfield Fighter Station. The smooth two-piece castings have no manufacturer's markings at all but were made by Tonka Polistil in Italy. They are fitted with black three-blade propellers, black wheels on a single axle and clear canopies. The gold paint finish is excellent and the upper wing surfaces are covered with clear stickers printed with a green camouflage pattern and red and blue roundels. Unboxed. Towards the end of the offer, Matchbox SB8 Spitfire, tampo printed, was also used to supply the demand. In 1991, the two castings, finished in the same way, became available in plain white boxes marked 'Tonka Polistil' which was by then owned by a Far East manufacturer. In 1993, the planes were offered by Kellogg's on boxes of Askeys ice-cream cones.

Hurricane
102mm. 1/120
A model of the Mark I of 1937–40 fitted with a Merlin II engine.

Spitfire
97mm. 1/115
A model of the Mark I of 1937–40 also fitted with a Merlin II engine.

SEGAL 1947

Segal manufactured figures in lead. Their 1947 catalogue lists 23 small aeroplanes.
They are so far unidentified.

SKYBIRDS 1936–1940

Skybirds was set up by A J Holladay at 3 Aldermanbury Avenue, London, near what is now the Barbican, in 1932. Until into the War, they produced accurate wood kits of contemporary and WWI aircraft, designed in 1/72 scale by James Hay Stevens. Some metal parts were used and eventually they were available fully finished. Many 1/72 scale airmen figures were issued. Two cast lead planes, called Skybird Junior Series, were produced in 1936. The unmarked fully finished solid castings are fitted with separate wheel spats and prominent cockpit glazing bars. Boxed in blue or brown card boxes with yellow labels on the lids, some emblazoned with 'Givjoy Copyright Design' or 'Givjoy' with a leaflet giving performance details. A selection of roundel and number transfer sheets was available. The Ships series contained a lapel badge of a Short R24/31 Flying Boat.

26 Percival Mew Gull Racing Monoplane 1935
99mm
Single casting, two-blade propeller.
Cream with '2' on fuselage, 'G' on tailfin.

27 Caudron C450/460 Racing Monoplane 1934/5
92mm
Fuselage with separate wings and cockpit, spring propeller.
Blue, '8' on fuselage, 'F' on tailfin.

27/1 Aeronca-Jap
A kit: cast fuselage supplied painted but all other parts unpainted.

TAYLOR & BARRETT c.1935

Taylor & Barrett commonly referred to as T&B. After being demobbed, Fred G Taylor, a lift engineer, decided to go into lead toy making with his brother-in-law A R Barrett, who worked for Britains. They set up business in 1920 in Scholefield Road, Holloway N19, moving in 1929 to Park Works, The High Road, East Finchley from where they sold direct to shops, via wholesalers such as Crescent or to middlemen like Kay (Sports & Games) Ltd, Carlisle Road, London NW9. The premises were destroyed by an air raid in 1940. In 1945, the moulds were divided between F G Taylor & Sons and A Barrett & Sons, both firms trading independently until about 1980. They produced two planes, a pilot and mechanic. The side view, windows, tail etc, show that the first was obviously based on the Armstrong Whitworth Atalanta. The second is a good model of the DH Comet Racer.

From 1935 to 1937, Kay (Sports & Games) Ltd bought in T&B products, probably without

the name T&B on them, and packaged them as Aerodrome Sets nos 0,1,2,3 in attractive boxes eg:
Airliner with petrol pump and pilot.
Two Airliners, One Comet, pump, pilot, mechanic.
Three Airliners, three road vehicles, two pumps, four figures.

There is a crude, heavy lead 'Comet' 103mm long, a modification of the Comet die (107mm) in which the nose has been shortened and the cockpit moved forward of the wings, which has no markings at all. The rivetting of the engines to the wings indicate that it is factory made – but in which factory is unknown.

Immediately after the war, a boxed set about 50cm square consisting of an Airliner and a Comet with eight road vehicles, road signs and a policeman on a horse, all of the castings as pre-war, was hung on the factory wall as a demonstration piece, where it became extremely dirty but survived. The lid has no label or markings.

A Barrett & Sons
A Barrett & Sons ended up with the 'Atalanta' Airliner and Comet Racer dies. They were re-released in about 1990. The trademark is a capital B with '&' in the upper loop and 'S' in the lower.

123 Aeroplane pre-1935
100mm
Lead fuselage and separate wing, both parts marked 'BRITISH T&B MADE'.
Two moulds: one marked 'ATALANTA' (including quotation marks) on the fuselage side centrally above undercarriage legs; one with no lettering but cabin door outline on port fuselage.
Large lead two-blade propeller. Lead wheel hubs pressed onto axle. White tyres.
Royal blue, silver wing, tail planes, red with silver or yellow with silver.

137 DH Comet after 1935
143mm
Large lead casting, with engine pod/undercarriage spat castings rivetted on, marked 'DH COMET' under wings and along top of fuselage, 'MADE IN ENGLAND COPYRIGHT' up inside fuselage.
Large lead two-blade propellers. Small lead wheels on individual axles.
Green and brown camouflage, red or mid-blue.

369 or 306 Aeroplane Set Contents unknown

FIGURES
160 Air pilot
161 Mechanic – renumbered 572

'Atalanta' Airliner

Trademark under wings. 'BRITISH B&S MADE' under centre wing. 'BRITISH T&B MADE' still inside fuselage.
Sprayed yellow with red-brown on nose, tailplane and wingtips, red propeller and wheels.

Comet Racer

Trademark under starboard wing. Wheels cast solid.
Sprayed matt white with red blown in on wingtips, fuselage top and tailplane. Red two-blade propeller.

TIMPO c.1945–c.1955

The name trade name Timpo derives from the firm's name: Toy Importers Ltd which was established in Westbourne Grove, Bayswater in 1941. Importing toys at the time being impossible, one wonders at the origin of the name. To give the firm a material to work with, the use of metal etc being prohibited, the managing director Mr Gawrylowicz invented 'timpolin' a light, strong, shatter resistant mixture of chalk, plaster of paris and glue, from which were moulded, for example, a Boeing Superfortress. Wood and fibreboard hangars were also made and figures were available. When the use of metal was permitted, some such as the Lightning were made in both materials to the same size. Metal plane production took place in the late 1940s. The trademark was TIMPOTOYS in a triangle or one word printed under the other sharing a large T between them. Not all their product is marked. The firm's name was changed to Model Toys in 1953 and it moved to Shotts in Lancashire. Elmont, a maker of plastic aeroplanes, coproduced with them for a time. Timpo ceased trading in 1979.

Boeing B17 Flying Fortress

130mm
Three-blade tinplate propellers. Dull brown/green camouflage.
White star on blue roundel on wingtips, or off white/cream.
A342 on starboard wingtip, large red, white and blue flash on tail.

Lockheed Lightning

101mm
Dull brown/green camouflage.
White star in blue circle on starboard boom and port wing.

SETS

Bomber Station (!) Set

Three Lightnings, four composition pilots strung to red or blue backing card. Dark blue box (25x18cm) with paper label with drawing of Fortress and Lightnings.

Bomber Station Set (large)

Three Lightnings, two B17 all in camouflage, six figures strung onto a backing card.
The yellow lid box measures 36x26cm.

Civil Airport (!) Set

Four Fortresses, six figures strung to green backing card.
Autumn colours on box lid with airport drawing.

The Timpolin 'Famous Aeroplane Series' included Fortress, Superfortress, Mosquito, Lightning, Spitfire, Typhoon and Jet Propelled Glider all in camouflage, silver or blue.

TREMO 1940–47

An emigré from Hitler's Germany, Herr 'Willi' Winkler, who had made some of the masters for the Wiking Ship range in 1935 set up a casting firm, Trefforest Mouldings, on a trading estate in South Wales to make lead warships. The name was contracted to Tremo Mouldings Ltd in 1940 and the firm moved to John Street, Cardiff. The trade mark is a T superimposed over an M. The ships were part toy part recognition model but they were not adopted as such by the Admiralty. In about 1939, a small group of good, one-piece, lead, Dinky-sized aeroplanes were produced some of which are not marked with the trademark. They were finished in either silver or camouflage and have a distinctive finish on the cockpits of the camouflaged versions: white with the support struts picked out in black. All have red, white and blue RAF roundels and three-blade tinplate propellers. At the end of the war (during which he was interned in the Isle of Wight as an enemy alien), Willi Winkler placed an advertisement in *Jane's* announcing the resumption of production in Cardiff. However, a fire in 1947 put an end to manufacture. The planes are not listed, even in the firm's ship catalogues. They are packed in brown boxes with a printed label on the lid.

Hurricane

52mm. 1/243. Good model.
'HURRICANE' under starboard wing. 'TM MADE IN ENGLAND' under port.
Detailed fixed undercarriage. Camouflaged upper, blue under or silver.

Bristol Blenheim Mark I
69mm. 1/252
No markings. Camouflaged or silver.

Handley Page Harrow
111mm. 1/243
'HARROW TM' under starboard wing. 'BRITISH MADE' under port.
Detailed fixed undercarriage. Camouflaged upper, black
under, white rear gun turret or silver.

UNIDENTIFIED

Many one-piece lead castings are not marked
with either manufacturer's name or country of
origin. Some are only marked 'Made in
England', or with the plane name, or even
both. In some cases it is possible to attribute
them to one particular manufacturer because
of some other identification feature such as the
white painted, black lined cockpits on Tremo,
but others have yet to be firmly identified. If
propellers are cast in with the wing or the
casting is extremely poor, they are probably
from casting moulds, but some good castings
were made for resale from these moulds.

Examples: One-piece castings of poor quality
with upper and lower surface detail. Plane
name under starboard wing, 'MADE IN
ENGLAND' under port. Two-blade tinplate or
two- or three-blade cast propellers. RAF
roundels may be red and blue, red, white and
blue or red, white and blue with yellow
exterior band.

Hurricane
84mm
Green and brown camouflage. Roundels.

Spitfire
76mm
Sand. Roundels.

Spitfire III (clipped wings)
52mm
Green and brown camouflage.

Blenheim Bomber MkIV
118/120mm
Green and brown camouflage. Red, white and blue roundels
or ditto with yellow high visibility external ring.

Fairey Battle
75mm
Composition (might be Timpo)
Orange tinplate three-blade propellers, RAF roundels.

USA production

Aero Mini, **Air Command** (see Dyna-Flites), **Bachmann**, **Barclay**, **Best Toy** (see Kansas Toy), **Casting Moulds** (see Introduction), **Cast Iron** (see Introduction), **Cragstan Wild Wings**, **'Dime Store'** (see Introduction), **Dyna-Flites**, **Erie**, **Ertl**, **Fairymark** (see also Lincoln Toys NZ), **Frankonia** (see Mail Box Series), **Gabriel** (see Hubley), **Goodee-Toy** (Excel), **Hobby Room** (see Dyna-Flites), **Home Manufacturing Co** (see Casting Moulds, Introduction), **Hot Wings** (see Dyna-Flites), **Hubley Kiddie Toy**, **Kansas Toy**, **Kiddie Toy** (see Hubley), **Mail Box Series** (Frankonia), **Midgetoy**, **MT**, **Modern Toy** (see Dyna-Flites), **Renwal**, **Revell**, **Road Champ Flyers**, **Slush cast toys** (see Introduction), **Tootsietoys**, **Unidentified** (see Introduction), **Wings** (see Dyna-Flites), **Zylmex**, **Zee Toys** (Intex) (see Dyna-Flites).

INTRODUCTION

Apart from cast iron, a material hardly ever used for toys in Europe, the methods and materials used on both sides of the Atlantic before World War II were similar. What differs is the terminology used and the relatively greater or lesser quantity of toys produced by each method. Cast iron was used for planes and airships up until the war and could fall within the scope of this book, being both cast metal and toys. However production is not well classified, is almost impossible to research without living in the US, was not exported, and is usually very expensive, so it has been excluded. Particularly in the 1920s and 1930s, there were many small unidentifiable toys made for sale in dime stores where, in principle, any item could be purchased for a cent or dime. They were usually slush cast or diecast lead and rarely based on an identifiable prototype. Thus a typical description might read 'a crude lead, high wing, open cockpit diecasting, embossed US-46 on squared fuselage side, span 55mm; has red wood hubs with white rubber tyres and is painted green with yellow tail plane, black stars on yellow roundels painted within cast outlines on wings.' In the early 1990s, Eccles, who specialise in reproductions of pre-war toys, re-issued some Dime Store toys.

Slushmoulding was a common casting method widely used before World War II for producing cheap toys, which was more frequently used for toys, other than soldiers, in the USA than in the rest of the world. Two-piece metal moulds with wall thicknesses designed to sink the heat from the molten lead to produce a casting of the required thickness were used. When the metal had cooled sufficiently, the surplus was poured back into the melting pot, producing the rough interior that typifies this method of production. Great detail could be obtained but makers marks could only be placed on the exterior of the toy. They were frequently omitted, leading to much difficulty in attribution. In addition, many of the moulds were passed around from firm to firm, further complicating the task. A recognisable DC2, with stars-in-roundels cast onto the upper surface of the wings was produced using this method.

Particularly during the war and in the 1950s, when toys were in short supply, a variety of casting moulds were sold for producting one-piece lead toys. Home Manufacturing Co, of Chicago Illinois, produced a 'Home Foundry' set. Amongst the moulds is one for a small (approximately 35mm) airship.

Recently, diecast aeroplane Toy Banks have been made. Though they could be given to a child, they are really aimed at the collector and are therefore excluded.

AERO MINI 1967–76, 1990

To quote from one of their brochures, 'The Aero Mini Collector's Series models are authentically detailed miniature reproductions of world-famous airplanes. Models are of ALL METAL construction and precision die-cast to an accuracy of five-thousands of an inch! The realism of flying is experienced through such features as retractable landing gear, ventral passenger stairways that raise and lower, cockpit canopies that open and close and meticulously duplicated airline and military identification. Built with the ACCURACY and PRECISION of collectors' demands, Aero Mini models are rugged enough for everyday play'. They were the inspiration of one Robert J Metchick, an ex-Navy pilot who couldn't find accurate toy planes for his children.

Some models were bought for children as playworn examples show, but, probably because they were expensive, the majority have always been in collectors' hands. Therefore, they mainly fall outside the scope of this book. However, since they were partly intended as toys, some brief notes and a listing follow.

The head office was in Farmingdale, New York and production started in Japan to keep costs down. After it was discovered that the Japanese were secretly producing models from the Aero Mini dies and distributing them in the Far East, production was transferred back to the US in 1974. The costs of the move were not recovered and the business failed in 1976. In 1990, the firm was reconstituted as Aeromini with a new President and it was planned to reproduce the models from the original moulds.

Apart from the Boeing 747 which is 1/290, the scale is 1/240. There are 10 beautiful, accurate, models in a variety of liveries. The following list is that of the 1967–76 issues and is not in chronological order. Usually, each livery has a different catalogue number.

2009 Super VC-10 BOAC

3006 A6M5 Zero Japanese Navy
3006 Japanese Air Force

4150 F-4E Phantom US Navy – USS Independence
4150 US Navy – USS America
4151 US Air Force

4152 Royal Navy
4156 Japanese Air Force

4251 F-104J Starfighter US Air Force
4257 German Air Force

7001 Boeing 707 Pan American
7002 TWA
7003 Northwest Orient
7005 American

7051 Boeing C-135 US Air Force
7051 US Air Force with black nose

7201 Boeing 727 Pan American
7202 TWA
7203 Northwest Orient
7204 JAL – unauthorised issue
7205 American
7207 Eastern
7210 Branif
7210 Braniff
7274 All Nippon – unauthorised issue

7306 Boeing 737 United
7316 Piedmont
7379 All Nippon – unauthorised issue

7400 Boeing 747 Boeing Dash-100
7401 Pan American
7402 TWA
7403 Northwest Orient
7404 JAL
7405 American
7405C American (in chrome)
7407 Eastern
7409 BOAC
7513 Air Canada
7451 USAF E4A
7451 Spirit of '76

8004 Douglas DC-8 JAL – unauthorised issue
8007 Eastern
8013 Air Canada

9002 Douglas DC-9 TWA
9007 Eastern
9008 Ozark
9013 Air Canada

BARCLAY 1930s

During the 1930s, Barclay produced soldiers and then cars, first slushmoulded later diecast. Some slush were marked 'MADE IN USA' on the outside, the diecast were usually marked 'Barclay'. They are fitted with white rubber wheels on a single axle.

US Army Plane (Northrop Delta)
97mm
Single lead diecasting marked 'BARCLAY USA' up inside the fuselage. Six windows and door both sides. Windows not properly pierced on some examples. Wings embossed with stars-in-roundels and 'US ARMY'.
Pressed steel large three- or two-blade propeller secured with nail.
Silver, red.

CRAGSTAN WILD WINGS SERIES 1968–

Cragstan Industries, a New York based firm, produced several small groups of planes, under the Wild Wings Series name, which were manufactured, sized to fit the packaging, in Hong Kong. Bubble packed onto stiff card printed with a standard bold decorative scheme colour coded for each group, eg International Jets with orange, shocking pink and deep purple, Airline Jets with purple, turquoise and blue etc. The castings are usually two piece with the split along the fuselage cheat line. Most are marked 'CRAGSTAN' in a block up underneath the fuselage or tail along with 'Made in Hong Kong'. Some have part of the name of the plane as well. The World War I Series have 'Cragstan' on a plastic bar between the wheels. They are not to scale but fit diagonally easily within the 110mm square plastic bubble, normally held in position with a plastic plug, with the result that many of the castings have an oblong plug hole underneath. The reverse of the backing cards is printed with a list of the planes in the range and with enthusiastic, reasonably accurate information about the plane enclosed. The wheels are small metal or black plastic circles. 1123 Airline Jets, 1121 World War II Series, three of 1128 Private Planes and 1129 International Jets have retractable landing gear, generally involving a flattish tin spring. Decals are usually paper stickers. The quality of the casting on the whole produced good surfaces but rough edges and the colours are rather toy-like. The decals are frequently poor. The accuracy of the models is good to average. However the choice of subject is interesting and many significant planes, some of which do not appear in other ranges, are represented. Though Mandarin (M) made in Hong Kong biplanes are superficially similar, their simple solid castings are not from the same dies, nor do the Mandarin planes appear to have been ripped off from Cragstan castings because some detail lines and the stagger of the wings is different.

In 1969, Airfix imported them into Britain direct from Hong Kong. Though they sold well, they mark the start of the diversification of Airfix away from plastic kits into areas in which they did not have expertise and the beginning of the decline of the company.

Packaging marked 1968 lists:	Packaging marked 1969 lists:
1120-3 World War I Series	1120-3 World War I Series
1121-3 World War II Series	
1122-3 US Jets Series	1122-3 US Jets Series
1123-3 Airline Jets Series	
1124-3 Helicopter Series	1124-3 Helicopter Series
	1127-3 Historic Series
	1128-3 Private Plane Series
	1129-3 International Jet Series

All propellers are black plastic. Decals are stickers.

1120-3 WORLD WAR I SERIES (Biplanes)

Spad XIII
115mm. 1/71
Yellow with black shading. Two-blade propeller. White edged RAF roundels, red and black stripes on upper and lower wings.

SE5 Scout
113mm. 1/72
Sky blue with black band in front of tailplane. Four-blade propeller, gun above upper wing centre. White-edged RAF roundels on upper and lower wings and side rear fuselage.

Sopwith Camel
122mm. 1/70
Sand with silver cowling. Two-blade propeller. Roundels as SE5, red and white V on upper wing, black and white stripes across rear fuselage.

Fokker D7
105mm. 1/85
Rear corners of upper wing flaps and tail plane flaps protrude beyond the edges of the fixed part. Red with white shading. Black and white iron crosses and stripes.

1121-3 WORLD WAR II SERIES

P-51 Mustang

Japanese Zero
122mm. 1/90
No markings. Dark green with silver cowling. White bordered rising sun stickers and red and white flashes on wings, suns on fuselage.

British Spitfire
115mm. 1/97
Dark blue. Red, white and blue roundels with white edges.

German Me.109 Messerschmitt
115mm. 1/87
Light green, red wing leading edges and tailplane tips. White edged red crosses on wings and fuselage sides.

1122-3 US JETS SERIES

F-105 Thunderchief
115mm. 1/93
Dark green with gold camouflage on upper surfaces, silver radome and tailfin. Star-on-bar on wings.

F-111 Swing Wing
87mm with wings extended. 1/150-170!
White, red nose, tail tips. Star-on-bar on wings.

F-86 Sabre Jet (Night Fighter version)
115mm. 1/103
Light grey, red radome nose, wingtips and upper tailplane tips. Star-on-bar on port wing, 'USAF' on starboard.

F-104 Starfighter
55mm including missiles. 1/121
Blue-green, silver nosecone, upper tailplane surface and wingtip missiles. Stars-on-bars on wings.

1123-3 AIRLINE JETS

Boeing 707

Concorde Supersonic

Boeing 727 Whisper Jet
90mm. 1/365
White, dark green nose, fuselage engines and tailplane. 'EASTERN', window and tail stripe in dark green.

British Vickers VC-10
90mm. 1/495
Grey, dark blue nose, tail fin and engines. 'BOAC' and windows on dark blue line.

1124-3 HELICOPTER SERIES

Piaseki Work Horse (H21)
115mm long including nose bubble. 1/139
Grey with yellow fins on tail. Star-on-bar on rear fuselage. Blue plastic blades on rotors. Clear door and hatch detail on the castings.

Huey Cobra (Bell 209)
115mm long. 1/118
All moss green with orange rotor tips and missile nose cones. Star-on-bar on rear fuselage.

Piaseki Twin Jet (YH16A)
115mm long including perspex nose. 1/206
Bright blue. White paper side strip with black windows. Orange top surface on tail pylon.

Sikorsky HO4S
115mm long. 1/110
Orange fuselage with silver roof. Dark blue plastic rotor blades. Star-on-bar on rear fuselage and nose.

1127-3 HISTORIC SERIES

Spirit of St Louis
120mm
Silver. Correct registration NX211 in black on clear tape sticker on starboard wing, incorrect Stars and Stripes on port.

Ford Trimotor
118mm. 1/191
Yellow with black sunray pattern on wings and stripe on tailplane.

PBY Catalina
118mm. 1/266
Lime green with white or red chord stripes on wings, fuselage and tail flaps.

Douglas DC3
116mm. 1/250
White with orange wing and tailplane surfaces. Black window stripe.

1128-3 PRIVATE PLANE SERIES

Beechcraft Super 18
124mm. 1/122
White with wide orange chord stripes on wings and flap on twin boom tail. Black and white chequered stickers on wings.

Cessna 180
130mm. 1/84
Dark blue with white scallops across high wing.

Lear Jet
90mm. 1/120
White with orange engines and rear tips of boom tanks. Orange sticker stripe along fuselage cheat line.

Cessna T37
120mm. 1/90
White with sand wing roots and leading edges of wings and tail with black chord stripe on inner edge of wing and tailplane tips.

1129-3 INTERNATIONAL JET SERIES

Russian MiG-21
70mm. 1/102
Orange with large white tips on the triangular wings, white trailing edges of the tail planes and band on nose. White edged orange stars on wings.

French Mystère B2
80mm. 1/126
Silver with red, silver and blue stripe stickers on the chord of the wings and round the nose.

British Buccaneer
72mm. 1/158
Mid blue with diagonal dark blue shading bands and a silver nose. White edged RAF roundel stickers on wings and tail fin.

Israeli Mirage IIIR
60mm. 1/137
Sand with brown diagonal shading stripes and silver nose. Blue on white Stars of David on wings.

DYNA-FLITES & SUPER DYNA-FLITES
Zylmex/Zee/Intex/Zyll/Fast Lane
Hong Kong/China, late 1970s–1990s

Many of the castings were initially issued by Zylmex and were made in Hong Kong. Some of the bubble packaging is marked 'HOT WINGS'. 30 castings, some in special liveries, were packaged by Modern Toys (MT) of Japan in window boxes (with different numbers from those on the toy) with either 'Trade Mark MT Modern Toys' logo or with 'MT' and 'HOBBYROOM'. Similar packaging, but with an oval window, marked only 'HOT WINGS' contained the early items in the range. Strictly, the Zylmex listing should be in the Far Eastern Produce section of this book, but c.1980 Zylmex appears to have been acquired by Zee Toys Inc., Long Beach, California. Special packaging, marked 'WINGS', for airliners, and 'AIR COMMAND', for military planes, was used by Woolco and distributed by FW Woolworth NY. In 1983, the Intex Recreation Corporation, Long Beach, Ca. marketed them, now made in China, as Zee Toys and Dyna-Flites. Further models were issued and eventually the trademark Zee was dropped. Some were also listed as Collavia. In 1993, Intex became Zyll Enterprises, still trading from Long Beach, Ca. SUPER DYNA-FLITES are a larger size. Some were marketed by Guisval (Spain). In 1993, some packaging was marked 'Fast Lane'. The list includes issues up to late 1994 but the range is ongoing.

DYNA-FLITES

The small one- or two-piece castings are approximately 90–100mm long and are bubble-packed onto card. The castings are simple but have clear hatch, window and panel markings and some have swing wings. Some of the air liners made in China suffer from bent wings. They are fitted with bright 'dumb-bell' wheels. The stickers are poor to adequate but there is some good tampo printing. Occasionally both occur on the same toy. Often the decoration bears a reasonable approximation to actual liveries. Also available in other countries with Japanese boxes being printed in that language.

All the catalogue numbers begin A1. The MT numbers are those on the boxes of the Modern Toy Japanese issues. There are several other variations but the main groups of castings in chronological order are marked:

1 Zylmex, name of plane, catalogue number, Hong Kong.
2 Zylmex, Zee, name of plane, catalogue number, Hong Kong.
3 Zee, name of plane, catalogue number, Hong Kong.
4 Name of plane, catalogue number (Intex, Zyll or Fast Lane, China on the packaging).

Models and colours on the same catalogue number are as far as is known in the order of issue.

SUPER DYNA-FLITES

A larger size with free rolling wheels with tampo printing were issued as Zee Toys. 110–120mm long, they usually consist of two castings, but sometimes the lower piece is plastic, as are any missiles. Most are numbered but some, including the numbers above 216, are not marked. Some (packaging copyright 1989) were painted in lurid, non-prototypical colours and sold as Wild-Flites Fantasy action toys (marked WF). 1994: some new colour schemes. Bubble packed onto card with photograph of the range on the back. Some (marked G) were marketed by Guisval (Spain). Others (marked FL) were sold in Fast Lane packaging copyright 1990 by Toys 'R' Us. The list covers issues up to late 1994 but the range is ongoing.

DYNAFLITES

A100 Sikorsky S55 Helicopter
Orange, chrome rotor. Black 'NAVY' sticker.

A101 Junkers Ju-87
Mid green, crosses on fuselage and wings, '87' on tailfin.
Dark green, yellow band round rear fuselage. Iron cross on wings and with 'F' on fuselage.
Black plastic cannon.

A102 Super Sabre F-100C

A102 C-54 Galaxy
White, 'US AIR FORCE' on fuselage or blue-grey upper casting, white lower.
'USAF' on starboard wing, star-on-bar on port and fuselage, flag on tail pylon.

A103 Thunderstreak F-84

A103 DC-9
All-over white. 'HAWAIAN AIR', red and pink tampo on top of rear half of fuselage (MT 13).
Alitalia.
White upper, silver lower and tailfin.
'AUSTRIAN' in orange with black windows.

A104 Sikorsky Jolly Green Giant
Olive green.

A104 Concorde
White, Air France with arrow on tail.

A105 Boeing 747
White TWA, Pan Am.
White upper, silver lower, Japan Air Lines (MT 2),
Air France with arrow on tail (MT 4),
'Alitalia' in green with green line and green and red tail flash (MT 3),
'Swissair' in red, brown and black line.

A106 Boeing SST (swing wing)
Metallic, greenish silver.
White, 'PAN AMERICAN' and blue window line, PAN-AM globe on tail,
Yellow, Pan Am (MT 1). Also metallic grey.

A106 Douglas DC-3
Silver with the orange, red and white of CP Air.

A107 Boeing 727 Whisper Jet
Three castings:
1 single piece with plug in undercarriage,
2 two piece with split along waist line,
3 separate piece for tail.
White, 'JAPAN AIR LINES', red and blue window line, sun on wings, Eastern.
White upper casting, silver lower, 'KLM ROYAL DUTCH AIRLINES' and window line in blue,
'ALL NIPPON AIRWAYS' in black with blue sticker stripes (MT 5).
Brown upper, silver lower, 'BRANIFF INTERNATIONAL', 'BI' on fin.

A108 Mustang P-51B
Silver, black and white D-day stripes on wings and rear fuselage, yellow nose.
Star-on-bar on port wing and rear fuselage. Black plastic bombs.
Also orange and white.

A109 P-38 Lightning
Metallic gold, olive green or silver with black and red, star-on-bar stickers.

A110 Star Fighter F104 J/G
Silver blue, 'USAF' in blue on fuselage and starboard wing, star-on-bar on port, flag on tail pylon.
Metallic grey, Japanese roundels (MT 15).

A111 N.A. OV10A Bronco
Light metallic olive green, 'USAF' and star-on-bar on wings, stars and stripes on fin.

A111 MiG-27 (swing wing)
Sand with dark green camouflage. Black plastic missiles.
Dark grey, red stars on wings and tail.

A112 Bell Huey Helicopter
Metallic blue.

A113 Spad (actually a Camel)
Silver, Japanese insignia. White, red stripes, 'FUTS Aeroplane Circus'.

A114 Mitsubishi Zero Fighter
Green, Japanese roundels (MT 23).
Yellow, orange sunray, 'sun air racing'.

A115 DC-10 Airliner
White, TWA. Silver, 'American' in red on red/blue window line, KLM (MT 7).
Red upper casting, silver lower, tampo 'NORTHWEST' in white on a mid-grey band.

A116 Vought Corsair F4U-4
Navy blue. White 22WR on starboard, star-on-bar on port.
'WR' on tailfin, MARINES star-on-bar 22 on fuselage. All tampo.
Black and white chequer band sticker round nose. Black plastic aerials, missiles.

A117 Messerschmitt Me 262A
Medium or dark blue, crosses on wings, sides and tail (MT 21).

A117 Grumman E-2A Hawkeye
Sand with white bar along flaps,
Star-on-bar on port wing, 784NG on starboard, 'NAVY' on fuselage,
Black plastic raydome with sand sticker (MT 21).

A118 F4E Phantom 2
White with blue and red lines, 'US AIR FORCE' and star-on-bar on sides, '1' on fin.
Silver, Japanese roundels (MT 16).
Blue/white/red, tan and brown camouflage, star-on-bar on wings, FG829 on tail.

A119 Spitfire IX
Bright green with yellow stripe on leading edge of wings.
Stickers: red, white and blue roundels on wings, flash on tail, GT roundel 'L' on fuselage.

A120 Vickers VC-10
BOAC, or British Airways.

A121 Hughes OH-6A Cayuse Helicopter
Shades of yellow, red cross, 'HUGHES500', (MT 24).

A122 Boeing-Vertol Chinook Helicopter
US Air Force camouflage, 21-6948 in white on upper sides.
Green, Japanese roundels (MT 25).

A123 ME 109E Messerschmitt
Black, 'GOOD GOOSE', N0186ME across wings, chequered band on nose, black and white crosses on fuselage (MT 29).

A124 MiG-21
Silver, red stars on wings and tail (MT 19).

A124 F-18 Hornet
White, 'Blue Angels'.
White, blue and yellow striped pattern.

A125 Republic F-105 Thunderchief
White, red, white and blue stickers, 'USAF' and star-on-bar on wing (MT 22).

A126 Dassault Mirage IV
Silver, red, white and blue stripes on wing, French roundels, flash on fin (MT 17).

A127 Lockheed SR71 Blackbird
Black, 'US AIR FORCE' star-on-bar on fuselage, flag on tail fin (MT 14).

A127 L-1011 Tristar
Pan Am.
Silver, EASTERN, duo blue cheat line.

A128 Boeing 707
White upper, silver lower casting, 'PAN AMERICAN'.
'ALL NIPPON AIRLINES' with blue sticker (MT 14).
'Lufthansa' in blue with blue line.
'CONTINENTAL', yellow fin stickers with logo in black.

A129 Saab AJ-37 Viggen
Light green/dark green.
Dark green and grey camouflage, Danish crown roundels (MT 18).

A130 Ryan NYP Spirit of St Louis
Metallic green, black N-X-211 sticker, or green, orange trim.

A130 Douglas A-4E Skyhawk
Blue-grey, 'NAVY AK' tampo on tail, star-on-bar sticker on side of fuselage or 'NAVY' and star-on-bar on wings, painted white flaps, 'NAVY' on sides (MT 11).
Light blue, NE.

A131 Bell Huey Cobra Helicopter
Light brown.

USA

A132 Hunter F.6
White, bright blue wing edges and roots, high visibility RAF roundels on wings, flash on tail.
Dark blue.

A133 Cessna Skymaster
White/orange.

A134 Cessna A-37A
Yellow. Leaping deer in grey five-point star tampo on wings and rear fuselage.

A134 Rockwell B1 Bomber
Light/dark brown/green camouflage.
White, USAF and star-on-bar on wings, red stickers on top of fuselage sides.

A135 Grumman HU-19B Albatross

A135 Gee-Bee
White with red flame pattern stickers, NR 2100 in black on starboard wing (MT 12).

A136 Curtiss P-40 Flying Tiger
Sand with mid-green camouflage.
Stickers: white star in blue roundel on wings, 38 on fuselage, shark smile on nose.

A137 Sikorsky H-19 Rescue Helicopter
White, US Coast Guard.

A138 MiG-25 Foxbat
Silver, red stars on wings and fins (MT 20).

A139 Sikorsky CH-54A Skycrane Helicopter
Olive green, red cross on plastic load, 'ARMY' and star-on-bar on sides.

A140 Bell 47 Helicopter
Yellow or metallic blue (MT 27), N32BPA.

A141 Boeing B-52 Bomber
Camouflaged, 'USAF' and star-on-bar on wings (MT 13).

A142 Fairchild A10A
Duo green and grey camouflage, shark nose decal and star-on-bar on sides.
Metallic blue, 'USAF' and star-on-bar on wings (MT 12).

A143 F-14 Tomcat (swing wing)
Light blue with silver flaps and tail planes, black fins, star-on-bar sticker below cockpit, white tampo skull and crossbones on fins.
Light grey/dark grey/white, grey-green, Jolly Roger.
Light grey, 'NAVY' and star-on-bar on wings, white stickers on control surfaces, 'NK' and two red stars on fins (MT 8).

A144 General Dynamics F-16 Falcon
White, red wings and top of tailfin, blue top on fuselage and band at bottom of tailfin, 'US AIR FORCE' on fuselage, F-16 on tail 'USAF' on starboard, star-on bar on port wing, all tampo, black plastic nose and missiles (MT 10).

A145 F-15 Eagle
Light brown with dark brown and dark green camouflage, star-on-bar on port, 'USAF' on starboard wing.
Silver banded with red and white (MT 9).
White, star-on-bar, red flashes on wings and tail.

A146 Harrier (not same die as A154)
Light/dark green, 'WF' and star-on-bar on wings (MT 11).

A147 Kaman YSH-2E Lamps
Dark blue.

A148 Space Shuttle
White (MT 6)

A149 Sikorsky HH-60D Nighthawk Helicopter
Olive green with dark green and grey camouflage, USAF.

A150 Grumman X-29
White/blue.

A151 Stealth Fighter
Incorrect shape: curved outline with turned up wings. Black.

A152 EF-111 (swing wing)
Grey, white flaps, tail fins, yellow tailplane.
Black lines and AB on tail all tampo.

A153 MiG-29 Fulcrum
Light grey with dark grey camouflage.
Tampo: red star on wings and tailfins.

A154 MD AV-8B Harrier (new die)
White, red bands, 'MARINES' on starboard wing and tail fin, star on bar on port, all tampo. Black plastic missiles.

A155 EA-6A Intruder (Grumman)
Grey with white flaps, lower fins, orange nose, all tampo, star-on-bar stickers.

A156 Lockheed S-3A Viking
Grey with white flashes, US 'Navy'

A157 Stealth Fighter F-117A
Correct shape. Black, grey exhaust slats, white tampo stars-on-bars on port wing and fuselage, USAF on starboard.

SETS

Airport Set 1982		A107 Boeing 727
		A112 Bell Huey Helicopter
		A116 Vought Corsair
		A143 F-14
		A144 F-16
Highway Patrol 1982		4 x road vehicles + Bell Huey Helicopter
1990 – date on packs		
WW II Fighters		A101 Junkers Ju-87
		A108 Mustang P-51
		A116 Corsair F4U-4
		A119 Spitfire IX
		A134 P-40 Flying Tiger
Famous Fighters		A130 Douglas A-4E Skyhawk
		A143 F-14 Tomcat
		A144 General Dynamics F-16
		A152 F-111
		A154 MD AV-8B Harrier
Desert Fighters		A117 E-2A Hawkeye
		A118 Phantom F-4C
		A145 F-15 Eagle
		A153 MiG-29 Fulcrum
		A157 F-117A Stealth
Famous Airliners		A103 DC9 Austrian
		A105 Boeing 747 Swissair
		A107 Boeing 727 KLM
		A115 DC10 Northwest
		A128 Boeing 707 Lufthansa

203

SUPER DYNA-FLITES

A201 Boeing 767
United.
White upper, dark blue lower, silver wings, 'BRITISH AIRWAYS'.

A202 McDonnell Douglas DC-10
Silver, 'American' in red above blue window line white red line below, 'AA' in red and blue on tail.

A203 General Dynamics F-16 Falcon
WF. G. FL.*

A204 F-18 Hornet
Dark blue and yellow, 'Blue Angels'. WF. G. FL.

A205 Boeing 727
White upper, silver lower, 'DELTA' in red and blue.

A206 Boeing 747SP
Panam.
White, mid-blue, silver, 'UNITED STATES OF AMERICA'.
As A201, British Airways.

A207 NASA Space Shuttle
White, Columbia. FL.

A208 Bell JetRanger Helicopter
White and red. White and black, 'PATROL'.

A209 MDD Apache AH 64A 'copter
Dark blue with white U6. WF. FL.

A210 Lockheed SR71 with drone
Black with silver drone 'US AIR FORCE' in white. WF. G. FL.

A211 F-15 Eagle
White with blue and red sticker on tail: American Revolution Bicentennial 1778–1978.
WF. G. FL.

A212 F-20 Tiger Shark
Metallic turquoise, 'F-20 Tigershark' in white. WF. G.

A213 Grumman X-29A
WF. G.

A214 Sikorsky HH-60D Nighthawk Helicopter
Grey/olive/green camouflage, 'USAF'. FL.

A215 Stealth Fighter
Concept shape: curved with turned up tips, black. WF.
Zylmex Sonic.

A216 Corsair II
Silver with orange and blue, 'USAF'. WF.

A217 F-14A Tomcat
Light grey, white rear wings, tail planes, red wing stripes in tampo, stickers on tail fin. WF. G. FL.

A218 MiG-29 Fulcrum
Light grey/dark grey soft edge camouflage. WF. G. FL.

A219 MD AV-8B Harrier
White with red tips etc, 'MARINES' in black. WF. FL.

A220 B2 Stealth Bomber
Black, G. FL.

A221 F-117A Stealth Fighter
Black. FL.

A222 B-17 Memphis Belle
Green, bright green camouflage splashes, Memphis Belle nose art decal, DF*A tampo.

Zylmex Sonic: A215 above with plastic base numbered SA215, Stealth finished in black. Pressing the base causes screaming and firing noises and a light to flash in the cockpit.

ERIE 1930s

Erie made a small selection of road vehicles and planes in the 1930s. The thin sectioned one- or two-piece diecasts have remarkably fine and crisp raised lettering cast in above and below the wings. Marked 'ERIE'. The axles, carrying small unpainted metal wheels, are crimped into the undercarriage stubs. Cast propellers are fixed to the engines with nails.

B.17 Flying Fortress Bomber
160mm
Large main casting with plug-in nose cone.
Three-blade propellers. Star-in-roundel US ARMY star-in-roundel cast across upper wings. Red (letters picked out in black), silver, chrome, chrome with red nosecone or grey.

Boeing 247D/B-9
102mm
Three-blade unpainted propellers.
Star-in-roundel US ARMY star-in-roundel cast across wings, 'BOEING' beneath both wings. Mid metallic green (roundels etc picked out in white).

Northrop Beta two seat low wing monoplane
102mm
Two-blade tinplate gold propeller. NC 25379 on both wings, 'NORTHROP' below. Silver, maroon.

Northrop Gamma single seat low wing monoplane
Two-piece casting. NC 17211 across wings.

Northrop Delta Airliner
Two-piece casting. NC 14211 across wings.

*WF = Wild-Flites Fantasy
G = Marketed by Guisval
FL = Fast Lane

ERTL 1980–

Fred Ertl Sr. of Dubuque, Iowa, found himself unemployed in 1945 and turned his hand to sand-casting aluminium toys in his basement, a skill that he had learnt in his native Germany. He was obsessed with accuracy and started working from the original blueprints of tractors etc. Later, in the 1980s, some of the diecast product was labelled 'Blueprint Miniature', though the term was more commonly used in connection with plastic kit production. Ertl has always worked closely with manufacturers, the agricultural equipment makers John Deere and International Harvester allowing him to release accurate toys as they announced the full size. In later years, this expertise with other firms enabled Ertl to enter licensing agreements for extensive character merchandising. The 1989 catalogue cover was aptly emblazoned 'Just like the real thing. Only smaller.'

From selling stock from the back seat of a car, the firm quickly expanded, branching out into products other than miniature farm equipment in 1962. As with many other US firms, the emphasis was on selling to the retailer in mixed cartons and leaving it up to the retailer to market to the end purchaser, and the catalogues, the first of which was issued in 1964, are trade catalogues. By this time the headquarters of the Ertl Company Inc. were in Dyersville, Iowa 52040.

By the 1980s, dies were being sent to wherever could produce and deliver the required quality and quantity at the right price. Some dies were moved part way through the production run. Suitable quality product eg Lintoy aircraft, was bought in and packed by Ertl – see list in Corgi/Lintoy section. Product has come from all over the Far East, Hong Kong, China, Korea, Singapore, Taiwan, Macau. Some sets contain produce of more than one country. Complete ranges with different names can suddenly appear and then disappear from the catalogue; ranges called 'Force One' were introduced in 1987 and the name 'Air and Space Replica' was coined in about 1990. Some existing toys were also included.

Availability has frequently been very patchy. For many years, there were no official European importers. Presence in a catalogue does not necessarily indicate availability, rather that it was intended that the item should be available. A popular model would become scarce because it would sell out before the rest of the group packaged with it and the retailer would not re-order until the less popular models were sold. Because of the lead time required, the illustration of a new model in the catalogue may be that of a mock-up or pre-production prototype. Several of these prototypes have been released to collectors. The catalogue numbers given are usually those of the trade pack, not of the individual item. Although a Collectors' Club was instituted from 1984 to date and a small subscription (which did not change) bought you a membership certificate, a membership card, a newsletter (six issues per year), a poster, a patch etc, it was not until the issue of the yellow RAF Rescue Helicopter 1011 in 1988 that a direct appeal was made to the retail customer with 'Collectors Edition' emblazoned on the packaging. This has no significance other than that Ertl was utilising one of the more recent marketing ploys. The retailer was still expected to order in mixed trade packs, say 24 helicopters, 12 of each of two types. The numbers and contents of retailer assortments have not been included in the listings. The packaging of the larger individual items is often in thick-walled open-fronted boxes. As the product size diminishes, the card is thinner and clear 'window' film is used. Smaller items are bubble packed onto card backing with good to excellent quality printing. As time passed, more items were bubble-packed.

A new style of packaging, very strong, with rigid sides, a clear front and with the plane lashed down to a slide-in card base decorated in blue with a pilot wearing an oxygen mask was introduced for the Force One range in early 1993. There were several recolours and some new castings were issued towards the end of the year.

In the 1990s, Ertl introduced banks in the shape of planes and a Prestige Series, both of which were made for the collector and do not fall within the scope of the book.

JET TRAN/AIR AND SPACE REPLICA AIRLINERS

Introduced in 1988 as Jet Tran, renamed Air and Space Replicas in 1990, and, to date, made in China. At first, details of the planes were printed on the back of the rigid bubble pack made with high quality card and printing. There are three castings: (usually) upper fuselage with tail fin, lower fuselage with tail plane, wings with centre lower fuselage. They are marked underneath with 'Ertl' and place of manufacture but there is no plane name. They are fitted with clumsy chromed metal retractable undercarriages with black wheels. The tampo printing is excellent. The scales are very variable.

ERTL FORCE ONE – 1/100 SCALE

Introduced in 1987, nominally in 1/100 scale, they were at first manufactured in Macau and then from 1989 in China. They are excellent smooth castings with highly detailed surface representations of flaps etc. The main upper casting has a clear canopy and small pilot figures attached, the lower is marked with 'Ertl' and country of manufacture but not the plane name. The number stamped on the undersurface is not the catalogue number but a manufacturing batch number. The earliest issues have silver painted wheels and landing gear. The wheels became plated and then the whole unit was plated. Lastly, black tyres were fitted. The paint finishes are good and there is some tampo printing. A small additional sheet of sticker decals and a white plastic sprue with rockets and missiles is enclosed in most packaging. The models were initially packed in a strong clear plastic bubble, the edges sandwiched between two firm sheets of card, a sort of double-bubble pack, enabling upper and lower halves of the toy to be examined before purchase. The plane names were at first in pink letters, then in yellow. In 1992 a very strong, clear fronted box pack was introduced.

HELICOPTERS

In common with the rest of Ertl production, the helicopters are reasonably accurate models, with, apart from the Bell Huey, a single diecasting for the main body with underpan and wheels or skids in plastic coloured to match the body paint. The manufacturer's name and country of production, say China or Macau, is typically on the plastic part. Liberties are taken with the decoration which is usually high quality tampo but they are most attractive models/toys. American liveries were often only available in the US and British ones only in the UK. Ertl frequently does not include the make of helicopter in the title or on the toy or packaging. For information and clarity, the make is included in brackets. The scale of the helicopters is claimed to be 1/64 but this is that of the road vehicles with which they were packed in sets and is not accurate. The dates given are the years in which the toys were first released. Each livery remained in production for about three years, though 1081 (Metropolitan) police helicopter was made for more than five. Large scale helicopters are said to be 1/16 scale. The Bell 222 is similar to the small version but has detail window differences. They are sturdy impressive toys with 'perceived value' appeal. Force One Helicopters first appeared in the catalogue in 1989, although it was some time before they were released.

FORCE ONE HELICOPTERS

Four helicopters were announced as part of the Force One range and shared their smoothness, accuracy and detail of casting. There are two castings, the upper of which is the larger and carries an excellent amount of good detail, the lower marked with 'Ertl' and country of manufacture but not the name of the machine. The cockpits are fitted with clear plastic glazing and two crew. The plastic rotors are individually and accurately modelled. The quality of the spraying and tampo printing is excellent. Packed with plastic missiles and rockets on a sprue and most with small sheets of self-adhesive sticker decals. Strongly bubble-packed onto firm card with information about helicopter on 'Cut and Collect Replica Card' printed on the back.

SPACE SHUTTLES

Shuttles featured in the 1980s' catalogues, some eg 1513 still being available in 1993. The quality varies depending on which part of the Far East was used for manufacture rather than length of time in the catalogue. Decals, various printings, clear backed self-adhesive tape: 'NASA', 'UNITED STATES' in blue with the stars and stripes flag but, later, stickers. Usually the boxes have a clear window but some models were bubble-packed and became increasingly so. In the 1989 catalogue packaging changed to a cleaner look using a darker blue.

AIRLINERS

The planes, all new castings, not Lintoy, are listed in alphabetical order. The date after the plane type is the date the casting was issued. The catalogue number and date of issue preceed the livery. The liveries are those in use by the airlines at the time.

Airbus A300 123mm. 1/364
2366 1990 'AIR FRANCE'
2367 1990 'BRITISH AIRWAYS', grey upper.
2368 1990 'Lufthansa'
2369 1990 'Alitalia'

Boeing 727
2370 1990 'Lufthansa'
2391 1990 'UNITED'

Boeing 737-200 1988. 126mm. 1/225
2380 1988 'BRITISH AIRWAYS', white upper
2392 1988 'TRANS WORLD' 'TWA'

Boeing 747-200 1988. 130mm. 1/458
2381 1988 'AIR FRANCE'
2390 1988 'UNITED'
2365 1990 'SWISSAIR'
2361 'OLYMPIC' – listed but not issued.

Boeing 747-400 1991. 130mm. 1/458
2362 1991 'BRITISH AIRWAYS'
2375 1991 'KLM'

Boeing 767 1990. 145mm. 1/328
2379 1990 'AIR CANADA'
2371 1990 'BRITISH AIRWAYS'
2372 1990 'SAS'

DC-9 (series 30) 1988. 106mm. 1/268
2383 1988 'Alitalia'
2393 1988 'CONTINENTAL'
2363 1990 'SWISSAIR'
2378 1990 'SAS'

DC-10 (series 30) 1988. 142mm. 1/354
2394 1988 'American'
2382 1989 'Lufthansa'
2364 1990 'SWISSAIR'
2379 1990 'SAS'

Introduced in 1989, similar in style and quality to Jet Tran but not part of the series:

1499 Boeing 747-200Bs Air Force One Presidential Jet 1989
130mm. Casting as 2381.
White upper fuselage with dark blue over nose, along window line and on leading edge of fin. Silver lower with gold line.
'UNITED STATES OF AMERICA' in black on fuselage. Presidential Seal on clear sticker either side of nose wheel.
Bubble-packed onto card depicting Presidential Seal.

FORCE ONE

The list is in introduction date, not numerical, order.
Different colours on the same model usually succeed each other. Sometimes the casting was unobtainable for a period between colours. Unless specified, the decals, stickers and later, tampo printing, are an abbreviated description of those applied by the factory. Additional stickers and plastic missiles were supplied with most models.
Undercarriage sequence to aid dating of long running castings: 1 all silver painted; 2 plated wheels, the rest painted; 3 all plated; 4 rubber tyres.

1160 A-10 Thunderbolt 1987
172mm. 1/102
Green and brown camouflage.
'US AIR FORCE' in black on starboard wing, star-on-bar on port.
1992 Sand and dark sand camouflage (Desert Storm). Star-on-bar, squadron markings, shark's mouth on nose.

1161 F-14 Tomcat 1987
115mm wings closed. 1/101
Operating swing wing. Silver. 'NAVY', star-on-bar.
Silver and barley grey.
1993 Light grey. 'NAVY', star-on-bar, 'NE' and wolf's head on tailfins.

1162 F-15 Eagle 1987
128mm. 1/105
Silver. Star-on-bar on port wing, 'USAF' on starboard.
Silver and grey/dark green.
1994 Semi-gloss light grey with matt dark grey patches, EG 33 TWF and badge on tailfins.

1163 F-16 Falcon 1987
115mm. 1/84
Light grey shading to dark grey, dark grey nose. Star-on-bar, 'USAF' across wings.
Silver.

1164 Stealth F-19 Fighter 1987
Non-prototypical pear-shaped outline. Black with 'US AIR FORCE', stars-on- bars in white.
Replaced by 1048, 1990.

1035 F-18A Hornet 1989
133mm. 1/86
Light grey or dark grey. Replaced by 1489.

1036 McDonnell Douglas F-4 Phantom II
1989
121mm. 1/97
Green and sand soft edge camouflage. Star-on-bar on port wing.

F-4G 'Wild Weasle' 1993
Matt dark grey with matt light grey forward fuselage, wing tips and tailfin. SP 274 in black on tailfin.

1061 Sea Harrier (RN) 1989
125mm. 1/79
Upper casting with plastic fold-down wing stabilisers. Matt dark grey, black nose. Red 'no walk' area markings, red and blue roundels on wings, mid-blue 'ROYAL NAVY' and winged fist outline on tail.
Dark grey and white.

1168 McDonnell Douglas AV-8B Harrier II 1989
125mm. Casting as 1061.
Grey and green soft edge camouflage.
'MARINES' in black on starboard wing, star-on-bar on port, red hatch markings centre wing.
1993 Gloss mid-grey with matt dark grey patch on upper surfaces.
'MARINES 80' in white on starboard wing, VMA-311 'TOMCATS' in white on fuselage, cat on tail.

1037 MiG-29 Fulcrum 1990
146mm. 1/79
Light grey with green camouflage, dark grey nose, tailfin tips. Red stars and 01.
1993 White, grey nose, black sticker stripe bordered in mid-blue down centre fuselage, mid-blue tail fins and planes.

1039 EFA Eurofighter 1990
134mm. 1/78
Mid-grey upper fuselage, remainder light grey. Multicoloured quartered, producer country roundels on wings.

1048 F-117A Stealth Fighter 1990
153mm, approximately 1/66
Matt black.
'US AIR FORCE', star-on-bar tampo printing.

1488 F-16 Viper 1991
Casting of 1063 F-16 Falcon.
White. Red, white and blue Thunderbirds display team decals.
1993 Gloss light grey lower and tail, matt dark grey upper. 'HOOTERS' SW17 TFS AMU in black on tailfin.
1994 Gloss light grey lower and tail, matt dark grey upper, 'NEW YORK GUARD' on tailfin.

1489 F-18A Blue Angels Hornet 1991
Casting of 1035.
Dark blue and yellow. 'Blue Angels' display team.
Cream, grey, pale blue (in 1981 Air Strike Command Joy Stick).
1994 Matt mid grey, light grey, star-on- bar on port wing, '410' on nose, arrow on tailfin.

1939 Tornado GR-1 1993
133mm wings closed. 1/64
Dark matt sand (desert pink for Desert Storm).
'Armoured Charmer' nose sticker, tampo kills on nose, red and blue roundels on wings, 'AC' in white on tail.

1564 Lockheed YF-22 1993
138mm. 1/95
Mid-grey with light grey nose, silver exhausts, star-on-bar tampo on wing, stickers on tailfins: YF-22, N22YX in white on outsides of tail fins, flashes across top of fins.

FORCE ONE SETS

1170 Military Three Piece Jet Set 1987
F-14 Tomcat (1161)
F-15 Eagle (1162)
F-16 Fighting Falcon (1163)

1491 F-16 Thunderbirds Gift Set 1990
Three F-16 Thunderbirds (1488)

1492 F-18 Blue Angels Gift Set 1990
Three F-18A Hornets (1489)

1431 Fighter Squadron Three Piece Gift Set 1990
F-4 Phantom II (1036)
F-18A Hornet Blue Angels (1489)
Harrier II (1168)

1981 Air Strike Command Joy Stick 1990
F-18A Hornet in light blue (1489)

DISPLAY MINIATURES

Two small models, single castings with a 40–50mm span, marked 'Ertl' and with plane name, tampo printed in camouflage colours, on oblong display plinth.

791 Air Force Fighters 1990
F-16 Falcon, three blues
F-15 Eagle, grey/grey

792 Adversaries 1990
MiG-29 Fulcrum, blue/grey
F-15 Eagle, brown/green/cream

793 Marine Fighters 1990
F-18 Hornet, three blues
McDonnell Douglas Harrier, blue/grey

794 Navy Fighters 1990
F-18 Hornet, grey/grey
F-14 Tomcat, brown/green/cream

FORCE ONE with plinths

Two large models each with two very large main castings with deeply incised surface detail (the B-1 has additional swing wing castings). 'Ertl' and country of manufacture but not plane name on lower casting. There is no glazing. Retractable undercarriages. Packed in an envelope of clear rigid plastic with card liner, with plastic plinth and additional sticker decals enclosed.

1165 SR-71 Blackbird 1988
134mm. 1/130
Black undercarriage. Matt or gloss black. Red upper surface lining.

1169 B-1 Bomber 1988
153mm with wings closed. 1/180
Chromed undercarriage. Gloss white, black cockpit window and nose. Star-on-bar on both wings.

1/40 SCALE MILITARY PLANES

Introduced in 1986, 1/40 scale planes with retractable landing gear, firing mechanism for bombs. Strong board carry boxes with handle. The scale is sometimes given, erroneously, as 1/20 or 1/16.

3390 F-15 Eagle Fighter 1986
Firing mechanism and eight bombs, four rockets, opening canopy to house 95mm figure (not included).
Silver. 'US AIR FORCE 613' in black, red, white and blue star-on-bar etc stickers. Still in 1989 catalogue.

3393 A-10 Thunderbolt Warthog 1987
Rotating 30mm nose cannon, fixed pilot.
Green and brown camouflage.

1/64 SCALE HELICOPTERS

1940 Helicopter (Bell UH-1 Huey) 1982
121mm long. 1/102
Two-blade rotor. White, NASA – see Space Shuttles.
Only available in sets?

1011 RAF Rescue Helicopter (Sikorsky/Westland) 1988
Casting as 1076.
Black rotors with red and white bands on tips. Yellow. 'RAF RESCUE', 'ROYAL AIR FORCE RESCUE XV729' and much other detail in black, red, white and blue roundel on fuselage sides.
UK issue.

1017 Royal Navy Wessex Search and Rescue Helicopter (Sikorsky/Westland) 1986
Casting as 1076.
Dark grey rotors. Dark blue with wide red band round nose and rear fuselage.
'14', red on white roundel, 'ROYAL NAVY RESCUE' in white on fuselage sides.
UK issue.

1019 Royal Navy Wessex Commando Troop Support Helicopter (Sikorsky/Westland) 1986
Casting as 1076.
Medium grey blades. Olive. 'ROYAL NAVY' in black with red and blue roundel on rear fuselage.
UK issue.

1076 'Screamin' Mimi' (Sikorsky/Westland) 1985
131mm long. 1/114
Grey main, white tail four-blade rotors. Pink.
'Screamin' Mimi', 'RIPTIDE' in red on sides, open mouth on nose in red, white and black, N698 on boom, all tampo. Eyes are stickers.
US issue.

1081 Police Helicopter (Bell 222) 1986
126mm long. 1/87
Medium grey blades. White. Red edged yellow stripe sticker with 'POLICE' in black and Metropolitan Police coat of arms superimposed on it.

1083 Black Widow Attack Helicopter (Bell 222) 1986
Casting as 1081.
Black. Spider and 'Black widow' in white.

Attack Helicopter Green.

1084 Commando Transport Helicopter (Sikorsky/Westland) 1986
Casting as 1076.
Olive and brown camouflage.
'Command Transport' and star in white. Later, green.

1085 Air Ambulance Helicopter (Bell JetRanger) 1986
102mm long 1/95
Olive green. 'AIR AMBULANCE' and cross in white.

1231 Airwolf Helicopter (Bell 222) 1986
Casting as 1081.
Dark metallic grey, with white plastic lower part and rotor. Black plastic missiles on spats and underbelly.
'AIRWOLF' in white.

1509 Coast Guard Helicopter (Sikorsky/Westland) 1990
Casting as 1076.
Dark grey rotor tipped with red and white.
White. 'US COAST GUARD' in black on rear fuselage, red nose with blue band, star-on-bar on sides of gear box.
US issue.

1511 Police Helicopter (Bell 222) 1990
Casting as 1081.
Mid grey rotor tipped with white and blue.
Dark blue. 'METRO POLICE', stripes on stabiliser fins, tail, etc, white.

1524 Ambulance Helicopter (Bell JetRanger) 1990
Casting as 1085.
Grey two-blade main and tail rotors. Red with black skids.
'Life Flight', dove and 'AIR AMBULANCE' in white.
US issue.

SETS

1014 Police Helicopter and Landrover 1988
Landrover and 1081 Metropolitan Police Helicopter (Bell 222)
UK issue.

1086 Chopper Squadron 1986
Sikorsky S-58 (1084)
Bell JetRanger (1085)
Bell 222 (1083)

1076 Westland Wessex 'Riptide' Three-piece set 1985
1960 Corvette, 4x4 pick-up and 'Screamin' Mimi' helicopter.

1230 Airwolf 1985
Jeep and Bell JetRanger white shading to blue on boom and tail, red stripes on white, white stars on blue, 'Santini Air' in blue behind windows.
Bell 222 as 1231 above

1415 The A-Team 1985
Two A-Team road vehicles and UH-1 Huey in red with white stripes.

1415 The A-Team 1986
Two A-Team road vehicles and Bell 206 Helicopter in red.
White lines along lower edge of fuselage and boom joined by wide white diagonal band across rear of body with 'THE A-TEAM' in red.

1482 Wrangler Set 1984
Three road vehicles and UH-1 Huey in yellow with black nose.
Wrangler and horse in black with multicoloured stripe

1561 Wranger Playmat Set 1984
Two road vehicles, playmat with ranch and rodeo scene, two horses and UH-1 Huey in red with white stripes.

1818 NASA Set 1984
See Shuttles for details +
Bell UH-1 Huey in white, with grey rotor.
Blue stripe with 'NASA' in black below window and in red on tail rotor pylon.
Blue stripe with 'NASA' in black below window and in red on tail rotor pylon.

4430 Coastal Rescue Landrover and Helicopter 1989
Landrover and 1011 RAF Wessex Helicopter in yellow.

FORCE ONE HELICOPTERS

1142 Hughes AH-64 Apache 1987
165mm long. 1/91
Four-blade main and tail rotors, moveable machine gun under cockpit, sprue with rockets in plastic.
All-over olive drab. Chromed, fixed wheels. '06' on cockpit sides, 'UNITED STATES ARMY' on boom in early: black numbers; later: white lettering. Later: black lettering.
Also: 'Firebirds' packaging.

1144 MIL Mi-24 Hind F 1989
175mm long. 1/96
Matt green and sand soft edge camouflage on upper casting, glass light grey lower.
Very light grey five-blade main, three-blade tail rotors.
Retracting tricycle undercarriage with chrome legs. Red star with white edge, '38' in yellow.
Decal sheet.

1146 Kamov Hokum 1989
170mm long.
Sand with dark sand soft-edge camouflage patches.
Two grey three-blade rotors on same shaft. Two retracting undercarriage legs with twin wheels. Red star with white edge, '08' in yellow on rear fuselage. Decal sheet.

1147 Bell UH-1D Huey 1989
144mm long. 1/88
Olive drab with shiny black nose top. Metal skids.
Grey two-blade main and tail rotors. 'UNITED STATES ARMY' in small black letters along boom.

1/16 SCALE HELICOPTERS

Two-piece diecast fuselage with plastic skids, five-blade main rotor, tail rotor, and interior. Overall length 440mm.
Decals are self-adhesive stickers.

Versions of the Hughes C500:

3579 A-TEAM Helicopter 1983
Red. Yellow diagonal stripe on rear cabin, with 'THE A-TEAM' in black, continuing as narrow stripe along boom.

3679 Wrangler Helicopter 1983
Yellow. 'Wrangler' and horse in black on multicoloured stripe.

3680 1st Cavalry Recon Helicopter 1983
Fitted with winch. Olive green. '1st CAV RECON', 'UNITED STATES ARMY' in yellow on olive sticker on rear cabin and boom.
Versions of the Bell 222:

3589 Police Helicopter 1985
White. Red edged yellow stripe with 'POLICE' in black superimposed, Metropolitan Police Coat of Arms.

3683 Airwolf Helicopter 1986
Metallic grey upper, white lower. 'AIRWOLF' in white.

3392 Viper X Attack Helicopter 1987
With missiles. Green/brown camouflage.
Red and white angular line decal with 'VIPER X' in white.

SPACE SHUTTLES

1512 USSR Space Shuttle 1991
As 1515 below but with CCCP decals.
Red backing card marked 'Bouran'.

1513 Space Shuttle and the 747/ Space Shuttle Package 1979
130mm
All castings with open cockpit windows as Corgi/Lintoy marked 'LINTOY Made in Hong Kong' with some alterations: upper fuselage and three supports for Shuttle, lower – one hatch, and tail fin stabilisers. Good metal dumb-bell wheels. White upper, silver lower. Red and blue stripe along fuselage, 'NASA' etc. on tail.
1990. 129mm
New casting with no cockpit windows and integral engines marked 'ERTL Made in China'. Poor plastic undercarriage.

Shuttle with 'ferry pod' tail cone
48mm
Marked 'Ertl Made in Hong Kong'
Three holes in lower casting to locate on supports on 747.
White upper with black stripe, black lower.
Later: slight casting changes due to cleaning of die, marked 'ERTL Made in China'.

1514 US Space Shuttle with Space Lab. 1991?
120mm. 1/196
Two heavy main castings with opening cargo doors. Grey and black plastic space lab. within.
More accurate paint scheme: white upper, black lower, black band across wings and on leading edge of tail fin, silver wing edges.
Sticker decal sheet for 'Columbia', 'Challenger', 'Discovery', 'Atlantis' in box.

1514 US Space Shuttle with removable satellite 1987
Casting etc of 1514 above but with sticker decals and white and grey plastic satellite.

1515 Orbiter Space Shuttle with booster rockets 1987
49mm. 1/500
Different, more accurate casting than 1513, with three holes in lower casting to locate onto rockets and tank.
Diecast booster rockets 91mm long. White fuel tank later prototypical brown.
Bubble-packed ensemble stands upright on black plastic plinth.

1534 NASA Space Shuttle Pullback 1984
84mm. 1/288 scale toy rather than model.
White diecast upper, black plastic lower creating wing borders. Pullback motor.

1534 USSR Space Shuttle 1990
As USA Shuttle 1534 above with CCP and Red Flag markings. (1991, USSR cancelled Shuttle Programme.)

1535 Columbia Space Shuttle 1987
Shuttle from 1515 packed on its own.

1818 NASA Playset 1982
Pickup truck, card playmat and buildings kit and Shuttle, booster and stand as 1515.
Bell UH-1 Helicopter, white with grey blades.
Black nose top sticker, blue stripe with 'NASA' in black below window and in red on tail boom.

CHARACTER MERCHANDISING

There is a lot of plastic in these toys.

1196 Smurf in Aeroplane 1984 catalogue
Noddy in Aeroplane 1987, 1988 catalogues
Bugs Bunny in Aeroplane 1989 catalogue

Batjet from the most recent Batman film. 1990.

Harold the Helicopter in the WH Audrey *Railway Book Series*. Seen 1991

FAIRYMARK

The country of manufacture is uncertain but because the model is of a US plane with US stars cast on its wings, it can be assumed to be American. The toy is identical to the Hubley. The die was also used by Lincoln Toys NZ.

Navy (Folding Wing) Fighter, Vought 4-FU Corsair
222mm
The centre sections are unpainted but the folding wings are red with silver roundels.

GOODEE-TOY 1950s

Excel Products, New Brunswick, NJ, made single castings consisting of the upper surfaces only with maker's and plane names cast underneath. They contrive to be neat in outline with good lettering, but crude in shape particularly at nose and tail with poorly cast open windows. No propellers. Black solid rubber wheels on a single axle.

Douglas C-54
132mm. 1/270 scale
N21981 on upper starboard wing. Name, '300 M.P.H., MILITARY TRANSPORT' under port.
Mid metallic blue.

Douglas Skyray F-4D

HUBLEY KIDDIE TOY 1936–1976

John Edward Hubley founded the company in 1893 in Lancaster Pennsylvania to make cast iron toys. During the 1930s they made several cast iron planes but in 1936 using the brand name Hubley Kiddie Toy, they branched out into diecasting. The first production was of two-piece, heavy-looking castings that could almost be mistaken for cast iron, though most castings were quite thin. Up until 1941, there was a great emphasis on packaging the planes in sets with other vehicles. Toy production ceased between 1942 and 1945.

In 1966, Hubley was purchased by Gabriel Industries. In the late 1970s Ertl bought some of the Hubley tools. The P-47 Thunderbolt is currently being made with a two-blade plastic propeller and a smoke grey canopy by Ertl in their Scale Model Line. The smaller Navy (Folding Wing) Fighter Vought 4-FU Corsair has been found in a Fairymark box and as a Lincoln Industries (NZ) Majormodel (*c*.1976).

Pre-war planes were fitted with white rubber wheels, on a single axle unless otherwise stated, postwar with black. Most of the toys are marked Hubley Kiddietoy and some have part or all of the address. The catalogue numbers are from internal records and are not usually on the castings, so the toys are listed in order of introduction.

PRE-WAR PRODUCTION

427 Airplane (Crusader) 1936–40
130mm
Two heavy castings with black pressed steel three-blade propellers.
TAT NC-31 embossed across wings and painted red.
Silver lower casting, red upper cabin, undersurfaces bare metal.

431 US Army Plane (Seversky P.35 with incorrect squared tail) 1938–41
147mm
Chromed cast iron two-blade propeller on two castings split along the waistline.
Star-in-roundel 'US ARMY' star-in-roundel heavily embossed across wings and painted red.
Pale blue or red upper casting, white lower, undersurfaces bare metal.

455 Air Plane (Seversky P.35 with rounded tail) 1939–41, 1946–48
165mm
Three versions of upper casting all with 'US ARMY' embossed across tail.
Cockpit canopy with: 1 six cut out panels; 2 four cut out panels; 3 four closed panels.
Lower casting with star-in-roundel embossed on tips.
Cast two-blade propeller. Silver upper, red lower.

470 Bell Airacuda XFM-1 (prototype) 1940–41
245mm
Four castings: upper fuselage and tail with 'US ARMY' across planes; lower fuselage and wings with K601 and roundels cast in; two engine/gun turret tops.
Silver upper casting, red lower. Stars in roundels, stripes on tailfin.
Individual box: 'Features – Retractable landing gear. Movable aerial guns. Three blade (pusher) propellers.'

440 US Navy Scout Plane (Lockheed B.34) 1940–41
135mm
Single casting with 'USN 3-B-4' cast across wings.
Three-blade pressed steel propellers.
Retractable undercarriage (folding inwards against a flat spring).

441 US Army Airacobra P.39 1941, 1946
133mm 1/78
Mazac fuselage and wing roots with fine detailing round cockpit area, seriffed 'US ARMY' across tail planes, otherwise unmarked.
Single piece printed tinplate wing/undercarriage secured by lugs in the casting. Very large pressed steel three-blade propeller.
Blue or silver fuselage, silver wing with red centred silver star on dark blue roundel.

PRE-WAR SETS

475 Kiddie Toys Set 1936
Contains six vehicles and 427 Crusader

490	1936	13 vehicles and 427 Crusader
482	1938	Six vehicles, 427 Crusader, 431 Seversky P.35
484	1938	Four vehicles and 431 Seversky P.35
485	1938	12 vehicles and 427 Crusader
486	1938	Eight vehicles, 427 Crusader, 431 Seversky P.35
125	1939	Seven vehicles, 427 Crusader, 431 Seversky P.35
483	1939	= 484 above
480	1941	Five 441 Airacobra
482	1941	Five 441 Airacobra and one 470 Airacuda
460	1941	Eight vehicles, 440 Lockheed B34, 441 Airacobra
484	1941	Four vehicles and 441 Airacobra
485	1941	Four different vehicles and 441 Airacobra
486	1941	Eight vehicles and two 441 Airacobra
488	1941	Eight vehicles and two 441 Airacobra

POST-WAR PRODUCTION

The new post-war castings are very big and usually chunky. Most are painted in bright primary colours. Undercarriages retract unless indicated. Black rubber wheels. The toys are not good models of the planes named but these are given because they are frequently used by collectors and help to distinguish the similarly named toys from each other.

441 Airacobra Re-issue, see above

455 US Army Plane Re-issue, see above

467/1468 Navy (Folding Wing) Fighter (Vought 4-FU Corsair) 1953–70
222mm
Seven castings: upper and lower fuselage including wing roots, folding wings embossed with star-in-roundel, four-blade propeller with spinner.
Fixed plastic cockpit cover.
Renumbered 1968. Silver with red wings.
Later: silver upper fuselage with dark blue, chromed propeller.

430 Airplane (Jet) with Folding Wings (Airacomet Prototype) 1955–62
200mm
Fuselage casting split horizontally. Cockpit cover cast in. Star-in-roundel on wings.

459/1495 Navy (Folding Wing) Fighter Bomber P.47 Thunderbolt 1956–76
295mm
Two-part fuselage casting, upper including tail, without or with lump to locate top of separate cast engine cowling.
Two-piece plastic sliding cockpit cover.
Silver with red wings and cowling.
Mid-blue upper, yellow lower, orange cowling, wings.
Later: black or dark blue upper, light blue lower and wings, red cowling.
All: star-on-bar transfers. Renumbered 1964.

483/1484/1484 Helicopter – twin rotor 1958–79
235mm long
Two main castings split longitudinally. Cast folding two-blade rotors.
Large clear bubble cockpit. Fixed undercarriage.
Yellow, star-on-bar decals. Forest Ranger.
Renumbered 1964, 1969.

751 (Delta Wing) Folding Wing Jet (Douglas Skyray) 1959–61. 153mm
Fuselage split horizotally. Clear plastic glazing.
Silver with red wings. Star-on-bar transfers.

761/1761 P-40 Fighter Plane 1962–70
210mm
Fuselage split vertically, separate wings, Three-bladed propeller with nosecone. Much fine rivet detail. Fixed undercarriage.
Orange with yellow wings. Later: plated with red wings.

881/1881 P-38 Lightning 1962–63
315mm
Casting split horizontally through fuselage and engine pods. Much fine rivet detail. Three-bladed propellers with nosecones.
Red upper, silver lower. Silver with red cockpit. Olive drab. Yellow and green camouflage.
Renumbered 1964.

767/1767 Piper Cub 1963–69
200mm. 1/53
Tinplate propeller. Black rubber wheels.
Red. Transfer on starboard wing NC4372.

SETS

The dates given are introduction dates. Sets could remain in the catalogue for several years.

45 Hubley Assortment 1954 Three vehicles, 467 Vought

10 Kiddie Toys 1955 Two vehicles, 430 Jet Airacomet

11 Assortment 1956 Three vehicles, 430 Jet Airacomet

46 Assortment 1956 Two vehicles, 467 Vought

55 Assortment 1956 Two different vehicles, 467 Vought

12 Airport Diner 1957 Three vehicles, 430 Jet Airacomet

53 Fighter Bomber Squadron 1957
459 Thunderbolt, four 420 Jet Airacomets

56 Army-Air Combat 1958
459 Thunderbolt, two 430 Jet Airacomets, two 467 Voughts.
Box forms a hangar.

80 Navy Airfield Set 1958
Two vehicles, 495 Thunderbolt, two 483 Helicopters.
Box forms a hangar.

522 Bomber Transporter 1958
Transporter vehicle and 495 Thunderbolt

54 Air Race Set 1959
459 Thunderbolt, two 430 Jet Airacomets, two 751 Delta Wing Jets.
Box forms control tower (with windsock).

49 Airport Set 1962 Four vehicles, 761 P-40, 881 P-38

16 Fighter Pilot Set 1963
Pistol, Pilot's wings, Air medal and 761 P-40

52 Aircraft Carrier Set 1963
Pistol, Pilot's wings, two medals and 495 Thunderbolt

1014 Airport Set 1965 Three vehicles, 767 Piper Cubs

1496 Fighter Plane Set, Famous Planes of World War II 1967
495 Thunderbolt, 761 P-40

1065 Air Rescue Squadron 1969
Three vehicles, 459 Thunderbolt, 483 Helicopter, 761 P-40

22113 America City 1972 Four vehicles, 483 Helicopter

21216 Flying Circus 1974 = 1496

GABRIEL

After the purchase of Hubley, Gabriel subsequently made two models under its own name.

26211 Helicopter 1976–77
255mm long

27218 Twin Engined Beechcraft 1976–77
228mm

SETS

26173 Rescue Team 1976
Two vehicles and 26211 Helicopter

26163 Smokey Bear Set 1976
One vehicle and 26211 Helicopter

KANSAS TOY & NOVELTY CO.
1920s and 1930s

Also known as Best Toy, the company was founded in Clifton, Kansas by John M. Best, probably in the early twenties. The mainly automotive items are slushmoulded from 35mm to 125mm long, some with excellent detail. Most items have a number cast into the outside. A wide variety of wheels were used. The plane die seems to have been used subsequently by other manufacturers.

32 High wing monoplane
56mm with radial engine, metal wheels

45 High wing monoplane
55mm with radial engine, white rubber tyres

MAIL BOX SERIES (FRANKONIA) 1968

Frankonia, about whom little is known, had four planes to 1/390 scale (eg Caravelle has 87mm span) made in Hong Kong, to be sold in mailable boxes in the US. The planes are solid single castings with dumb-bell wheels marked: 'Frankonia Products Mail Box Series Hong Kong'. All are finished in silver with transfer decals. The standard colourful box, 80 x 90mm, has a detachable hanging card with mailing instructions and a illustration of the box, dominated by red and blue airmail colours, being put in a US Mail Box. The back of the box has lines drawn for the address to be filled in. A plastic stand was enclosed. The box illustrates the planes in the following liveries, but it is probable that they were all available in all liveries, eg DC-7 is also in TWA.

Serial No. 4506 Caravelle Air France, United
DC-7 Eastern, American
DC-8 KLM, Delta
Boeing 707 Pan Am, TWA

MIDGETOY 1950s

Midgetoy made planes from single thin diecastings similar to those being made at the same time by Tootsietoy. They are marked 'MIDGETOY ROCKFORD ILL.' up inside the casting and have 'USAF' or 'NAVY' cast on the starboard wing with a star-on-bar on the port, but they are not marked with the plane name. They are crude but recognisable models. Several types of solid black rubber wheels are fitted to a single axle. Nose wheels are not fitted, but there is a peg at the rear for additional support. The average to poor castings are painted a single colour, orange, blue, etc. The colours given in the list are examples.

Cutlass (NAVY)
82mm
Swept wing twin jet, tail fin half way along trailing edge. Bright blue.

Grumman F9F Cougar (NAVY)
80mm
Swept wing single jet with high tail. Orange, red.

F86 Sabre (USAF)
99mm
Swept wing single jet with tip tanks. Light blue.

Martin B-57 (Canberra) (USAF)
90mm
Straight centre wing section between engines, conventional tail with flat top to fin. Olive.

Boeing 707 Transport (USAF)
113mm
Four-engined, low swept-back wings, tail fin curving to meet fuselage.
Dark green, light blue.

RENWAL 1950s

Renwal are known for plastic kits, but they made a small group of planes – single castings fitted with German friction motors powering the black rubber main undercarriage wheels. The upper fuselage is embossed with the name of the plane and performance data is cast under the wings, but not the manufacturer's name. The span is approximately 200mm. All were silver. The propellers are red or blue plastic.

Lockheed Constellation
TWA cast on port wing, F15243 on starboard.

Boeing Stratocruiser
PAA cast on port wing.

XB-52 Bomber
No name on fuselage. Star-on-bar on port wing, 'USAF' on starboard.

Sabre Jet

REVELL AIR ACES 1990–91/3

Originally known as a manufacturer of high quality plastic kits, Revell, Des Plaines Illinois and D-4980 Bunde 1, launched a range of diecast up-to-date military jets. These were very fine quality light castings made in China, fitted with a plastic pilot in the clear glazed cockpit. The plastic underpart, which incorporates a slotted fitting for a handle supplied with the Sonic Air Aces version, is marked: 'Copyright Revell 1990 All Rights Reserved Made in China'. The plane name is not included. The retractable undercarriages are black plastic, the engine exhausts red. Grey clip-on missiles are packed within the sturdy bubble packing which is printed with details of the range in four languages. Though well made and reasonably accurate, these models have a disappointingly wide spread of scales to make the toys conform to a size. Sales did not fulfil expectations perhaps because of competition from Ertl and the models were remaindered in Europe in 1991 and in the States in 1993. European and American bubble-packaging have different backing cards and catalogue numbers.

US numbers in brackets.

8301 (8639) EFA Eurofighter
120mm. 1/91
Dark grey fuselage, mid-grey wings with light grey edges. Multicoloured quartered producer-country roundel on wingtips, cockpit sides, 'EFA Eurofighter' on tail fin in black and white.

8302 (8637) MiG-29 Fulcrum
118mm. 1/101
Light grey and lighter grey shading with red stars on wings and tail fins, '23' in blue on engine intakes.

8303 (8638) SU-27 Flanker
120mm. 1/121
Light grey and lighter grey shading with red stars on wings and tailfins, blue '05' either side of nose and on tail fins.

8304 F-15 Eagle
118mm. 1/110
White with red and blue wingtip and nose stripes.

8305 F-16 Fighting Falcon
114mm. 1/82
White. Red and blue stripes on wings and tail plane, red scallops and blue stars on tail and nose, star-on-bar on port wing and rear fuselage, 'US AIR FORCE' on wing roots (Thunderbirds Display Team).

8306 F/A-18 Hornet
120mm
Dark blue with yellow central fuselage stripe, tail fin and plane tips and yellow missiles on wingtips. 'Blue Angels' (display team) on lower fuselage, emblem on nose.

There is a report that 8307 was to be an F-14 Tomcat and that 8308 was to have been a Tornado.

8351–8356 Sonic Aces
As above but with fittings under the fuselage to make quiet engine noises and exhaust flashes operated by a button protruding through the top of the fuselage. In the packaging is a separate handle to twist into the slot in the fuselage so that it can be more easily 'flown'.

ROAD CHAMPS FLYERS

Road Champs took over some of the Flyers dies (see Hong Kong and China) and marketed them as Road Champs Flyers. Most of the airliners are ex-Flyers but the Fighters and Combat Jets are all new castings of very variable quality. Marked 'Road Champs' under fuselage or wing. Red or blue backing card marked 'Copyright 1988'. Some liveries were also packed for Woolworths in the States (marked 'W' in list) and others for YDC, York, Penn 17402 (marked 'YDC'). Later packaging, marked 1993, has a map on the backing card and the plane colours are new.

6201 Airliners: white upper casting, metallised silver lower

Boeing 747 United (also W), Pan Am (YDC)

Douglas DC9 Delta, TWA, Swissair with red arrow (YDC)

Airbus A310 (not Lintoy) Eastern

Boeing 727 Continental, TWA, People Xpress, Pan Am (W)

Douglas DC10 American, United (W), (YDC)

Douglas DC8 Air Canada (YDC)

Boeing 707 (all new die) Delta (W), Air Canada, Pan Am (YDC), no labels

Simplified castings with spurious liveries issued after 1990:

Boeing 747 Red and purple, Western

Boeing 727 Grey and maroon, Eagle

Douglas DC9 Blue and yellow, Meridien

A300 Airbus Green and gold, Global Air

6202 WWII FIGHTERS: all new castings

B-17G Flying Fortress
149mm
Upper casting shared with Tootsietoy. 'Road Champs' on replaceable lower casting of part wings and centre fuselage. Pale blue, orange bar on wingtips, tail. Star-on-bar. Later, silver.

F4U-1A Corsair
132mm
'US Navy' blue, red and white chequered band round nose and on tailfin, 'NAVY' and star-on-bar on dark blue on fuselage, star-on-bar on wings.

Thunderbolt P-47D
125mm
Mid and dark green camouflage. G9 star-on-bar on fuselage. 1993: Silver 'Lil Friend' and star-on-bar stickers.

B-52J Mitchell
129mm
Green. Star-on-bar on wings, yellow flashes on fuselage and tail.
Later, silver, 'Panchito' on nose.

6203 COMBAT JETS: all new castings

F-16XL Fighter
Silver, red edges to wing and tail fin. Star-on-bar on wings, 'F-16' on tail.

F/A-18 Hornet
Green and sand camouflage. Bright star pattern on wings, ditto incorporating 'F-18' on tail.

SR-71 Blackbird
66mm
Black with yellow lightning flashes on tail.

EF-111 Raven
Silver, or bluish silver. Star-on-bar on wings, chequers on tailfin.

TOOTSIETOYS 1910 – present day

The United States was the birthplace of aviation, the Wright Brothers' plane taking to the air for all of one minute at Kittyhawk in 1903 for the first powered flight with a pilot at the controls. However, aero-fever did not grip America as it did Europe. Indeed, the Wrights spent much of their time in Europe promoting their Flyer which, with its patented wing-warping control system, outshone the indigenous product on the competitive circuits of the European air shows until everyone else incorporated wing-warping as well. It was not until 1918 that there was a plane with the stamina to cover the long distances between towns that typified the population spread in the States, and a Curtiss JN-4 Jenny biplane was used to set up the first significant airmail service between New York and Washington. It offered no load and no speed advantage over the railroads which networked the country and air development was slow. Even so it was initially much more profitable to carry the mails with lucrative contracts from the US Mail service than to try to find passengers. Curtiss Flying Boats won the Daily Mail Atlantic Crossing prize of £13,000 for the first flight (west to east) across the North Atlantic in 1919. In the unregulated 1920s there was sudden exponential growth as the entrepreneurs grabbed at the new idea of air transport, so that by 1926 there were over 400 operators. In Lindberg, after his first solo Transatlantic flight in 1927, the States got its own hero and the important US manufacturers and airlines, Douglas, Boeing, Lockheed, Pratt & Whitney, all developed during the decade. 1929 saw the amalgamation of many of the smaller lines into the Big Four – TWA, United, Eastern and American Airlines which had the territory divided up between them. The secret of the success of the whole industry was the Trimotor from the car manufacturer, Ford, which flew commercially in 1930. Douglas ensured its continuation with its DC range. The foundations of world dominance of the air by the US aviation industry were thus laid, though Ford later withdrew because of the effects of the depression. So significant was the industry that Pan Am and its founder Von Trip were regarded as synonymous with US foreign policy. There was no wartime hiatus and the new Lockheed Constellation was pressed first into military service in 1943. In the immediate post-war years, Douglas, Boeing and Lockheed were pre-eminent throughout the world.

The toy industry of the United States was well developed and well used to producing transport items by the time that the aeroplane was invented. Cast iron in particular had been used to make pull along bell toys and mechanical banks in many complex forms, as well as modelling horse-drawn fire pumpers and early motor vehicles. Pressed steel, a most suitable material for producing aeroplane wings, was also commonly used. Both types make robust toys! Diecasting with lead based alloy had also been developed producing more fragile items. One of the leading exponents was Theodore Samuel Dowst trading as the Dowst Brothers Company. In 1926 he sold out to Nathan Stone but remained the President of the Dowst Manufacturing Company of Chicago until he retired. Nearly 40 years later, in 1964, Stone's grandsons bought out the Strombecker Corporation under which name they now trade. Originally in publishing, Dowst experimented with producing small lead objects, instead of lead type, on a new 'linotype' machine and, from the 1890s, the firm manufactured small items in vast quantities with strict regard to the formula of the metal to enable the quality of production to be closely regulated. This enabled accurate weights to be calculated both for the cost of materials and for shipping, factors of overriding importance in this vast country, especially since profit margins on goods retailing at 10 cents were in fractions of cents. In 1910, Dowst added to his range of trinkets and game pieces a small aeroplane, a model not of the Wright Flyer but of Bleriot's famous Channel-crossing monoplane. Whether this is a copy of the French SR model, or the SR a copy of this, or both were created independently, has kept collectors arguing for years.

In 1921, as the identity of the toy range began to develop, Dowst decided to call a range of dolls' furniture 'Tootsie', after a granddaughter of the family. The name 'Tootsietoy', all one word, was registered retrospectively at the US Patents Office as a trademark in 1924, though it is found used both as one word and as two. The name was added to the product in 1932 while lead and tin were still being used. The change from lead to mazac, alias zamac, a zinc alloy, was phased over 1932/3 and all mazac toys are marked 'Tootsietoy'. Dowst was fiercely protective of the trade name and product, filing patents in 1927, and went to law vigorously to defend them against copyists, even overseas ones such as Johillco. The accurate model of the DC2 launched in 1935 was marked 'PAT. APL. F.' in addition to the full 'MADE IN UNITED STATES OF AMERICA', in an attempt to protect its unique method of construction.

The pre-war range consists of only about 20 planes, several of which are merely versions of each other but, for most of the time, the ones modelled are significant and famous ones. The selection of some subjects, for instance, a model of The Spirit of St Louis in the guise of the Aero Dawn, was controlled by how well they were expected to sell straight off the counter, Dowst having no truck with the French and English idea of the 'young collector'. The willingness of firms to pay Tootsietoy for making the models and for putting their names on them, as general promotional products, was a major factor in product selection. This is typified amongst the planes by the Douglas DC-4 which has 'Super Mainliner – Another Tootsietoy' clearly embossed underneath the fuselage.

COLOURS By 1931, in the quest for economies of scale, the colours had become almost always standard: red, green, silver and blue.

PROPELLERS Most production was fitted with large lead two-blade propellers, early production having large paddle-shaped blades and later ones a thinner section. In 1935 a large three-blade propeller was introduced for use on some models. Later production, including some of the four-engined Super Mainliner had tinplate three-blade propellers.

WHEELS A wide variety of wheels were fitted. Solid metal ones were chemically gilded or coloured in early production and bare metal in later. The same type sometimes had an integral short axle. Metal hubs fitted with white tyres feature and the five cent product often had solid white rubber wheels on a single axle. Most of the post-war planes have solid black rubber wheels.

MARKINGS   Decals, whether sticker or transfer were not commonly used on US toys. Keeping costs down, Dowst opted for embossing the decoration, stars-in-roundels, US NAVY, registration numbers, etc, onto the surface as part of the casting.

DATES   Tootsietoy factory records give the prewar introduction dates of the toys. From 1928, the name 'Tootsietoy' was marked onto all the new plane castings. From 1934, mazac was used for all new diecastings. Most of the deletion dates are not recorded. Because they were not advertised directly to the public in itemised catalogues, it was easy to drop a toy just as soon as the sales figures dropped too low. Production carried on into the war but at a reduced rate as the government prohibited the use of strategic materials even before America entered the war after Pearl Harbour in December 1941. Most of the planes were still in production at this time and were listed in sets in the 1941 Trade Catalogue. Manufacturing continued to slow down until all production of metal toys was stopped by Government Edict on 30 June 1942. The impetus was lost. When production started again in 1945, pre-war issues were re-released until 1947 when new ones were issued. Tootsietoy production became a shadow of its former self. Most of the new production did not have the charm or the quality of the pre-war toys and some, such as the Boeing 707, are very poor. Plane production stopped in the late 1950s. In the late 1980s, with Tootsietoy now being a division of the Strombecker Corp. of Chicago, bubble-packed sets of small fighters made in China were issued, though diecast toys were still being made in the USA.

NUMBERING   Individual catalogue numbers were only allocated if a toy was available separately. In the plane listing no number indicates that the toy was only available in sets. The listing is therefore in the order of the year of issue, not in numerical order. The numbers in the catalogues were for trade orders and were not publicised generally. Most of the planes do not have numbers cast on them. Looking at catalogue captions, Biplane and Autogiro seem to share the number 4650 (or possibly the Autogiro caption is incorrect and should read 4659). Set numbers seem to have been used to designate the size or type of set, the contents varying over the years. The sets are not well documented.

ADVERTISING AND BOXES   Marketing and the catalogues were aimed at the trade. A 1921 example lists a 'Grab Bag' assortment, the items to be enclosed in penny bags of sweets. Two sizes of the Bleriot are featured, the smaller coming in an even bigger bag (12 gross) than the larger which was sold by the gross (144). The Aero Dawn, in 1928, was repackaged in eyecatching individual boxes, with a red model in a red box etc. but the advertising was still aimed at the retailer: ' . . . worthwhile merchandise of educational value to sell at a popular price and thru any channel of distribution, you have an item that moves, and moves rapidly'. These individual boxes were enclosed in a dealer counter display pack into the backing card of which an example of the toy was slotted. Most of the planes were sold without individual boxes from retailer assortments. The 1940 catalogue, for instance, lists two: 575 Aeroplane Assortment contained small planes selling for five cents each; 1075 Aeroplane Assortment was of the large planes selling for ten cents each.

SCALES The scales are very variable because the toys were being made to a price and quantity of material was of overwhelming importance.

SETS With the needs of the retailer in mind, so called 'Perfection Packaging', a flat box with a colourful lid containing and displaying a selection of toys – 'strong, well made, brightly coloured . . . safely and securely packed in a strong box' – was introduced in the 1929 Catalogue 'to meet the demand for department store packing of our small toy line'. The lids with 'Highly colored and varnished lithographed labels cover a box that marks another step forward in the always perfect packing of Tootsietoys' were emblazoned with 'Tootsietoy Playtime Toys'. Each letter was positioned on a different coloured counter like an uneven row of balloons above a scene of children waiting before a door marked 'Entrance to Playtime'. These, usually mixed, sets were good value for money with, for instance, the $1 set consisting of 11 vehicles that retailed individually at ten cents each. They were to remain a feature of Tootsietoy marketing through into the 1950s. The planes usually retailed at ten cents, but cheaper five cent Miniatures appeared sporadically. The box lids of the plane sets frequently have beautiful Art Deco designs. Assortments from which individual sets were made varied from time to time. The 1941 Catalogue has a Five Cent Assortment consisting of eight each of 119 Army Plane, 4660 Aero Dawn and 125 Electra. The Ten Cent Assortment was made up of four each of 718 Waco Bomber, 721 Pursuit Plane Curtiss P-40, and the new 722 Transport Plane. Normally the Five Cent type were packed 24 of each and the Ten Cent 12 of each to a box.

MIDGETS A smaller, cheaper range of vehicles, Midgets, was introduced in 1936 using the same packaging formula. These single-piece fixed-wheel novelties came in sets of up to 12 vehicles in various combinations. There were four different small planes, all finished in bright colours. They had more detail and were better made than the game pieces and party cake favours. A ten-piece set cost a mere ten cents. Both are known as 'Cracker Jacks', snack givaways, to US collectors. Post-war the lid decoration changed, for instance to a striking yellow and black New York scene. Other titles, such as the ugly Rol-Esy Toys, were used as appropriate for sales purposes. Records are not complete so the set listing is partial.

PROTOTYPES The original unmarked handmade prototype of the Ford Trimotor created by Frank Bischof Jnr, who made most of the prototypes for the beautiful Tootsietoys in the 1920s and 30s, still exists. The fuselage, which has less detail around the windows and nose than the zamac toy, is lead. The spine of the fuselage is marked with an indentation, not a raised line. The undercarriage is cruder and roughly tacked together with solder. Small gilded metal wheels are fitted. There is only a slight difference in the tinplate wing. The whole is finished in white and fitted with red propellers.

REPLACEMENT PARTS Parts, cast in white metal, have been available for pre-war planes for many years. In addition, cast iron and slush-moulded propellers have been made. It can be very difficult to tell the new parts from the originals.

COPIES AND REPRODUCTIONS

Tootsietoys were copied at home and abroad and Dowst chased such offenders with litigious vigour, even beginning a case against one of the worst offenders, Johillco, in England. Some planes are so distinctive that all models of them, if approximately the same size, look similar, so that it is difficult to say whether they are copies or not. The 'copies' are not usually marked – that would have been asking for trouble – so it is often difficult to ascribe manufacturers. Many of the Tootsietoy dies were legitimately used in the 1970s/80s by Accucast. The toys are slightly heavier than the originals and the bare metal parts have a high shine. They can be difficult to distinguish because not all the Tootsietoys reproduced were marked with the name and not all the Accucast have had the original name removed. All the following are cast lead toys or lead with tin wings. Other copies/lookalikes in tin fall outside the scope of this book.

Ford Trimotor
Dyson, England. The whole toy has been copied accurately except that cast lines are proud, not indented. Marked 'BRITISH MADE DYSON' up inside fuselage. All lead – made in France. Accucast

Bleriot Monoplane
SR France. At least one other version.

Autogiro
Dyson, England. This has to be a copy as the Kellett autogiro was confined to the USA. The whole toy has been copied but it is unmarked. The lines cast along the fuselage are proud not indented and the whole is thinner and less crisp.

Aerodawn Biplane
Dyson, England. The Tootsietoy was copied right down to the registration UX214, but is marked 'BRITISH MADE' inside the fuselage. All the lines are less fine than the original and the lead casting is poor round the radial engine.

Aircraft Carrier
Possibly by Charbens, marked 'MADE IN ENGLAND 891'.

THE AEROPLANES

Aero Dawn High Wing Monoplane, and with pontoons (Spirit of St Louis) – 4660

The neatly-made toy, cast fuselage with tinplate wing, is a representation of the plane flown by Lindberg from New York to Paris in 1927 but was not called Spirit of St Louis for legal reasons and the 'real' number NX211 was represented on the fuselage side as UX214. It is not to scale as the toy's wing is too short: scale span 1/147; scale length 1/84. Individually boxed and available in sets. The toy, fitted with pontoons, a single piece of tin with float shapes fixed on the axle, instead of wheels, was unnumbered and probably only available in sets.

Aeroplane Carrier – 1036

Now known as an aircraft carrier, a fine diecast ship, with indented portholes and metal wheels on rollers, was fitted with two planes with a span of 17mm and three smaller ones with a 7mm span. They carry small cast stars on each wingtip and are painted bright blue. Though rivetted on to the deck, they sometimes become detached. An English copy marked 'Made in England 891' has the portholes proud on the casting. It carries four 8mm span planes with roundels on the wingtips, all painted a drab grey.

Autogiro – 4659

This good model of the Kellett Autogiro has the engine cylinders well represented on the single casting which is marked 'TOOTSIETOY'. The tinplate wing slips up over the undercarriage legs and is held on by deforming the casting slightly. The two tinplate pieces of the rotor are pinned to the stanchion. The toy was copied in Europe.

Biplane – 4650

The 1926 catalogue describes it as 'A toy to arouse the imagination of every boy. Educational as well as a means of play'. It's difficult to see its educational benefits! The box-section wing cast in one piece is quite a technical achievement for the time. A pretty toy, with the same propeller and wheels as the Bleriot.

Bleriot Monoplane – 4491, 4492, 160

There are two sizes of Bleriot produced by Tootsietoy, the smaller, a 22mm long charm with a ring at the end of its tail, was sold unnumbered to the retailer by the mixed gross. The larger, in 1/134 scale, has a span of 58mm. Described in the 1921 catalogue as a 'Reproduction of a well-known make of monoplane. Strongly made with moveable wheels and propellor. Finished in bronze gilt with silver plated propellor and coloured wheels. Packed 2 doz. to the box'. More lyrically the 1925 catalogue says, 'Any boy will understand the fine points of this reproduction of a well-known make of monoplane. Propellor and wheels turn. Bright gilt finish with coloured wheels. A sure sale to any boy who sees it.' The next version was released in 1925. A loop was cast into the top of the fuselage so that four could be hung from a Carousel, 160. The two crossed wires with a different coloured plane hanging from each extremity twirl prettily down a twisted pole which is supported by a circular tinplate stand. The third type has the same dimensions and casting characteristics, the lattice spars of the fuselage being more square than rounded and a smooth upper wing embossed with 'SPIRIT OF ST LOUIS'. The rear fuselage at the tail has been filled in and a squared loop added at the end. There is some discussion as to whether these are copies of the SR toy (France) or vice versa or whether they are similar because they are models of the same plane. SR produced both marked and unmarked Bleriots. The Tootsietoy has 13 regular dash marks between the ribs on the two centre panels on the wings and has six-spoke wheels and squarer section spars. The two-blade paddle-shaped propellers are indistinguishable. Grey paint typical of SR is not a Tootsietoy colour. Because the real Bleriot was not seen in the United States, it is possible that Dowst contracted a French firm to make the original.

Crusader Plane –719

The lower casting of this accurate 1/84 scale model is fine and intricate, incorporating everything (including wheel housings) except the top half of the cabin which is secured in place by interference spigots.

Curtiss P-40 Pursuit Plane – 721

This is a scarce model because it was introduced in 1941 and production ceased in 1942. The two castings have neat incised panel lines covering the whole of the upper surfaces and indented roundels on the wings.

Electra (Lockheed) – 125

Apart from the rudimentary single-axle undercarriage, this 1/166 scale, one-piece casting is quite a good model with an Eastern Air Lines (EAL) registration. Neville Chamberlain flew in one to see Hitler, returning with the famous 'Peace in our time' document which he waved from the aircraft steps.

5 Cent Miniatures

Smaller toys introduced in 1932, retailing at half the price of the normal range. (See also 5 Cent and 10 Cent Assortments)

Low Wing Two-Seater Monoplane – 106
A pretty curvy cast lead fuselage has a single engine and twin open cockpits to the rear of the wing. The undercarriage legs slot though the tinplate wing which is painted above and chemically blacked or browned below.

High Wing Cabin Monoplane – 107
The square-edged fuselage has a row of cabin windows indented and the radial engine has prominent exhausts. The same tinplate wing that is fitted to 106 above is insecurely held on by deformed lead lugs projecting from the top of the main casting.

Fly-n-Giro – 720
It has a diecast body incorporating two pulley wheels designed to run along a taught string. As it moves, the rough string rubs against the offset central pillar supporting the four tinplate rotor blades, the friction causing the rotor to turn. Very few have survived.

Los Angeles (Airship) – 1030
Rather a late introduction (1937), the model, scale length 1/1063, diameter 1/890, is embossed with 'USN LOS ANGELES' along both sides of the envelope though the original was lettered only 'US NAVY' and carried the star-in-roundel aft. Two castings sandwich pulley wheels (hubs from Graham cars) between them. Only two of the engines are represented.

Super Mainliner – DC-4E, Long Range Bomber – DC-4, 722
Douglas and United Airlines must initially have had confidence in this unsuccessful plane, the DC-4E (experimental), as presumably they paid for the underneath of the fuselage to be embossed 'SUPER Mainliner' and the wings 'UNITED NC20100'. Tootsietoy had their difficulties too and this 1/320 scale model with its thin section is prone to casting faults. The windows on the upper casting tend to mould badly and the lower casting is prone to tailfin failure. The difficulty of filling the undercarriage legs led to the mould having thick ribs added beneath the wings between undercarriage and fuselage. In 1941, the casting was modified: the letters were removed from the upper wings, and cast roundels were added. The underfuselage now reads 'LONG RANGE BOMBER TOOTSIETOY'.

Trimotor (Ford) – 4649
This pretty 1/171 scale model consists of one large main fuselage casting with an intricate second one for the undercarriage and two underwing engines. The two castings are very neatly held together by a clip which is part of the tinplate wing.

TWA Douglas Airliner (DC-2) – 0717
The Tootsietoy is a good 1/196 scale model of the DC2 with the sharp junction between the leading edge of the tailfin and the fuselage cast cleanly. The underneath has 'Pat. Apl. F.' embossed, no doubt to protect the casting method which splits the fuselage in two vertically down the centre line instead of horizontally. Each half requires a three-part die and, despite a tendency to mismatch around the cockpit windows, the whole indicates no mean skill on the part of the toolmaker.

US Army Plane (Northrop Gamma) – 119
The wings of the 1/138 scale model are embossed with stars-in-roundels and 'US ARMY'.

Waco Navy Bomber – 718
The 1/84 scale model is accurate particularly in the plan view and the tail. The upper casting consists of part of the engine cowl, top wing, cabin with window uprights and tail; the lower consisting of the front of the engine, lower fuselage, wings and undercarriage legs. The castings are particularly smooth with some good detail, including a rear gun position above the rear of the cabin and a rack of bombs below.

Wings Biplane, and with pontoons – 4675
Wings, the name of this diecast toy with twin tinplate wings, derives from the title of an exciting if biased film featuring several different types of biplane used around the time of the First World War and showing how the Americans won the war in the air single-handed. The boxes feature

scenes of trenches. It must be one of the earliest marketing spin-off diecast toys, but there was nevertheless a dispute with Parker Bros Inc of Salem, Mass. who were marketing a card game of the same name. A truce was agreed however, probably because Dowst was supplying Parker with games pieces. Wings Biplane with Pontoons does not seem to have a catalogue number leading one to suppose that it was only available in mixed sets. The pontoons, or floats, are neatly pressed from a single piece of tin and fixed on to the main casting with an axle.

POST-WAR PRODUCTION 1947–60+

Production started again with some pre-war toys being available for December 1945, the first peacetime Christmas. New product first appeared in 1947. The models were no longer sold individually but in fairly cheap sets: 7000 Playtime Set containing 10 pieces was priced under US$3. Early production had many similarities to pre-war but as time passed, the castings became simpler and more representational. Many of the models were one-piece castings with simple bar axles. Black rubber wheels were fitted. The latest catalogue containing these planes and helicopters that I have seen is dated 1960. Most of the castings are marked 'Tootsietoy', though in some it is indistinct, and many have the plane name. There are few individual catalogue numbers. Some were bubble-packed onto card, eg Airport Set has a Boeing 707 plus small plastic accessories. If a specific year is listed in the date column, the toy was known to be in the catalogue for that year. The wheels are solid black rubber on a single axle, unless specified.

MADE IN USA AND CHINA 1970–1985

As manufacturing costs rose in the 1970s and 1980s, in common with many other established firms, Tootsietoy, now a division of the Strombecker Corp., Chicago, had some of their product made in the Far East. This list is of poorer quality models, the earlier of which were made in the USA and the later in China.

1910–42

4491 Bleriot Monoplane charm 1910–25+
22mm
Lead with small ring cast on the end of the tail. Bronze coloured.

4482 Bleriot Monoplane 1910–25+
58mm
Lead, two-blade propeller, six-spoke wheels.
Silver or gold, purpled wheels and propeller or propeller unpainted.

Bleriot Monoplane with ring on top 1925
As 4482 with ring for attaching it to 160 Carousel. Yellow.

Bleriot 'Spirit of St Louis' 1927
As 4482 with smooth upper wing surface cast with 'SPIRIT OF ST LOUIS'.

160 Four Bleriot Monoplanes on a carousel 1925–25+
4482 above with ring on top, one each red, green, blue and silver. Tinplate carousel.

4650 Biplane 1926–34
58mm
Lead fuselage and box wing. Two-blade propeller. six-spoke wheels.
Yellow fuselage, propellers, wheels with red wings or orange with blue wings, also green wings.

'Tootsietoy' marked onto all new plane castings

4660 Aero Dawn High Wing Monoplane (Spirit of St Louis) 1928–41/2
95mm
UX 214 on fuselage. Lead fuselage, tinplate wing. Two-blade propeller. Silver, red, blue or green. Individual boxes.

Aero Dawn High Wing Monoplane with pontoons 1928–41/2
95mm
As above but pontoons instead of wheels.

4675 Wings Biplane 1929–36
95mm
Lead fuselage, tinplate wings, two-blade propeller. Blue, red, silver or green.

Wings Biplane with pontoons 1929–36
95mm
As above but pontoons instead of wheels. Blue or yellow.

4649 Trimotor (Ford) 1930–41
132mm
Lead fuselage, tinplate wing. Silver, red, black or yellow. Two-blade propellers, silver, gold, black or blue.
Silver or black hubs with flat boss with white rubber tyres or gold all-metal wheels. Some with oval paper label under wing 'Made in USA'.

106 Low Wing Two-Seater Monoplane 1932–41
89mm
Lead fuselage, tin wing shared with 107 below.
Purple two-blade propeller. Green with orange wing, red with gold or gold with red, undersurfaces chemically blackened or browned. Purple or gold metal wheels. Five Cent Miniature.

107 High Wing Cabin Monoplane 1932–41
89mm
Lead fuselage, tin wing shared with 106 above.
Green with red wing, red with green or red with gold. Purple or gold metal wheels.
Five Cent Miniature.

All subsequent new plane castings are in mazac and are marked 'Tootsietoy'.

4650 Number given in one catalogue for 4659 Autogiro below.

4659 Autogiro 1934–41
110mm across wing/121mm rotor.
Mazac fuselage with engraved lines, tinplate wing and rotor blades. Silver with red or blue rotor.
White rubber tyres on black hubs, or white rubber wheels.

0717 TWA Douglas Airliner (DC2) 1935–41/2
135mm
TWA NC101Y across wings. Marked: 'TOOTSIETOY MADE IN UNITED STATES OF AMERICA PAT.APL.F.'
Red, silver, green or yellow with black letters or, red or orange fuselage and silver wings or silver fuselage with red wings. Three-blade propellers.

119 US Army Plane 1936–41/2
105mm
Star-in-roundel 'US ARMY' star-in-roundel across wings.
Red, silver, yellow or green. Also brown with green camouflage.
Three-blade propeller. Five Cent Miniature.

718 Waco Navy Bomber 1937–41/2
127mm
Star-in-roundel US NAVY, star-in-roundel across wings.
No. cast under wing. Silver, dark blue lower or red, silver lower. Casting and colours split around top of engine and along lower edge of windows. Two-blade propeller. White rubber wheels. Grey with brown camouflage with black wheels.

Waco Dive Bomber 1942–46
As above but with 'DIVE BOMBER' cast across wing.
Silver upper, red lower or khaki and green camouflage.

719 Crusader Plane 1937–41
130mm
'CRUSADER X110' across wings. Red upper, silver lower or dark blue upper, silver lower. Casting and colour split around waistline of cabin.
Large or small three-blade propellers. Black metal wheels.

125 Electra (Lockheed) 1937–41/2
102mm
EAL NC1011 across wings Green, silver, yellow or orange. Two-blade propellers.

1030 Los Angeles (Airship) 1937–41
127mm long
'US LOS ANGELES' on envelope. Silver. Individual dark blue box.

DC-4 Super Mainliner (DC4E) 1939–40
134mm
Two castings split along lower window edge. Later casting has ribs from fuselage to undercarriage to assist metal flow.
'UNITED NC 20100' across wings, 'SUPER MAINLINER-ANOTHER TOOTSIETOY' under fuselage. Silver or red. Three-blade tinplate, later diecast propellers.
Individual boxes.

720 Fly-n-Giro 1938–40
72mm
A single casting with 'USN' on port side of fuselage, XOP-1 on the other and 'TOOTSIETOY MADE IN THE UNITED STATES OF AMERICA' under wings.
Four tinplate blades made from two strips of tin are held up on a diecast pillar secured through the casting with a long nail. Black three-blade propeller. Two white rubber wheels on a single axle.
Green or yellow with red and white striped blades. Individual box.

721 Curtiss P-40 Pursuit Plane 1941–42
?mm
Silver. Three-blade propeller. Two white rubber wheels on a single axle.

722 Long Range Bomber 1941–42
134mm
Second casting of DC-4 modified: lettering on upper wings removed, replaced by cast circles. Underfuselage re-engraved 'LONG RANGE BOMBER TOOTSIETOY'.
Brown and green, light blue and cream or brown and grey dull camouflage. White centred red star on blue roundel (in cast circles).

1036 Aeroplane Carrier (ship) c.40–41/2
154mm long
Blue planes rivetted on. Silver, red funnel etc. detail.

MIDGETS

All marked Tootsietoy except 1636 2-engined bomber.
Single-engined plane
Spirit of St Louis
Four-engined Atlantic Clipper

1636 Two-engined bomber (DC2) 1936–41
Approx. 60mm
Single castings with fixed propellers. Red or silver.

SETS

Most of the sets are mixed road vehicles but some have planes in them as well. The loose descriptions of some of the toys occasion some difficulties in establishing their contents. There is no problem with 'Trimotor' as there is only one, the Ford, in the range but 'Scouting Combat Planes' could be either of the two Wings Biplanes, or both, or even the Aerodawn, eg, 5061 Aerial Defense Set contains four vehicles, five figures and three Pursuit Planes comprising two Aerodawn (red) and one Wings Biplane (silver). There is a US Army Plane and a miniature bomber, and a US Army Transport Plane which could be referred to as an Army Plane, and so on. 189 Air Raiders Set either has two different groups of contents or one is on the wrong number. Some of the sets, however, were exclusively aerial and these are listed below. The set box lids were often eyecatchingly and beautifully designed. The interior backing card was usually dark cream card with slots to hold the planes. Some of the sets contained metal badges: Toosietoy Airlines Pilot, Co-pilot and Stewardess; United Airlines (a minor modification to the logo of the real company) Jr Stewardess and Future Pilot.

SETS OF PLANES ONLY – PRE-WAR

5100 Airport Set
1930/31 catalogue: contains 'Attractively coloured metal hangar with two of the new Trimotor planes in red and silver. Beautifully lithographed in four colours', ie two 4649 Ford Trimotor, one red, one silver and a tin curved-top hangar, brown with white and green star in white, gree. red, white concentric circles, tin flag with 'T' on it.
Chequer-edged, multi-coloured box lid depicting hangars, searchlight and child aeronauts.

Aces of the Air
1931 catalogue: contains '2 Biplanes and 2 Monoplanes – one each for land and sea (both versions of Aerodawn and Wings Biplane?).
New Playtime Perfection packaging. Silver, red, green and blue planes in each set as illustrated'.

Aerial Offense Set
1931 catalogue: contains '3 Trimotored bombers, 4 Scouting Combat and Observation Planes (both versions of Aero Dawn and of Wings Biplane?), all differently coloured'.

Aerial Offense Set
Three Trimotors and four Scouting Combat Planes

Set 1935?
Aero Dawn High Wing Monoplane with pontoons, 4675 Wings Biplane with pontoons, 4649 Trimotor, 0717 TWA Douglas Airliner, 4659 Autogiro

Speedy Aeroplanes c.1939
719 Crusader Plane, two 125 Electra, Wings Biplane with Pontoons, 718 Waco Navy Bomber, two 119 Army Plane, 4659 Autogiro, DC-4 Super Mainliner, 0717 TWA Douglas Airliner, Aero Dawn with pontoons, 4649 Trimotor. Also in box: three badges, Tootsietoy Airlines Pilot, Tootsietoy Airlines Co-pilot, Tootsietoy Airlines Stewardess.
Art Deco Box lid showing seven planes flying along parallel air corridors.

189 Air Raiders Set 1941/2
Two 125 Electra, two 119 US Army Plane, seven small bombers

189 Air Raiders Set
718 Waco, DC-4 Super Mainliner, 125 Electra, 0717 TWA Douglas Airliner, 721 Curtiss P-40, 119 US Army Plane

1407 Air Defense Set 1941/2
10 miniature bombers (0717 DC2) in varying colours mounted on a card.

6100 Aeroplane Set 1941
Wings Seaplane, 4660 Aero Dawn Aero Dawn with pontoons, two 718 Waco Navy Bomber, two 119 U.S. Army Plane, 721 Curtiss P-40 Pursuit Plane, two 125 Electra, 722 Army Transport Plane, DC-4 Super Mainliner.

6150 Aeroplane Set 1940/1
722 Long Range Bomber or 0717 TWA Douglas Airliner, 718 Waco Navy Bomber, 125 Lockheed Electra, 712 Curtiss P-40 Pursuit Plane or 719 Crusader, 0717 TWA Douglas Airliner, 119 US Army Plane.
In Art Deco Box.

PLANES AND ROAD VEHICLES – PRE-WAR

The sets listed here contain planes and road vehicles. They are featured in Trade Catalogues or are in collections that the author has had access to. There are more to be added to the list as more catalogues are found. The contents most likely varied from year to year.

5031 Playtime Toys Set $1 1929–31+
10 road vehicles, 4660 Aero Dawn High Wing Monoplane

Playtime Toys Set $1.50 1929–31+
14 different road vehicles, 3660 Aero Dawn High Wing Monoplane, 6475 Wings Biplane

Playtime Toys Set $2.00 1929
21 pieces including three? planes (Aerodawn Monoplane, Wings Biplane + one other?)

Playtime Toys Set $2.50 1929
28 pieces including four? planes (all available?)

4051 Air Mail Set 1931
Catalogue: 'Trimotor, 2 Monoplanes (Aero Dawn), 2 large and 2 small Mail Trucks, 6 men and a Pylon with revolving and tilting beacon. A complete unit of modern Air Mail service that has infinite possibilities for big sales.'

7004 Motor Set 1931
Catalogue: 'Five Items of Motor Transportation, Aero Dawn Monoplane, Sedan, Coupe, Delivery Van, Touring Car'.

5061 Aerial Defense Set 1931
Catalogue: 'Scout Car, 2 Anti-aircraft Guns and 2 searchlights each mounted for rotation and elevation on a big truck. 3 Pursuit planes (2 x Aero Dawn monoplanes, 1 x Aerodawn biplane) with crew of 6 men as illustrated'.

7005 Playtime Miniatures 1932
101-110 (10) vehicles including 106 Low Wing Monoplane and 107 High Wing Monoplane.

0510 Playtime Midgets Set 1936–41/2
12 small single castings including up to four Midgets Series Planes. Contents vary.

5450 Buck Rogers Set 1938–39
Three different Buck Rogers Rocket ships, two figures, a spool of cord and 1030 Dirigible Los Angeles

1404 Land Defense Set c.1940

199 Playtime Set 1941–42
Four road vehicles and 119 US Army Plane

650 Army Set 1941–42
Seven military pieces, soldiers and 718 Waco Navy Bomber

750 Jumbo Set 1941
Four large vehicles and 718 Waco Navy Bomber

5000 Rol-Ezy Motor Set 1941–42
16 road vehicles, two 119 Army Planes, two 125 Electras

5050 Playtime Set 1941–42
Seven road vehicles, 119 Army Plane, 125 Electras

5100 Playtime Set 1941–42
All the Torpedo road vehicles, larger ladder and hose trucks, 718 Waco Navy Bomber, DC-4 Super Mainliner

5210 Commercial Set 1941
10 commercial vehicles and 718 Navy Bomber

5220 Army Set 1941
Seven military pieces, two 119 US Army Planes, 718 Waco Navy Bomber, two Miniature Bombers

5400 Jumbo Set 1941
Eight large vehicles, 718 Waco Navy Bomber, 722 Army Transport Plane

POST-WAR PRODUCTION 1947 – 60+

Beechcraft Bonanza 1953
106mm. 1/94
Single casting with 'TOOTSIETOY' under starboard wing, 'BEECHCRAFT BONANZA' under port.
Orange, dark blue or silver. Two-blade dark blue or silver propeller, usually contrasting with the body.

Boeing 377 Stratocruiser 1954
170mm. 1/260
Upper casting, fuselage and tail with 'PAN AMERICAN WORLD AIRWAYS' along fuselage sides. Lower casting with 'PAA N1025V' across wings. Plug in undercarriage legs. Silver. Four blue three-blade propellers.

2941 Boeing 707 1958
150mm. 1/282
Three castings: upper and lower fuselage with little detail, wings with flap outlines.
Plug in undercarriage legs. Blue with silver wings.
1960/1 and 1964/66: bubble-packed with small diecast baggage trucks etc.

Constellation
154mm. 1/246
Upper casting has 'PAN AMERICAN WORLD AIRWAYS' along fuselage sides. Lower casting has 'PAA' and 'N88846' across wings.
Silver. Four blue three-bladed propellers. Plug in undercarriage legs.

Convair 240 Airliner 1952
128mm. 1/220
Two castings split along the bottom edge of the 10 square cabin windows. Marked 'TOOTSIETOY MADE IN USA'.
Silver or white. Blue or black three-blade propellers.
Plug-in undercarriage legs with double wheels.

Cutlass F7U3 1960
92mm. 1/123
Single casting. Star-on-bar on port upper wing, 'NAVY' on starboard (reversed below). Under casting also marked 'F7U3 CUTLAS, TOOTSIETOY USA'. Red.

Douglas F-4D Skyray
72mm
Single delta wing casting with raised star-on-bar on port wing, 'NAVY' on starboard above, and reversed below. Under post wing marked 'F40 (error for F-4D) SKY RAY'. 'TOOTSIETOY R USA' marked up inside fuselage. Dark blue or red.

Shooting Star (Lockheed F-80C)
108mm. 1/111
Star-on-bar cast on wing tips, 'Shooting Star' in script on starboard side of nose. Marked under wings: 'TOOTSIETOY MADE IN USA' (S reversed on some/all?), under fuselage: 485004.
Upper fuselage and tail casting silver, lower fuselage and wing unit red.

Grumman F9F 2 Panther
95mm
Two castings: upper with wings, star-on-bar on port; lower marked 'TOOTSIETOY MADE IN USA'.
Wheels pressed onto stubs on lower casting.

Hiller 12c Helicopter
Blue or light blue. Silver tinplate four-blade rotor.

P-38 Lightning
130mm. 1/122
Single casting with circle 'USA' on port wing, 'P-38' circle on starboard, '1' or '2' up inside nose.
Silver. Blue three-blade propellers.

Piper Cub
105mm
Single non-prototypical casting. 'PIPER CUB MADE IN USA' under port wing. 'TOOTSIETOY' under starboard. Green.

Ryan Navion
110mm. 1/92
Single casting. 'MADE IN USA NAVION' under port wing. Not marked Tootsietoy. Orange, red. Two-blade propeller.

F-86 Sabre
97mm. 1/122
Two castings. Marked 'F-86 Sabre' below.
Upper fuselage and tail red, lower fuselage and swept wings silver. Red, green.

Sikorsky Amphibious Seaplane
Circle 'US COASTGUARD' Circle across wing casting. Fuselage casting incorporates floats.
Silver wing, red lower. Two three-blade propellers.

Sikorsky S58 Helicopter 1958
Red. Four-blade rotor.

F-94 Starfire 1960
93mm
Single casting with wingtip tanks with star-on-bar on port wing, 'USA' on starboard and reversed below. Named up inside fuselage. Green or red with silver tanks and tailfin.

POST-WAR SETS

7000 Playtime Set 1947+
Eight road vehicles, Convair 240, P.38 Lightning
1954: eight road vehicles, Convair, Stratocruiser
Box: yellow and black.

7500 Planes 1947+
Two Lightnings and Convair 240
Piper Cub, F-86 Sabre, Shooting Star, Beechcraft Bonanza, Navion
United Airlines Badges: Jr Stewardess, Future Pilot.
Box: planes flying against background of yellow sun with 'TOOTSIETOY' in silver, light and dark blue arc.

7200 Motor Set 1952
Eight road vehicles and Convair

5149 Playtime Motors Set 1953
Nine road vehicles and Beechcraft Bonanza

3198 Land and Air
Six military vehicles, F-86 Sabre, F-94 Starfire

4398 Combat Set 1960
Six miliary vehicles, gun, soldiers, Cutlass F7U3 and two others

6500 Pan American Airport Set
One vehicle, four airside accessories, Constellation, Stratocruiser, Navion, Sabre, Convair and two badges. Box lid has airport scene with nose of Stratocruiser coming in from the left with the name of the set in seriffed Pan Am style.

1970–1985

2552 Bell 206 JetRanger Helicopter 1975
115mm long
Main cabin and tail boom casting with 'TOOTSIETOY on boom in red, undercabin, interior and skids in white. Two-blade cast rotor in blue. Bubble-packed.

2980 F-16 Plane 1977
Silver fuselage with red wings. Star-on-bar on tips. Bubble packaging.

3185 F4U Corsair 1979
Dark blue upper fuselage and tail with light blue underfuselage and wing ends. Star-on-bar stickers. 'Air Aces' thick card open-topped box locating wingtips.

3260 Fokker TriDekker 1978
Red. Black and white German crosses on upper wings. 'The Red Baron' thick card open-topped box.

2220 Scorpion Helicopter 1977
95mm long.
Diecast non-proto-typical upper, metallic purple. Rotor and base marked 'Tootsietoy Scorpion made in USA' yellow plastic. Bubble-packed.

3166 Sport Airplane 1979
Light brown fuselage with white wing ends. Brown and yellow feather decals.

3150 TV News Helicopter 1978
Cast non-prototypical metallic purple upper, white plastic lower.

WW II AND JET FIGHTERS

Small (the F-15 is 55mm in length with a span of 40mm) single diecastings with a peg nose wheel and superfast main wheels are marked under the fuselage with 'Tootsietoy China' and an abbreviated plane name. The recognisable toys are sprayed the approriate colour and have sticker decals. They are bubble-packed four to a card. The reverse of the card shows the selection of:

WW II FIGHTERS: Zero, Stuka, P-40, F-4U Corsair, Spitfire, P-51, B-17 Bomber

JET FIGHTERS: F-14 Tomcat, F-16 Falcon, F-106, B-1 Bomber, F-15 Eagle, F-4 Phantom, Tactical Fighter (Stealth) Example: Pack 2925 contains B-1 Bomber, F-15 Eagle, Tactical Fighter, F-106 or B-17 Bomber, Spitfire, Zero, Stuka

B-17 Bomber
139mm
Upper die shared with Road Champs Flyers, lower die (part of wings and centre fuselage) marked 'Tootsietoy'. Light blue. Orange sticker flashes on wing tips, tail planes and fin, blue star-on-bar on wings.

2919 Advanced Tactical Fighter (Stealth)
70mm
Gloss black upper, grey one-piece plastic lower, cockpit surround and fins. White star-on-bar decals, F71138 on fins. The shape is a poor likeness. Bubble-packed onto card.

HARD BODY Made in China. Copyright 1992 on bubble packs.
The models consist of cast uppers with plastic lowers marked 'Tootsietoy'. Sticker decals.

2927 F-14 Swing Wing Fighter
130mm with wings extended.
Silver with pale blue lower. Stars-on-bars on wings, '104' on fuselage.

2927 MiG-27 Swing Wing Fighter
95mm with wings retracted.
Sand and green camouflaged upper, pale blue lower. White edged red stars on wings.

2928 AH-1W Super Cobra 'copter
160mm long
Yellow and brown camouflaged upper. Black plastic two-blade rotors and lower with skids. 'US ARMY COBRA' in red with drawing of the same on the sides.
Similar to Hard Body.

B2 (Stealth Bomber)
185mm
Mid metallic blue upper. The shape is a poor likeness. Small low quality models. Various non-prototypical colours with national markings available individually or in three-packs at different times:
Saab J35 'Dragon', Northrop F5A 'Little Tiger', McDonnell F4C 'Phantom', Dassault IIIC 'Mirage'.

138 *top:* Major Models (Hubley, Fairymark) Vought Corsair Navy Folding Wing Fighter (222mm);
bottom: Londontoy Hawker Hurricane (repainted, non-original propeller), Micromodels Vickers Viscount

139 *top:* Bento float plane (59mm), Crescent (UK) plane from Aircraft Carrier 'Eagle';
centre: Mollberg Sikorsky S.55 helicopter;
bottom: Unknown Spitfire pin brooch, stud lapel badge

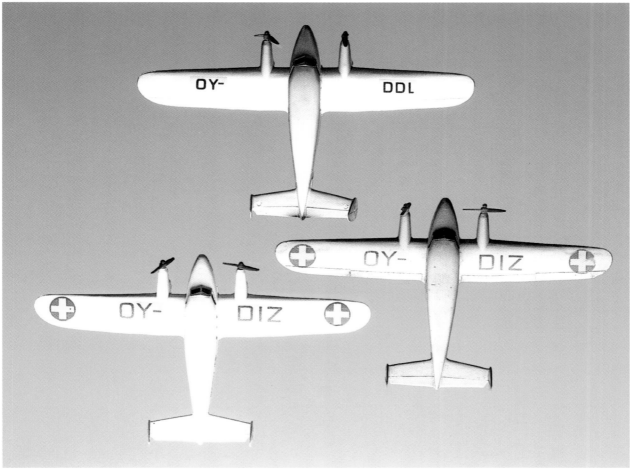

140 *top:* Tekno Transport-flyver (201mm); *bottom:* Ambulance-flyver, silver, scarcer blue

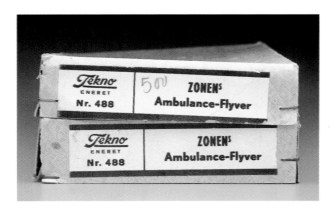

141 Boxes for the Tekno Ambulance-flyver

142 Tekno 401 B-17 Flyvende Fæstning (Flying Fortress) (143mm) USAF

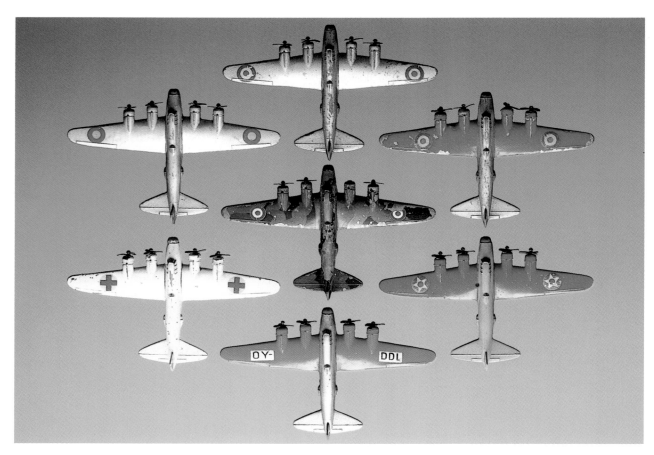

143 Tekno 401 B-17 Flying Fortress (143mm) in seven different liveries

144 Tekno 402
Bombeflyver (Blenheim
BB-1) (91mm) in five
different liveries

145 Tekno 403 Dauntless SBD-1 (87mm) in a variety of non-US liveries

146 Tekno 403 Jager DSB-1 (Douglas Dauntless SBD-1) (87mm) in various US liveries

147 Tekno Douglas DC-7C (193mm) Scandinavian, SAS

148 Tekno Douglas DC-7C (193mm) KLM old livery, KLM new livery

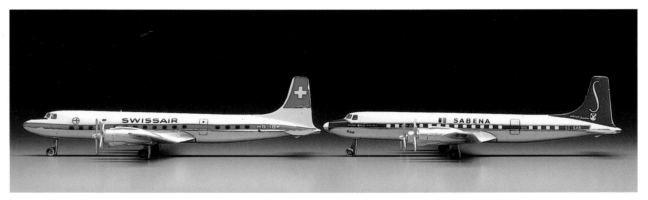

149 Tekno DC-7C (193mm) Swissair, Sabena

150 Tekno DC-7C (193mm) Alitalia, Sudflug

151 Tekno 766 Caravelle SE210 (169mm) with shaped plastic box
containing display stand; *top:* Scandinavian, Scandinavian Air Services;
bottom: Air France, Swissair

152 *top:* Tekno 785
Hawker Hunter (82mm);
centre: 788 Super Mystère
B-1, 787 F-100 Super
Sabre;
bottom: 786 MiG-15

153 *top:* Aviation Su-11 (43mm), Yak-25, Tu-24; *centre:* M-50, Il-62; *bottom:* Su-7, Tu-144

154 *top:* Metallix Breguet 690 C3 (150mm), L.R. Trimotor; *bottom:* A.R. Spirit of St Louis

155 A.R. Spirit of St Louis (126mm): note hole for motor on right-hand version

156 *top:* C I J Boeing 707 (136mm) Air France, Boeing 707; *bottom:* Caravelle Air France, Caravelle

157 *top:* C I J Noratlas (107mm), Breguet Deux Ponts, Fouga Magister; *bottom:* Douglas DC-6 UAT, Douglas DC-7, Norécran

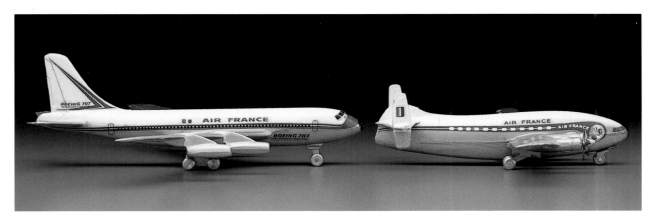

158 C1J Boeing 707 (136mm) Air France, Breguet Deux Ponts Air France

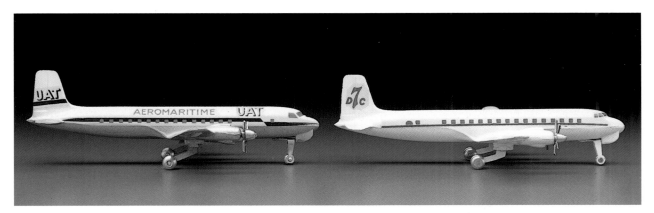

159 C1J DC-6 (118mm) in UAT livery, DC-7 in plain

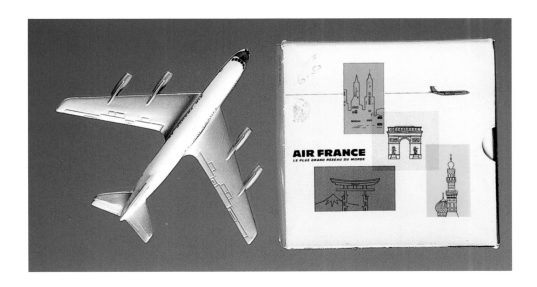

160 C1J Boeing 707
(136mm) Air France with
special box

161 C I J Fouga Magister
(65mm) with and without
blue cockpit and tip tanks
with original plastic bag
packaging

162 C I J standard box
for DC-7, special box for
DC-6 UAT

163 C I J undersides of Caravelles: earlier (left), later with added detail and different undercarriage mountings

164 C I J Caravelle (114mm): one side with Roman letters 'Royal Air Maroc' (above); the other with Arabic (below)

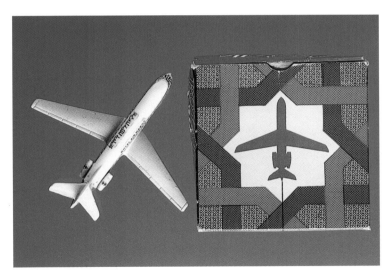

165 C I J Caravelle (114mm) Air Maroc with box

166 C I J box sides for Caravelle Air Maroc and Boeing 707 Air France

167 *top:* Majorette Douglas MD80 (78mm), Airbus A300, Boeing 767; *bottom:* Douglas DC-10, Boeing 747-400

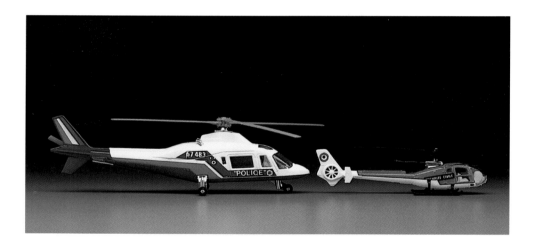

168 Majorette Super Mover Agusta Police (200mm), Gazelle Securité Civile

169 Majorette Sonic Flasher F-15 (91mm)

170 *top:* Pennytoys S.R. Rumpler Taube (65mm), Breguet I, Morane Saulnier; *bottom:* Bleriot ('feathered' wing), Bleriot, Farman F.60

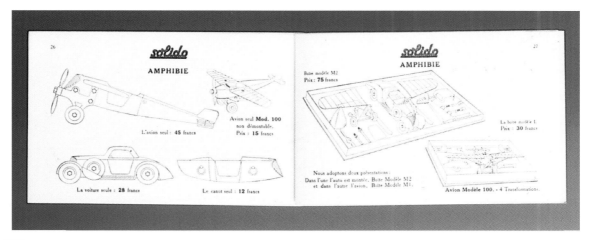

171 Solido 1935 catalogue: the left page illustrating the Amphibie plane available built (L'avion seul: 45 francs) and the High Wing Monoplane 'chromé' (Mod 100. 15 francs); the right page showing the Amphibie Set above the Avion Modèle 100 Set

172 Cover of the 1935 Solido catalogue

173 Solido High Wing Monoplane 'chromé' 1933–39 (162mm)

174 Solido High Wing Monoplane 'chromé' 1933–39 (162mm)

175 Solido Avion Set 1935–c.1939. Contains High Wing Monoplane (173–4) disassembled

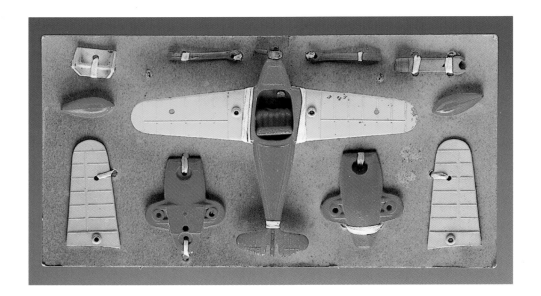

176 Solido Set Avion 3 1949–c1958. High Wing Monoplane is bottom right

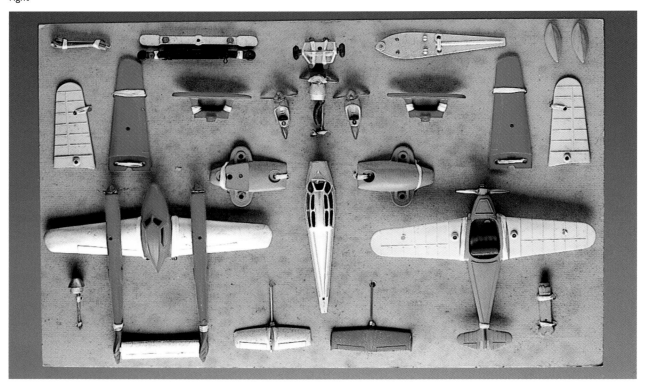

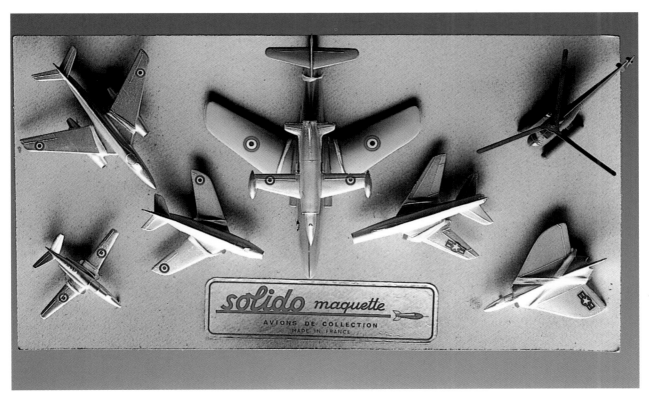

177 Solido Set: Shooting Star with swept wings (140mm) carrying Leduc 021 with;
top: Vautour, Sikorsky S.55; *centre:* Mystère IVA, Super Sabre; *bottom:* Fouga Magister, Douglas Skyray

178 Solido label from box lid of set

179 Solido Piaseki with three windows painted

180 Solido Piaseki with five windows painted

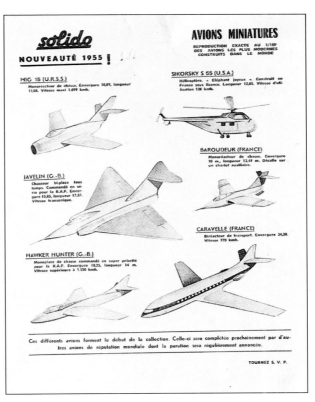

181 Solido 1955 instruction leaflet enclosed in set (Shooting Star carrying Leduc)

182 Solido Set: Shooting Star with tip tanks and pilot (140mm) with
top: Leduc 021, Fouga Magister; *bottom:* Douglas Skyray, Mystère IVA

183 Solido: three versions of the Super Constellation (151mm) with catalogue

184 Solido Super Constellation (151mm) (all silver), Tupolev Tu104 Aeroflot

185 Solido: two Javelins (104mm) showing 'hard' and 'soft' camouflage, Hawker Hunter

186 *top:* Solido Etendard (64mm), Breguet Alizé; *bottom:* Aquillon

187 *top:* Solido Morane-Saulnier (67mm), Fouga Magister; *bottom:* Trident, Thunderjet

188 *top:* Solido Super Mystère B2 (69mm), Super Sabre 100; *bottom:* Fairey Delta, Baroudeur

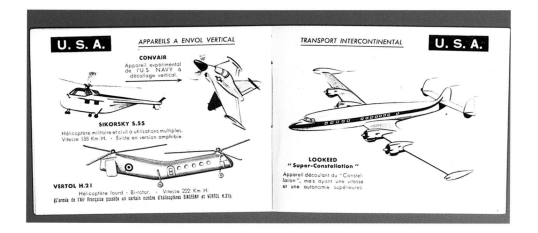

189 Solido: the USA plane pages from the 1958/9 catalogue

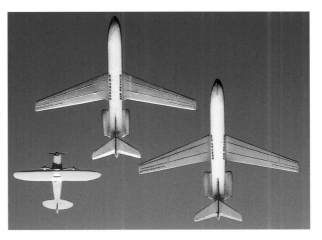

190 Solido MiG-15 (78mm), Tupolev Tu-104

191 *top:* Solido Caravelle (114mm) 'Air France' silver;
bottom: Super Cigale, Caravelle 'Air France' blue

192 Solido: various Super Cigale (62mm) colours with underside showing Solido transfer (the star-on-bar decals are dubious)

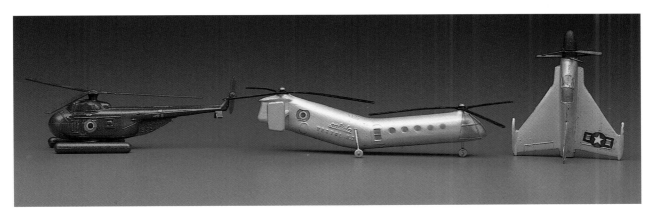

193 Solido Sikorsky S.55 (85mm), Vertol, Convair XFY-1

194 Solido helicopters Alouette III (170mm) Gendarmerie, Gazelle military

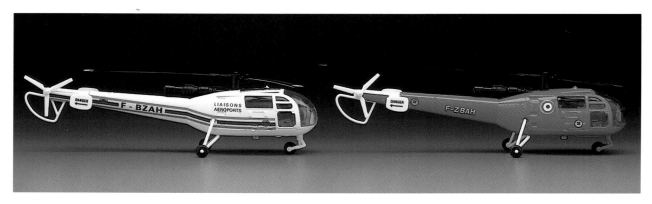

195 Solido helicopters Alouette III (170mm) Liasons Aeroports, Securité Civile

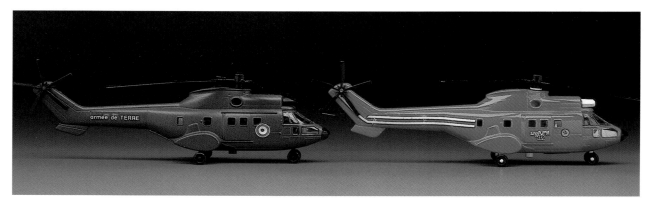

196 Solido helicopters Super Puma (185mm) Armée de Terre, Aerospatiale

197 Solido helicopters Gazelle PHI (175mm), Gendarmerie

198 *top:* Gescha Comet Racer (98mm), Crescent Comet Racer (for comparison); *bottom:* Märklin Hydravion (Dornier Wal)

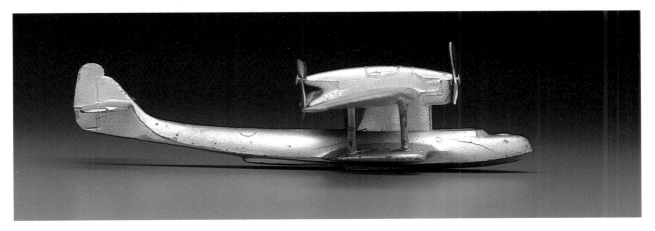

199 Märklin Hydravion (Dornier Wal) (120mm)

200 *top:* Schuco Piccolo Douglas F4D-1 (45mm), Super Sabre F100;
centre: Schuco Micro-Jet Super Sabre (repaint);
bottom: Schuco Piccolo Magister 170R with box, Thunderjet

201 *top:* Schuco Boeing 707 (76mm), Boeing 727, Lintoy Boeing 727, Schuco 784/4 Boeing 747;
bottom: Schuco Junkers F13, 784/5 Concorde, 789 Concorde (longer tail), Junkers Ju.52

202 *top:* Schuco Douglas DC-8 (78mm), 793 Boeing 747, Douglas DC-10;
bottom: Douglas DC-9, Airbus A300B, Ilushin Il-62, Lear Jet

203 *top:* Siku Boeing 767-200 (96mm), Boeing 747-400, Siku Club Airbus A320;
bottom: Siku Lockheed TriStar, Space Shuttle, Airbus A340-200

204 Siku helicopter MBB BO105 (175mm) Polis, Feuerwehr

205 Siku helicopter MBB BO105 (175mm) Polizei, Sussex Police

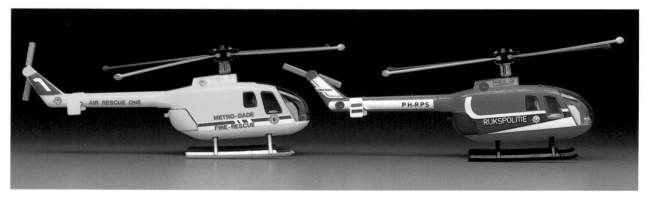

206 Siku helicopter MBB BO105 (175mm) Metro-Dade, Rijkspolitie

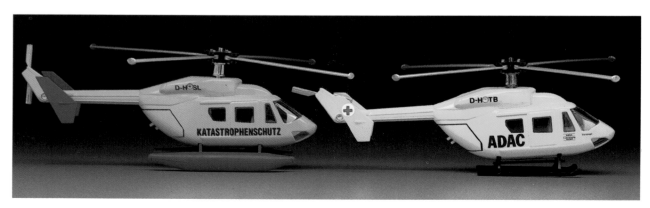

207 Siku helicopter Bk117 (175mm) Katastrophenschutz, ADAC

208 *top:* Polfi Bell 222 (82mm), Concorde; *bottom:* Pilaz Concorde, Tornado

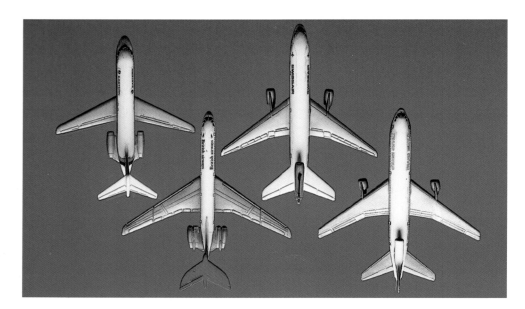

209 *top:* Lintoy DC-9 (102mm), Corgi DC-10; *bottom:* Corgi Vickers VC10, Ertl Lockheed TriStar

210 *top:* Lintoy Boston Havoc (132mm), Lintoy Spitfire; *bottom:* Corgi Zero-Sen A6M2

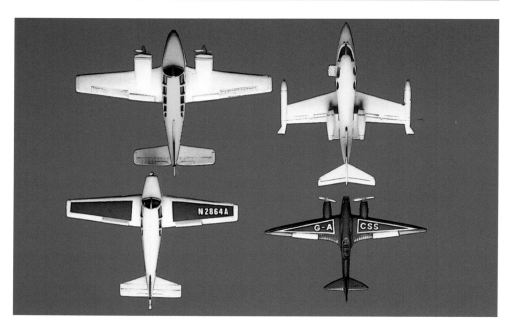

211 *top:* Corgi Piper Navajo (150mm), Corgi Lear Jet; *bottom:* Corgi Piper Cherokee, Lintoy Comet Racer

212 *top:* Lintoy Messerschmitt
Me262 (132mm) (die 1);
bottom: Flyers Messerschmitt
Me262, Lintoy Me262 die 2)

213 *top:* Corgi
Messerschmitt Me410
(135mm); *bottom:* Corgi
Messerschmitt Me410,
Flyers Me410

214 *top:* Corgi P-51D Mustang
(133mm) (with flaps), Flyers P-
47D Thunderbolt (horizontal
casting split);
bottom: Lintoy P-51D Mustang
(no flaps), Lintoy P-47D
Thunderbolt (vertical casting
split, with flaps)

215 *top:* Flyers MiG-21, Lintoy Grumman F11F (die 2); *bottom:* Corgi MiG-21(69mm), Flyers Grumman F11F

216 *top:* Flyers Jaguar (80mm), Lintoy Phantom F-4E; *bottom:* Lintoy F-104A Starfighter, Lintoy Saab 35X Draken

217 *top:* Bachmann
Boeing 707 (113mm)
TWA, Corgi Boeing 747
Wardair; *bottom:* Corgi
Boeing 747 CP Air, Lintoy
Boeing 727 Braniff

218 Corgi Boeing 747 (130mm) Wardair, CP Air

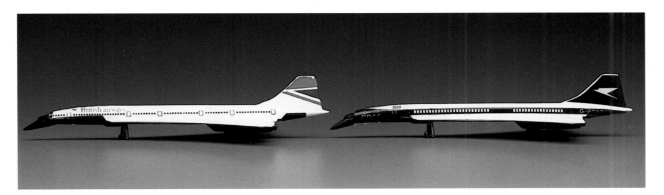

219 Lintoy Concorde (73mm) British Airways, Corgi Concorde BOAC

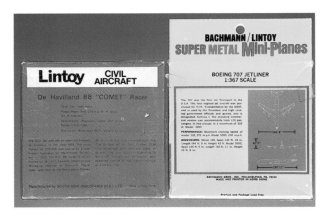

220 Corgi/Lintoy boxes for Hong Kong and Singapore product

222 *top:* Imperial Diecast Mini Jets A-10 Thunderbolt;
centre: TU-26 Backfire, F-19 Stealth; *bottom:* F-4E Phantom

221 Lintoy 'Civil' and Bachmann/Lintoy boxes

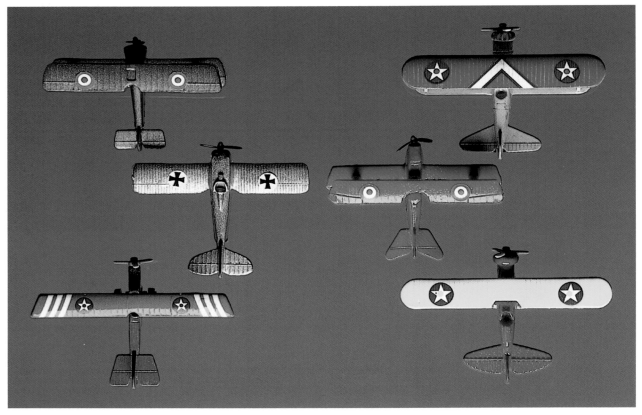

223 *top:* Benkson Sopwith (72mm), BiPlane Boeing PT-17;
centre: Benkson Junkers J10, R.A.F. RE.8;
bottom: BiPlane JN-4D, Boeing P-12E

224 *top:* Die-Cast Miniatures F-16 (70mm) (pencil sharpener), Imperial Die Cast A-4F Skyhawk;
bottom: Flight-of-a-Gun Phantom, Home Toys/Freda F-16

225 *top:* Home Toys (85-90mm) Boeing 727, Airbus A300B; *bottom:* Douglas DC-10, Lockheed TriStar

226 *top:* Mandarin (M) (small) Nieuport 17 (89mm), Phantom F-4K, Mitsubishi Betty;
centre: MiG-21, Mirage 4A; *bottom:* Boeing 727, Albatross D111, Lockheed P-38 Lightning

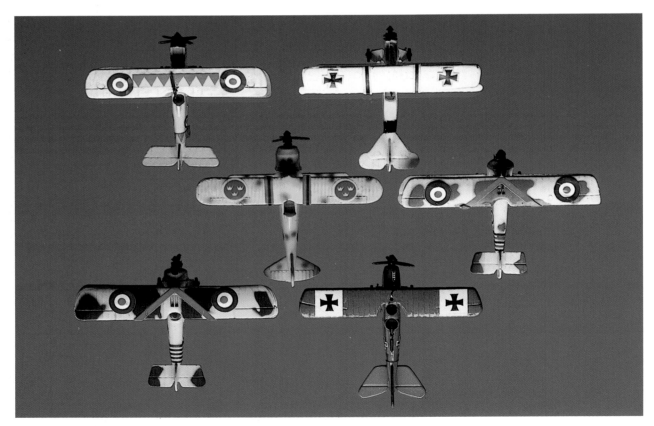

227 *top:* Mandarin (M) (large) S.E. 5 Scout (105mm), Fokker F.7;
centre: Forch CR-42, Sopwith Camel; *bottom:* Sopwith Triplane, Roland C11

228 M Pull-back Shuttle,
Unknown China Shuttle,
Road Tough Hughes
helicopter, Wondrie Puma
helicopter

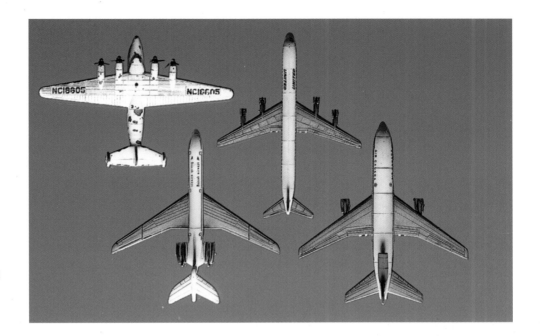

229 *top:* Playart Fast Wing
Boeing Clipper (121mm),
Douglas DC-8-61;
bottom: Vickers VC-10,
Lockheed TriStar

230 *top:* Playart Fast
Wing Spitfire (115mm)
bottom: P-51B Mustang,
Il-2M3 Stormovik

231 *top:* Playart Fast Wing Messerschmitt Me410 (120mm), A.W. Seahawk; *bottom:* MiG-21 PF

232 *top:* RacingChampion P-51D Mustang (130mm) *bottom:* Super Wings Phantom, Concorde

233 Soma Microjets. Six US Jet Fighters on card aircraft carrier play base

234 Tintoys MiG-21 (71mm), Vickers VC-10, F-4EJ Phantom II

235 *top:* Maxwell Boeing 747 (99mm) 'Air India', Milton Caravelle SE210
centre: Milton Concorde BOAC (copy of Corgi)
bottom: Maxwell Boeing 747 'British airways', MiG Fighter

236 *top:* Edison Airlines Heroes' Wings (Le Ali Degli Eroi) 1002
Fokker Dr.l(100mm), 1003 Spad S XIII
bottom: 1001 RAF SE 5A, 1004 Macchi Nieuport II

237 Edison Airlines: inside of box lid of Heroes' Wings set

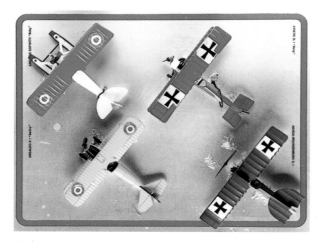

238 *top:* Edison Airlines Italian Sky (Cielo Tricolore) 1103 Ansaldo
Sopwith Baby (106mm), 1102 Aviatik D.I. Berg
bottom: 1101 Ansaldo A.I. Balilla, 1104 Hansa-Brandenburg

239 Edison Airlines: inside of box lid of Italian Sky set

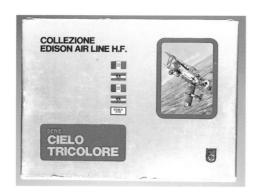

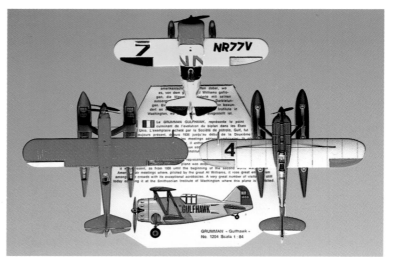

240 Edison Airlines: box lid of Italian Sky set

241 *top:* Edison Airlines Records in the Sky 1203 Gee Bee Super
Sportster (105mm)
bottom: 1202 Macchi Castoldi M.C.72, 1201 Supermarine S.5 on
leaflet showing Grumman Gulfhawk which was not issued

242 Edison Airlines 'stamps' and leaflet: when you had got all four of the Heroes' Wings planes you sent off for club membership, a magazine and a draw entry, the stamps being proof of purchase

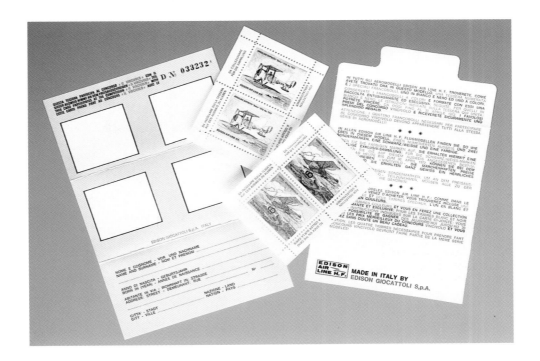

243 Undersides of (*below*) Edison Airlines 1104 Hansa Brandenburg and (*top*) Pyranglo/Toyway reissue showing deletion of 'Made in Italy'

244 Mercury 416 Convair RB-36E (234mm)

245 Mercury box for Convair RB-36E

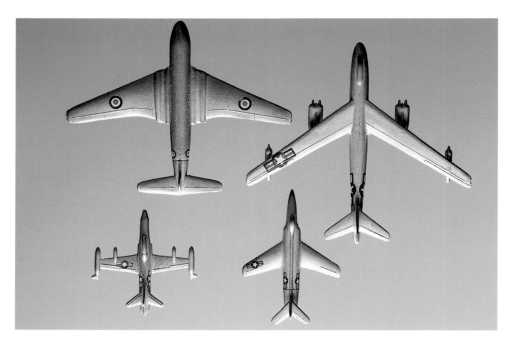

246 *top:* Mercury 407
DH Comet (138mm),
418 Boeing B-47 Stratojet
bottom: 424 Lockheed
F94C Starfire, 405
Lockheed F.90

247 *top:* Mercury 402A
Fiat 212G Ambulance
(145mm), 402 Fiat 212G
bottom: 415 Boeing B.29
marked under as B.50

248 *top:* Mercury 401
Fiat G.59 (59mm), 414
Piaggio 136, 411 Piaggio
P.148
bottom: 425 Lockheed
Lightning P.38, 423 Vought
Corsair F4U-5N

249 *top:* Mercury 403
Fiat G.80 (55mm), 408
Mystère, 410 Sabre
bottom: 412 MiG-15, 420
MiG-19, 419 Douglas D-
558-2 Skyrocket (missing
nose probe)

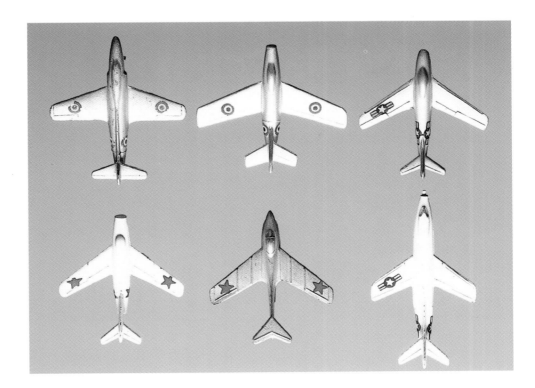

250 *top:* Mercury 406
Avro 707A (51mm), 426
Republic XF.91, 422
Cutlass F7U-3
bottom: 413 Convair
XF92A, 409 Missile, 404
Vampire

251 Mercury 426
Republic XF.91 (48mm),
417 Sikorsky S.55, 421
Convair XFY-1 Vertical
Riser, 422 Cutlass F7U-3

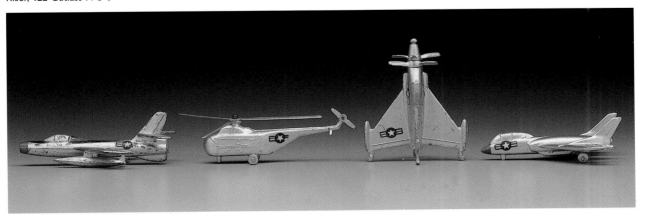

AEROMODELLINI

400/A Scatola 8 aerei assortiti
400/B Scatola 7 aerei assortiti
400/C Scatola 14 aerei assortiti
401 Monomot. «Fiat G 59 »
402 Trimotore «Fiat G 212»
402/A «Fiat G 212» tipo Cr. R.
403 Reattore «Fiat G 80 »
404 Reattore «Vampire »
405 Reatt. «Lockheed F 90»
406 Reattore «Avro 707 »
407 Reattore «Comet »
408 Reattore «Mystère »
409 Missile
410 Reattore «Sabre F 84 »
411 Aereo «Piaggio P 148 »
412 Reattore «Mig 15 »
413 Reatt. «Convair XF 92 A»
414 Idrov. «Piaggio P 136 »
415 «Boeing B 50 »
416 «Convair B 36 »
417 Elic. «Sikorsky S 55 »
418 «Boeing B 47 Stratojet»
419 «Douglas D 558-2Skyr.»
420 Reattore «Mig 19 »
421 Reatt. «Convair XFY-1»
422 Chance Vought Cutlass
423 Chance Vought Corsair
424 Lockheed F 94 C Starfire
425 Lockheed P 38 Lightning
426 Republic Thunderceptor

Le illustrazioni di queste due pagine corrispondono ad un terzo circa del vero.

252 Mercury pages from the 1960 catalogue

253 *top:* Polistil (42-56mm) AZ-3 Mirage, AZ-6 Hustler, AZ-4 MiG-21C
bottom: AZ-2 Starfighter, AZ-5 Thunderchief, AZ-1 Phantom F4

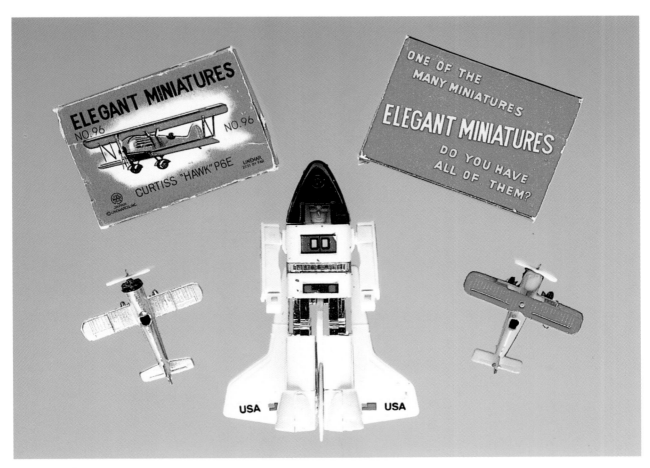

254 Linemar Boeing
P-26A, Bandai Robmachine
Shuttle (82mm), Linemar
Curtiss P6E 'Hawk'

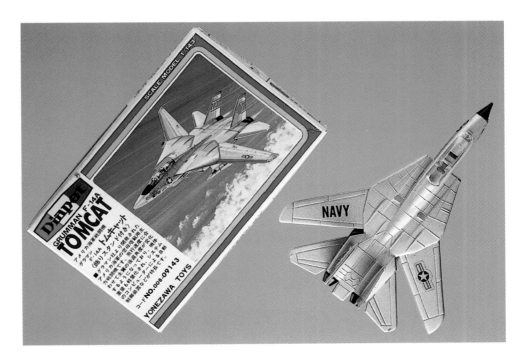

255 Diapet Grumman
F-14 with box

256 *top:* Dieca Hobby
P-51D Mustang (160mm),
Messerschmitt Me109E
bottom: Mitsubishi A6M5

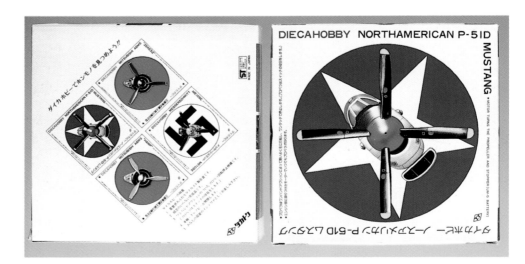

257 Dieca Hobby: bottom
and lid of box

258 Edai Grip F-15 Eagle (150mm)

259 Edai Grip F-16A Falcon

260 Edai Grip F-15 Eagle (150mm)

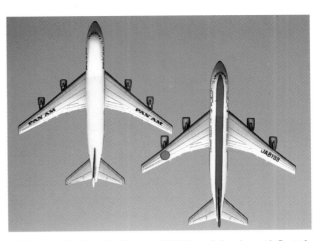

261 Miniair (Modern Toy) Boeing 747 (171mm), Pan Am with Pratt & Witney engines, All Nippon Airways with Rolls Royce engines

262 Miniair (Modern Toy) Boeing 747 (171) All Nippon Airways

263 Miniair (Modern Toy) Lockheed TriStar (170mm), All Nippon Airways

264 Miniair (Modern Toy) Concorde (116mm), British airways

265 Nakajima F-4 Phantom

266 Nakajima boxes for F-4, F-15

267 Nakajima boxes for F-16A, F-14A

268 Tomica Superwings F-15A Eagle

269 Tomica Superwings F-16A Falcon, F-14A Grumman Tomcat (*above right*)

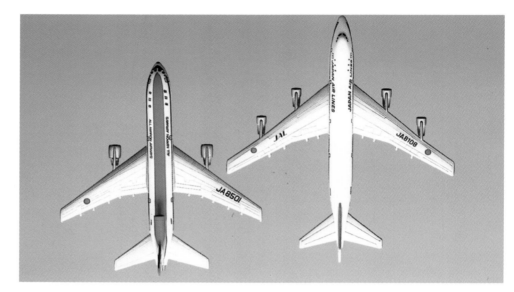

270 Tomica Superwings Lockheed L-1011 TriStar (144mm), Boeing 747

271 Tomica Superwings Lockheed L-1011 TriStar (144mm), Air Canada, British airways

272 Tomica 19 Kawasaki-Vertol KV-107 II with box

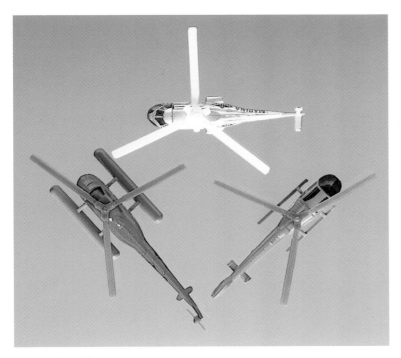

273 *top:* Guisval Puma helicopter (80mm)
bottom: Pilen helicopters Sikorsky H-19, Gazelle SA-341

274 Pilen (60-95mm) – dealer's cardboard wall dispenser with the complete range of planes (*above right*)

275 Joal Agusta helicopter (217mm) SAR, Poste

276 *top:* PlayMe Casa C212 Aviocar (115mm), Lockheed F-104 Starfighter, Boeing 747 Iberia
bottom: Mirage IIIc, Junkers Ju52

277 *top:* PlayMe Polikarpov I-16 (114mm), Spitfire
centre: Cierva C.30 on box base
bottom: Fiat CR32, Dornier Wal Seaplane

278 *top:* Mira HS125 Executive Jet (112mm), Boeing 747
bottom: Cessna, (small series) Twin Jet

279 *top:* Charbens (114mm) Blenheim, Hurricane
bottom: Acorn Spitfire, Cap bombs

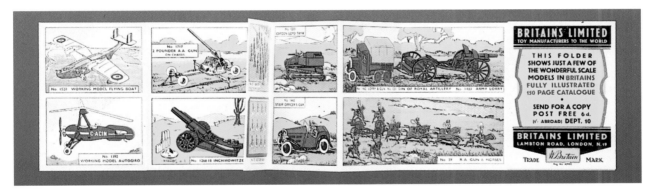

280 Britains catalogue showing Autogiro and Seaplane

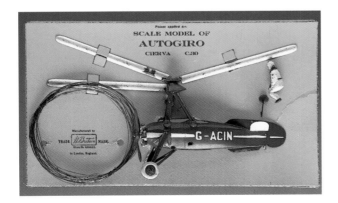

281 Britains Autogiro (142mm) in its box complete with wire for it to 'fly' down

282 Britains Civilian Autogiro box lid demonstrating how to 'fly' it

283 Britains Army Co-operation Autogiro (142mm) in brown and green. Note the pilot's lever to alter the inclination of the rotor instead of the wheel which enables the civilian version to 'fly' along a wire

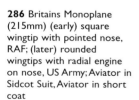

284 Britains box lids for the Army Co-operation Autogiro

285 Britains (early) Monoplane (215mm) with square tips and pointed nose, RAF; (later) Monoplane with rounded wingtips and radial engine (*centre right*)

286 Britains Monoplane (215mm) (early) square wingtip with pointed nose, RAF; (later) rounded wingtips with radial engine on nose, US Army; Aviator in Sidcot Suit, Aviator in short coat

287 Britains Biplane (225mm) (based on later Monoplane) with three RAF Regiment figures

288 Britains Biplane (225mm) (based on later Monoplane)

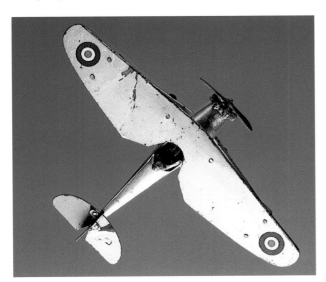

289 Casting moulds (60-140mm) assorted lead cast toys on H Buckley leaflet

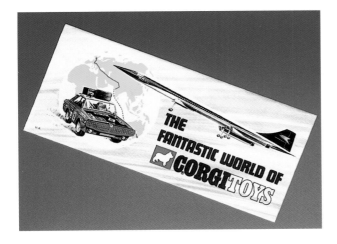

290 Corgi 1969 catalogue featuring Concorde

291 *top:* Unidentified – all marked 'made in England' Spitfire (76mm), Spitfire III
centre: Blenheim Bomber
bottom: Hurricanes

292 Milton Concorde (85mm) Air France a copy of, Corgi Concorde BOAC

293 Corgi photomontage supplied to Corgi by BAC, Filton, with Concorde in first Corgi livery

294 *top:* Milton Concorde box, a copy of the Corgi Concorde box below

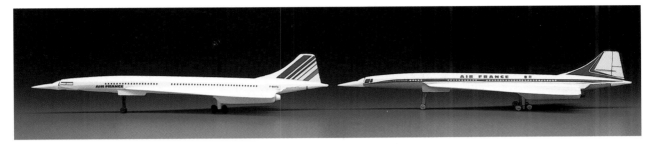

295 Corgi Concorde (85mm) later Air France livery, early Air France

296 Corgi Concorde (85mm) later British Airways livery, earlier British airways

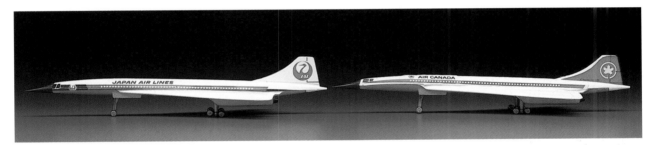

297 Corgi Concorde (85mm) Japan Air Lines, Air Canada

298 Corgi helicopter 920 Bell AH-1G (130mm), 921 Hughes 369 Police

299 Corgi helicopter 9212 Hughes 369 (143mm) Politie, 9921 Polizei, both with 'small' early tailfins

300 Corgi helicopters 9216 Hughes 369 (143mm) Swiss Air Rescue, 9214 ADAC, both with 'large' later tailfins

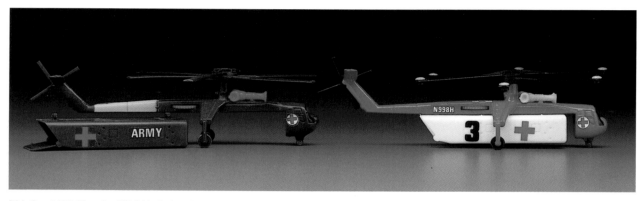

301 Corgi 923 Sikorsky CH-54A (160mm) US Army helicopter, 922 Casualty helicopter

302 Corgi 924 Bell 205 (150mm) Rescue helicopter late (orange) and early (blue) liveries

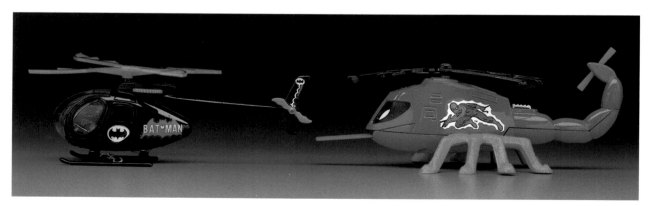

303 Corgi 925 Batcopter (143mm), 928 Spidercopter

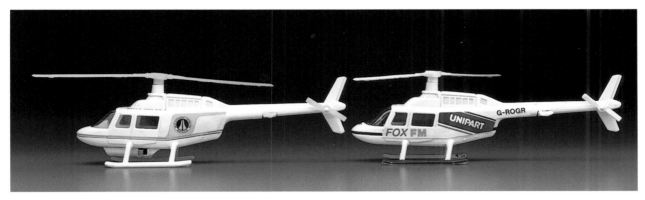

304 Corgi 930 James Bond 007 Drax JetRanger (156mm), Unipart JetRanger

305 Corgi 926 Stromberg Helicopter (156mm) (The Spy Who Loved Me), 929 Daily Planet Jetcopter

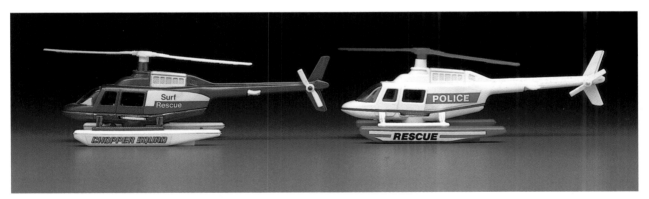

306 Corgi helicopter 927 Chopper Squad JetRanger (156mm) Surf Rescue, 931 JetRanger Rescue (Police)

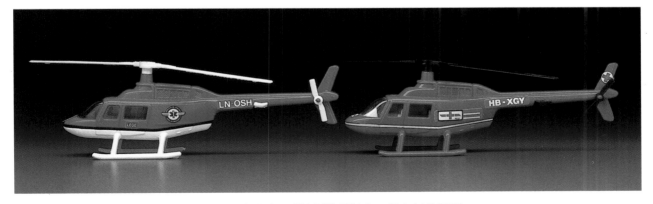

307 Corgi GS65 JetRanger (156mm) Norwegian Air Ambulance LN-OSH, GS54 Rega (Swiss) HB-XGY

308 Corgi GS1412 JetRanger (156mm) Polizei (Swiss) HB-XCU, GS77 JetRanger Police

309 Corgi for Marks & Spencers Wings Flying Club Nipper Aircraft, Hughes 369 Helicopter (143mm)

310 Corgi for Marks & Spencers Spindrift JetRanger (156mm)

311 *top:* Corgi box art 9216 Swiss Rescue, 952 Batcopter
bottom: 929 Superman, 930 Moonraker (Drax)

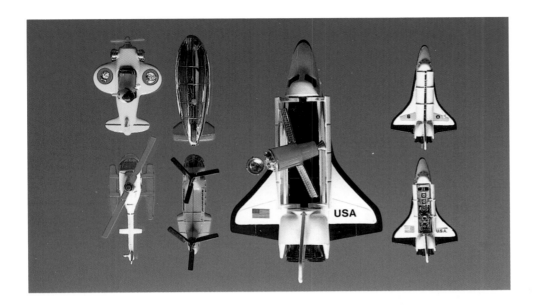

312 *top:* Corgi Junior E79 Olive Oyl's Plane, E83 Goodyear Blimp, E41 Bond Shuttle
centre: Corgi 648 Space Shuttle (102mm) and Satellite
bottom: Corgi Junior E98 Police Helicopter, E35 Airbus Helicopter, J1 Nasa Shuttle

313 *top:* Crescent 'Bomber' (94mm) (Comet), Spitfire, 'Hurricane'
bottom: Mosquito, Lightning (large), Lightning (small)

314 *top:* Johillco DC2 (133mm), Airship R80
bottom: Dyson (Wings) Biplane, Autogiro

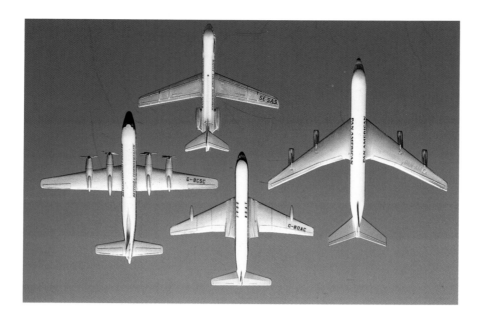

315 *top:* Lone Star Caravelle (137mm), Boeing 707
bottom: Bristol Britannia, DH Comet

316 Lone Star Viscount (114mm) with box and instruction sheet for painting and decalling

317 Lone Star Comets (138mm), one showing detailed inscription underneath

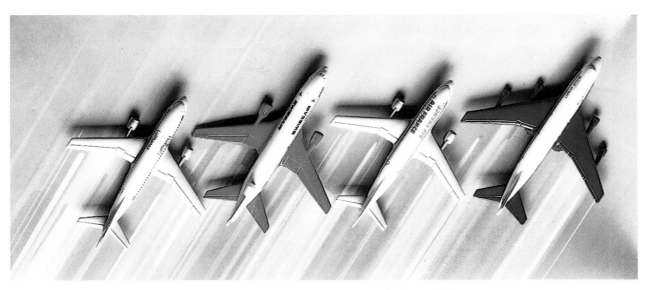

318 Matchbox Skybuster Sky Giants set G-16: Airbus A300, Douglas DC-10, Airbus A300, Boeing 747

319 Matchbox Skybuster aircraft from Sets JCB, Virgin, 007 Licence to Kill

320 Matchbox Skybuster aircraft from Japanese Airport Gift Set, Boeing 747 ANA, Airbus A300B Air France arranged on the back of the box

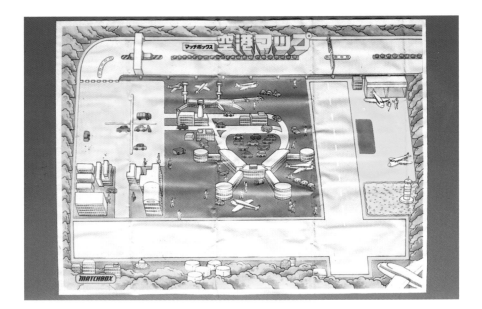

321 Matchbox Skybuster playmat from Japanese Airport Gift Set

322 *top:* Matchbox Skybuster SB10 Boeing 747 Aer Lingus, SB13 DC10 American
centre: SB820 DC10 Sabena with badge, SB31 747-400 Cathay Pacific, SB28 A300 Airbus
bottom: SB38 BAe 146 Dan-Air, SB40 Boeing 737 Britannia

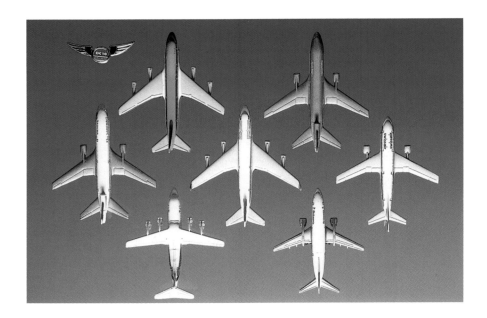

323 *top:* Matchbox Skybuster SB20 RAF Helicopter, SB35 MIL Hind, SB33 Bell JetRanger
bottom: SB12 Mission Chopper, Matchbox MB2 S-2 Jet

324 *top:* Matchbox Skybuster SB36
F-117A Stealth, SB3 Nasa Shuttle
bottom: SB23 Supersonic Airlines
Concorde, SB29 SR-71 Blackbird,
SB23 Concorde Air France

325 *top:* Matchbox Skybuster SB22
Tornado, SB24 F-16, SB30 F-14
Tomcat, SB27 Harrier (Marines)
bottom: SB37 Hawk Trainer Red
Arrows, SB27 Harrier (RAF), SB32
A-10 Thunderbolt

326 *top:* Matchbox Skybuster SB8
Spitfire, SB16 Corsair F-4U, SB19
Piper Comanche
bottom: SB1 Learjet, SB29
Stearman, SB34 C-130 Hercules

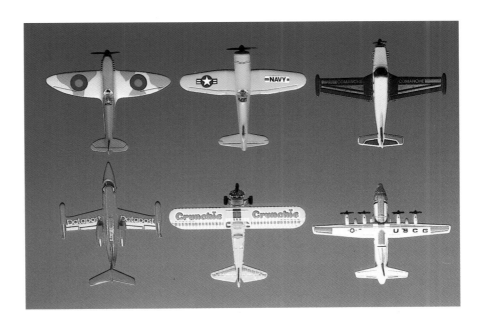

327 Matchbox Skybuster SB10 Boeing 747 SAA, MEA, El Al

328 Matchbox Skybuster SB13 DC10 UTA, aeroméxico, SB28 A300 Airbus Air Malta

329 RAF/Tonka Spitfire (97mm) and Hurricane on Kelloggs Corn Flakes promotional packet

330 Skybirds Caudron C460 (92mm), Percival Mew Gull with boxes and leaflets

331 *top:* Unknown copy of Taylor & Barrett Comet (143mm), Taylor & Barrett Comet Racer *bottom:* Taylor & Barrett (Atalanta) Aeroplane

332 Timpo Bomber Station Set:
3 x P-38 Lightning (101mm) with
personnel

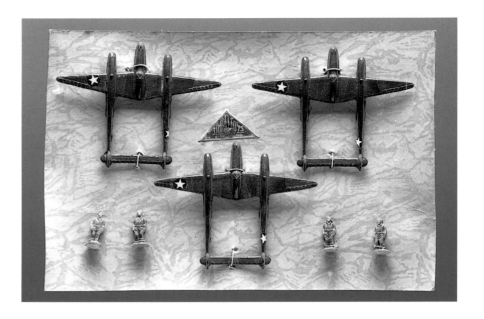

333 Timpo Fairey Battle (75mm)
and Boeing B.17 on Bomber
Station Set lid

334 *top:* Tremo Handley-Page
Harrow (111mm) camouflaged,
Bristol Blenheim Mk 1
bottom: Hawker Hurricane, Harrow
in silver

335 *top:* Goodee Toy Douglas C-54 (132mm), Barclay Northrop Delta, unidentified lead monoplane
bottom: Erie Boeing 247D/B-9, B-17 Flying Fortress

336 *top:* Cragstan Douglas DC-3 (116mm), Cessna T37, Lear Jet
centre: Spirit of St Louis, Ford Trimotor, PBY Catalina
bottom: Fokker D7, Cessna 180, Beechcraft Super 15

337 *top:* Cragstan Mystère B2 (80mm), Buccaneer, Mitsubishi A6 Zero
centre: VC10, Piasecki Work Horse, Boeing 727
bottom: F-111 Swing Wing, Mirage IIIR, MiG-21

338 *top:* Dyna-flites (90-100mm long) A106 Boeing SST, A103 DC-9, A128 Boeing 707, A128 Boeing 707 *bottom:* A107 Boeing 727, A105 Boeing 747, A115 DC-10, A107 Boeing 727

339 *top:* Dyna-flites A130 Douglas Skyhawk A-4E, A145 F-16 Eagle, A153, MiG-29 Fulcrum, A129 SAAB AJ-27 Viggen
bottom: A143 F-14 Tomcat, A152 EF-111, A127 Lockheed SR-71 Blackbird, A110 Lockheed F104 Starfighter, A111 MiG-27

340 *top:* Dyna-flites A154 MD AV-8B Harrier, A114 F-16, A155 Grumman EA-6A Intruder, A156 S-3A Viking
bottom: A118 Phantom F-4C, A157 F-117A Stealth, A132 Hunter F6, A102 C-54 Galaxy

341 *top:* Dyna-flites A119 Spitfire IX, A108 Mustang P.51, A136 P.40 Flying Tiger
bottom: A123 Messerschmitt Me109, A116 Corsair F4U-4, A101 Junkers Ju-87

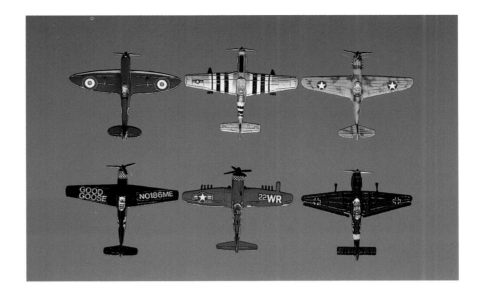

342 *top:* Dyna-flites A109 Lockheed P.38 Lightning, A113 Spad, A114 Mitsubishi Zero
bottom: A130 Spirit of St Louis, A118 E-2A Hawkeye, A106 DC-3

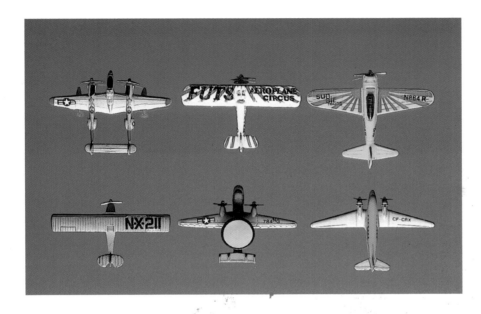

343 Dyna-flites helicopters A140 Bell 47, A121 Hughes OH-6A, A100 Sikorsky S.55, A149 Sikorsky HH-60D

344 *top:* Super Dyna-flites
(110-120 long) A216 Corsair
II, A218 MiG-29, A211 F-15
Eagle, A219 MD AV-8B
Harrier
bottom: A204 F-18 Hornet,
A221 F-117A Stealth, A222
B-17 Memphis Belle, A212
F-20 Tiger Shark

345 *top:* Super Dyna-flites A217
F-14 Tomcat (Wild Flites), A215
Stealth Fighter (Wild Flites),
A210 Lockheed SR-71 with
drone (Wild Flites), A213
Grumman X-92A (Wild Flites)
bottom: A217 F-14 Tomcat (Fast
Lane), SA215 Stealth (Sonic),
A210 Lockheed SR-71 with
drone, A203 F-16 Falcon (Wild
Flites)

346 *top:* Super Dyna-flites
A206 Boeing 747 Air Force
One, A205 Boeing 727
bottom: A202 Douglas DC-10,
A201 Boeing 767

347 Super Dyna-flites helicopters: A208 Bell JetRanger, A209 Apache, A214 Sikorsky HH-60D; A207 Nasa Space Shuttle

348 *top:* Ertl Jet Trans
Douglas DC-9 (106mm),
Boeing 737
bottom: Boeing 747, Boeing
747 US Presidential

349 *top:* Ertl Jet Trans
Boeing 767 (145mm),
Airbus A300B
bottom: Douglas DC-10,
Boeing 747-400

350 *top:* Ertl Force One 1987 castings F-16 Falcon (115mm), A-10 Thunderbolt
bottom: F-15 Eagle, F-14 Tomcat

351 *top:* Ertl Force One 1989 castings Douglas AV-8B Harrier (125mm), F-18A Hornet
bottom: Sea Harrier, F-18A Hornet, F-4 Phantom II Wild Weasle

352 *top:* Ertl Force One MiG-29 (146mm) (1990 casting), Tornado GR-1 (1993)
bottom: Stealth Fighter (1990), Lockheed YF22 (1993), EFA Eurofighter (1990)

353 *top:* Ertl Display Miniatures (40-50mm) – the six castings used for the four sets – F-14 Tomcat, MiG-29 Fulcrum, F-18 Hornet
bottom: F-16 Falcon, AV-8B Harrier, F-15 Eagle

354 Ertl large scale SR-71 Blackbird (134mm), B-1 Bomber

355 Ertl Chopper Squadron: Bell 222 (126mm) 'Black Widow', Bell JetRanger, Sikorsky Westland

356 Ertl Airwolf Set: Bell 222 (126mm), JetRanger; Riptide Sikorsky 'Screamin' Mimi'

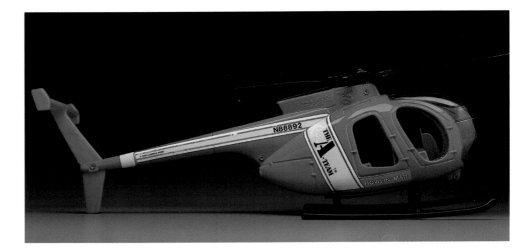

357 Ertl 1/16 scale 'A-team' helicopter (440mm)

358 Ertl Force One Helicopters Apache (165mm), Bell UH-1D Huey

359 Ertl Force One Helicopters Kamov Hokum (170mm), MIL Mi-24 Hind

360 Ertl Nasa Playset:
Bell UH-1 (121mm),
Orbiter Space Shuttle
with booster rocket;
Russian Shuttle

361 Ertl 1534 Shuttle
with pull-back action
(84mm), 1514 Space
Shuttle with space
laboratory

362 Ertl/Lintoy 1513
Boeing 747 (130mm) with
Nasa Shuttle

363 *top:* Hubley Kiddie Toy Lockheed B.34 Navy Scout Plane (135mm), P.39 Airacobra
bottom: Crusader, Seversky P.35 (rounded tail)

364 Hubley Kiddie Toy lid for set showing Seversky and Crusader

365 Hubley Kiddie Toy P.47 Thunderbolt Folding Wing Navy Plane (295mm), P.40 Fighter Plane, both playworn

HUBLEY MIGHTY-MITE AIRCRAFT

**STAPLE STAND-BYS,
EVERY ONE WITH ACTION FEATURES...**

- FOLDING WINGS
- SPINNING PROPELLERS
- RETRACTABLE LANDING GEAR
- SLIDING CANOPIES
- FOLDING, TURNING ROTORS
- DETAILED DIE CAST METAL
- HIGH GLOSS COLORFUL ENAMEL FINISHES

NO. 1495 NAVY FIGHTER BOMBER
Husky all-metal carrier plane, folding wings open down to 11½ inch wingspan, prop spins, wheels retract for "in-flight" realism, canopy slides open. Blue with red cowling.

12 PER CARTON: 18 LBS.

NO. 1496 WORLD WAR II FIGHTER PLANE SET
Two true-to-life aircraft, in a shrink-wrapped display package. No. 1495 Navy Fighter Bomber plus a bright silver and red P-40 fighter plane, with realistic rivet detail, spinning plated prop.

6 PER CARTON: 14 LBS.

No. 1484 FOLDING ROTOR HELICOPTER
Mighty-Mite helicopter in bright yellow, plastic canopy, plated folding rotors. Over 14 inches long, modeled after the big can-do 'copters used throughout the world.

12 PER CARTON: 13 LBS.

NO. 1468 CARRIER FIGHTER PLANE
Lots of fun in this 8½ inch wingspan navy fighter, with folding wings, retractable landing gear, spinning prop. Silver and blue, all metal with plastic canopy.

12 PER CARTON: 8 LBS.

366 *top:* Hubley 1970 catalogue illustrating P.47 Thunderbolt Folding Wing Navy Plane, P.40 Fighter Plane
bottom: Folding Rotor Helicopter, Carrier Fighter Plane (die used by Major Models, Fairymark)

367 *top:* Mail Box Series
(box 80 x 90mm) Caravelle
Air France
bottom: Douglas DC8 Delta,
Boeing 707 Pan Am

368 *top:* Midgetoy Cutlass
(82mm), F-86 Sabre, F9F Cougar
(repaints)
bottom: Martin B-57 (Canberra),
Boeing 707 Transport

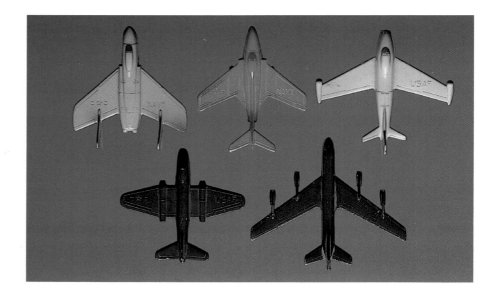

369 Revell F-16 Fighting Falcon
(114mm), F/A-18 Hornet (Sonic
Aces), F-15 Eagle

370 Revell SU-27 Flanker (120mm),
EFA Eurofighter, MiG-29 Fulcrum

371 *top:* Road Champs Flyers
P-47D Thunderbolt (125mm),
F/A-18 Hornet
bottom: B-17F Flying Fortress,
F4U-1A Corsair

372 *top:* Road Champs Flyers
spurious liveries DC-9, Boeing 727
bottom: Boeing 747, Airbus A300

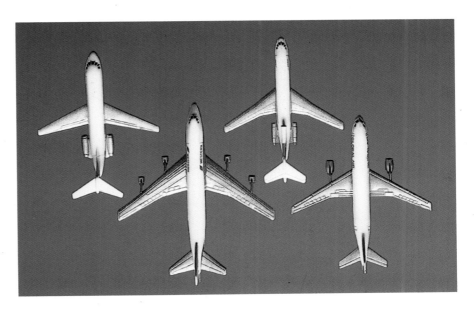

373 *top:* Tootsietoy Vought Biplane (58mm), Bleriot
bottom: two 'Miniatures'

374 *top:* Tootsietoy U S Army Plane (105mm), Lockheed Electra
centre: 'Wings' Biplane with pontoons
bottom: High Wing Cabin Monoplane, Low Wing two-seater Monoplane

375 Tootsietoy 'Wings' Biplane (95mm) with wheels, and (right) with pontoons

USA

376 *top:* Tootsietoy DC-2
(135mm), DC-2
centre: Long Range
Bomber (modification of
DC-4)
bottom: Long Range
Bomber, DC-4 Super
Mainliner

377 Tootsietoy DC-4 Super Mainliner (134mm) with its box showing
that it was 'licensed by United Airlines'

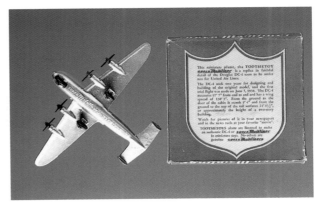

378 Tootsietoy DC-4 Super Mainliner underside with the reverse
of its box

379 *left:* Tootsietoy Waco
Navy Bomber (127mm)
right: (Sikorsky) US
Coastguard Amphibion
(*sic*)

380 Tootsietoy P-39 Airacobra (132mm) (post-war), Crusader

381 Tootsietoy Trimotor (132mm), Trimotor prototype created by Frank Bischof Jr

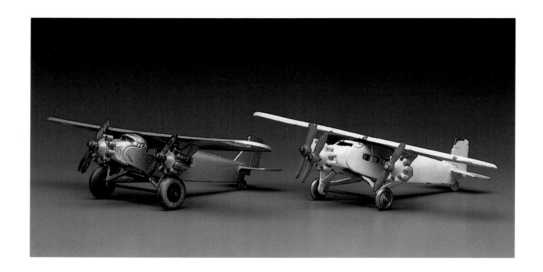

382 Tootsietoy – four of the colours on the Trimotor (132mm)

383 Tootsietoy 'Made in USA' paper sticker under the wing of a Trimotor

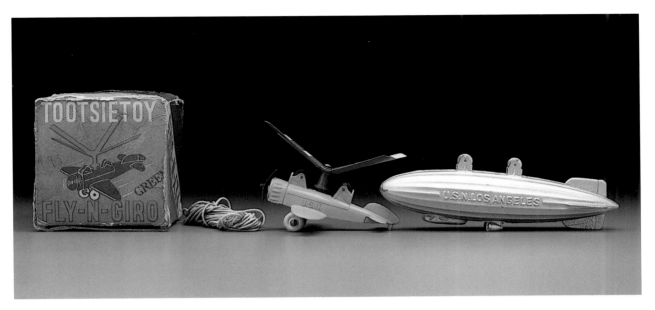

384 Tootsietoy Fly-n-Giro
(72mm) with box and
cord, Airship 'Los Angeles'

385 Tootsietoy Aero
Dawn High Wing
Monoplane (95mm),
Dyson Aerodawn Biplane
(copy, with additional
lower wing)

386 Tootsietoy Autogiro
(110mm), Dyson Autogiro
(copy)

387 Tootsietoy lid for set no. 05051 Aerial Defense

388 Tootsietoy lid for set 4200

389 *top:* Tootsietoy Set (post-war). Planes set 4200 Navion (110mm), Convair 240, Beechcraft Bonanza
centre: Piper Cub, Lockheed F-80 Shooting Star
bottom: P-38 Lightning, F-86 Sabre, P-38 Lightning

390 *top:* Tootsietoy (post-war) Lockheed Constellation (154mm), Boeing Stratocruiser
bottom: Boeing 707

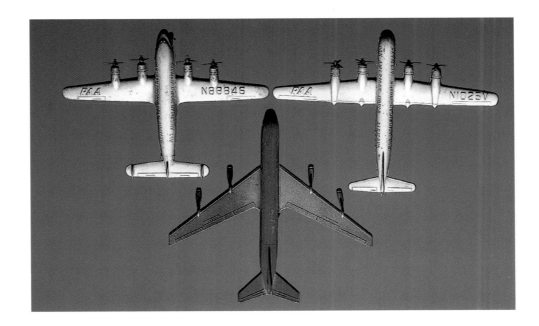

391 *top:* Tootsietoy (post-war) Grumman F9F2 (95mm), Douglas F-4D Skyray
bottom: F-94 Starfire, Cutlass F7U3

392 Tootsietoy Helicopters, Scorpion (95mm), Super Cobra, Bell 206

393 *top:* Tootsietoy (China) Stealth Bomber (185mm) *centre:* MiG-17, F-14 Tomcat *bottom:* Stealth 'Advanced Tactical Fighter'

394 Tootsietoy (China) Stealth Bomber, B-1 Rockwell Bomber, B-17 Flying Fortress (139mm) with assorted small WWII and modern fighters

Bibliography

Model books

Britains Toy Soldiers 1893–1932, James Opie, Gollancz, 1985, ISBN 0-575-03741-5

British Tin Toys, Marguerite Fawdry, New Cavendish Books, 1990, ISBN 0-904568–86-5

Collecting Dinky Toy Model Aircraft, John Marshall. Out of print

Collecting Matchbox Diecast Toys – The First Forty Years, Kevin McGimpsey and Stewart Orr, published for Matchbox International by Major Publications, 1989

Collectors' Guide to Tootsietoys, David E Richter, Shroeder Publishing Co Inc, 1991, ISBN 0-89145-442-X

Dinky Toys & Modelled Miniatures, Mike and Sue Richardson (section contributed by Alan Dimmock), New Cavendish Books, 1981, ISBN 0-904568-33-4

Hubley Die-Cast Toys 1936–1976, Charles A Jones 1994, private publication

Les Dinky Toys et Dinky Supertoys Français 1933–1981, J M Roulet, EPA, 1982, ISBN 2-85120-216-2

Price Guide to Metal Toys, Gordon Gardiner and Alistair Morris, Antique Collectors Club, 1980, ISBN 0-902028-92-8

Skybird Notes, A G Sinclair 1994, private publication

Solido 1957–82, Bertrand Azema, EPA, 1983, ISBN 2-85120-184-0

Solido 1932–57, Bertrand Azema, EPA, 1991, ISBN 2-85120-375-4

Tekno Made in Denmark, Dorte Johansen, Togbørsen, ISBN 87981684-4-4

The Book of Pennytoys, David Pressland (section contributed by Ian Leonard), New Cavendish Books, 1991, ISBN 0-904-568-54-7

The Complete Book of Building and Collecting Model Automobiles, Louis H Hertz, Crown Publishers Inc., 1970

The Great Book of Corgi 1956–1983, Marcel R Van Cleemput, New Cavendish Books, 1989, ISBN 0-904568-53-9

The Great Book of Hollow-cast Figures, Norman Joplin, New Cavendish Books 1993, ISBN 1-872727-26-3

The Story of American Toys, Richard O'Brien, New Cavendish Books, 1990 ISBN 0-904568-68-7

Toy Soldiers, Andrew Rose, Salamander Books, 1985, ISBN 1-85501-023-2

Reprint catalogues

Crescent, November 1940

Britains, 1940

Model magazines

Antique Toy World, editor Dale Kelly, 1970–

Argus de la Miniature, editor E Flamant, 1978–

Collecting Toys, editor Jim Bunte, 1993–

Die Cast & Tin Toy Report, editor Doug Kelly, 1993–

Meccano Magazine, 1930–1969

Model Collector, editor Richard West, 1987–

Model Cars, c.1965–70

Modelisme, 1960–70s

Modellers' World, 1971–85

The Plane News, editor G R Webster, 1989–

The Miniature Vehicle, USA, c.1975